FAILED STATE

A PORTRAIT OF
CALIFORNIA
IN THE TWILIGHT OF EMPIRE

CHRISTOPHER MORITZ

Skyhorse Publishing

Skyhorse Publishing books may be purchased in bulk at special discounts for sales promotion, corporate gifts, fund-raising, or educational purposes. Special editions can also be created to specifications. For details, contact the Special Sales Department, Skyhorse Publishing, 307 West 36th Street, 11th Floor, New York, NY 10018 or info@skyhorsepublishing.com

Skyhorse® and Skyhorse Publishing® are registered trademarks of Skyhorse Publishing, Inc.®, a Delaware corporation.

Visit our website at www.skyhorsepublishing.com.
Please follow our publisher Tony Lyons on Instagram @tonylyonsisuncertain.

10 9 8 7 6 5 4 3 2 1

Library of Congress Cataloging-in-Publication Data is available on file.

Hardcover ISBN: 978-1-5107-8447-5
eBook ISBN: 978-1-5107-8448-2

Cover design by Brian Peterson

Printed in the United States of America

CONTENTS

FOREWORD

THE FIRE THEY INVITED

From high ground on San Vicente Boulevard in Santa Monica, my neighbors and I gathered in stunned silence, our faces bathed in the inferno's baleful yet otherworldly radiance. Phones were raised in futile attempts to capture a reality too vast, too profound to confine within a frame. The air seemed charged with a haunting confluence of dread and reverence as we witnessed not only the tangible destruction of homes but also, in the abstract, a vision both apocalyptic and sublime.

The fire arrived without subtlety or hesitation; it came roaring over the ridgelines, driven by the ancient devil wind—the Santa Ana—that propelled its destructive force with terrifying precision and unbridled rage. What began as a distant, fiery glow on the horizon—a harbinger of something vast and inevitable—advanced with a ferocity that defied comprehension. In its wake, the world became unrecognizable: a hellscape where the boundaries between the natural and the manmade collapsed into ash and flame.

Smoke billowed in towering columns, choking the sky and blotting out the sun until day fell into a sepulchral twilight. The air pulsed with a suffocating heat, tainted by the acrid stench of burning wood, melting plastic, and scorched metal. Every breath carried the taste of destruction, each toxic inhalation a reminder of the fire's insatiable hunger.

In the distance, the hills blazed, their contours alive with molten reds and searing oranges, a once-verdant expanse consumed in its agonizing death throes. The inferno moved with remarkable intelligence, leaping across canyons and devouring everything in its path. Palm trees, those icons of Southern California, became death pyres in an instant. A single ember would strike, and the tree would erupt into a towering torch, its fronds crackling as flames raced up its spine. Embers, the size of sparrows, spiraled through the air like incendiary missiles, carried by the tempestuous wind that scattered destruction indiscriminately, igniting rooftops and dry brush while spreading chaos, terror, and ruin. A survivor recalled how they rolled through the streets like glowing tumbleweeds, leaving trails of fire that reduced entire neighborhoods to ash; even the sidewalks were aflame.

Survivors fled in all directions, clutching children, pets, and whatever they could carry, while others stood frozen, unable to comprehend the speed and enormity of the destruction.

Firefighters, their silhouettes spectral against the haze, worked with a desperation that teetered on madness. They moved with relentless precision, hoses spraying dwindling water supplies as they battled against an inferno that exhaled searing gusts like the very breath of damnation. Hydrants sputtered and ran dry, forcing them to improvise, yet they pressed on, their resolve as unyielding as the flames' advance.

Houses fell not with the grandeur of cinematic destruction but with the slow, tortured collapse of lives dismantled. Roofs caved inward, walls crumbled, and windows burst outward, releasing plumes of flame that illuminated the skeletal remains of homes reduced to ruins. Each collapse was accompanied by a grotesque symphony: the shrill whine of fire meeting glass, the groan of bending steel, and the muffled roar of timbers succumbing to the heat. In minutes, these symbols of affluence and the California dream were reduced to smoldering footprints, marked by blackened chimneys rising like solemn grave markers from the ash and rubble.

The streets bore the scars of panicked escapes. Cars, abandoned in haste, sat gutted by the fire's relentless touch. Tires had melted into pools of blackened rubber, their interiors reduced to charred voids—the hollowed remains of hurried lives abandoned to chaos. Strewn among the ash were half-packed suitcases and singed clothing. In one driveway, a child's sneaker lay singed but intact, a haunting symbol of innocence lost. Sirens wailed, helicopters droned overhead, and the once-pristine streets of the Pacific Palisades lay strewn with the fragmented remains of lives undone.

Amidst the chaos, there was a queer order to the destruction. The fire advanced with grim purpose, as if driven by an unyielding force intent on erasing not just structures but the very memory of what had been. This was not just a disaster; it was a reckoning—a harbinger of something far darker. Nature, wielded by human folly, had unleashed a calamity that defied comprehension. More than a natural disaster, it was a fiery indictment of systemic failure—a blistering emblem of a state adrift, its foundations crumbling under the weight of negligence and hubris.

The Pacific Palisades is one of several suburban citadels within Los Angeles. It is secluded physically, but also culturally (even temporally perhaps), and thus shielded from the decay consuming the city below. Today, it stands as a wasteland, a vision torn from another world and another time: Gaza, Hiroshima, Dresden. The world now knows its name not for its prestige or singular beauty, but for horror; a community burned alive, abandoned by a city that ignored the mounting risks of decaying infrastructure, deferred critical fire prevention measures, and drained essential resources in favor of ideological gestures. The negligence was as deliberate as it was deadly, turning a preventable disaster into a nightmare of unimaginable proportions.

The Palisades was a memory of a Los Angeles that clung to the gossamer web of the California dream. It was largely white, affluent, orderly—a haven of single-family homes and exclusivity, antithetical to the vision of radical environmentalists and leftist city organizers like Mayor Karen Bass. Their belief in high-density urban life—a mandated intensity and squalor in the name of equity and environment—was intensely hostile to the Palisades' generational estates and capacious living. When the fires came, the Santa Ynez reservoir that supplies the Palisades with 117 million gallons of water was bone-dry, empty since February 2024 pending repairs to its floating cover by the Los Angeles Department of Water and Power (LADWP).[1] In the darker, whispered recesses of the city's DEI eco-cult, I suspect the Palisades' destruction was not only a convenient clearing of space, but a just and fitting end for a paragon symbol of white privilege.

The Shell station at the edge of town off Sunset Boulevard was a scene of violent devastation. The canopy over the pumps had collapsed, its steel supports twisted and buckled by the searing heat. Flames licked at the remaining fuel, sending plumes of black smoke spiraling into the ashen expanse above. Propane tanks exploded sporadically, each detonation fracturing the ominous stillness with deafening booms that ricocheted across the hills like wrathful thunder.

Above it all, the sky churned with smoke and embers, its colors bleeding between deep orange and suffocating gray. The sun was no longer a source of light but a blood-red orb, looming, judging, monstrous—a disquieting reflection of the fire's celestial ambition. The wind carried more than embers; it carried despair and especially, it carried fear. In harrowing and violent gusts, unusually angry for the Santa Ana, wind fanned the fire's tendrils beyond the mountains and into a defenseless city below; with its life it would pay for a mismanagement yet to receive justice. Even the trees, stripped of their leaves and dignity, stood like spectral keepers, their charred trunks clawing skyward in futile defiance.

As the blaze swept through Los Angeles with near-sentient malevolence, a counterforce emerged—Los Angeles firefighters and police officers, rising above the ineptitude and disgrace of city officials to confront a catastrophe of staggering proportions. Survivors looked on in awe as these front-line defenders charged into battle, armed with little more than dwindling water supplies and an unshakable resolve. Their uniforms and soot-streaked faces bore silent witness to their exhaustion, but they pressed on with a determination that was as relentless as the inferno itself. They were Hispanic, they were Filipino, but honestly they were mostly white—fireman physiognomy. This was not heroism romanticized but heroism realized—a raw, unyielding commitment to defend the city and its people.

The challenges these firefighters faced were unparalleled and, in many ways, avoidable. Despite forecasts of extreme Santa Ana wind, internal records revealed that the Los Angeles Fire Department (LAFD) failed to pre-deploy critical resources. As the fire ignited, hundreds of firefighters and essential water-carrying engines sat idle.[2] The geography of the Pacific Palisades—its steep canyons and dense chaparral vegetation—compounded the crisis. Narrow, winding roads hindered the movement of personnel and equipment, while hydrants ran dry, a damning reminder of municipal neglect and California's pathetically strained water systems.[3]

Amid these obstacles, the human toll was profound. Firefighter Chief Freddy Escobar, a thirty-five-year veteran and president of Los Angeles United Firefighters, stood amidst the charred ruins he had long warned were at risk. On live television, his voice cracked with emotion as he described the lack of resources that had turned this catastrophe from inevitable to inescapable.[4]

Yet, even as the fire surged forward with every parching gust, mocking their efforts, the firefighters kept at it. Hydrants sputtered uselessly, but they improvised, commandeering private pools, redirecting scarce resources, and crafting makeshift water tanks to sustain their fight. Armed with little more than axes and resolve, they held their ground as walls of flame roared toward them, their actions embodying the existential defense mounted by a city under siege.

The contrast was glaring. While firefighters and residents risked everything to defend their homes, those entrusted with governance were morally and physically absent. Mayor Bass was apparently attending an inauguration in Ghana—which would be in Africa. . . . Politicians who had long promised proactive wildfire strategies and infrastructure improvements were silent as their failures erupted into tragedy. Their absence stood as a scathing indictment—a bitter reminder of systemic negligence within California's progressive leadership, where incompetence and corruption had grown increasingly, glaringly lethal.

For all its devastation, the fires laid bare not only the failings of a broken system but also the unyielding strength of those who refused to succumb. It was a stark tableau of contrasts: heroism and neglect, resilience and abandonment—a reflection of humanity at its finest and institutions at their most bankrupt, a dichotomy that defines our unraveling state.

In the void left by absent leadership, acts of quiet bravery and unexpected kindness emerged as fragments of hope. Neighbors banged on doors to rouse the sleeping, ferried elderly residents to safety, and carried individuals out of senior centers threatened by the inferno.[5] Groups organized spontaneously to clear brush and extinguish smoldering embers, working together to shield their communities from further destruction.[6] Volunteers provided meals and supplies to evacuees and firefighters, with organizations like World Central Kitchen serving thousands of meals to those on the front lines.[7] Meanwhile, animal rescue groups mobilized to save pets left behind in the chaos, reuniting them with their families or offering them shelter.[8] Among the heroes were even state prisoners participating in California's Conservation Camp Program, who volunteered to fight the fires, seeing it as an opportunity for redemption. One inmate reflected, "I love doing this, helping the community by making up for the bad decisions I made in life. . . . It's a chance to redeem myself."[9]

All of that—that is at least what the media reported; hopefully truly. But the few survivors I spoke to and know well paint a different picture: everyone was terrified, panicked, and fled desperately with no thought other than not being burned alive. I could only watch from across the canyon.

The fire burned through more than just homes and hillsides—it torched the illusion of California's stability, revealing a state where leadership is divorced from accountability, and where rhetoric, not results, dictates policy. This was not simply a failure of governance; it was a forewarning of what lies ahead for a nation that continues to neglect the foundations of its own survival.

This calamity was an act of God, yes, but not an unpredictable one. It was a reckoning made inevitable by years of systemic negligence and chronic mismanagement, perpetuated by a political system resistant to scrutiny or reform. Convenient as it is to pin the blame on climate change—an ever-present canard for state policy failures—the reality is far more damning: the force which set the Palisades ablaze was as old as the land itself, while the policies that left it vulnerable were unmistakably modern and reckless.

For years, experts issued urgent and unequivocal warnings about the escalating wildfire risks in California, emphasizing the deadly convergence of environmental mismanagement, deferred infrastructure maintenance, and bureaucratic inertia. These warnings were not merely ignored; they were dismissed as alarmist or politically inconvenient by a single-party system that prioritized ideological purity over good governance and, therein, public safety. The inferno that consumed the Palisades was no surprise—it was foretold and disregarded.

Central to this disaster is the Santa Ana wind, a force as intrinsic to Southern California as its coastline and earthquakes. The wind is born in the Great Basin, where cold, dry air pools before descending toward sea level. As it falls, the air compresses, warms, and sheds its remaining moisture, becoming hot and dry.[10] Funneled through the narrow passes of the San Gabriel Mountains, the wind gathers speed and power, transforming sparks into infernos and fire-prone landscapes into fields of ash.[11]

The Santa Ana has been a defining feature of the region's history, recognized for both its destructive power and the psychological unease it brings. On January 6, 1847, Commodore Robert Stockton recorded its ferocity while camped near Santa Ana Canyon:

"The wind blew a hurricane (something unusual in this part of California), and the atmosphere was filled with particles of fine dust, so that one could not see and but with difficulty breathe."[12]

Joan Didion, in her essay *Los Angeles Notebook,* captured the existential unease brought by the Santa Anas:

"To live with the Santa Ana is to accept, consciously or unconsciously, a deeply mechanistic view of human behavior. . . . The violence and the unpredictability of the Santa Ana affect the entire quality of life in Los Angeles, accentuate its impermanence, its unreliability. The wind shows us how close to the edge we are."[13]

Didion's reflections evoke the elemental despair that seems to rise from Los Angeles itself during moments of crisis. The winds were not merely weather; they were a force that unmoored the city, leaving its inhabitants teetering on the edge of reason. She captures this visceral dislocation, writing:

"I recall being told, when I first moved to Los Angeles and was living on an isolated beach, that the Indians would throw themselves into the sea when the bad wind blew. I could see why."[14]

The Santa Ana is unsympathetic and eternal, but its capacity for destruction has gone nuclear with systemic negligence and the complacency of local and state leadership. This is the bitter irony of the Palisades Fire. The Santa Ana, for all its ferocity, was not the proximate cause of the destruction. At the heart of this tragedy lies a cascade of preventable failures, each compounding the last. Politicians, chasing short-term accolades, championed performative environmental policies while neglecting the essential, unglamorous work of fire prevention. Policies that eschewed proactive fire management, deferred infrastructure maintenance, and prioritized ideological distractions over essential safeguards created conditions where a natural force could become an anthropogenic apocalypse. The wind merely revealed the cracks in a system too fractured to withstand it.

Environmental policies, celebrated as progressivist milestones, ultimately deepened a growing crisis. Reckless (and extremist) preservation—not true and responsible conservation—supplanted proactive forest management, creating vast expanses of overgrown land ready to ignite. The refusal to support controlled burns—a proven, time-tested method for mitigating wildfire risk—left ecosystems dangerously overburdened, where even minor sparks could ignite uncontrollable blazes. Prescribed burns and underbrush thinning were underfunded or delayed, dismissed as environmentally harmful despite their proven necessity. In California, the environmental review process of controlled burns can take three to seven years.[15] Inaction was the policy.

For instance, the California Environmental Quality Act (CEQA), often lauded as a regulatory safeguard, routinely delayed or obstructed critical measures like brush clearance or controlled burns, allowing dead trees and dry underbrush to accumulate unchecked.[16] In one glaring example, the California Coastal Commission prioritized the preservation of an endangered shrub over the safety of the nearby communities, blocking life-saving fire-prevention efforts with devastating consequences.[17]

Bureaucratic inertia magnified these failures. Residents attempting to clear fire-prone vegetation found themselves entangled in labyrinthine permitting processes, clearly designed to placate radical environmental lobbies rather than address the immediate and obvious danger of seasonal wildfires. These restrictions rendered basic safety measures impractical, leaving communities exposed while officials adhered to eco-puritanical dogma at the expense of public safety. The result was a landscape primed for catastrophe, overseen by leaders who abdicated their moral and legal responsibilities to the people.

In a cruel irony, the environmentalists obliterated the very ecosystems they claimed to protect, reducing habitats to ash, releasing unfathomable amounts of carbon and carcinogens into the air, and rendering California's green agenda not just feckless but actively self-defeating.

California's water crisis is not a story of scarcity but of waste—an almost pathological refusal to treat water as the critical resource it is. Every year, 740 billion gallons of stormwater are flushed into the Pacific, enough to sustain over 9 million households annually.[18,19] Water management and sourcing is a perennial challenge (and controversy) in Southern California, particularly Los Angeles, where the issue has plagued the city for well over a century, and yet in LA, on a daily basis more than 437 million gallons of runoff are funneled into storm rains and out to the Pacific rather than recycled into use.

The infamous delta smelt, a three-inch fish with outsized political significance, has come to symbolize California's regulatory psychosis. Environmental protections for the smelt restrict water diversions from the Sacramento-San Joaquin Delta, the hub of the state's water supply. This means 95% of the Delta's fresh water—critical to two-thirds of the state's population and millions of acres of farmland—flows directly into the ocean. These policies have been sacrosanct for decades, yet their defenders have no answer to the simple fact: the state is running out of water while letting billions of gallons slip away every day.[20]

In January 2025, President Trump issued a directive to increase water deliveries from the Delta to Southern California, bypassing the entrenched environmental priorities that have throttled the state's ability to provide for its residents.[21] His move exposed a glaring truth: California's water crisis is not inevitable but constructed, sustained by a bureaucracy that privileges ideological gestures over practical solutions. While aquifers run dry and farmers' fields wither, California's leaders remain committed to policies that prioritize symbols over survival.

The consequences of the state's psychotic water policies ultimately left fire hydrants dry during the worst fire in the history of Southern California, crippling firefighters' power to combat the flames. Developer and 2022 LA mayoral candidate Rick Caruso, owner of the Palisades Village mall (the only major property to survive the blaze), expressed his outrage at the madness: "The firefighters are there, and there's nothing they can do—we've got neighborhoods burning, homes burning, and businesses burning. . . . It should never happen."[22]

Instead of addressing water shortages, Governor Gavin Newsom has exacerbated them. Last October, he oversaw the demolition of four dams on the Klamath River.[23] Declaring the move a win for salmon and tribal communities, Newsom touted, "By taking down these outdated dams, we are giving salmon and other species a chance to thrive."[24] To residents in fire-prone areas, however, his message was clear: *Your safety is expendable for fish.*

Misallocated resources underscore the systemic failures that fueled the Palisades Fire. As wildfire threats grew, California's budgets increasingly diverted funds from essential services to symbolic initiatives. In the 2024–25 budget, Newsom approved a $101 million reduction in funding for wildfire and forest resilience funding, despite mounting warnings about escalating fire dangers.[25] Meanwhile, spending priorities reflected a pattern of ideological profligacy: the state committed $3.1 billion annually to expand Medi-Cal to cover illegal aliens; it allocated $430 million over three years in Rapid Response Funding for illegal aliens ineligible for federal aid; and Sacramento directed up to $500 million toward diversity, equity, and inclusion (DEI) programs.[26,27,28] These choices epitomized a governance model where leftist political religion overshadowed practical investment in the infrastructure and emergency preparedness desperately needed to underwrite public safety.

Even as California faced worsening fire threats, resources were ludicrously squandered. State leaders made headlines by offering up, as if in penance, firefighting equipment and medical supplies to Ukraine, gestures which played well in the Bay Area but were starkly misaligned with the real desperation afflicting California.[29] The result was a perilous lack of preparation, with critical infrastructure and emergency services neglected in favor of political priorities detached from the immediate realities of those living in the shadow of inferno.

In a further blow to fire prevention efforts, the Biden administration, in October 2024, ordered the U.S. Forest Service to halt prescribed burns in California, the last effective tool for reducing fuel loads in volatile dry brush.[30] This decision revealed a stunning disregard for the growing wildfire threats facing the state.

Despite Californians overwhelmingly approving a $7.5 billion water bond in 2014 to build reservoirs and dams, not a single reservoir has been constructed. The deadline for completion passed in January 2022, and still the state has failed to deliver on its promise. California has not built a major water reservoir since 1979, underscoring decades of negligence.[31]

The Los Angeles Department of Water and Power (LADWP) exemplified the institutional dysfunction, failing to maintain vital infrastructure critical to fire containment. Decades of deferred maintenance on water systems led to fluctuating hydrant pressure at the height of the crisis, hampering firefighters' efforts to contain the blaze. LADWP's outdated pipelines and lack of redundancy in water distribution systems turned a perhaps manageable blaze into a definitive, uncontrollable conflagration.[32]

At the helm of this derelict institution was General Manager Janisse Quiñones, a controversial appointee of Mayor Bass. Quiñones, who has a sing-song ethnic accent that grates, receives a staggering annual salary of $750,000—nearly double that of her predecessor; presumably because she is double-plus competent. Quiñones has been widely criticized for prioritizing political allegiances over substantive reforms. Her prior tenure at Pacific Gas and Electric (PG&E), an entity infamous for its wildfire-related negligence, most evident in the incineration of eighty-five people and the town of Paradise, CA, during the Camp Fire of 2018, has drawn further scrutiny. Her appointment is emblematic of the cronyism and entrenched corruption within the city's leadership, where political connections predictably overshadow competence.[33] Under Quiñones's watch, LADWP's failures stood as a testament to the devastating consequences of prioritizing image and nepotism over operational competence.[34]

The failures are so glaring and predictably destructive that one has to consider whether Los Angeles officials might simply be pyromaniacs. The city routinely fails to enforce brush clearance laws that could mitigate wildfire risks, citing resource shortages as the excuse. Bass slashed the Fire Department's budget by $17 million while allocating funds for projects like the $100,000 "Midnight Stroll Transgender Café," $8,670 for the "One Institute International Gay and Lesbian Archives," and $170,000 for "Social Justice Art-Worker Investments."[35] This absurd and decadent misallocation of resources left overgrown brush as kindling for the firestorm to come.

The Los Angeles Fire Department's own strategic plan prioritized "diversity, equity, and inclusion" and creating a "progressive work environment" over technological innovation and disaster recovery capabilities, which it ranked as its lowest priority.[36] Such was the wholesale rot within the body of city leadership on the eve of the worst wildfire in the region's history.

The broader implications of a single-party state came into sharp relief as the Palisades disappeared into the smoke. The absence of meaningful opposition stultifies California's political leaders who operate in an echo chamber of perverse delusion, insulated from accountability and judgment. This dynamic fosters a culture of complacency, where governance is dictated by ideological purity rather than pragmatism and public safety. The Palisades Fire laid bare the vulnerabilities created by this system, exposing the brittleness of California's infrastructure, the rot within its institutions, and the indifference of its leadership.

For those who lived through it, the fire was more than a natural disaster—it was a crucible. It burned away the illusion of safety, revealing the harsh reality of a state in decay. The ashes of the Palisades stand as both a grave and a warning: a testament to the human and environmental toll when leaders abandon their responsibilities. California's unraveling governance turned what should have been a preventable disaster into a searing indictment of systemic failure.

The devastation unleashed by the January 2025 fires is staggering in both scope and detail. Across LA County, more than 40,000 acres were incinerated, with the Palisades Fire alone consuming over 23,000 acres.[37] Entire neighborhoods were obliterated, as more than 10,000 structures—including iconic landmarks—were reduced to rubble.[38] Simultaneously, the Eaton Fire ravaged the eastern side of Los Angeles, scorching 14,000 acres and leveling 9,000 structures.[39] As of January 20, 2025, the wildfires have claimed at least twenty-seven lives, a grim toll that underscores the magnitude of this catastrophe.[40] By comparison, the Woolsey Fire in November 2018, previously the most destructive wildfire in Los Angeles County history, destroyed 1,643 structures and claimed three lives.[41] For survivors of the current fires, the loss extends far beyond the physical destruction. Sifting through ash and debris in search of fragments of their former lives, they confront a profound and disorienting grief—a sense of dislocation and despair that no statistics can capture.

The economic toll of the fires mirrored the human devastation, with damages across Los Angeles County estimated to exceed \$150 billion.[42] Insurance companies, inundated with an avalanche of claims, struggle to process payouts, leaving countless residents in financial limbo.[43] Those without sufficient coverage face an insurmountable path to recovery, as rebuilding costs will likely surge in the aftermath of the disaster. Even for those with the means to rebuild, haunting questions remain: Would it ever be safe to return? Could a semblance of home and normalcy be restored?

A crisis of displacement soon emerged from the ruins. Thousands of residents, now homeless, sought refuge in a housing market already strained to its limits. Rental demand surged, with prices skyrocketing by as much as 64% in some areas, forcing families into temporary accommodations far from their communities and support systems.[44] The emotional toll of this dislocation has been profound. Children, torn from familiar surroundings, grappled with the upheaval of new schools and neighborhoods—many of them already bearing the lingering psychological scars of the Pandemic. Adults, burdened by the dual weight of financial uncertainty and the psychological trauma of sudden loss, face a future overshadowed by the daunting challenges of rebuilding their lives and the ever-present fear of recurrence in a state that never seems to learn.

A survivor poignantly described the disorienting aftermath:

"You're always looking for something. Packing in haste disturbs the order of life. Before the fire, I had a simple life, but behind it there was a very complicated system to support the simplicity I took for granted. When the simplicity was incinerated, the complex system behind that began to appear. That system has to be managed, and because the fire happened so suddenly, there is a sense of overload—an unraveling of mental order. What was established over decades was consumed in moments, leaving only chaos in its place."

This profound sense of dislocation was compounded by the knowledge that the fire's devastation extended far beyond individual lives and homes—it scarred the very environment that had once defined the region, once again exposing the bitter irony of California's much-touted environmental policies. Vast expanses of vegetation were reduced to ash, leaving the landscape vulnerable to erosion and landslides. Wildlife habitats were annihilated, and the unchecked release of toxins into the atmosphere undermined the very ecological goals policymakers claimed to champion. Even the firefighting efforts themselves were hindered by misguided regulations, such as restrictions on the use of saltwater, which further desiccated communities at a time when every available water resource was salvation. For many, the ashes of their communities were a personal loss, but they were also part of a broader collapse that would ripple across the natural world.

Meanwhile, the aftermath of the fire brought a secondary crisis: contamination of drinking water supplies in surrounding areas. Toxic runoff from charred debris, combined with chemicals used in firefighting, seeped into reservoirs and aquifers, threatening the safety of the water supply. Residents were forced to rely on bottled water and temporary filtration systems, further compounding the challenges of recovery and underscoring the long-term consequences of the fire.

For survivors, the challenge was not merely rebuilding—it was confronting whether rebuilding was even possible in a meaningful sense. The fires had destroyed not only homes and property but had also fractured the community's sense of security and trust. In their aftermath, residents grappled with anger, grief, and the bitter realization that their suffering was not caused by an unpredictable natural disaster but by preventable, human folly. Such disillusionment is a natural reaction to governmental negligence—a corrosive force that erodes faith in institutions, undermines civil society, and weakens the social contract itself. Systemic incompetence, ideological rigidity, and misplaced priorities had transformed what should have been a manageable crisis into an unimaginable catastrophe.

The fire blackened not only the landscape, but the soul of Los Angeles; the blaze revealing a dark, moral decay in the chaos that followed. The looters came swiftly, descending from the distant corners of the city like vultures drawn to death. They were systematic and merciless, as if summoned by the same forces that had unleashed the inferno. They moved with alarming velocity, their convoys of tinted SUVs cutting through quiescent streets in packs of two or three, fast and deliberate. I stood in the midst of it, watching as Santa Monica police wrestled hooded suspects from their vehicles in broad daylight. During and after the peak of the blaze, the SMPD's presence in my neighborhood, situated in an Evacuation Warning Zone, was both unrelenting and resolute. They guarded homes and the street with a sense of purpose that had felt absent for years. For the first time in a long time, I saw a police force that seemed to have rediscovered its calling—its backbone.

This wasn't the same SMPD that had once stood down as George Floyd rioters torched and looted downtown Santa Monica in 2020. From my vantage point, the shift was palpable and stark—a return to a policing style we hadn't seen in LA since the 1990's. The hesitant racial calculus that had paralyzed action for years seemed gone, replaced by a deadly seriousness that brought genuine protection. For many of us, this moment felt like an overdue correction, the kind of policing we had been waiting for—not with cynicism, but with a desperate and long-dormant hope.

But even with the heightened police presence, the streets were dangerous. My brother had a harrowing encounter just two blocks from our family home on Georgina Avenue, an area designated as an Evacuation Warning Zone. Around 11 p.m., while walking on the street we grew up on—a street we'd always associated with safety—a dark sedan passed him, stopping briefly at the end of the block before reversing ominously toward him. He froze as the car pulled alongside him.

"Do you need help?" one of the passengers, a young Hispanic male, barked with thinly veiled aggression. My brother replied cautiously, "No, I'm fine, thanks." The situation escalated as the man snapped back, "Because it looks like you were looking at us!" It wasn't a question—it was a threat. As the car idled, he could make out three, maybe four gang members inside, their black eyes blazing with hatred, boring into him like predators sizing up food.

Armed with nothing but a tactical flashlight, he aimed its beam into the vehicle, the only semblance of defense he had. "Are you from here?" he challenges, trying to reclaim some control over the situation. One of the men in the back, slouched low, sneered, "Nah, we're from far from here." Then, the passenger in the front seat erupted: "Now get that fucking light off us!"

Tension hung heavy in the air. My brother, standing firm yet fully aware of the danger, took a step back, refusing to break eye contact. "You should get out of here," he said, voice steady despite the pounding in his chest. After a long, loaded silence, the car finally sped off deeper into the neighborhood.

He called 9-1-1 immediately and flagged down an SMPD patrol car, relaying everything he had witnessed. The officers responded rapidly, taking off in the direction he had pointed—a striking departure from the inaction and indifference that had come to characterize policing in Los Angeles in recent years.

Yet even this swift action couldn't obscure a deeper, more unsettling truth: the streets of our hometown, once sanctuaries of safety and familiarity, had become contested ground. The fire exposed more than systemic failures; it revealed the fragility of the city's authority and the emboldened criminality it had allowed to fester. Bad policy had carved a vacuum of order in Los Angeles, and the predators tore into it with feral savagery.

The looters who descended upon Los Angeles weren't opportunistic thieves driven by desperation. They were soldiers of organized crime— tactical, armed, and ruthlessly methodical. They moved through the chaos with the precision of a predatory force, exploiting the crisis with a level of planning that spoke to both experience and boldness. A witness recounted to *KTLA 5*, "Cars pull up, doors open, and groups of men running up our street, going up to the doors of these houses. There were at least 100 people who came up on scooters, trying to get into any and all houses." When pressed about law enforcement's response, the witness delivered a chilling indictment: "I didn't see any."[45]

The impudence of these criminals was matched only by the scale of their operation. In Mandeville Canyon, three men were accused of stealing $200,000 worth of valuables from a home just three days into the crisis.[46] This was not simply opportunism—it was premeditated exploitation, executed in the midst of a disaster. The lawlessness wasn't confined to one neighborhood; it was pervasive, targeting white communities already on their knees, where police, stretched thin, were often unable to intervene.

The looters were also ingenious in their depravity—beyond belief actually. In the Pacific Palisades, two individuals, Dustin and Jennifer Nehl, criminals from Oregon, were arrested for impersonating firefighters using a firetruck they had purchased at an auction. Donning CAL-Fire uniforms, they attempted to breach secured areas under the guise of emergency responders, aiming to pilfer valuables from deserted homes.[47]

Amid the devastation of the Eaton Fire in Altadena, looters were caught trying to steal a 2002 Emmy Award from a burned-out home. Posing as concerned neighbors, they attempted to blend into the chaos but were intercepted by firefighters and later charged with burglary. The incident underscored the depraved opportunism that surfaced in the wake of the disaster.[48]

On January 9, the City of Santa Monica declared a local state of emergency and ordered a curfew for residents in the evacuation zones owing to the continued threat of theft and looting in areas subject to evacuation orders.[49] Curfews were also imposed on the Pacific Palisades and Altadena, ravaged by the Eaton fire. On January 10, the National Guard was deployed to some burn zones for added protection from the onslaught of criminal predation.[50]

In Santa Monica, police chased away at least 150 suspects from evacuation zones near the Palisades in the course of a week, making forty-two arrests in the process. According to Lt. Erika Aklufi, the suspects, mostly from South LA, had swarmed affluent, vacated neighborhoods under evacuation orders, seizing the opportunity to loot and pillage.[51] Of those arrested, ten faced burglary charges, while six were caught with burglary tools. The rest were detained for curfew violations, drug possession, driving offenses, outstanding warrants, and parole or probation violations. Not a single suspect was a Santa Monica resident, underscoring the sense of targeted besiegement characterizing the crime spree.[52] The gangsters were now *in our neighborhood*, and far from their turf. They asserted territorial dominance with menace, and until recent years this would have been unthinkable. Yet, in the era of Soros DAs and woke equity politics, this violent presence had to some extent become both normalized and habitual.

Sergeant Michael Maher (ret.), a thirty-two-year veteran of the Los Angeles County Sheriff's Department and former Detective Sergeant with twelve years in the Major Crimes Bureau, offered this sobering reflection: "Over thirty years I've been in the trenches for large violent riots, many large brush fires, flooding, earthquakes, and madness . . . All pale in comparison to last week. Honestly."

Police reports from the Palisades and nearby evacuation zones documented over fifty incidents of theft, ranging from stolen jewelry to firearms.[53] As of January 21, 2025, the Los Angeles County District Attorney's Office had formally charged nine individuals with looting in connection to the Palisades and Eaton fires.[54] Despite these measures, the pervasive sense of insecurity further traumatized evacuees, who already faced the daunting prospect of returning to decimated neighborhoods.

On January 13, six days after the outbreak of the Palisades Fire, prosecutors charged nine individuals with looting in the evacuation zones.[55] Additionally, authorities accused a homeless man of deliberately starting a blaze in Azusa, two miles from the dry brush of the San Gabriel Mountains. Though this fire didn't link directly to the wildfires that ravaged Los Angeles County, Police Chief Rocky Wenrick noted its dangerous potential, stating that it could have easily spread given the fierce winds that week.[56]

Jose Gerardo Escobar, thirty-nine, was charged with three counts of arson in connection with the Azusa fire. Officials have not disclosed his motive, but the timing and malevolence of the act reflect a chilling and evil disregard for the ongoing disaster. This marked the second alleged arson incident during the wave of January wildfires.[57] Days earlier, Ventura County authorities arrested thirty-three-year-old Juan Sierra, a "person of interest" in the Kenneth Fire, which scorched nearly 1,000 acres and endangered homes in Calabasas.[58] Sierra was apprehended after residents in West Hills saw him attempting to start a fire with a blowtorch in their neighborhood.

Sierra, a homeless illegal alien from Mexico, became a flashpoint in the debate over California's sanctuary state policies. Despite Immigration and Customs Enforcement (ICE) issuing a detainer request for his deportation days after his arrest, sources for the New York Post indicated the federal agency did not expect compliance due to state law.[59] California's sanctuary policies, reinforced by a Los Angeles City Council ordinance passed in November 2024, prohibit local resources and personnel from aiding federal immigration enforcement.[60]

Sierra's criminal history is as alarming as it is extensive. Records reveal multiple convictions in Los Angeles County, including assault with a deadly weapon in 2023. Collectively, he has spent over two years in jail yet was repeatedly released back into the community—a testament to the revolving door of California's justice system.[61] His case underscores a system where public safety is secondary to ideological posturing, leaving citizens exposed to preventable dangers while policies prioritize shielding individuals like Sierra from deportation.

In the City of Industry, twenty minutes east of Downtown LA, thirty-seven-year-old Jaime Mota was arrested after allegedly setting a stack of wooden pallets ablaze behind a shipping yard on the afternoon of January 11, five days after the fires erupted. Mota's flames quickly spread, consuming a tractor-trailer and igniting nearby brush before authorities contained the fire. Currently, he is being held on $350,000 bail and faces up to seven years in prison if convicted.[62]

In Irwindale, twelve miles southeast of the Eaton Fire, twenty-seven-year-old Ruben Michael Montes allegedly set another fire under the shadow of the Interstate 605 overpass at Rivergrade Road. Already on probation at the time, Montes now faces charges that could result in a fourteen-year sentence. His actions, deliberate and calculated, underscored the insidious criminal element that capitalized on chaos. Authorities have held him on $400,000 bail, but the larger question remains: How many others like Montes are emboldened by a system that fails to deter repeat offenders?[63]

On January 14, the LAPD arrested a woman suspected of lighting multiple piles of rubbish ablaze. At a press conference, LAPD Chief Jim McDonnell revealed her chilling confession: she enjoyed "causing chaos and destruction." Earlier that same day, officers arrested a man who admitted to starting a tree fire simply because he liked the smell of burning leaves.[64] Authorities have detained at least eight individuals accused of setting smaller fires since the larger infernos erupted at roughly 10:30 a.m., and 6:18 p.m. on January 7, 2025. These incidents are stark reminders of how a fractured justice system and unchecked criminality can further inflame an already devastated landscape.

Human activity accounts for approximately 95% of California's wildfires, according to a report by Cal Fire Law Enforcement, a division of the California Department of Forestry and Fire Protection. Whether sparked intentionally, by negligence, or through accidents like downed power lines and reckless backyard barbecues, these seemingly small and isolated acts have borne enormous destruction across Southern California.[65] Cal Fire statistics show that in 2024 alone, 109 arson-related arrests were made across the state.[66] In 2020, wildfires caused by arson burned 44,609 acres—a sobering testament to the fact that California's wildfire crisis is as much anthropogenic as it is a feature of the weather.[67]

Furthermore, the looting crisis triggered by the LA fires extended far beyond the ransacking of homes, exposing something far more deliberate and sinister. Classified intelligence from the LA County Sheriff's Major Crimes Bureau reported a major breach at the Army Reserve Center in Tustin, a city in Orange County but within the greater Los Angeles metropolitan area. On January 8, 2025, unknown suspects infiltrated an Army storage warehouse and absconded with a staggering haul of military hardware: three Humvees—one of them armored—along with eight machine gun vehicle mounts, seven standing machine gun tripods, forty binoculars, and eighteen bayonets. This wasn't mere opportunism; it was a calculated, high-stakes raid carried out with chilling precision under the cover of wildfire-induced chaos. The question of where the Army was during this breach remains unanswered—and profoundly unsettling.

The theft didn't just strip a federal facility of military assets; it shattered any remaining illusion that California retained control over its institutions. The state's governance, already exposed as brittle, now appeared irreparably hollow. When the Army itself becomes a target for plunder, the message is brutally clear: the state is defenseless. This wasn't the work of desperate thieves or opportunistic looters; it bore the unmistakable hallmarks of a highly organized and well-funded operation—sophisticated criminal networks exploiting systemic collapse with unnerving audacity and reach. The brazenness of the Tustin heist underscores a deeper, more disturbing reality that transcends the chaos: California's gangs have metastasized into shadow paramilitary forces, mirroring the dynamics endemic to Mexico—if not direct extensions of Mexican organized crime. Emboldened by the same corruption and state impotence that fostered their rise south of the border, these forces have extended their influence unchecked into the very heart of California—and this infiltration has been underway for years.

In a region where cartel influence has entrenched itself as a shadow economy and captured the machinery of organized crime across the state, the implications are dire. The precision and coordination behind this heist suggest something far beyond opportunistic theft—it was a calculated strike by professional networks adept at exploiting failing states. Tucker Carlson, a California native and no stranger to the state's decline, encapsulated the gravity of the moment with chilling clarity: "It sounds like a war."

And perhaps it was—though this war had been raging long before the fires of January 2025 erupted. For years, California has been quietly losing its battle against organized crime, a war that most state leaders have lacked the courage to confront. But the fires left no room for denial. They exposed the raw and unvarnished truth: criminal networks are not merely exploiting chaos—they are thriving in it, flourishing in a state gutted by mismanagement, failed policies, and an institutional paralysis that emboldens the most dangerous predators in the hemisphere. California has become their hunting ground, and its leaders have ceded the fight.

The audacity of these criminals was compounded by the backdrop of California's Proposition 47, the so-called "Safe Neighborhoods and Schools Act," which decriminalized theft under $950. Proposition 47 and other soft-on-crime policies have predictably fostered a climate of lawlessness and violence, emboldening criminals during times of crisis. This wasn't chaos. It was collapse. The looters didn't fear the state because the state no longer existed in any meaningful form. Laws like Proposition 47, drafted for voters by Kamala Harris, had already ensured that theft wasn't a crime worth punishing. The looters understood what so many Californians had come to accept: there were no consequences anymore, only opportunities. They weren't acting outside the system—they were the logical end of it.

The January fires didn't just consume land and property; they revealed a county caught in the crucible of chaos, its institutions forced into a trial of competence and will. Amid the flames and the aftermath, Los Angeles County was compelled to confront its fragility, exposing fractures in governance and law enforcement. Yet, within this chaos, contrasts emerged—contrasts that told a deeper story about the state of policing and civic resilience across the region.

XXXII   ·   FAILED STATE

In Santa Monica, an independent city within LA County, the SMPD demonstrated an unyielding commitment to their charge. Their swift, coordinated response in the Evacuation Warning Zones inspired trust that bordered on nostalgia—a vision of law enforcement that felt almost bygone with its clarity of purpose. Residents, many of whom still bore the scars from the unchecked destruction of 2020, saw in the SMPD a stark and reassuring contrast to the paralysis that had defined so much of LA's law enforcement in recent years.

Meanwhile, in the Palisades, where jurisdiction fell to the LAPD, the response faltered. Waves of looters descended on evacuation zones unchecked, reports of burglary and vandalism continuing for days. Arrests were made, but they were sporadic, and enforcement gaps left many residents feeling exposed and abandoned. Faced with this escalating threat, surviving households in the Palisades even began pooling resources to form private security forces. These weren't simply concerned neighbors keeping watch; they were armed patrols—a modern echo of the militias that emerged in past eras of frontier lawlessness. Similar reports of nascent private policing efforts surfaced across LA County, underscoring the growing sense of disillusionment with public institutions.

Even in Santa Monica, where the SMPD had proven itself reliable, residents in Evacuation Warning Zones felt the weight of self-defense. Some joined informal street patrols to safeguard their homes, while others fortified their properties in anticipation of further threats. These citizen-led efforts, occasionally coordinated with law enforcement, revealed an uncomfortable but enduring truth: when public systems falter, the burden of safety inevitably shifts to the people themselves.

The fires laid bare the consequences of a collapsing social contract. As public safety eroded, those with means turned to privatized solutions. A former senior law enforcement officer, now running a private security firm, described the surge in demand for his services: "I've taken calls from all over LA—the Palisades, Brentwood, La Crescenta, Flintridge—regarding our company providing armed neighborhood patrols. Sadly, this has been good for business." His sober conclusion was as revealing as it was troubling: "Only the ultra-wealthy can afford protection." In a state lauded for its progressivism, the disparity in safety became yet another indicator of societal decline.

As Sergeant Maher observed, "Following the fires the press erupted with stories of looting and how evil it is (and it is). But let's be clear—this sort of looting has been happening daily for years. Even if there had never been a fire, burglars would still be victimizing and pillaging homes all over the Southland, with the media ignoring it." The fires may have briefly brought attention to this rampant criminality, but as the flames die down and the city begins its recovery, the media will likely return to overlooking the entrenched lawlessness that has become a fixture of life in California.

The fires didn't create this wave of criminality—they merely stripped away the façade, exposing the unchecked erosion of public safety. Looting during the crisis was not an aberration; it was a stark reminder of the deeper failures that have allowed lawlessness to thrive in the state.

The limitations of law enforcement during times of crisis were also laid bare. Maher's pointed critique illustrated this disparity: "I wish the police on LA's West Side were as motivated in fighting and preventing crime as they are in holding an intersection during evacuations. Holding a road-block is mindless, easy, and sexy when it's on national news. But actively preventing crime—that's hard work. It takes skill, effort, and persistence, and it doesn't make for good TV." His words highlighted a troubling pattern—performative displays of order taking precedence over the hard, unglamorous work of crime prevention, leaving communities vulnerable to the very conditions the fire revealed so starkly.

What burned in the Palisades wasn't just homes or brush. It was the pretense of order, the lie of safety. These were insolated neighborhoods that had believed, until that moment, in the myth of California's prosperity, in its veneer of governance and control. Significantly, these were voters of Kamala Harris, Gavin Newsom, and Karen Bass. But in the blaze that wiped their world from the map, they found amongst the ashes a state stripped bare of its responsibilities, exposed for what it had become: an empty husk, incapable of defending even its most basic functions. The looting wasn't a symptom. It was the inevitable outcome of a state that had long since ceased to care.

Survivors described streets devoid of any authority, neighborhoods left to fend for themselves. Families who stayed behind, unwilling to abandon the only lives they had ever known, armed themselves with whatever weapons they could find—shotguns, crowbars, even kitchen knives. Fear and fury overtook desperation as they guarded their shattered homes, no longer trusting the hollow promises of a system that had already abandoned them.

The fire's aftermath, much like its apocalyptic fury, revealed a deeper rot within the structures meant to safeguard society. What burned in the Pacific Palisades wasn't just the landscape—it was the last illusion of order in a state crumbling under the weight of its contradictions. California, for all its wealth and innovation, had become a grim microcosm of national decline—a dystopian theatre where hollow ideology posed as governance, and the innocent paid the price. As the embers cooled and the smoke began to clear, the true scale of the crisis revealed itself—not merely in the ruins of the Palisades but in the hearts of its survivors, who now bore the weight of a terrifying realization: the fire was not the end. It was the beginning. The prelude to a failed state.

Donald J. Trump ✓
@realDonaldTrump

The actual irony... A home owner consents to pay property taxes that will go to the fire department. The funds are diverted to illegal immigrants because LA is a Sanctuary City. An illegal immigrant comes and sets your house on fire and the fire department doesn't have the resources to put it out. The home owner paid for their own destruction. On top of that, the government is so inept that the insurance companies won't insure houses here anymore, so the home owner is left with nothing.

2.83k ReTruths 6.54k Likes   1/14/25, 3:35 PM

PREFACE
HOME INVASION

On the weekend of September 9, 2023, my family home in Santa Monica, CA, was burglarized on two consecutive nights while my brother and I slept inside. The first night, the intruder broke through a gate and slipped into the backyard, past sensor lights, and breached the well-lit house through a back door. We have neighbors on either side several feet away. This did not deter him, nor did the numerous signs indicating an alarm system, which coincidentally, and known only to us, was inactive. The second night, he dismantled a first-floor street-facing window, again, into the well-lit house, this time a dining room—a place of many cherished Thanksgiving and Christmas dinners. I believe he returned a third night, as I observed an individual idling outside the house at 2 a.m. I would later discover that this person matched the suspect and his vehicle. He took everything of value, irreplaceable items from our grandparents, but also odd, seemingly worthless items—sunglasses, a letter opener, Easter eggs. The electronics were left untouched, however, the sanctity of a home, with generations of memories, was desecrated.

We live in an affluent neighborhood, but our house is the most modest on the block, unchanged since my grandparents bought it after World War II. The neighbors were stunned that we had been targeted—the house with the dilapidated roof. We, too, were incredulous until we realized that the handicap parking spot out front, a relic of my grandparents' time, probably made the burglar think it was an easy mark. Predators go for the weak.

Burglaries gut you. The violation and the plunder evoke emotions akin to assault: shock, rage, helplessness, and a creeping, insidious shame. It's a persistent dread, a stain on the house that never quite looks the same. For my brother and me, knowing it happened inches from us while we slept—and then happened again—brought disbelief and an enduring paranoia. In time, I came to realize that our response was wholly warranted by the stark reality of our circumstances and the broader downfall of a city.

After the first break-in, the Santa Monica police showed up ten hours later. On the second day, they took fifteen hours. The officer said they were overwhelmed with homeless overdoses. A forensic team eventually dusted for prints and DNA, assuring us they'd take it seriously. We were given an incident number. We were ghosted. To this day, SMPD hasn't followed up, despite California Penal Code (§ 667.5(c)) classifying burglaries of inhabited dwellings as violent felonies. It became evident that SMPD's inaction was part of a broader policy of inaction, especially concerning so-called property crimes on the westside. This is the same department that ordered officers to stand down when downtown Santa Monica was torched during the BLM Riots in the summer of 2020.

A month later, Detective Chris Mulligan from Simi Valley Police called. My wallet and driver's license were found during the arrest of a convicted felon linked to numerous home invasions in Southern California.

The suspect, called Eduardo Rodriguez, is a 30-year-old illegal alien—a Dreamer, actually—who came to Los Angeles when he was 5 years old from El Salvador. According to Detective Mulligan, Rodriguez is also MS-13. Rodriguez was matched to the burglaries by fingerprints, surveillance footage, stolen property, and DNA.

At his arrest during a traffic stop in Sylmar, Rodriguez had his wife and two-month-old son in the car. He was found with a stolen loaded Kimber handgun, 19 hollow-point rounds, a large quantity of Fentanyl pills, various jewelry, and $1,200 in cash. Also discovered in his vehicle, oddly, was an Armenian bachelor's degree diploma, a book of blank checks, and foreign currency.

At Rodriguez's home, officers found more weapons: another stolen handgun, two shotguns, and tactical plate carrier with level four body armor. Possession of body armor by a felon is a federal offense (18 U.S.C. 981). The Kimber handgun had been reported stolen, along with three other firearms, during an August burglary. The checkbook belonged to LA Superior Court Judge Michael Pastor, who presided over the Michael Jackson death trial. He had the judge's Seiko watch too.

While booking Rodriguez, an officer "thanked him for not using the recovered firearm against police during the operation." Rodriguez replied that if his wife and child hadn't been in the car, he would have engaged in a shoot-out and attempted to kill officers. He told them he had no intention of going back to prison, having already lost seven years of his life. He reiterated that he was "serious about his statement," and would have "gone 'Eric's' to initiate his last stand."

In 2019, ICE deported Rodriguez to El Salvador after he served seven years in a California State Prison for felony weapons and drug offenses. Upon release, Rodriguez stated that "he was immediately picked up by the Feds" and sent back. While in El Salvador, he had his MS-13 tattoos removed from his face. He then made his way to France, living there for two years before slipping back into the United States in 2021. The police reports do not reveal how he reentered the U.S.

Rodriguez addmitted that he used fentanyl to dull the pain from a 2021 stabbing and meth to stay sharp enough to work. He married Dorrin Muniz two years ago. They had a son, Ezekiel. He helped raise her two daughters from a previous relationship and considered them his own. Rodriguez confirmed an LAPD report listing him in a battery investigation, stating he fought Dorrin's ex-boyfriend and "knocked his bitch ass out." Rodriguez worked construction with his father, specializing in finish carpentry.

During interrogation, Simi Valley Detective Shane Johnson asked Rodriguez if he knew what a burglary was. He stated it was "when someone broke into a house and stole stuff," adding that he too had been a burglary victim after returning to California from El Salvador. He said if someone broke into his house, he would "beat their ass."

Rodriguez was caught on surveillance footage and partly identified by his clothing. In his interview, he admitted to visiting a victim's house to ask for a job but denied committing the burglaries. Flippantly, Rodriguez asked Detective Johnson if he thought he would commit a burglary while wearing sandals. Detective Johnson responded, "Yes, which is why you're arrested." Johnson added, furthermore, "that it scared him that he would be so brazen to commit these crimes in the middle of the day in the manner for which he did and that was why he was arrested." Indeed.

Another month passed. Detective Mulligan gave me a final update before Simi Valley closed the case. He shared many details from the official police files. Reluctantly, he confirmed Rodriguez's MS-13 affiliation after I inquired about the El Salvador connection. Mulligan was swamped with cases of Asian donut shop owners being followed home and robbed by South American burglary crews. These immigrant merchants, distrustful of banks, tend to carry excess cash and gold, and are undefended. The South Americans know a score. Mulligan expressed frustration that Rodriguez had only been convicted of two burglaries. He explained that Rodriguez's prosecution had been fast-tracked because Ventura County was dealing with so many homicides.

Santa Monica ghosted Simi Valley. No charges were filed against Rodriguez by SMPD or LAPD. Mulligan remarked that we were lucky it happened in Ventura, not Los Angeles County. There, Rodriguez would have been "released on no bail with a ticket to show up in court two years later."

Rodriguez stole at least $100,000 worth of goods. The thefts were vicious, reckless, and cruel. He took everything and anything, from wedding rings to a Catholic rosary box. He pled guilty to a burglary charge under section 459 of the Penal Code and was sentenced to two years in the Department of Corrections. He also pled guilty to a third burglary count, receiving another two-year sentence, to be served concurrently. In total, he will serve just two years. He was credited with 69 days already spent in custody.

The court acknowledged his history of drug abuse and recommended counseling. A $300 restitution fine was imposed, with another $300 stayed pending parole completion.

INTRODUCTION

FALL FROM GRACE

Failing by Design

When I spoke to Kathleen Cady, a victim's rights advocate and former Los Angeles Deputy District Attorney, she remarked with pointed clarity:

"What is so important about your story is it is something where people go, Oh, crap, that could have been me. And so I think it is more relatable to many people. The thought that, Wow, I could be in my house and an MS-13 gang member with a loaded gun who's already been deported could break in and take all my stuff and nothing happens. Wow. So, yeah, there are, of course, many horrific cases. But I think what's so important about your case is that it is so relatable."

Relatable. That word captures a grotesque new reality in California. How did we arrive at a point where an armed, previously deported, illegal alien—a hardened gangster no less—could twice invade a suburban home in one weekend? Where a violent criminal could be so emboldened and face only trivial consequences? And this is now "relatable" to the average Californian?

The case of Rodriguez exposes systemic rot eroding law, justice, and public safety in California. Violent, brazen, felonious, a member of a transnational death cult—yet, he will serve less jail time than a veteran who walked into the Capitol on January 6; veterans who, in one case, met execution. Rodriguez will serve less prison time than an American ensnared by the IRS. It leaves one to wonder: Did he ever pay taxes? Did he or his family receive state benefits? Was he mailed a voter registration card—perhaps more than one?

This is not an isolated instance of bureaucratic failure; it is emblematic of a system adrift from its purpose. Rodriguez should never have stepped foot here. Yet he roamed this state with impunity—armed, dangerous, and secure in the knowledge that California's justice system prioritizes foreign criminals over protecting citizens.

He sired at least one U.S. citizen, cost the state millions, and terrorized families. He stole memories—wedding rings, graduation presents, family heirlooms. With brazen disregard, he threatened to murder police officers. To his credit, he spoke primarily English—thanks DREAM Act. The systemic collapse that allowed Rodriguez to thwart our laws repeatedly highlights a glaring divide between the government and the citizenry. Yet, as one peels back the layers of decay, a grim reality emerges: the policy functions precisely as designed.

At its core, this is not mere negligence—it is gross negligence, a reckless disregard for public safety so blatant it borders on criminality. By definition, gross negligence is not just failure—it is willful neglect, an abdication of duty so extreme that the harm is not just possible but inevitable. In Rodriguez's case, as in countless others, California's refusal to enforce its laws and prosecute violent offenders is not passive incompetence—it is active dereliction, a betrayal so severe it meets the threshold of criminal negligence.

What we are witnessing in California is not simple bureaucratic incompetence but the deliberate enactment of a radical ideology that elevates offenders above victims, criminals above citizens, and illegal aliens above Americans. This is government no longer failing by accident but failing by design.

A Civic Order in Freefall

We now live in a state where safety is an illusion, shattered by bureaucratic paralysis and the pathological mismanagement of justice. Half of our wealth is surrendered to a government that prioritizes foreign criminals over its own citizens. Our safety, well-being, and welfare are sacrificed on the altar of "equity," a tribute to the foreign hordes in our midst.

The handling of Rodriguez's case—his expedited prosecution amid a backlog of homicides and the indifference of local law enforcement—exposes a state that has abandoned its most fundamental duty: public safety. California no longer enforces the law; it selectively applies it, prioritizing optics over the protection of its own citizens.

The consequences of this dereliction are dire. The social contract—the foundation of a civilized society—has fractured. As trust in government disintegrates, citizens are left to fend for themselves, navigating a landscape where lawlessness is tolerated and justice is arbitrary. A dangerous transformation takes hold when people see that their leaders are more invested in ideological posturing than protecting lives. The boundaries between right and wrong dissolve, and the rule of force replaces the rule of law.

This is not simply a failure of governance—it is the systematic dismantling of order itself. And its repercussions will not be confined to California. A nation that refuses to uphold its own laws will not remain a nation for long.

The Ideology of Collapse

This collapse is no accident. It is the inevitable outcome of a radical ideological project designed to dismantle law and order, deliberately transforming California into a reflection of South Africa's failed state—a calculated "South Africanization" of our society. California has become the staging ground for this social experiment, where policies like Proposition 47 and Proposition 57, alongside sanctuary city laws, have rendered law enforcement impotent while emboldening the criminal class.

At the core of this collapse lies a malignant offshoot of the equity cult, a doctrine I term "crime-equity"—a grotesque perversion of justice that recasts criminal behavior as the inevitable result of societal oppression and redefines offenders as victims. Justice is no longer about maintaining order but about redressing historical grievances, whether real or imagined. The legal system, once a bulwark against chaos, has been repurposed into a tool for social engineering, where punishment gives way to leniency, and accountability is erased by excuses.

Figures like Kamala Harris, George Gascón, Pamela Price, and their benefactor, George Soros, have led the charge to gut the criminal justice system, turning it into a grotesque caricature of itself. Their policies shift the focus from public safety to rehabilitation of offenders, no matter how dangerous or unrepentant. The result is a two-tiered system where the criminal is liberated and the victim is forgotten.

The intellectual foundation for this radical project rests on the belief that traditional justice is inherently oppressive and that law and order are relics of a discredited past. Offenders like Rodriguez are painted as casualties of an unjust system. At the same time, ordinary citizens—real victims—are left to piece together their shattered lives, abandoned by the very institutions meant to protect them.

A Warning to the Nation

California's collapse is not confined to its borders. The policies responsible for this state's descent into chaos are being systematically exported nation-wide. What begins as "reform" under the guise of social justice inevitably culminates in the dissolution of order. California's ruling elites haven't failed; they've succeeded in implementing their vision of social justice—of crime-equity: a society where the law no longer serves the law-abiding, where criminals operate without consequence, and where justice itself is turned upside down.

This is California's legacy: a failed state, not by incompetence but by intention. It stands as a stark warning to America. The story of Rodriguez is not merely the story of one man—it is the story of a state, and perhaps a nation, on the edge of collapse.

PART I

KILL SWITCH

CHAPTER 1

MACRO VIEW

A System in Freefall

California, once the vanguard of American optimism and innovation, now plunges into alarming disrepair with a speed and severity impossible to deny. The collapse—long apparent to those whose roots run deep and others chasing the dream—has seeped into daily life with urgent force. A state once famed for its cultural vitality and infrastructure now festers under layers of bureaucratic neglect, inefficiency, and escalating criminality. California exemplifies how societies unravel when governance devolves into dysfunction—cloaked in the language of progress but devoid of accountability—leaving behind a brittle façade while the foundations of law and order crumble beneath it.

A net exporter of culture and cutting-edge manufacturing for much of the 20th century, California now exports its people. Over eight million residents fled the state between 2010 and 2022, driven out by crushing taxes, sky-high housing costs, and decaying infrastructure.[1] Those who remain either tacitly acknowledge the crumbling foundations or, more cynically, become complicit in sustaining the rot, driven by political allegiance or personal gain. Newcomers, drawn by the lingering mythos of the Golden State, are quickly disillusioned. Instead of vibrant metropolises, they find open-air drug markets and sprawling encampments masquerading as downtowns. Conversations about crime, homelessness, and political failure are no longer whispered; they are spoken with urgency, embedded in daily discourse, fueled by lived experiences and an intensifying climate of fear.

The visible decay is matched only by the state's reluctance to confront it. Crime, once contained within the so-called "bad neighborhoods," has metastasized across the urban landscape. Homeless encampments multiply, seizing sidewalks and parks as city leaders peddle platitudes, promising vague solutions that never materialize. This is no temporary inconvenience; it is a structural failure that reflects the collapse of governance itself.

Take Los Angeles, for instance—once the embodiment of ambition, beauty, and opportunity. Today, it is a grotesque tableau of destitution, lawlessness, and decay. The City of Angels has become a nightmare for many—a monument to the profound failures of modern governance. Homicides surge, aggravated assaults have become the norm, and organized crime targets businesses and residents alike with impunity. And what is the response from civic leaders? Blank stares from podiums, platitudes masquerading as solutions, and a disconcerting detachment from the violence unfolding under their watch.

Consider the testimony of a Turkish Uber driver, recently settled in Los Angeles, who, after surviving two violent attacks in a single year, remarked: "Los Angeles is a scary shithole compared to Istanbul." His story is far from anomalous, emblematic of a broader, more pervasive trend. California's urban centers now mirror the endemic criminality typically associated with failing states, where both petty and violent crime challenge the very notion of public safety. The state that once promised prosperity now offers a grim lesson in how power, detached from responsibility, can turn paradise into purgatory.

Demography Engineered for Hegemony

California's current political landscape did not emerge by chance or through natural social evolution. It is the product of deliberate policy decisions that have reshaped the state's demographic composition, influencing its political trajectory. Policies such as the sanctuary state designation, ostensibly promoted under the banner of humanitarian concern, have had the desired effect: altering the electorate, increasing reliance on public resources, and entrenching political alignment with the Democratic Party. This shift has contributed to a consolidation of single-party dominance, neutralizing political competition and fostering a feedback loop of power that serves the interests of the ruling establishment rather than the broader population.

This project dates back to the early 1990s, coinciding with California's shift toward a more liberal immigration policy. The state promoted policies encouraging an influx of low-wage, foreign-born laborers, not out of benevolence but to create a new voter base aligning with the state's progressive agenda. By offering social services and protection to these populations, the state created an electorate that is not only more likely to support the Democratic Party but also more reliant on government programs. The calculus was obvious: replace disaffected middle-class voters fleeing the state in droves with a new electorate that would be more reliant on public services—and, therefore, more politically pliant.

The numbers underscore the scale of this transformation. Foreign-born residents now comprise roughly 27% of California's population—the highest proportion in the nation, according to the Public Policy Institute of California (PPIC).[2] Meanwhile, over six million residents have fled the state from 2010 to 2020, many of them middle and upper-class households driven out by crippling taxes, skyrocketing housing costs, and deteriorating infrastructure.[3] The exodus of these voters, who once constituted the backbone of California's economy and fostered political moderation, has solidified the Democratic Party's control and furthered the left's directional radicalism.

Studies from the Pew Research Center and the National Bureau of Economic Research show this new electorate overwhelmingly favors permissive immigration policies and expanded social welfare programs.[4] As the foreign-born population grows, so too does its political influence, consistently bolstering candidates who align with these positions.[5] This creates a recursive cycle: the larger the immigrant population, the more entrenched the Democratic Party becomes, consolidating a one-party system.[6]

The success of this demographic engineering comes at a staggering cost. California's once-vaunted middle class is rapidly receding, replaced by a bifurcated social structure of landed gentry and working poor—if not generational peasants. *Forbes* reports that California experiences some of the worst income inequality in the nation, with top earners benefiting from the tech boom and real asset appreciation.[7] At the same time, the poor are left to navigate one of the highest living costs in the United States that worsens every year.

Victor Davis Hanson of the Hoover Institution at Stanford University notes that the influx of low-wage workers has suppressed wages for native-born residents, creating a permanent underclass that depends on government welfare.[8] California has become what Hanson calls a "cruel medieval state," where serfs serve the interests of the elites, who remain insulated from the very chaos their policies perpetuate.[9] In this paradigm, the ruling class consolidates power as the middle class withers, giving rise to a bifurcated society dominated by a plutocratic elite and an inexorably destitute underclass

The political implications are evident. The Republican Party, once competitive in California, has been relegated to irrelevance, with Democrats holding every statewide office and supermajorities in both legislative chambers continuously since 2012. According to the Public Policy Institute of California, California's foreign-born population grew by 61% from 1990 to 2022, while the native-born population has steadily declined.[10]

The state's infrastructure, once the envy of the world, is collapsing under the weight of its unsustainable and increasingly destitute population. Public schools are overwhelmed by the influx of non-English-speaking students, with the California Department of Education reporting that nearly 20% of California's K-12 students do not speak English.[11] The healthcare system is similarly buckling, with overcrowded hospitals and long wait times becoming the norm. The state's Medicaid program is stretched to its limits, serving over 13 million residents—many of whom are recent immigrants.[12] As of January 1, 2024, illegal aliens ages 26–49 are eligible for full Medi-Cal benefits.[13]

The physical decay of California's cities is the most conspicuous manifestation of the price exacted by single-party rule, a political hegemony engendered by this radical demographic experiment. Sprawling homeless encampments metastasize along the coastline, a stark testament to the erosion of civic order. The state's once-modest social safety net stretched beyond capacity, now buckles under the weight of an ever-growing population reliant on its provisions. Consequently, basic services have deteriorated, public spaces devolved into cesspools of squalor, and the middle class has all but receded—leaving behind an increasingly dependent population ensnared in the web of government aid.

California's political leaders have realized their ultimate ambition: a permanent political majority. Yet this triumph has come at the expense of the foundation upon which the state's prosperity once stood. The price of this engineered hegemony is the systematic erosion of the middle class, the collapse of infrastructure, and the disintegration of social cohesion.

As the Biden-Harris administration presses forward with increasingly permissive immigration policies, California offers a grim preview of America's political future: a nation where demographic engineering is wielded as the primary instrument for maintaining power, no matter the societal costs. What was once the nation's beacon of innovation and opportunity has deteriorated into a cautionary tale of political stagnation, where the absence of genuine opposition has permitted the entrenchment of a grotesque status quo.

Corruption, once confined to hushed conversations, now weaves itself seamlessly into the fabric of state governance, normalized by the complacency of a population anesthetized by decades of one-party rule. The policies crafted under this regime are not solutions to the state's myriad crises; rather, they are designed to entrench power, ensuring that the rot remains obscured by the hollow optics of "progress." In California, Orwell's warning finds its chilling embodiment: "Power is not a means; it is an end."[14]

Exodus from Neo-Feudalism

California's urban decay is a merciless rebuke to its political stewards, a once-gilded realm now corroded by profound, inescapable mismanagement. Downtown boulevards, once brimming with the confidence of peak civilization, are awash in misery and debasement, with tent cities rising like America's favelas—a deep stain on the state's conscience. Even iconic beaches and boardwalks, once the living postcards of a sun-drenched paradise, have devolved into scenes of destitution unimaginable just a generation ago. No amount of polished rhetoric can blot out this glaring failure of governance, which reflects not a mere lapse in policy but a deeper moral collapse—an unbridled nihilism now fracturing the social contract.

The homeless crisis is emblematic of a deeper ideological decay. The so-called "people experiencing homelessness" are not merely casualties of economic misfortune or ill fate; they are the sacrificial lambs of a ruling ideology that has abandoned the pretense of real solutions. Poverty, addiction, and mental illness are no longer viewed as crises demanding resolution but as perpetual conditions to be managed—sustained for the benefit of bloated social bureaucracies that grow fat on their very persistence yet solve nothing. Meanwhile, California's wealthy elites—Silicon Valley's tech oligarchs and Hollywood's self-righteous moralists—reside safely behind fortified walls, applauding their own progressive virtues from afar. They champion policies that manufacture and perpetuate the misery they claim to abhor, insulated from the very chaos their ideologies spawn.

What is now marketed as the "new normal" is nothing less than a descent into barbarism—where gang members are recast as victims of systemic oppression, and public spaces devolve into open-air asylums. The state's pathological obsession with "equity" exacerbates the inequities it purports to remedy, entrenching chaos under the guise of social justice. Once the embodiment of the American Dream, California has become a grotesque caricature of its former self, a parody in which virtue is signaled, but rot runs unchecked beneath the surface.

Perhaps the most damning indictment of California's decline is the exodus of its own residents. Between 2010 and 2022, approximately 8.5 million people fled the state, while only 6.3 million arrived from other parts of the country.[15] This mass departure is not an anomaly but a wholesale repudiation of the political and economic model California has championed. Middle-class families, crushed by soaring housing costs, draconian regulations, and crumbling infrastructure, are being replaced by two distinct groups: affluent tech professionals and low-wage migrant laborers—a deliberate demographic shift engineered to create a more dependent electorate.

The financial implications of this outmigration are stark. According to IRS data, California hemorrhaged $24 billion in personal incomes across

2021 and 2022 alone, as departing residents were wealthier, more likely to have families, and were replaced by poorer individuals seeking their version of the California Dream.[16] The state lost a net 144,203 tax filers in two years, along with their substantial adjusted gross incomes, signaling the flight of prosperity from the state.

At the same time, foreign immigration swelled from 90,300 in 2022 to 114,200 in 2023—excluding those seeking asylum at the border. Yet despite these new arrivals, California's birthrate continued to decline, from 420,393 births in 2022 to 399,368 in 2023, suggesting that while families leave, the newcomers have fewer children, further underscoring the erosion of a stable, thriving middle class.[17]

As middle-class families flee, they leave a void threatening California's future. According to the Hoover Institution, 352 companies relocated their headquarters out of the state between 2018 and 2021—further evidence of California's failure to sustain a functional economic environment.[18] This exodus underscores a deeper systemic breakdown that vitiates economic vitality and undermines broad-based prosperity. What remains is a hollowed-out economy increasingly reliant on a polarized workforce of tech elites and low-wage laborers, eroding the foundations of long-term growth and stability.

A stratified society remains, fractured between the ultra-wealthy and the inexorably poor. Even high-income households are increasingly fleeing to tax-friendly states like Texas and Arizona, as Forbes reports—a trend that directly threatens California's fiscal viability.[19] The state's tax system, disproportionately reliant on the top 1% of earners, now teeters on the brink of collapse as the exodus of wealth accelerates, leaving an unsustainable tax burden on the dwindling middle class.

The tragedy of California lies not merely in the exodus of its people but in the loss of its soul. The once-promised land of opportunity has devolved into a stark cautionary tale, illustrating the dangers of governance that elevate ideology above reality. As infrastructure crumbles and public services buckle under strain, the middle class—the lifeblood of any functional society—steadily vanishes. What was once a beacon of American idealism has been reduced to a hollow shell, a stark reminder of the perils that arise when power is prized above the welfare of the people.

As California bleeds, so too does the narrative that once defined it. The rule of law crumbles alongside decaying infrastructure, and with that decay comes the collapse of trust—a trust once placed in a government that has now forsaken its most fundamental responsibilities.

Civilizational Homicide

California's precipitous decline is not merely a regional tragedy but a stark warning to the United States and the broader global community. Once celebrated for its natural beauty, economic vitality, and cultural influence, California now stands as a masterpiece defaced by those entrusted with its preservation. For generational Californians, the loss is deeply personal—more than just economic or aesthetic, it is the erosion of a state that once embodied possibility, freedom, and progress, replaced by chaos, dysfunction, and betrayal at the hands of the ruling class.

This degradation is no accident; it is the result of a deliberate campaign of exploitation by political elites whose ambitions have gutted the state while setting a dangerous precedent for the nation. Policies enacted under the guise of "equity" have only consolidated power among a wealthy oligarchy, leaving California's infrastructure to decay and its people to suffer the consequences. In a system sustained by demographic manipulation and divisive rhetoric, California has become a test case for national policies that erode the social contract and fracture communities.

California's collapse is not an isolated failure—it is the vanguard of a broader civilizational decline, a blueprint for managed dissolution that extends far beyond its borders. The same sociopolitical forces dismantling California are at work across the West, particularly in Europe, where political elites prioritize power over the welfare of their citizens. Through mass migration, the erosion of national sovereignty, and the deliberate fragmentation of cultural identity, Western nations are being transformed from within—not by conquest, but by design.

This is not just political malpractice; it is demographic warfare—a calculated effort to dilute, displace, and ultimately erase indigenous European populations under the guise of humanitarianism. Such policies are not merely reckless; they constitute ethnic cleansing, orchestrated by domestic actors whose betrayal demands nothing less than proportional justice in the tradition of Nuremberg, 1945.

To dismiss California's decline as a localized crisis is to misunderstand its gravity. As the world's fifth-largest economy, its collapse has seismic implications—not just for the United States but for global markets. A state of this economic magnitude cannot implode in isolation; its failures will reverberate across the nation, accelerating the trends that threaten America's future. Any so-called "Conservative Republican" who cheers California's downfall without grasping its national consequences is not a nationalist but a fool—blind to the systemic forces that will soon engulf the rest of the country.

The unraveling of California is a case study in the perils of unchecked oligarchy, where concentrated wealth, political corruption, and mass migration are weaponized to dissolve national cohesion. The state's ruling elite, insulated from the chaos they've created, have used California as a testing ground for policies that hollow out the middle class, undermine public safety, and fracture civil society. If the United States is to survive intact, it must confront the forces that turned California into a failed state—before they metastasize nationwide.

Criminal Negligence and Malice Aforethought

What is happening in California is not mere mismanagement—it is deliberate. This is not simply incompetence; it is criminal negligence, carried out with full knowledge of the destruction it would unleash—particularly on middle-class neighborhoods once considered safe. The communities now besieged by crime, addiction, and economic collapse were not abandoned by accident—they were sacrificed.

These are not policy missteps; they are acts of systemic betrayal:

- **Lawlessness by Design:** Under the pretense of "justice reform," violent criminals are emboldened while law-abiding citizens are stripped of police protection. Cities that once thrived have become free-for-all zones, where theft is normalized, fentanyl flows unimpeded, and law enforcement is ordered to stand down.

- **The Manufactured Homelessness Crisis:** Public spaces have been surrendered to squalor and criminality, as so-called housing policies do nothing to fix homelessness but instead reward dysfunction, erode property values, and drive families out of their own neighborhoods.
- **Deliberate Economic Strangulation:** The middle class, once the backbone of California's prosperity, is being crushed by confiscatory taxation, mass migration, and bureaucratic sabotage—forced either into permanent dependence or permanent exile.

This collapse is no longer contained within urban decay and failed policies—it has spread to middle America, where once-secure families now face the same government-engineered chaos. The rule of law has disintegrated, bureaucracies have grown parasitic, and the institutions designed to uphold civil order have been weaponized against the public.

California Is the Warning; America Is Next

California is not just collapsing—it is being collapsed. It is the prototype for a post-national America in which lawlessness, demographic upheaval, and economic vassalage are not accidents but intended outcomes. To ignore this reality is to invite catastrophe—not just for California but for the nation at large.

If this trajectory is not reversed, California's fate will become America's. The only question is how much time remains before the nation follows.

CHAPTER 2

STREET VIEW

Los Angeles is dying in slow motion. The fault lines of its collapse run through every neighborhood, from the hollowed-out streets of South Central to the manicured avenues of Brentwood. Where prosperity once masked decay, the pretense has vanished. Smash-and-grab robberies are now routine in Beverly Hills, and tourists at Hollywood's Walk of Fame shuffle past open-air drug markets, sidestepping the discarded needles and broken lives. In a phrase that has come to enshrine the Obama and Biden years, this is LA's "new normal"—a slow, grinding descent where affluence no longer insulates and chaos is met with weary acceptance.

This isn't just neglect; it's a deliberate failure of governance. Policies enacted in the name of equity have hollowed out the legal system, reducing law enforcement to bystanders and deterrence to an afterthought. Theft under $950 is effectively legalized, drug possession carries no consequence, and violent offenders cycle in and out of jail with grim predictability. The people these policies claim to help—those in the city's most vulnerable neighborhoods—are their greatest victims, enduring rising assaults, theft, and an ever-present sense of insecurity.

Law enforcement has been reduced to triage. Veteran officers describe a city where arrests feel pointless, prosecutions are slipping, and morale is at an all-time low. One LAPD sergeant said bluntly: "We've been told to stand down, so that's what we do. The streets aren't ours anymore." 2023 property crimes spiked by double digits while arrest rates plummeted—a deliberate byproduct of reforms championed by figures like District Attorney George Gascón. Under his tenure, punishment is seen as regressive, and accountability has become a dirty word.

The economic toll is just as stark. High-crime neighborhoods now host rows of shuttered businesses, their owners driven out by losses too steep to absorb. In Santa Monica, where retail theft has become a full-time industry, corporate chains are packing up, and local shops are closing without ceremony. Insurance rates skyrocket, commercial vacancies rise, and what remains of the middle class quietly makes plans to leave.

The collapse has been normalized. What was once unthinkable—mobs looting jewelry stores in broad daylight, wealthy residents in Brentwood assaulted on their own doorsteps—barely registers as news. The shock has faded, replaced by a quiet, resigned acceptance. Lawlessness is no longer an aberration but the cost of doing business in California.

This is what happens when the social contract dissolves—not in a single cataclysmic event but through steady erosion, where chaos becomes routine. Survival depends not on the law but on one's ability to navigate the wreckage of a failed state. Outrage has given way to fatigue, and governance to abandonment. The unraveling of a civilization does not always announce itself with a bang. Sometimes, it happens with a slow, deliberate shrug.

The streets of Los Angeles offer a grim warning. The collapse unfolding here is not an anomaly but a reflection of broader systemic failures, policies designed not to preserve safety or order but to dismantle them. These policies do not represent reform; they represent surrender. Policies framed under the guise of equity have failed disastrously, resulting in widespread lawlessness and eroded public trust in law enforcement. As Los Angeles teeters, the question remains: how far can a city fall before it becomes irretrievable?

This chapter examines the alarming rise in crime statistics, the societal impacts of these policies, and the urgent need for decisive action to restore order and safety in one of America's greatest cities and icons.

Reality on the Ground

The unraveling of Los Angeles becomes starkly evident at ground level, where the abstract failures of policy materialize as daily despair. On

Melrose Avenue, shopkeepers weigh the cost of another burglary against the futility of filing a police report. In South Central, families fortify their homes, though even steel bars seem a fragile defense against the unchecked chaos outside. Once shielded by affluence, Brentwood residents now hold neighborhood watch meetings with a seriousness that betrays their rising fear. Across the city, the boundaries that once separated safety from danger are dissolving.

This isn't merely lawlessness; it's entropy by design. Policies prioritizing equity over deterrence have transformed the city into a theater of dysfunction. Crimes that would once provoke outrage—mob-style thefts, brazen assaults in daylight—are now shrugged off as predictable fixtures of life. "Our job isn't to stop it anymore," one LAPD officer admitted. "It's to clean up after it."

What remains unspoken is the weariness that pervades the city, the quiet capitulation of its residents to a system that has abdicated its responsibility to protect them. Local business owners whisper about relocating to safer states. Longtime Angelenos, once dismissive of the notion of leaving, now quietly scout neighborhoods in Austin or Phoenix. These aren't rash reactions—they are the rational calculations of people who no longer trust the city to recover.

For those unable to leave, the normalization of fear is a cruel reality. In minority neighborhoods, where crime has long been a chronic affliction, the escalation feels personal. Single mothers walk their children to school past abandoned lots that have become open-air drug markets. Elderly residents avoid evening strolls, their lives confined by an invisible curfew imposed not by laws but by lawlessness.

Veteran prosecutors and officers agree that this collapse is unlike anything the city has seen before. "We've abandoned the idea of deterrence," explains John Lewin, a respected senior prosecutor in Los Angeles. "We're sending a message that there are no consequences, and criminals know it." Lewin's frustration echoes across jurisdictions, where demoralized officers wrestle with the futility of arrests leading nowhere and cases prosecutors decline to pursue. "There's no question the crime rate is much higher than reported," Lewin asserts. "The lack of reporting of crime is a huge problem. Companies now understand nothing will happen to these people if they report theft. They're just spending time and money, reporting it, going to court, etc., that isn't going to amount to anything."

And so the city adapts, not by solving the problem but adjusting to it. Businesses invest in private security as a cost of doing business. Wealthier neighborhoods expand gated communities and hire patrols, creating micro-fortresses within the collapsing whole. Meanwhile, communities without resources are left to fend for themselves; their neighborhoods are steadily drained of vitality by the ever-present threat of violence.

Trust in law enforcement, governance, and even neighbors has given way to a pervasive skepticism that undermines civic life. People no longer believe that justice will be served, their property will be protected, or the streets will ever be safe again. It's not simply that crime has risen; the social contract has unraveled, leaving behind a hollowed-out city.

Crime on the Westside

The Westside of Los Angeles—long synonymous with gated communities, tree-lined streets, and quiet affluence—now bears the same scars as the city's most neglected neighborhoods. Beverly Hills, once the zenith of security and status, has become a preferred hunting ground for gangs and thieves. Santa Monica, with its postcard-perfect coastline, is now home to brazen daylight robberies and the unrelenting churn of petty theft. The veil of privilege has been ripped away, leaving exposed a fragile reality: no neighborhood is safe.

The calculus of crime has shifted. The same gangs that once killed over drug corners now trade violence for precision, targeting neighborhoods where victims are less likely to fight back and where the rewards—watches, jewelry, designer handbags—are worth the risk. "The open-air robberies on the street—that didn't exist before," says Detective Sam Bailey, a gang investigator with the Inglewood Police Department. "The Westside is virgin ground, and all the gangs have found it." What was once unimaginable in Beverly Hills—the brazen mugging of a socialite outside a restaurant, the violent robbery of a homeowner in their driveway—is now chronic and unremarkable.

LA prosecutor John Lewin explains the ruthlessness behind this trend: "A lot of LA gangs have realized there's more money in wealthy areas.

That's where they're going to get it."[1] Though it's not just about wealth—it's about visibility. Social media has turned high-end crime into a spectacle. Stolen Rolexes are flaunted online within hours of their theft, and gangs use Instagram to scout their next marks, with photos of luxury dinners and high-end purchases serving as unintended invitations. The wealth that once insulated the Westside now paints a target on its back.

For Sergeant Michael Maher, recently retired from the Los Angeles Sherriff's Department, the Westside's vulnerability signals something deeper: the unraveling of civic order. "Twenty years ago, gangsters were killing each other for corners to sell dope. Today, they're victimizing all of us, all the time, everywhere." The streets no longer distinguish between the poor and the wealthy, the vulnerable and the protected. As Maher puts it, "It's less violent for the gangs, but it's more dangerous for everyone else. Crimes that would have shocked us twenty years ago are now what I hate to say—routine."

But it's not just the novel criminality that causes such alarm—the perpetrators have also changed. Detective Bailey notes the shift in demographics, with teenagers driving this wave of violence. "Back in the '90s, the guys doing big robberies were hardened criminals, thirty or forty years old, fresh out of prison. Now you've got fifteen and sixteen-year-olds snatching Rolexes off people sitting at Starbucks. And it's happening here, on the Westside. That has never happened before."[2]

This is what societal collapse looks like in real time. Gangs once hidden in alleyways now stalk coffee shops. The reassuring sight of a patrol car no longer deters; it barely reassures. Residents are left with a creeping understanding that the boundaries have disappeared, that their lives are no longer insulated from the chaos unfolding just a few miles away. Fear has seeped into daily life, the kind that doesn't scream but whispers, persistent and unrelenting.

Even the homes themselves—once symbols of safety—feel like little more than facades. Gated communities and private security firms proliferate, but the walls they build are psychological as much as physical. Every break-in and every mugging reminds homeowners that the line between them and the disorder is tissue-thin. In the face of a justice system unwilling to protect them, they are left to protect themselves—or leave entirely.

The Westside was supposed to be the exception, the last bastion of stability in a city slipping into chaos. Instead, it has become the clearest proof that Los Angeles has no boundaries left. Crime doesn't respect affluence, privilege, or power. It goes where the opportunity is, and Los Angeles, for all its wealth, offers it in abundance.

Lawlessness of the Street

Detective Jamie McBride, a veteran of the Los Angeles Police Department and Director of the Los Angeles Police Protective League, doesn't mince words; his warning is as stark as it is unsettling: "I tell everybody, don't come to LA. We can't keep you safe." This isn't hyperbole or rhetorical flourish—it is a grim admission from a man who has spent decades on the frontlines. "It is the worst in my career," McBride continues. "When I was working the streets, I worked South Central, all over the place, and if a gangster had a gun, they would run nine out of ten times. Now, they stop, let you take the gun off them, and let you take them to jail because they know nothing is going to happen to them."

This is the new rhythm of the streets: criminals emboldened not by chaos but by the calculated predictability of a system that has abandoned consequences. A gangster's arrest is no longer a setback but a detour. McBride's reflection captures the unnerving evolution of lawlessness—one where fear has shifted from the criminal to the civilian, leaving the latter exposed to a city that no longer enforces its rules.

The anarchy is impossible to ignore. "Every day, people are blatantly trying to steal shit," McBride explains with grim frankness. "Blatantly, and getting violent too, by the way. Absolutely violent. I live in Ventura County for a reason because I don't want to deal with the LA shit. It is absolutely insane." The tone of his lament is not just one of frustration but of resignation—an acknowledgment that Los Angeles has passed the point of manageable disorder.

For John Lewin, who has prosecuted homicides in Los Angeles since the 1990s, the scale of the collapse defies comparison. "In terms of just, for instance, the thefts and the homelessness and the rampant drug use, and the retail theft and smash and grabs . . . I don't remember it ever being this bad." Lewin's words reflect a declining city and a system utterly incapable of responding to the crisis. Crimes that once carried consequences now go unanswered, eroding not just public trust but the very idea of deterrence.

The streets of Los Angeles have become a theater of open defiance, where the unspoken rules that once restrained criminality have dissolved entirely. Theft is no longer concealed but flaunted, the criminal's confidence a stark indictment of the city's impotence. Retail theft has evolved into smash-and-grabs so brazen that shop owners have stopped reporting them. Drug markets thrive with no pretense of evasion, their patrons sprawled across sidewalks in plain sight. Homeless encampments, fueled by addiction and untreated mental illness, now form shadow communities that stretch for blocks, encroaching on residential neighborhoods and commercial districts alike.

For many in law enforcement, this isn't just a crisis of crime—it's a crisis of purpose. Officers who once worked to maintain order now manage its absence. Arrests feel like exercises in futility, prosecutions an afterthought. McBride's warning to visitors is grim but accurate: in Los Angeles, safety is no longer a guarantee but a gamble.

Crime Statistics: Los Angeles Is Raging

Los Angeles is grappling with a troubling rise in crime, where each statistic tells a story of a city under increasing strain. Homicides have reached their highest point in over a decade, while property crimes and organized theft are becoming a daily reality for many. These numbers are more than just data—they reveal a growing sense of vulnerability that touches every corner of the city. As violent crime escalates and theft rings operate with alarming efficiency, Los Angeles finds itself facing a deepening crisis that raises critical questions about safety, justice, and the future of its communities.

Crime in Los Angeles is no longer an abstraction measured in yearly reports—it is a constant, visceral presence. Each statistic reflects a reality that residents confront daily: the sound of gunfire in the night, the smashed glass of a looted storefront, the resigned look of a business owner filing yet another futile police report. The numbers, stark as they are, barely capture the atmosphere of unease that permeates the city. They tell a story not just of rising violence but of a system that has abdicated its most basic responsibility: to protect its citizens.

Historic Homicide and Violent Crime Rate

Los Angeles recorded 397 homicides in 2023, marking a 26.7% increase since 2018.[3] Aggravated assaults surged by 15%, totaling 13,673 reported cases.[4] These figures are not just spikes on a graph—they are the shattered families, the victims of senseless violence, and the neighborhoods grappling with fear. The streets have grown colder, not just in violence but in their indifference to it.

Property Crimes Unchecked Surge

Property crimes in Los Angeles have become almost routine, further amplifying the sense of lawlessness. In 2022, the LAPD reported 85,182 property crimes, a 10% rise from the previous year.[5] Burglaries and vehicle thefts have surged, no longer confined to high-crime neighborhoods but spreading into once-secure areas. For many residents, a locked door or a gated driveway now feels like little more than a flimsy suggestion, easily ignored by those who see little risk in taking what they want.

Organized Retail Theft: Big Business

Perhaps nowhere is the breakdown of deterrence more evident than in the epidemic of organized retail theft. In 2022, these crimes spiked by 20%, carried out by sophisticated networks operating with impunity.[6] Luxury stores in Beverly Hills and Santa Monica have become regular targets, their smashed glass and emptied shelves standing as monuments to a system that no longer enforces its laws. The financial toll is staggering, but the psychological impact on business owners and employees—who now face these brazen heists as part of their daily reality—is immeasurable.

Shoplifting soared 81% in Los Angeles in 2023—11,945 reported incidents. Ten years ago, that number was 4,885—a 114% increase.[7]

Los Angeles's Drug Crime Epidemic

The proliferation of narcotics, particularly fentanyl and methamphetamine, has fueled a surge in drug-related crimes. Los Angeles recorded over 5,000 drug-related arrests in 2022, a 15% increase from the prior year.[8] Open-air drug markets, once relegated to the city's fringes, now operate openly in broad daylight, from Downtown to Venice Beach. These drugs, often trafficked by cartels who exploit the city's porous enforcement, are not just fueling addiction but driving ancillary crimes, from petty theft to violent assaults.

Overall Crime Rate: Fallen Angel

In 2022, Los Angeles reported a crime rate of 36 per 1,000 residents, one of the highest in the nation.[9] The likelihood of falling victim to either violent or property crime in Los Angeles now stands at 1 in 28—statistics that paint a grim picture of a city in the throes of a public safety crisis.[10] California as a whole fares no better: its robbery and assault rates far exceed national averages, a damning indictment of policies that prioritize leniency over accountability.

The numbers are sobering, but they do not capture the full scope of the crisis. Rising crime is not just a failure of enforcement; it is a collapse of public trust, a signal to residents and businesses that the system cannot or will not protect them. For every burglary reported, countless others go unrecorded, as victims grow weary of reporting crimes that lead to no arrests, no prosecutions, no consequences.

The economic ramifications are equally dire. High-crime areas see businesses shuttered, investments stalled, and insurance premiums skyrocket. The exodus of retailers from neighborhoods like Melrose Avenue and Downtown LA is not just a statistic—it's a visible wound, an open acknowledgment that safety, once taken for granted, is no longer guaranteed.

But beyond the economic and statistical toll is the psychological erosion—the quiet despair of residents who now view crime as an inevitability rather than an aberration. Los Angeles has become a city where people think twice before walking at night, where families lock their doors earlier, and where the simple act of parking a car feels like a gamble.

These statistics do not just demand attention—they demand action. Without decisive intervention, Los Angeles risks descending further into lawlessness, its residents left to fend for themselves in a city that has abandoned them. The numbers are a warning, but the reality behind them is a stark and urgent call to rebuild what has been lost.

Crime Statistics: California's Disturbing Outlier Status

The crisis in California is not an abstraction—it is a measurable reality, reflected in crime rates that exceed those of every other large state in the nation. The numbers paint an unambiguous picture: California is the most violent and crime-ridden of all major U.S. states, outpacing Texas, Florida, New York, Illinois, and Pennsylvania by significant margins.

According to the FBI's Uniform Crime Reporting (UCR) Program, in 2023, California reported a violent crime rate of 5.19 per 1,000 residents and a property crime rate of 23.10 per 1,000—figures that position it as the most crime-plagued large state in America.[11] A comparison with other populous states makes this disparity undeniable:

State	Violent Crime per 1,000	Property Crime per 1,000
California	5.19	23.10
Texas	4.47	21.53
Florida	3.85	15.60
New York	4.04	20.74
Illinois	4.04	20.74
Pennsylvania	3.15	17.58

The disparities are not marginal—they are foundational. California's violent crime rate is 16% higher than Texas, 35% higher than Florida, and nearly 65% higher than Pennsylvania. Its property crime rate is higher than every other large state, with 48% more property crime than Florida and 31% more than Pennsylvania.

A Crime Problem Unlike Any Other

California stands alone as the nation's most crime-ridden major state. It is not merely struggling with crime—it is setting the benchmark for lawlessness.

The numbers alone, however, fail to capture the full weight of what this means for daily life in the state. Unlike in previous decades, where high crime was often confined to specific urban pockets, California's lawlessness has spread outward, seeping into areas that were once considered insulated from urban decay.

- Violent crime is no longer concentrated in a few inner-city districts—it has become a statewide phenomenon.
- Theft is so widespread that it has altered business models, with major retailers shuttering locations not due to lack of demand, but because the basic assumption that businesses can operate without mass looting has collapsed.
- Homicide rates, while slightly below the national average, are hyper-concentrated in cities like Los Angeles and Oakland, where killings occur at rates comparable to some of the most dangerous places in the Western Hemisphere.

The Hidden Crime Crisis: Underreported Data and Missing Numbers

Even these staggering statistics do not tell the full story. Several law enforcement agencies—including San Jose PD, Orange County PD, and the Los Angeles Sheriff's Department—failed to provide complete crime reports for 2023. Given that these jurisdictions contain some of the state's most dangerous areas, California's actual crime rate is almost certainly higher than what is officially reported.

The absence of full data is not a technical oversight—it is a fundamental flaw in how crime is recorded and acknowledged. It allows officials to claim that crime is stabilizing or declining, when in reality, many of the most dangerous incidents go untracked or unclassified. This statistical manipulation serves only to obscure the gravity of the crisis while offering no relief to the people who live under its shadow.

A State Consumed by Violence

California's rising crime rates are not abstractions. They are not "perceptions" shaped by media narratives or political rhetoric. They are the lived reality of millions who now move through a state where violence is no longer contained but ambient, where the specter of danger is as much a part of daily life as traffic or the weather.

The state's *assault rate of 350.95 per 100,000 residents* is not merely high—it is exceptional, far surpassing the *national average of 271.19 per 100,000*.[12,13] The nature of these assaults has shifted. They are more random, more indiscriminate, more feral. Women indiscriminately raped. Strangers stabbed in broad daylight. Elderly men beaten to the point of unconsciousness outside their own homes. These are not outliers. They are part of the fabric of life in a state where the expectation of safety has eroded to the point of irrelevance.

The consequences are psychological as much as they are physical. Californians now live with an altered sense of space, an unconscious recalibration of how they move, where they go, what they avoid.

Endemic Brigandry

Robbery in California has become so frequent, so unchallenged, that it no longer elicits shock. The state's *robbery rate—127.8 per 100,000 residents—nearly doubles the national average of 66.5 per 100,000*, marking a profound collapse in the deterrence of violent crime. Robbery is not simply theft; it is the use of force or fear to seize what belongs to another. It is not committed in the shadows but in full view—on sidewalks, in stores, at bus stops, in parking garages. The victims are not just businesses but individuals going about their daily lives, accosted at gunpoint or knifepoint, stripped of their belongings with impunity.

The nature of these crimes has changed. Criminals no longer flee in haste; they linger, comfortable in the knowledge that intervention is unlikely. Armed holdups unfold in gas stations and convenience stores as though they were routine transactions. Restaurant diners are relieved of their wallets and watches mid-meal. Commuters are assaulted and robbed on public transit as fellow passengers avert their gaze. The brazenness is not the exception but the rule.

This ubiquity has produced a kind of mass resignation. Pedestrians, once confident in their ability to navigate city streets unmolested, now move with quiet vigilance, anticipating the moment when they, too, might be targeted. Shopkeepers and clerks no longer resist, understanding that physical confrontation invites greater harm than surrender. The term *crime wave* suggests a temporary surge, something that will crest and recede. But what California is experiencing is not a wave—it is a new equilibrium, a redefinition of normalcy in which forceful takings are an expected part of life.

The public's adaptation to this disorder is perhaps the most unsettling development of all. The psychology of avoidance—of looking away, of making oneself small, of surrendering without resistance—is now embedded in daily existence. This is not merely lawlessness; it is an environment in which law and order formally exist, yet functionally do not. The mechanisms of the state remain intact, but the basic expectation that criminals will be punished has eroded to the point of irrelevance. The result is a society where violent predation is not merely tolerated but, in effect, accommodated.

Murder: The Grim Arithmetic of Urban Violence

California's *murder rate of 4.92 per 100,000 residents* sits just below the national average of *5.5 per 100,000*, a figure that offers a misleading sense of parity. This number is diluted by the sheer size of the state, obscuring the stark reality of concentrated violence in its major cities. The geographic disparities are staggering:

- **Los Angeles: 8.8 per 100,000**—a level of bloodshed that has become so routine it barely registers as a crisis.
- **Oakland: 30.2 per 100,000**—a homicide rate that places the city among the most dangerous in the developed world.

This is not a matter of crime "spikes" or seasonal fluctuations. It is a permanent condition, a structural feature of life in cities where the body count rises but the urgency to address it does not. The most violent neighborhoods in Los Angeles and Oakland do not just suffer from high murder rates—they are defined by them. To live in these areas is to live with the knowledge that death is not an abstract possibility but a daily risk.

A Life Redefined by Fear

What does it mean when an entire population is forced to adjust to violence as a constant? Californians no longer move through their cities with the assumption of safety—they move with strategies for avoidance. They know which streets are safest to walk at dusk, which gas stations to avoid after dark, which blocks they should never cross under any circumstances.

They scan subway cars for potential threats. They park their cars in well-lit areas, not to prevent break-ins, but to increase the chance of witnesses if they are attacked.

Fear has become a defining feature of life in California, but unlike fear in times of war or natural disaster, this fear is not met with mobilization or outrage. It is met with accommodation. The people who can afford to do so buy private security, build higher walls, and relocate to enclaves where crime is kept at a tolerable distance. Those who cannot afford such measures are left to fend for themselves in cities where the streets belong, not to the public, but to those most willing to wield force.

A Reality That No Longer Shocks

The most unsettling part of California's crime crisis is not just the scale of the violence—it is the growing indifference to it. There is no sense of emergency, no meaningful attempt to reverse course. The public reacts with momentary outrage when a particularly brutal murder makes the headlines, but the outrage fades, replaced by resignation. The assumption, increasingly, is that this is just the way things are now.

Property Crime: Widespread and Growing

California's property crime rate of 23.10 per 1,000 residents exceeds the national average of 19.17, with alarming increases in key categories:

Burglary: At 3.45 per 1,000 residents, burglary is significantly higher than the national rate of 2.51.[14] This figure reflects homes and businesses left vulnerable to frequent and often devastating invasions.[15]

Motor Vehicle Theft: Perhaps the most troubling statistic, California's car theft rate is 5.12 per 1,000 residents—nearly double the national average of 3.19.[16,17] This underscores the state's growing struggle with organized theft rings and the lack of effective deterrence.

The high incidence of these crimes is more than an economic drain—it is a constant reminder of the fragility of security in California. For residents, the prospect of theft has shifted from an occasional risk to an expectation, driving a profound sense of disillusionment and insecurity.

Implications of California's Crime Epidemic

The implications of these numbers are profound, touching every aspect of life in the state:

Economic Instability: High crime rates deter business investment and increase operational costs for those who remain. Retailers face rising insurance premiums, while small-business owners grapple with the constant threat of theft and vandalism.

Social Fragmentation: Communities across California are fracturing under the weight of unchecked crime. Residents retreat behind locked doors, creating pockets of isolation that erode the sense of shared responsibility and trust.

Public Disillusionment: The data reflects more than just crime—it reveals a governance failure. Policies that prioritize leniency over accountability have stripped the justice system of its ability to protect, leaving residents to fend for themselves.

A Crisis Without Boundaries

The crime crisis in California is not confined to its cities or its poorest neighborhoods. It is a statewide phenomenon that transcends class, geography, and politics. From rural towns struggling with rising methamphetamine addiction to affluent suburbs battling organized theft, the collapse of public safety is felt everywhere. The statistics are damning, but the lived reality they represent is even more harrowing—a state where lawlessness feels inevitable and justice increasingly unattainable.

California's crime surge is not just a story of numbers; it is a story of people—of lives disrupted, communities destabilized, and a future increasingly uncertain. The path forward demands more than policy tweaks; it requires a fundamental reckoning with the state's approach to crime and punishment. Without decisive action, California risks becoming not just a warning but a cautionary tale for the nation.

Erosion of Trust

The social contract underpinning any civilized society rests on a fragile premise: that citizens relinquish their right to self-defense in exchange for protection by the state. Kathleen Cady, a seasoned Los Angeles

County Deputy District Attorney and victims' rights advocate, captures the gravity of what happens when this agreement collapses: "My concern is that in living in society, I give up my right to street justice when I say, 'Police, I want you to come in and take care of me' and 'Prosecutor, I want you to do the right thing.' But if victims start feeling like that's not happening, then they could start taking the law into their own hands."

This erosion of trust is no longer a hypothetical concern—it is an unfolding reality in Los Angeles. As law enforcement struggles to respond effectively to rising crime and a paralyzed justice system undermines accountability, residents increasingly feel abandoned. The result is desperation—a slow, dangerous shift toward vigilantism.

A study by the Pew Research Center reveals the scope of this trust deficit: only 30% of Americans report having a great deal of confidence in the police, a staggering decline from previous decades. In Los Angeles, this erosion is even more pronounced. Internal reports from the LAPD detail a sharp drop in public cooperation. Fewer residents are willing to report crimes or serve as witnesses, convinced that their efforts are futile in a system that rarely delivers justice.

This growing cynicism is not unwarranted. The *Los Angeles Times* has documented a rise in cases where residents take matters into their own hands, a grim testament to the breakdown of law and order. One incident stands out—a stark warning of where this trajectory leads. A local business owner, targeted by thieves multiple times and exasperated by the indifference of law enforcement, decided to defend his property himself. Armed with a high-caliber rifle, he waited for the burglars to strike again. When they returned, the confrontation turned into a violent shootout. One burglar was fatally shot, another fled with severe injuries, and the owner himself was critically wounded and hospitalized in intensive care.

The aftermath of this incident ignited a fierce debate. For some, the business owner was a hero—an embodiment of resilience in the face of systemic failure. For others, his actions were reckless, a tragic escalation born of desperation. But no one could ignore the underlying truth: this was not an isolated incident. It was the natural outcome of a city where trust in law enforcement has crumbled, leaving citizens to fend for themselves.

The implications of this erosion extend far beyond individual cases. When residents no longer believe that the system will protect them, they withdraw their participation in it. They stop reporting crimes, stop cooperating with investigations, stop engaging with a justice system that seems increasingly irrelevant to their lives. This withdrawal accelerates the breakdown of public safety, creating a feedback loop of lawlessness and isolation.

For law enforcement, the consequences are dire. The ability of police to function depends on the trust and cooperation of the communities they serve. Without that, even the most dedicated officers find themselves adrift, fighting battles they cannot win. And for the broader city, the cost is nothing less than the unraveling of civic life itself.

As Cady warns, the rise of vigilante justice is not just a symptom of lawlessness—it is its ultimate consequence. Once citizens lose faith in the state's ability to maintain order, the social contract is irreparably damaged. In such a world, violence becomes the currency of justice, and chaos is no longer confined to the margins. It seeps into every corner, eroding not just trust but the very idea of a shared society.

Impact on Public Perception

The rising crime rates in Los Angeles have shattered the city's sense of safety, leaving residents gripped by a profound unease. Surveys reveal that a majority of Angelenos feel less secure than they did a year ago, highlighting not just a crisis of governance but a deep fracture in public trust. This breakdown in perception isn't unfounded—it's rooted in the lived realities of a city that appears to have lost control of its streets.

A recent *Los Angeles Times* survey found that 70% of residents believe crime has increased in their neighborhoods, with over half expressing little confidence in the city's ability to address it. The data corroborates their fears. LAPD reports show a 13.9% increase in robberies in the first two months of 2024 compared to the same period in 2023.[18] Homicides have climbed nearly 30% since 2020, intensifying public anxiety and straining the already demoralized ranks of law enforcement.

The economic fallout of this insecurity is devastating. Businesses are increasingly reluctant to invest in areas perceived as unsafe, leading to economic stagnation and compounding unemployment. A report by the

Los Angeles Chamber of Commerce revealed a 25% spike in commercial vacancy rates in high-crime areas, far outpacing the citywide average increase of 8%. A *Los Angeles Business Journal* survey found that 60% of small business owners in these neighborhoods are actively considering relocation, citing crime as their primary concern. For those who remain, rising insurance premiums—up 20% in high-crime zones—add yet another financial burden, creating a cycle of decline that chokes economic recovery.

Even property values, long a bulwark of stability in Los Angeles, are plummeting. Hard-hit neighborhoods have seen drops of up to 15%, further eroding the tax base that funds public services. As businesses shutter and residents leave, the infrastructure that holds communities together begins to crumble, leaving behind pockets of despair and lawlessness.

This erosion of safety isn't confined to statistics or economic trends; it is deeply felt in the daily lives of residents. For many Angelenos, the streets no longer offer a sense of freedom or community—they are battlegrounds where fear dictates behavior and where the belief that the system will protect them has been all but lost.

Criminality Affecting Minorities

"The worst part of all this," says John Lewin, "is that the people paying the price for this movement are primarily people of color. Law-abiding citizens who happen to be poor are stuck in communities where crime is rampant. Prosecutors like George Gascón don't want to address it for political reasons. They want to free as many criminals as possible."

This brutal assessment underscores an often-overlooked reality: the communities most impacted by rising crime are those least equipped to endure it. Minority neighborhoods, already grappling with systemic disadvantages, now find themselves abandoned by a justice system that prioritizes offenders over victims.

Kathleen Cady paints an unflinching picture of the cycle of criminality and bureaucratic neglect:

"If I go and speak at victims' rights clinics, especially in South Central or downtown LA, the people I speak to certainly feel like shootings are out of control. If you're a victim of crime and it takes the police 14 hours to respond, why would you bother reporting it? Nothing is going to happen. And that's not even a criticism of the police—they've been defunded and demoralized. But what happens is, when people stop reporting crimes, the stats go down, creating the illusion that things are improving. Meanwhile, the reality on the ground gets worse."

Store owners in these neighborhoods echo the same frustrations. For many, reporting theft feels pointless. "Why would I bother?" one shopkeeper asked. "I'll have to take time off work, file a report, maybe even go to court—and for what? The thief will be back in my store the next day."

This resignation perpetuates a vicious cycle. When crimes go unreported, they are excluded from official statistics, masking the extent of the problem. This allows policymakers to claim progress even as the streets grow more dangerous. In the meantime, minority communities—caught between rising crime and systemic indifference—are left to fend for themselves, their plight ignored by a justice system that no longer serves them.

Conclusion

The crime crisis in Los Angeles represents a broader systemic failure, one that has left residents abandoned, businesses fleeing, and trust in governance at a historic low. To reverse this descent into chaos, city officials must confront the policies that have emboldened criminals and demoralized law enforcement. This means abandoning leniency, bolstering police resources, and enforcing punitive measures with the full weight of the law.

Community policing and crime reporting initiatives, while important, are not enough. These efforts must be paired with aggressive enforcement strategies and judicial reforms that prioritize accountability over ideology. Restoring safety requires dismantling the bureaucratic impediments that prevent officers from doing their jobs and replacing failed policies with a steadfast commitment to deterrence.

Kathleen Cady's warning looms large: when trust in law enforcement collapses, the social contract dissolves, paving the way for vigilantism and disorder. The path forward must begin with rebuilding that trust—through swift justice, uncompromising enforcement, and an unyielding defense of public safety.

CHAPTER 3

CRIME-EQUITY

The collapse of a society is rarely marked by a single, cataclysmic event. Instead, it is a slow, insidious poisoning—a kind of arsenic coursing through the bloodstream of civilization. It beings with an intellectual corruption that seeps unnoticed into the system, vitiating language and corroding weak institutions. Over time, the rule of law buckles under the weight of incremental ideological subversion, until justice is no longer recognized as justice, and crime is no longer treated as crime.

When justice ceases to be a neutral arbiter and is instead weaponized, subordinated to ideology, or transformed into an instrument of redistribution, the moral scaffolding of society collapses. California, long the avant-garde of political and cultural experimentation, now stands as a case study in collapse—not through war or disaster, but through the deliberate subversion of law. Central to its decline is ***crime-equity,*** a term I use to encapsulate an ideology that does not merely corrupt justice—it inverts it entirely.

Crime-equity is not about deterring criminality but rationalizing it. It redefines crime not as a violation of law, but as an expression of justified resistance. Punishment is reframed as oppression, deterrence dismissed as unjust, and the criminal transformed into the victim. This is not a malfunction of governance—it is governance repurposed, where justice is wielded not to uphold order, but to redistribute criminal accountability along ideological and racial lines.

This chapter dissects crime-equity as both an ideology and a policy doctrine, exposing how it has corroded deterrence, dismantled public trust, and weaponized the justice system against itself. In California's pursuit of radical egalitarianism, it has not merely reformed governance—it has hollowed it out, replacing law and order with an arbitrary and selective regime of ideological enforcement. Crime-equity is not just a crisis of public safety—it is a crisis of civilization.

Defining Crime-Equity: The Ideology of Retributive Justice

Crime-equity is a radical ideological construct that seeks to redefine justice, shifting the focus from individual culpability to collective societal responsibility. It begins with the premise that traditional criminal justice systems are inherently oppressive, disproportionately targeting marginalized communities. Advocates of crime-equity propose recalibrating justice to emphasize equity over equality, often arguing that the consequences of crime must be redistributed as a form of social reparation. This reframing not only undermines core principles of Western legal philosophy but deliberately erodes the foundations of the rule of law.

Crime-equity is therefore not merely an approach to criminal justice reform; it is a radical ideology that subverts the principles of deterrence, punishment, and justice in favor of ideological redistribution. It reframes criminal behavior not as individual wrongdoing but as a *necessary rebellion* against systemic oppression. By inverting moral responsibility, crime-equity rationalizes lawlessness as a legitimate response to historical grievances, rendering the legal system an instrument of sociopolitical engineering rather than impartial justice.

Both as an abstraction and policy doctrine, crime-equity harnesses lawlessness as a tool of ethno-social redistribution, redefining crime not as a violation of law but as an expression of justified resistance. It is an ideological sleight of hand that transmogrifies criminality into a form of retributive justice, where punishment is reframed as oppression, deterrence is dismissed as unjust, and the criminal is lionized while the victim is erased.

Although crime-equity represents an insurgent, even terroristic worldview, it is not necessarily an external force; quite often it is a virus within the system, a doctrine that operates through policy to erode and subvert justice. Under its framework, governance is no longer tasked with upholding order but with redistributing criminal accountability along ideological and racial lines.

Under this framework, justice is no longer blind, nor is it neutral—it is weaponized, meting out punishment not on the basis of guilt, but on the basis of political and racial considerations. Crime-equity redefines crime itself, transforming it from an individual act of wrongdoing into a collective political grievance:

- Punishment is reframed as oppression.
- Deterrence is dismissed as unjust.
- The criminal is recast as the victim of oppressors.

This is not a rogue movement attacking the system from without; it is a virus hollowing it out from within. Crime-equity operates not as an external insurgency, but as an embedded doctrine, disseminated through policy, academia, and bureaucracy, steadily corroding the mechanisms of justice until governance itself ceases to uphold order and instead redistributes criminal accountability along ideological lines.

Core Tenets of Crime-Equity

At its core, crime-equity dismisses personal agency, recasting offenders as victims of circumstance rather than perpetrators of harm. It frames crime not as a choice but as an inevitable reaction to systemic failings, paving the way for policies that subordinate deterrence and accountability to ideological objectives. In this paradigm, crime is no longer viewed as an aberration to be prevented but as a tool for rectifying historical injustices. This reimagining of justice transforms the legal system into a mechanism for political and social engineering, where theft and violence are rationalized, even valorized, as acts of redistribution. The law, once a bulwark against disorder, is repurposed to balance an imagined scale of historical inequities.

1. **Redefinition of Criminality:** Crime is reinterpreted not as a voluntary act but as an unavoidable reaction to systemic injustice.

2. **Elimination of Consequences:** Punishment is framed as oppression; deterrence is dismissed as an outdated tool of social control.
3. **Reallocation of Victimhood:** Criminals are recast as victims of systemic bias, while actual victims are marginalized or ignored.
4. **Destabilization of Law Enforcement:** Traditional policing is systematically dismantled in favor of "community-based" alternatives that prioritize rehabilitation over accountability.

Crime-equity does not seek justice in the traditional sense—it aims to dismantle accountability as a means of redistributing power.

Crime-Equity within the Broader Equity Movement

Crime-equity is the logical extension of the broader equity movement, which abandons the principle of equality under the law in favor of outcomes engineered along racial and social lines. It is not about fairness or impartiality but about redistribution—of power, of punishment, and ultimately, of criminal accountability. Under this framework, justice is no longer neutral; it is a weaponized instrument of political reordering, where law and order become expendable obstacles to ideological objectives.

Rooted in Critical Race Theory (CRT), neo-Marxist legal thought, and abolitionist criminology, crime-equity treats the criminal justice system not as a mechanism for maintaining civil order, but as an instrument of historical oppression that must be dismantled. Its adherents argue that crime is not a matter of personal agency, but a structural inevitability— an affliction visited upon "marginalized" groups by an unjust society. Deterrence is reframed as oppression, accountability as victimization, and punishment as an act of systemic violence.

Crime-equity functions as a strategic weapon within the broader ideological war, applying racialized quotas to policing, prosecution, and incarceration to produce politically desirable demographic outcomes. By shifting the focus from individual responsibility to collective guilt, these policies replace the concept of justice with an activism-driven model that prioritizes retribution against perceived historical injustices rather than public safety.

This shift is not incidental; it is calculated. The widespread embrace of decarceration initiatives, the elimination of sentencing enhancements, and the non-prosecution of entire categories of crime are not unintended consequences but deliberate efforts to hollow out legal structures under the guise of equity. The result has been the emboldenment of criminal networks, the erosion of deterrence, and the steady destabilization of public safety.

The Weaponization of Lawlessness: Crime-Equity and the Shifting Social Contract

Crime-equity is not merely an ideology—it is a calculated effort to reengineer society by manipulating criminal behavior. Crime, once viewed as an aberration to be punished and deterred, is reimagined as a political tool, weaponized to challenge and destabilize the existing order. By redistributing the effects of criminality across communities, crime-equity seeks to dismantle the traditional structures of law and order, effectively unraveling the social contract that underpins civil society.

Ideological Substitution of Law and Order

Under crime-equity, the mechanisms of justice are no longer designed to uphold societal stability. Instead, punishment is reframed as oppression, while criminal acts are rationalized as inevitable responses to systemic inequality. Deterrence, prosecution, and sentencing—the foundational barriers against lawlessness—are deliberately weakened in the name of equity. The justice system is transformed into a platform for ideological activism, prioritizing political objectives over its core mandate to protect and maintain order.

This reimagining subverts the rule of law, turning the criminal justice system into an instrument for advancing radical agendas. Justice becomes a secondary concern, replaced by a fervent commitment to ideological conformity. The result is not reform but a collapse of the mechanisms that ensure accountability and safety.

The Dismantling of Public Safety Mechanisms

Crime-equity manifests in policies that systematically erode the effectiveness of law enforcement, reduce deterrence, and undermine public safety. Measures such as defunding police departments, abolishing cash bail, and curtailing prosecutorial discretion have not only failed to address root causes of crime but have actively fostered environments where criminal activity thrives.

This breakdown is not an accidental byproduct of misguided policies—it is a deliberate strategy. By redistributing crime and insecurity, crime-equity seeks to level societal disparities, albeit at the expense of safety and public trust.

Defunding Police Departments

The defunding of police, touted as a remedy for systemic inequality, promises to reallocate resources to social services to address the root causes of crime. In practice, it often results in reduced police presence, slower response times, and diminished capacity to deter or investigate crime. The consequences are particularly severe for the very communities these reforms claim to help.

Ironically, the abolition of cash bail and reduced police funding disproportionately harm poorer neighborhoods. At the same time, these policies facilitate the spread of crime into previously stable areas, triggering a new form of "de-gentrification," where insecurity transcends socioeconomic boundaries. The ideological aim of redistribution is achieved, but at the expense of leaving both marginalized and affluent communities vulnerable to rampant criminality.

Abolition of Cash Bail

The abolition of cash bail, promoted as a step toward equitable pretrial outcomes, removes financial barriers for low-income defendants. However, its indiscriminate application enables individuals charged with serious crimes to return to the streets almost immediately, often reoffending before their trials. This revolving door not only jeopardizes public safety but also undermines public trust in the justice system, eroding its deterrent function and fostering a perception of lawlessness.

Pretrial detention, once a critical safeguard against recidivism, is rendered toothless in this new framework. Offenders cycle in and out of custody with impunity, emboldened by a justice system seemingly incapable—or unwilling—to enforce meaningful consequences. This emboldens criminality, exacerbates public disillusionment, and deepens the divide between the state's ideological commitments and the practical needs of the communities it governs.

In its place, a new order emerges—one of so-called revolutionary justice, arbitrated by ideological frameworks that redefine crime and punishment according to the dictates of equity. Under this system, the law ceases to function as a neutral arbiter and becomes instead an instrument of redistribution, where the focus shifts from protecting society to addressing historical grievances, often at the expense of safety and order. The result is a justice system stripped of its foundational purpose, leaving communities vulnerable to escalating disorder and fostering a cycle of insecurity that deepens societal fragmentation.

Weaponizing Prosecutorial Discretion

Under the banner of reducing incarceration, certain district attorneys have embraced a policy of deliberate inaction, declining to prosecute entire categories of offenses. Framed as a remedy for systemic inequities, this selective enforcement signals to offenders that their actions carry little to no consequence. The result is a justice system that increasingly appears indifferent to crime, fostering an environment where lawlessness thrives and accountability is eroded.

This shift undermines the foundational principle that justice must be both impartial and enforceable. By refusing to prosecute what are deemed "low-level" offenses, prosecutors create a cascading effect: minor crimes escalate unchecked, communities are destabilized, and the perception of impunity emboldens more serious criminal behavior. Public trust in the rule of law fractures, as citizens witness a justice system seemingly abandoning its duty to protect.

Moreover, this deliberate retreat from prosecution accelerates societal disorder. By reframing criminal acts as symptoms of systemic oppression rather than individual culpability, the justice system is recast as an ideological apparatus, prioritizing abstraction over accountability. The result is not merely a weakening of enforcement but an active dismantling of the social contract, where the law ceases to function as a deterrent and instead becomes a tool for excusing behavior that destabilizes the very communities it claims to serve.

In this paradigm, prosecutorial discretion is no longer a measured exercise of judgment—it becomes a weaponized ideology, signaling that justice is malleable, contingent upon political and cultural narratives rather than a commitment to public safety and order. The long-term consequence is a justice system stripped of coherence and credibility, fostering a climate of insecurity that undermines the bedrock of civil society.

Crime Redistribution and Equalizing Insecurity

The redistribution of criminality represents one of the most unsettling manifestations of crime-equity. Unlike overt reforms, this strategy operates subtly, dismantling the traditional mechanisms of accountability—policing, prosecution, and sentencing—to allow crime to metastasize across societal boundaries. What was once concentrated in marginalized communities is now deliberately diffused into previously secure neighborhoods. This engineered expansion of insecurity transforms crime into a societal equalizer, blurring the lines between the protected and the vulnerable.

In this paradigm, crime is no longer treated as a breach of the social contract but as an instrument of ideological justice. The state abdicates its protective role, reframing harm as an unavoidable consequence of addressing historical imbalances. Vulnerability becomes a collective burden, redistributed under the guise of fairness. This reordering of priorities fosters a system in which prevention is de-emphasized, and harm is normalized, creating a society where the erosion of safety is seen not as failure but as progress.

This "equalization of insecurity" is not an unintended consequence but the ultimate aim of crime-equity—a radical reconfiguration of justice with far-reaching consequences. Stable neighborhoods, once insulated by effective governance, are forced to confront the chaos that unchecked crime brings—eroding property values, fracturing social cohesion, and generating widespread fear. The ideological ambition of dismantling systemic inequality through "shared experience" produces not equity, but mutual disillusionment, as communities across the socioeconomic spectrum lose faith in institutions that no longer serve their most basic purpose: protection.

Far from uniting society, this redistribution deepens fragmentation. It pits communities against one another, fosters resentment, and breeds a cynical view of governance as prioritizing abstract ideals over real-world outcomes. In this way, crime-equity does not merely undermine public safety—it deconstructs the concept of justice itself, replacing it with a system that sacrifices order and security to the dictates of ideology.

Historical Parallels: Crime-Equity's Bloody March for Justice (Power)

Throughout modern history, the deliberate destabilization of societal order through the exploitation of criminal behavior has emerged a recurring strategy among radical movements seeking to redistribute power and dismantle established hierarchies. This reminiscent of the principles underlying crime-equity, reframes crime as a means to advance ideological objectives, cloaked in the rhetoric of equity and justice. By weaponizing disorder, such movements aim not merely to challenge authority but to reengineer the very foundations of society under the guise of redressing historical grievances.

The French Revolution (1789–1799)

The French Revolution offers a profound example of how revolutionary fervor can weaponize crime to dismantle existing social structures. During the Reign of Terror (1793–1794), the revolutionary government, led by the Committee of Public Safety under figures like Maximilien Robespierre, institutionalized violence against perceived enemies of the revolution. The Law of 22 Prairial (June 10, 1794) epitomized this radicalization, suspending suspects' rights to public trial and legal representation. Juries were left with only two choices: acquittal or death. This draconian framework resulted in approximately 17,000 executions and an additional 10,000 deaths in prisons or without trial.[1]

The French Revolution stands as a cautionary tale of what unfolds when ideological zealotry and vengeance usurp the rule of law. At its most radical phase, the revolution did not merely aim to dismantle the aristocracy—it sought to annihilate the very concept of societal order, weaponizing crime as a tool of social reengineering. The abolition of feudal privileges and the erosion of legal protections, ostensibly pursued in the name of justice, gave way to a far darker agenda: the systematic obliteration of social hierarchy, where criminality was recast as a grotesque vehicle for equity. Justice, the cornerstone of civilized society, was not simply eroded—it was commandeered to legitimize mob violence, mass executions, and the wholesale collapse of legal order.

The Reign of Terror was no chaotic accident but a calculated campaign to suppress dissent and redistribute suffering across all levels of society. The guillotine, far from being a mere symbol of revolutionary fervor, became an instrument of ideological conformity, wielded not only against the aristocracy but also against citizens from all classes deemed counter-revolutionaries. In this systematic machinery of fear, crime was redefined—not as an affront to justice but as a sanctioned method of achieving perceived social equality.

The French Revolution's descent into violence offers a stark reminder of how revolutions that subvert the rule of law can ultimately dismantle the very fabric of civilization, leaving in their wake a legacy of destruction masquerading as progress. It reveals the peril of conflating justice with retribution and of sacrificing order at the altar of ideology, where the pursuit of equity becomes indistinguishable from the perpetuation of chaos.

The Bolshevik Revolution (1917–1923)

The Bolshevik Revolution offers a compelling example of how crime can be weaponized to dismantle existing social and legal structures in the pursuit of ideological goals. Following the October Revolution of 1917, the Bolsheviks, led by Vladimir Lenin, undertook a systematic effort to eradicate the remnants of Tsarist Russia and suppress any opposition to their rule. In September 1918, the Council of People's Commissars issued the decree that launched the Red Terror, an organized campaign of mass executions, repression, and fear designed to eliminate enemies of the revolution. This decree explicitly sanctioned the execution of those accused of anti-revolutionary activities and mandated the public disclosure of their names and alleged crimes.[2]

The Red Terror was not an unintended consequence of revolutionary upheaval but a deliberate strategy to consolidate power through the
calculated redistribution of violence. Under the guise of protecting the
revolution and achieving a classless society, the Bolsheviks reframed acts
of state-sanctioned brutality as necessary instruments of social transformation. This systematic dismantling of the existing order extended beyond
political rivals, targeting entire classes of people—aristocrats, bourgeois
landowners, and intellectuals—under the banner of retributive justice.

The breakdown of law and order was integral to this strategy. The
Bolsheviks normalized land seizures, state-sanctioned theft, and widespread violence, repurposing crime as a mechanism for redistributing
wealth and inverting established hierarchies. The deliberate destruction of
Tsarist judicial and police systems was not simply an act of revolution but
a means to destabilize society and fill the resulting vacuum with chaos and
fear. Released prisoners—ranging from political dissidents to hardened
criminals—were weaponized to instill terror and suppress dissent, blurring the line between ideological enforcement and outright anarchy.

This approach served dual purposes: it legitimized the Bolsheviks as
champions of the oppressed while simultaneously positioning them as the
sole arbiters of order amidst the chaos they had unleashed. Criminal elements, now empowered under the regime, became instruments of state
control, their violence exploited to dismantle opposition and enforce
ideological conformity. By hollowing out traditional institutions and co-
opting crime as a tool of governance, the Bolsheviks ensured that power
was centralized, and resistance was crushed beneath the weight of state-
sanctioned brutality.

The Red Terror epitomized this calculated use of crime as a means of
societal reengineering. Far from a reactionary campaign, it was a meticulously orchestrated assault on the foundations of law and civil order,
designed to redistribute harm in alignment with revolutionary ideology.
The suffering it inflicted was not incidental but deliberate—a grim realization of crime-equity's core principle: dismantling established hierarchies
by ensuring that insecurity and fear permeate all levels of society.

The Bolshevik Revolution demonstrates the perils of a justice system
repurposed to serve ideological ends. In their quest to impose equality, the

Bolsheviks destroyed the mechanisms of accountability and protection, replacing them with a regime of terror where criminality was exalted as a means of revolutionary justice. The result was not a classless society but a fragmented and fearful populace, ruled by a state that thrived on violence, repression, and the annihilation of order.

Anti-Colonial Movements

In numerous anti-colonial movements, the principles of crime-equity found expression through the use of insurgent violence and expropriation as instruments to dismantle colonial power structures and redistribute authority to indigenous populations. During the Algerian War of Independence (1954–1962), the National Liberation Front (FLN) utilized guerrilla tactics such as targeted assassinations, bombings, and urban warfare to destabilize French colonial control. These acts of insurgent violence were framed as a necessary retributive justice, challenging the legitimacy of colonial rule and asserting the right of the colonized to reclaim political and territorial sovereignty.[3]

Similarly, the Mau Mau uprising in Kenya (1952–1960) employed a comparable strategy of violence and land seizures. Targeting British settlers and colonial infrastructure, the Mau Mau sought to expel foreign domination and restore ancestral lands to indigenous communities. These actions, while denounced by colonial authorities as criminal, were portrayed by the insurgents as acts of legitimate resistance against systemic oppression and economic exploitation. In both cases, traditional notions of criminality were inverted, redefined as revolutionary justice aimed at rectifying historical grievances.[4]

This redefinition of crime as a tool of liberation had profound and often paradoxical consequences. While insurgent tactics were instrumental in achieving political independence, they also unleashed prolonged periods of instability, social fragmentation, and internecine violence. The normalization of criminal methods in pursuit of revolutionary goals blurred the line between resistance and lawlessness, leaving post-independence societies grappling with deep-seated divisions and weakened institutions.

In many cases, the destabilizing effects of such movements outlived the colonial regimes they sought to overthrow. The redistribution of power through violent expropriation and insurgent tactics often undermined the very foundations of governance necessary for stability in the aftermath of liberation. The elevation of crime to a mechanism of social transformation did not merely challenge colonial hierarchies—it created enduring cycles of conflict, where the tools of resistance became entrenched as instruments of control within the newly independent state.

The use of crime-equity within anti-colonial movements illustrates the double-edged nature of retributive justice. While these movements sought to rectify historical injustices, the reliance on criminal tactics to achieve ideological objectives often imposed devastating costs on the societies they aimed to liberate. The legacy of such strategies underscores a central paradox: crime, even when wielded for the purpose of equity, risks leaving behind not liberation, but fragmentation and enduring instability.

Rhodesia (1979) and South Africa (1994)

The transitions in Rhodesia (now Zimbabwe) and post-apartheid South Africa provide stark illustrations of how crime-equity principles have been employed to disrupt entrenched hierarchies and pursue ideological goals. In Rhodesia, the end of white-minority rule in 1979 marked the beginning of aggressive land reform policies designed to redistribute land from white farmers to black citizens. These policies, often enforced through the forcible seizure of property, were framed as necessary reparations for colonial-era injustices. However, the implementation was marred by violence, economic disintegration, and social chaos. The mass expropriation of white-owned farms destabilized agricultural production, leading to famine, hyperinflation, and the collapse of Rhodesia's once-thriving economy.[5,6]

In this context, criminality became a state-sanctioned instrument of retributive justice. Acts of violence and property seizure were legitimized as part of the revolutionary goal of rectifying historical inequities, regardless of the broader societal costs. The pursuit of equity through the dismantling of legal and economic order left Rhodesia crippled, its institutions hollowed out and unable to support the very populations the reforms purported to uplift.

Similarly, in post-apartheid South Africa, the dismantling of institutionalized racial segregation was accompanied by an explosion in crime rates. While the redistribution of political power in 1994 ended decades of apartheid, it failed to deliver immediate economic equity, leaving millions of black South Africans in poverty. This disparity, combined with widespread unemployment and social discontent, created fertile ground for the proliferation of criminal activity. In some circles, these acts of theft and violence were rationalized as retributive justice, targeting the wealth and privilege of the formerly dominant white minority.[7]

This normalization of criminality, framed as a means of addressing historical grievances, has had profound consequences for South Africa. The erosion of the rule of law and the inability to contain escalating crime rates have perpetuated insecurity and deepened societal divisions. The very communities these policies sought to empower remain mired in poverty and violence, trapped in cycles of instability exacerbated by a justice system ill-equipped to balance equity with order.

Both Rhodesia and South Africa demonstrate the inherent dangers of employing crime as a tool of social reengineering. While the ideological aim of dismantling historical hierarchies may seem just, the practical outcomes often prove devastating. The breakdown of legal and economic systems undermines not only the rule of law but also the stability necessary for long-term progress.

These historical instances reveal a recurring paradox: the pursuit of equity through criminality often results in outcomes that are antithetical to justice. Far from creating harmonious or equitable societies, these approaches leave behind fractured institutions, widespread disillusionment, and enduring cycles of violence and instability. They serve as a sobering reminder that dismantling oppression without building a sustainable framework for governance risks replacing one form of dysfunction with another.

The Radical Left and Crime-Equity: A Continuum of Subversion

The historical precedents of weaponized criminality—from revolutionary France to Bolshevik Russia and anti-colonial insurgencies—find their modern ideological counterpart in crime-equity, a doctrine advanced not through paramilitary struggle but through the subversion of law itself. Where past revolutions openly embraced violence as a means of overturning power structures, today's radical left wields crime as an instrument of political reordering, not through barricades and bayonets but through the systematic dismantling of deterrence, prosecution, and punishment.

Crime-equity is not an anomaly within leftist thought but its latest and most refined iteration, an ideological descendent of the radical movements of the 20th century that sought to destabilize Western legal and economic systems under the guise of justice and liberation. The guiding principle remains unchanged: law and order are instruments of oppression, criminality a form of resistance, and justice an arena for ideological warfare.

Unlike past revolutionary factions that sought to overthrow the state through direct insurrection, modern crime-equity adherents operate within the system, repurposing legal and policy mechanisms to erode its foundations from within. Their objectives are achieved not with bombs or barricades, but through legislative activism, prosecutorial inaction, and linguistic manipulation, ensuring that the consequences of crime are redistributed to serve ideological aims rather than deter lawlessness.

From Armed Insurrection to Institutional Subversion

The intellectual lineage of crime-equity is evident in its parallels with the radical leftist movements of the 1960s and '70s, which sought to delegitimize state authority by normalizing violence and subversion:

- **The Weather Underground (1969–1977):** A militant leftist faction that openly declared war on the United States, engaging in bombings, assassinations, and robberies as part of a revolutionary struggle against capitalism and law enforcement.
- **The Black Liberation Army (BLA):** A radical offshoot of the Black Panther Party that assassinated police officers and robbed banks, justifying its actions as resistance against systemic oppression.
- **The Symbionese Liberation Army (SLA):** Infamous for kidnappings, bank heists, and targeted killings, the SLA rejected conventional politics in favor of armed struggle,

mirroring the ideological justifications of crime-equity in framing violence as a means of rectifying historical injustice.

- **The Red Brigades (Italy, 1970s–1980s):** A Marxist-Leninist terrorist organization that sought to dismantle the Italian state by executing government officials, judges, and business leaders—a philosophy echoed today in the targeted dismantling of law enforcement through progressive legal frameworks.
- **The FARC and ELN (Colombia, 1960s–Present):** Communist insurgents who combined guerrilla warfare with organized crime, using drug trafficking, extortion, and kidnappings as tools of revolutionary justice—an approach eerily mirrored in modern policies that excuse or redefine violent criminality as a response to systemic inequities.

Unlike these violent precursors, today's crime-equity adherents do not storm government buildings or hijack planes—they occupy DA's offices, legislative bodies, and university faculties, embedding their ideology into the very institutions that were once tasked with preserving law and order. Their revolution is not waged with bullets but with policies that erode enforcement, eliminate sentencing, and repurpose the legal system into an engine of retributive justice. By framing legal consequences as inherently racist and unjust, crime-equity proponents leverage existing democratic institutions to achieve the same long-term goal that leftist paramilitary groups once sought through direct violence: the destabilization of law and order in pursuit of ideological dominance.

The Pathology of Crime-Equity: How Linguistic Subversion Enables Ideological Control

The most effective revolutions do not announce themselves with gunfire or manifestos; they begin in the quieter realm of language, where meaning is diluted, inverted, and ultimately reprogrammed. Crime-equity is not merely a policy shift but a paradigmatic reordering of how society understands crime, justice, and responsibility. It does not seek to alter outcomes within the existing framework of law and order but to dissolve the framework itself.

This dissolution is achieved not through argument but through linguistic sleight of hand. A criminal is no longer a criminal but a justice-involved individual, a term so abstract that it suggests entanglement with the legal system rather than direct engagement in wrongdoing. A repeat offender is rebranded as a system-impacted person, as if victimhood and criminality were interchangeable. Burglary is downgraded to survival crime, implying that the offender was compelled to act by conditions beyond his control, rendering moral culpability irrelevant.

Traditional Term	Crime-Equity Rebrand
Criminal	Justice-involved individual
Non-violent offender	Repeat burglar, fentanyl trafficker
Restorative justice	The systematic elimination of consequences
Community-based interventions	The dismantling of policing

This is not linguistic evolution; it is ideological warfare. Crime-equity's vocabulary is not meant to clarify but to disable resistance by stripping language of its moral and legal weight. Words that once denoted criminal acts now describe social conditions, diffusing responsibility and redirecting outrage away from offenders and toward an amorphous concept of systemic injustice.

The Political Utility of Reprogramming Language

Crime-equity's rhetorical project follows a familiar historical pattern. Every revolutionary movement that has sought to reorder human society—whether Bolshevism, Maoism, or the various iterations of leftist cultural upheaval in the West—has begun by restructuring language to reshape reality. The goal is not just to introduce new terms but to render old ones unusable. The criminal ceases to exist as a category, and without the word, the concept itself erodes.

This tactic is not theoretical. The Soviets did not imprison political dissidents; they confined enemies of the people who had deviated from socialist orthodoxy. Mao's Red Guards did not denounce individuals; they waged war against counter-revolutionary elements. The Khmer Rouge did not exterminate civilians; they engaged in reeducation and purification.

Each of these regimes understood that language does not merely describe reality—it conditions thought, suppresses dissent, and preemptively invalidates opposition.

Crime-equity operates on the same premise. If criminality is redefined as an imposed condition rather than an act of agency, then prosecution becomes an injustice, policing becomes repression, and punishment becomes cruelty. The legal system itself is transformed from an instrument of public safety into an instrument of oppression.

From Words to Policy: The Dismantling of Law Under the Guise of Equity

Linguistic reprogramming is never a passive exercise. It is a mechanism of power, deployed with surgical precision to redefine social reality and justify ideological imperatives. Nowhere is this more evident than in the criminal justice system, where the manipulation of language has served as a prelude to the systematic dismantling of legal order. The crime-equity movement does not seek to *reform* law—it seeks to render it obsolete.

By redefining criminality as a structural inevitability rather than an individual choice, crime-equity inverts the moral foundation of justice. Guilt becomes a social construct, consequences are framed as persecution, and the legal system itself is recast as the true transgressor. This shift is not an abstraction; it has direct, measurable consequences.

Downgrading Serious Offenses: The Manufactured Illusion of Non-Violence

Language is the gateway to policy, and crime-equity has used linguistic manipulation to reclassify violent offenses as "non-violent," paving the way for mass decarceration. Proposition 57 in California provides a case study in this semantic sleight of hand. Under this law, violent crimes—including sexual assault of an unconscious person, human trafficking of a child, and hostage-taking—were legally reclassified as "non-violent" for parole purposes. The result? A pipeline for early release, not based on rehabilitation but on rhetorical maneuvering.

This is not merely a failure of policy—it is a calculated act of deception. The redefinition of violence is not intended to reflect empirical reality but to facilitate a predetermined political outcome: the emptying of prisons, irrespective of the consequences for public safety.

Manipulating Crime Statistics: How Reclassification Hides Criminality

If the crime-equity movement cannot eliminate crime, it can at least eliminate the appearance of crime. The statistical decline in felony offenses following California's Proposition 47 was not evidence of progress but an act of bureaucratic fraud. By reclassifying a broad range of felonies as misdemeanors—including shoplifting up to $950, grand theft, and drug possession—California engineered a statistical drop in felony crime while actual criminal activity surged.

The public was told crime was declining. Retailers, facing rampant theft and brazen looting, knew better.

This pattern extends beyond reclassification to outright statistical manipulation. The crime-equity movement routinely presents racial disparities in arrest and incarceration rates as *prima facie* evidence of systemic bias, omitting the behavioral patterns that drive these disparities.

Consider the FBI's Uniform Crime Reporting (UCR) data from 2019:

- 53% of homicide offenders and 60% of robbery offenders were Black, despite Black Americans comprising roughly 13% of the U.S. population.
- Rather than engaging with these figures, crime-equity advocates strip them of context, using raw disparities as self-evident proof of racial injustice while ignoring factors such as socioeconomic conditions, education, family structure, and urban crime concentration.

By framing disparities as the product of systemic oppression rather than criminal behavior, the crime-equity movement shifts the conversation away from deterrence and accountability toward reparations by another name: the selective suspension of law enforcement.

Another facet of statistical manipulation involves redefining what constitutes a crime or altering reporting practices to produce desired statistical

outcomes. In California, following the implementation of Proposition 47—
which reclassified certain felonies as misdemeanors—there was a reported
decrease in felony crimes. However, this did not necessarily reflect a true
decrease in criminal activity but rather a reclassification that artificially
deflated felony statistics.

Erasing the Victim-Offender Distinction: The Deconstruction of Justice

Justice requires moral clarity. Crime-equity thrives on moral ambiguity.

A functioning legal system operates on the fundamental distinction
between victim and offender. The crime-equity movement seeks to blur,
and ultimately erase, that distinction. Criminals are rechristened as
justice-involved individuals, a term that strips crime of its moral gravity
and recasts it as an incidental bureaucratic entanglement. The victim, in
turn, becomes a footnote—often referred to in abstract statistical terms,
if at all.

This inversion of justice is not accidental; it is a feature, not a bug. If
the primary focus is no longer the harm inflicted but the systemic forces
that allegedly produced the offender, then culpability ceases to exist.
Punishment becomes persecution. Accountability becomes oppression.
The law itself is reframed as an instrument of violence rather than a safeguard against it.

The end result is a perverse moral economy in which sympathy flows
inexorably toward those who commit harm, while those who suffer it are
discarded as inconvenient obstacles to a broader ideological agenda. This
is the trajectory of crime-equity: it does not reduce crime, nor does it
rehabilitate offenders. It erases the concept of crime itself, replacing it with
an ideological abstraction that functions as a pretext for dismantling the
institutions that uphold law and order.

Conclusion: The Ideological Engine of Collapse

Crime-equity is not a theoretical abstraction—it is the ideological skeleton
upon which an entire movement has been constructed. It does not operate
as a series of isolated legal experiments but as a comprehensive reordering of justice itself—one that is neither accidental nor haphazard but the

logical extension of a worldview that sees law not as a safeguard of order but as a tool of oppression.

At its core, crime-equity is the theoretical justification for a system that no longer punishes crime but rationalizes it, that does not seek to deter offenders but to redistribute the burden of criminality in accordance with ideological dictates. It is not an aberration within California's criminal justice system—it is the foundation upon which the state's most destabilizing policies have been built. The dismantling of deterrence, the erosion of sentencing, the retreat of law enforcement—none of these developments exist in a vacuum. They are the direct consequences of a doctrine that has transcended theory and metastasized into governance.

What began as an intellectual abstraction has now been operationalized into law, reshaping prosecutorial discretion, legislative priorities, and public safety itself. As we turn to the next chapter, we examine how crime-equity has been embedded within the broader criminal justice reform movement, driving the policies that are unraveling the very concept of justice—not by accident, but by design.

CHAPTER 4

REFORM IS REVOLUTION

Criminal justice reform, as it is framed today, is not reform at all—it is the operational arm of an ideological revolution, concealed behind the language of equity and progress. What its advocates sell as fairness and modernization is, in truth, a deliberate dismantling of the legal and moral architecture that underpins civil society. Beneath the rhetorical veneer of "compassion" and "fairness" lies a movement that is not content with improving the justice system but seeks to abolish it altogether.

At its core, this movement is driven by the conviction that the criminal justice system is irredeemably racist, classist, and structurally oppressive. Emerging from Critical Race Theory (CRT), abolitionist criminology, and neo-Marxist legal thought, it does not aim to make the system more just or effective—it aims to erase it as a means of reordering society itself. Crime-equity, as explored in chapter 3, provided the intellectual scaffolding for this shift, redefining criminality as an expression of systemic oppression rather than an act of individual agency. Now, those same radical principles have been operationalized into policy.

The legal and policy changes that have destabilized California—eliminating cash bail, gutting sentencing enhancements, refusing to prosecute entire categories of crime, and decriminalizing theft and drug offenses—are not a series of isolated missteps. They are deliberate, calculated measures designed to deconstruct the mechanisms that uphold social order. The ultimate objective is a justice system that ceases to function as a barrier against crime and instead redistributes its consequences in accordance with ideological imperatives. Criminals are reframed as victims, while law-abiding citizens are cast as complicit in a system of historical injustice.

This chapter will expose the false promises of "reform" and dissect the philosophies that animate it—philosophies that, taken to their logical conclusion, seek to strip the law of its moral authority and replace it with an arbitrary system of ideological enforcement. The data is unambiguous: leniency does not foster rehabilitation, and decarceration does not enhance public safety. Instead, these policies embolden criminals, erode deterrence, and weaken the very institutions that sustain order, leaving society vulnerable to the predation of those whom the system now refuses to restrain.

The Evolution of Reform: From Civil Rights to Revolutionary Subversion

The trajectory of criminal justice reform in America is not one of linear progress but of ideological capture. What began as a necessary and measured response to genuine disparities in sentencing, police conduct, and prison conditions has metastasized into a campaign to dismantle law and order itself. Reform has ceased to mean refinement; it now means eradication. The movement that once sought to ensure justice is applied fairly now seeks to ensure it is not applied at all.

At its core, this shift is not about crime or justice in any conventional sense but about power—who wields it, how it is distributed, and, ultimately, how it is dismantled. The modern criminal justice reform movement is the product of a radical ideology that regards the very concept of crime as a construct of oppression. This ideology is not new; it is merely the latest iteration of a Marxist-Leninist framework that has, for over a century, sought to delegitimize Western institutions by recasting order as tyranny and punishment as persecution.

What was once a demand for proportional sentencing and accountability in law enforcement has morphed into a wholesale rejection of criminal culpability. Crime is no longer viewed as an individual moral or legal failing but as an inevitability produced by an unjust social order. This rejection of agency—rooted in the deterministic fantasies of Marxist social theory—has profound consequences, for it transforms the legal system from an instrument of justice into an arena of revolutionary struggle.

From Class War to Crime War: The Intellectual Roots of Criminal Justice Reform

The modern reform movement draws heavily from the ideological currents of the 1960s and 1970s, when radical leftist theorists—frustrated by their failure to ignite a proletarian revolution in the West—began repurposing Marxist class struggle into racial and legal struggle. The Soviet-backed subversion of the American legal system during the Cold War planted the seeds for this transformation, with organizations like the National Lawyers Guild and figures such as Angela Davis serving as conduits for Leninist legal theory repackaged for domestic consumption.[1,2]

At the heart of this shift is the principle that the rule of law is not an impartial system but a mechanism of oppression, designed by the powerful to maintain their dominance. This notion, championed by legal theorists such as Derrick Bell, Richard Delgado, and Kimberlé Crenshaw, forms the intellectual backbone of Critical Race Theory (CRT) and its juridical offshoots, including abolitionist criminology.[3] These movements frame the American justice system as an extension of white supremacy, arguing that crime itself is not a breach of moral order but a reaction to racial and economic inequality.[4,5]

From this premise, criminality is no longer a question of personal responsibility; it is a structural inevitability. Punishment ceases to be an act of justice and instead becomes an extension of oppression. Law enforcement is no longer seen as a guardian of order but as an occupying force of systemic repression. The logical conclusion of this worldview is not reform—it is abolition.

Restorative Justice: The Rejection of Punishment and the Normalization of Crime

The movement's intellectual roots were not confined to university lecture halls; they were actively injected into policy through progressive legal academia, activist-backed district attorneys, and legislative overhauls disguised as racial justice initiatives. The transition from theory to policy was seamless—what began as radical legal scholarship became governing doctrine, implemented through prosecutors who saw their role not as enforcing the law but as dismantling it. The concepts of "crime-equity" and "restorative justice" became the new standard, transforming courts, sentencing laws, and law enforcement priorities under the guise of reform.

The vehicle through which these ideological objectives are being implemented is restorative justice, an alternative framework that replaces deterrence and punishment with dialogue, mediation, and rehabilitation. The language of restorative justice is deliberately euphemistic, designed to obscure its true purpose: to eliminate incarceration, decriminalize entire categories of offenses, and dismantle the capacity of the state to enforce law and order.

Proponents argue that restorative justice "addresses the root causes of crime" rather than simply punishing offenders. In reality, it achieves neither. Instead, it replaces accountability with therapeutic intervention, reducing sentencing, refusing to prosecute repeat offenders, and systematically emptying prisons under the pretense of equity. The consequences of this shift have been disastrous:

- **Non-Prosecution of Entire Categories of Crime:** Progressive district attorneys, backed by activist organizations and leftist donors, have ceased prosecuting a wide range of offenses. In cities like San Francisco, Los Angeles, and Chicago, crimes such as shoplifting, drug possession, and resisting arrest have been effectively decriminalized, leading to spiraling disorder.
- **Elimination of Sentencing Enhancements:** Measures like California's Proposition 57 and the abolition of cash bail have ensured that repeat offenders are treated as first-time criminals, eroding the deterrent effect of legal consequences.
- **Decriminalization of Theft and Drug Offenses:** Proposition 47 reclassified theft under $950 as a misdemeanor, fueling a surge in organized retail crime. Meanwhile, so-called harm reduction policies have led to the mass distribution of needles and the open-air fentanyl markets now endemic in major cities.

These policies are not failures of governance; they are its deliberate negation. The objective is not safety but the dissolution of legal structures that uphold it.

The Rejection of Deterrence and the Political Utility of Crime

One of the most insidious aspects of this ideological shift is the rejection of deterrence-based justice. The premise that punishment dissuades crime—one of the oldest and most empirically sound principles in legal theory—is now derided as regressive, even racist. Instead, modern reformers insist that criminal behavior is best addressed through social intervention, economic redistribution, and rehabilitation.

But this is not naïveté—it is strategy. The erosion of deterrence serves a political function, for when crime is no longer met with consequences, its effects become universal. The destabilization that follows is not an unfortunate byproduct but an ideological objective, part of a broader effort to weaken the mechanisms of state authority and to cultivate a sense of perpetual crisis that justifies further leftward transformation.

The criminal justice reform movement, as it exists today, does not seek to correct injustices; it seeks to engineer them. It does not wish to protect society but to restructure it through disorder. Its policies are not misguided—they are calculated, designed to redistribute criminal accountability, undermine confidence in law enforcement, and fracture social cohesion.

Addressing Racial Disparities: A Narrative Built on Deception

The criminal justice reform movement's fixation on racial disparities in arrest and sentencing data fundamentally misrepresents the realities of crime and enforcement. By framing law enforcement as a racialized mechanism of oppression, reformists divert attention from the actual drivers of criminal behavior—family breakdown, economic instability, and cultural decay. The singular focus on racial statistics, without accounting for crime rates and offender patterns, transforms law enforcement into an exercise in demographic engineering rather than a function of public safety.

The Myth of Systemic Racial Bias in Law Enforcement

Reformers exploit racial disparities in arrests to frame the justice system as inherently racist while deliberately omitting the underlying cause—crime rates. According to FBI Uniform Crime Reporting (UCR) data, disparities in violent crime mirror disparities in policing, yet activists push for policies that treat enforcement as the problem rather than criminal behavior. This manipulation has driven a wave of reforms prioritizing racial quotas over effective policing, ensuring that enforcement is not dictated by crime data but by ideological mandates.[6,7]

Racial Quotas and Public Safety

By prioritizing racial quotas over crime data, these reforms have weakened law enforcement in high-crime areas, emboldened offenders, and made policing a political liability. A clear example is the New York Police Department's controversial decision to reduce stop-and-frisk practices.

Initially framed as a measure to address racial disparities, the policy shift led to a rise in violent crime, according to a Manhattan Institute report.[8] The NYPD's emphasis on reducing racial discrepancies came at the cost of effective crime deterrence in high-crime neighborhoods.

In Chicago, the city's efforts to adopt community policing strategies aimed at reducing racial tensions have been criticized for leaving high-crime areas underserved. As a result, law enforcement's reluctance to engage proactively in these areas, out of fear of racial backlash, has led to increased violence.

After stop-and-frisk practices were significantly reduced in 2016, an 80% decrease in pedestrian stops was recorded. This shift led to an increase in violent crime, particularly in minority neighborhoods, where police interactions with civilians were most needed for proactive crime prevention.[9]

Similarly, in San Francisco, where policies have emphasized racial equity in policing, the city's homicide rate has risen, with authorities struggling to balance demographic goals with the need to curb escalating violence.

San Francisco saw a sharp increase in homicides in 2021, with fifty-six homicides compared to 2019, which had only forty-one. San Fracisco's Mission District experienced an 82% rise in shootings from 2020 to 2021. While some of the spike is attributed to broader national trends and the impacts of the pandemic, local reforms and racial equity-driven policing strategies also contributed to challenges in addressing violence effectively. Law enforcement officials, including Police Chief Bill Scott, have highlighted staffing shortages and shifts in police focus as complicating factors, particularly as policies sought to balance equity goals with maintaining public safety.[10]

The reality reformers ignore is this: crime is not evenly distributed across racial demographics, nor is victimization. The primary victims of these equity-driven policies are minority residents in high-crime areas who bear the brunt of weakened law enforcement.

The Weaponization of Racial Disparities

By redefining disparities as proof of systemic bias rather than behavioral trends, reformists have manufactured a crisis that does not exist in the data. The solution they propose—reducing enforcement in high-crime areas and eliminating sentencing disparities—removes the last barriers preventing those communities from descending into lawlessness. The push to eliminate racial gaps in incarceration is not about fairness; it is about engineering equal criminal outcomes at any cost, even if that cost is more crime, more victims, and the systematic erosion of justice.

The Radical Takeover of the Criminal Justice System

The movement to "reform" criminal justice is not an organic response to societal needs but a top-down ideological project. It is driven by a network of radical theorists, activist academics, and elected officials who wield disproportionate influence over how crime, punishment, and public safety are defined. These figures do not merely propose adjustments to the legal system; they seek to dismantle it entirely, recasting criminality as victimhood and law enforcement as an instrument of oppression.

Operating under the guise of equity and compassion, they manipulate legal structures to erode accountability, weaken deterrence, and strip the law of its moral and functional authority. The result has not been greater fairness but growing disorder, as law-abiding citizens bear the brunt of policies designed to shield offenders from consequence. These architects of criminal anarchy operate on two fronts: the commissars of crime-equity, who supply the intellectual and ideological framework, and the progressive prosecutors, who execute it from within the justice system itself.

Commissars of Crime-Equity: The Ideologues Behind Criminal Justice Reform

The modern criminal justice reform movement did not emerge organically; it was engineered by a cadre of ideological enforcers—commissars of justice—who view law not as a safeguard of order but as an instrument of systemic oppression. These theorists do not seek to improve the justice system but to dismantle it, replacing punishment with grievance-based redistribution and deterrence with rehabilitationist dogma.

Through their work, incarceration is rebranded as a vestige of racial and economic tyranny, prosecution as an extension of state violence, and crime as an unavoidable consequence of structural inequity. Their influence has transformed criminal justice policy from a means of protecting the public into an ideological project that prioritizes abstract notions of equity over real-world safety, ensuring that laws are rewritten, reinterpreted, or ignored altogether in pursuit of a revolutionary legal order.

Michelle Alexander: Incarceration as a Racial Construct

In *The New Jim Crow* (2010), Michelle Alexander reframed mass incarceration as a direct continuation of slavery and segregation, arguing that the criminal justice system is designed not to punish wrongdoing but to uphold systemic racism. By reducing crime to a mere byproduct of racial injustice, Alexander's work has fueled policies that prioritize racial "equity" over public safety. The logical consequence of this worldview is that laws should be selectively enforced—or ignored altogether—to balance incarceration statistics rather than prevent crime. Her rhetoric has provided ideological cover for decarceration policies that prioritize statistical parity over deterrence, ensuring that punishment is no longer tied to criminal behavior but to racial quotas.

Angela Davis: The Mainstreaming of Prison Abolition

Angela Davis, a Marxist revolutionary and former Black Panther, has long advocated for the complete abolition of prisons and police, contending that they exist solely to uphold white supremacy and capitalist exploitation. Her vision is not one of reform but of total dismantling—she does not argue for fairer sentencing or improved policing, but for their elimination altogether. Davis's influence has mainstreamed the idea that incarceration itself is an illegitimate response to crime, directly shaping policies that release even violent offenders under the guise of "restorative justice." Her work has served as an intellectual blueprint for radical district attorneys and activist policymakers who view crime not as an act requiring accountability but as a justified rebellion against systemic oppression.

Dorothy Roberts and the Rejection of Deterrence

Dorothy Roberts, along with other theorists steeped in Critical Race Theory (CRT), rejects deterrence-based justice outright, arguing that punishment is a social construct designed to reinforce power hierarchies rather than maintain order. Under this logic, incarceration is never a matter of public safety but an instrument of racial and economic control. Her work has influenced policies that replace incarceration with ineffective "community-based interventions," ensuring that career criminals cycle in and out of the system without meaningful consequences. The result has not been a reduction in crime but its proliferation, as habitual offenders recognize that the state no longer possesses either the will or the mechanisms to enforce order.

The Abolitionist Movement: The Campaign to Eradicate Law Enforcement

The Abolitionist Movement, spearheaded by organizations such as Critical Resistance, takes these ideas to their logical extreme, arguing that true justice can only be achieved by dismantling all carceral institutions—including prisons, policing, and probation. This is not a rhetorical flourish but a literal call to abolish law enforcement altogether, replacing it with vague notions of "community accountability." These ideas have directly influenced policies aimed at defunding police departments, eliminating cash bail, and restricting prosecutorial discretion, ensuring that criminal behavior is met with little to no consequence. What began as an academic fantasy has now been operationalized into legislation, with devastating consequences for public safety.

The Intellectual Vanguard of Crime-Equity

These theorists have not reformed the justice system; they have undermined it. Their ideas have been weaponized into policy, ensuring that crime is excused, punishment is abandoned, and law-abiding citizens are left unprotected. What they call "justice" is, in reality, the systematic dismantling of the rule of law.

Crime-equity is the ideological scaffolding of this movement, subordinating criminal accountability to grievance-based redistribution. These abolitionist academics and legal activists do not seek fairness; they seek to replace deterrence with ideological adjudication. Their work provides the justification for policies that erase enforcement, strip away consequences, and subordinate public safety to the dictates of historical redress. Their influence is not theoretical—it is the blueprint for the unraveling of justice itself.

The Enforcers of the Revolution: Progressive Prosecutors

The implementation of crime-equity policies has not been left to chance. It has been systematically embedded into the legal system by a new class of prosecutors who do not view their role as enforcing the law but as redefining it to serve an ideological agenda. These district attorneys—many installed through the financial backing of left-wing megadonors such as George Soros—have used their offices to dismantle deterrence, eliminate cash bail, and refuse to prosecute entire categories of crime.

George Gascón (Los Angeles, CA): A Fake Lawyer Who Broke Los Angeles

Gascón has not reformed prosecution—he has dismantled it. By eliminating sentencing enhancements for violent criminals, refusing to try juveniles as adults, and ensuring mass early releases, he has systematically erased the last vestiges of deterrence in Los Angeles. Under his tenure, violent crime has surged, with *carjackings up 200%* and businesses crippled by unchecked looting. His policies have not merely weakened law enforcement; they have signaled to criminals that punishment is now an abstraction, an outdated relic of a justice system that no longer functions.

Chesa Boudin (San Francisco, CA): A Politician Too Left for SF

Boudin, raised by Weather Underground terrorists and steeped in radical legal activism, did not see prosecution as a mechanism of justice but as an extension of his ideological mission to dismantle it. His tenure turned San Francisco into an urban wasteland where property crime was de facto decriminalized, fentanyl markets operated in broad daylight, and public safety became a privilege reserved for those wealthy enough to escape. The city decayed so rapidly under his watch that even its overwhelmingly left-wing electorate ejected him in a landslide recall, a rare admission that his experiment in non-prosecution had gone too far.

Kim Foxx (Cook County, IL): The Prosecutor Who Made Chicago Deadlier

Foxx has not simply refused to prosecute crime—she has stripped prosecution of meaning altogether. By dismissing thousands of felony cases, including violent assaults, carjackings, and homicides, she has ensured that crime in Chicago operates without meaningful consequence. Retailers have shuttered, mob-style looting has become commonplace, and gang violence now rages with near-total impunity. Under her policies, the city's justice system has become an empty shell, where law exists in theory but not in practice.

Larry Krasner (Philadelphia, PA): Defense Attorney First, DA Second

Krasner did not take office to enforce the law; he took office to erase it. A former criminal defense attorney with open contempt for law enforcement, he has presided over the deadliest years in Philadelphia's history, with homicides soaring to historic highs. His refusal to prosecute gun crimes has turned the city into a war zone, where violent offenders walk free while their victims are buried. His legacy is not reform but carnage— an entire city sacrificed to a theory that punishment is worse than crime itself.

Alvin Bragg (New York, NY): Make New York Scary Again

Bragg has not merely deprioritized prosecution—he has actively ensured that repeat violent offenders remain on the streets. By downgrading serious felonies to misdemeanors and refusing to seek pretrial detention for danger-ous criminals, he has turned Manhattan into a playground for predators. The explosion of random street attacks, robberies, and violent assaults under his tenure is not an accident but an inevitability—a direct result of his belief that prosecution itself is the problem, not the crime it was designed to address.

THE EXECUTIONERS OF LAW AND ORDER

The installation of progressive prosecutors has not reformed the justice sys-tem—it has hollowed it out. These officials were not elected to uphold the law but to selectively dismantle it, ensuring that prosecution is no longer a safeguard against crime but a mechanism for advancing ideological objectives.

Through non-prosecution policies, the elimination of cash bail, and the refusal to seek meaningful sentences, they have rendered entire cat-egories of crime effectively legal. Criminals are emboldened, deterrence is nonexistent, and communities—particularly the most vulnerable—are left defenseless. These prosecutors are not reformers; they are enforcers of a system in which law-abiding citizens are collateral damage in the pursuit of ideological purity.

Their legacy is not justice—it is the systemic deconstruction of law itself.

The Policy Manifestations of Criminal Justice Reform

The radical policies masquerading as reforms have not improved the crim-inal justice system—they have dismantled its core functions, eroding pub-lic safety and systematically neutering law enforcement. From sentencing rollbacks and reckless bail reform to ideologically driven policing policies and diversionary loopholes, these changes have crippled the justice sys-tem's ability to deter crime and hold offenders accountable. This is not the unintended consequence of misguided compassion but the calculated work of zealots determined to upend the structures that maintain order. Their policies have not merely failed; they have actively empowered crimi-nals while leaving communities defenseless.

Sentencing Reform: The Deliberate Weakening of Deterrence

The gutting of mandatory minimums and the dilution of three-strikes laws are not adjustments to sentencing guidelines but an explicit dismantling of the legal framework that underpins deterrence. In the radical creed of reform advocates, habitual offenders are not dangerous criminals but casualties of systemic oppression, to be released rather than punished.

A Heritage Foundation report reveals the stark consequences: states that have embraced these "reforms" now suffer a 15% increase in violent crime—the inevitable outcome of eroding the consequences of repeat offenses. This is not justice; it is a controlled demolition of deterrence, ensuring that predators remain free under the banner of equity, or more precisely, *crime-equity*. By unleashing habitual offenders onto the streets, these policies do not advance fairness—they orchestrate the disintegration of civil order, inviting chaos to spread unchecked.

Bail Reform: Legalized Recidivism

The elimination or reduction of cash bail, sold as a moral imperative to prevent discrimination against the poor, has functioned instead as a state-sanctioned guarantee of repeat offenses. These policies do not ensure fairness; they ensure that criminals cycle endlessly through the system without consequence.

Nowhere is this clearer than in New York, where the abolition of cash bail for countless offenses triggered a 24% increase in recidivism. This is not an unfortunate oversight—it is a fundamental recalibration of the justice system, designed to prevent incarceration rather than crime.[11]

For the high priests of *crime-equity*, habitual criminals are not dangers to society but foot soldiers in a broader struggle against an unjust system. Their release is not a matter of rehabilitation but a strategic redistribution of harm, ensuring that the burden of crime falls not on the guilty but on a society deemed culpable by history. This movement does not seek reform—it seeks to obliterate the foundations of the existing order and reduce it to rubble, leaving revolution to rise from the ruins.

Policing Practices: The Systematic Neutralization of Law Enforcement

The assault on policing is not about improving public trust—it is about rendering law enforcement powerless. Reformists, cloaked in the sanctimonious language of *equity and de-escalation*, have methodically stripped police of the authority and tools necessary to combat crime.

Defunding and Resource Diversion

Reform advocates push to slash police budgets and divert funding to social services. The consequences have been dire: in Minneapolis, after the police budget was cut and over 200 officers left the force, violent crime surged 21%, leaving entire neighborhoods at the mercy of criminals.[12]

The Death of "Broken Windows" Policing

The once-effective strategy of targeting minor offenses to prevent major ones has been abandoned under pressure from activists. In New York, after it was scaled back under the disastrous mayorship of Bill de Blasio, shootings and violent crime increased by 22%.[13]

De-Escalation Training as a Liability

While billed as a necessary reform, these training programs often leave officers hesitant to act in high-risk situations. The assumption that violent criminals can be talked down ignores the brutal realities of law enforcement. Officers conditioned to second-guess themselves hesitate in moments where force is required, creating dangerous openings that criminals readily exploit.

Replacing Police with Unarmed "Community Responders"

Reformers propose replacing law enforcement with social workers for "non-violent" incidents such as mental health crises. In cities like San Francisco, where this approach has been tested, response times have increased, and many situations have escalated into violence beyond the capacity of untrained civilians to manage.[14]

These reforms do not make policing more effective—they convert officers into passive facilitators rather than enforcers of law. The goal is not to enhance public safety but to strip the police of their authority, ensuring that criminality is not deterred but tolerated. Reformists are not interested in maintaining order; they seek to dissolve it.

Diversion Protocols: The Revolving Door of Crime

Diversion programs, billed as a humane alternative to incarceration, have become yet another mechanism for repeat offenders to evade meaningful consequences. Prosecutors and defense attorneys alike have witnessed firsthand how these initiatives function as an endless reset button, allowing criminals to cycle through the system indefinitely.

Los Angeles prosecutor Kevin Swartz lays bare the absurdity:

> A first-time shoplifter with no prior record is automatically given a diversionary offer—typically two days of community service and an anti-shoplifting program. If they complete it, the case is dismissed and wiped from their record. The problem? They can be re-arrested for the same crime, get another diversion offer, and repeat this indefinitely. Unless a prosecutor meticulously examines their arrest record, they appear as a first-time offender every time.[15]

This perversion of justice creates a perpetual cycle where career criminals accumulate no formal record of their offenses, ensuring that courts treat them as first-time offenders forever. The effect is not rehabilitation but a total subversion of accountability. This is not a justice system—it is an assembly line of lawlessness, where victims are forgotten, consequences are erased, and the machinery of the state exists not to deter crime but to guarantee its survival.

A System Built for the Criminal, Not the Victim

Every policy examined here shares the same underlying philosophy: the notion that criminality is an inevitable product of systemic oppression and that the primary function of justice is not deterrence but redistribution. Sentencing reductions, bail elimination, police disempowerment, and diversionary loopholes all serve the same purpose—to shift the consequences of crime away from those who commit it and onto the society they prey upon.

These policies are not merely misguided; they are the calculated mechanisms of an ideological movement that sees justice not as an impartial principle but as a tool of political transformation. The resulting devastation is not collateral damage—it is the point.

Recidivism Data: A Cycle of Criminality and Systemic Failure

The claim that "non-violent" offenders pose little threat upon release collapses under scrutiny. A Bureau of Justice Statistics (BJS) study tracking offenders across thirty-four states found that over 60% of non-violent criminals were rearrested within a decade, with a significant proportion committing violent crimes.[16] Similarly, the BJS's 2018 report revealed that 68% of drug offenders were rearrested within three years, climbing to 83% within nine years. While not every drug offense directly escalates to violence, the data confirms a pattern: habitual offenders rarely remain confined to one type of crime.[17]

This exposes the fallacy of treating offenses such as drug trafficking and burglary as "low-risk." These are not isolated crimes but gateway offenses, destabilizing entire communities and frequently leading to more severe criminal activity. Sentencing reductions, decarceration initiatives, and lax parole policies have turned the justice system into a revolving door of repeat offenders, undermining both public safety and trust in law enforcement.

A Comparative Analysis: Stricter Sentencing and Public Safety

Empirical data consistently shows that stricter sentencing correlates with lower recidivism rates. Florida's Prisoner Release Reoffender (PRR) law, which mandates harsh penalties for habitual offenders, has significantly reduced recidivism—only 25% of PRR offenders are rearrested within three years, far below the national average. Similarly, Texas's tough-on-crime policies, which prioritize incarceration for repeat offenders while maintaining selective rehabilitative measures, have achieved similar declines.[18]

By contrast, California's decarceration policies, enacted under the pretense of prison overcrowding, have fueled a cycle of reoffending. The California Department of Corrections and Rehabilitation (CDCR) consistently reports high recidivism rates, worsened by sentencing rollbacks and mass early releases.[19] These policies are not reducing crime; they are reintroducing it into the public sphere at an industrial scale.

The Scandinavian Illusion: Why Rehabilitation Fails for Violent Criminals

Scandinavian countries are often cited as models of rehabilitative justice, with proponents pointing to their relatively low crime rates. However, these systems collapse when applied to violent offenders. A *Journal of Quantitative Criminology* study on Norway's penal system found that while short sentences (typically under six months) have minimal impact on recidivism, violent offenders continue to reoffend at disproportionately high rates, despite extensive post-release programs.[20]

This underscores a crucial point: rehabilitation and leniency alone cannot contain serious criminal behavior. Soft-on-crime policies fail not because they lack resources, but because they operate on a false premise—that offenders can be reformed simply through economic and social intervention. When applied broadly, as in California, these policies produce only one result: increased victimization.

The Fallacy of Rehabilitation: When Reform Becomes Delusion

The reform movement operates on a dangerous assumption: that crime is a mere function of circumstance, and that offenders—regardless of their history—are malleable, capable of rehabilitation if given the right interventions. This belief ignores both behavioral science and lived reality.

A National Bureau of Economic Research study confirms what law enforcement professionals have long known—violent offenders are significantly less responsive to rehabilitative programs compared to non-violent criminals.[21] The idea that a career criminal, hardened by years of violent behavior, will be fundamentally reformed by job placement or therapy is not just naïve—it is demonstrably false.

The National Institute of Justice found that reentry programs such as the Second Chance Act, which offer job placement and housing assistance to felons, have failed to meaningfully reduce recidivism.[22] This underscores a critical reality: while rehabilitation has its place, it is not a panacea—especially for criminals predisposed to violence. Without strong deterrents, high-risk offenders cycle through the system, using leniency as an opportunity rather than a second chance.

The consequences of this ideological fixation are not theoretical; they are borne by the public, particularly victims. Reformers place the offender's narrative at the center of the justice system while sidelining the moral and societal imperatives that demand accountability. Punishment is dismissed as outdated, while society is expected to absorb the escalating costs of recidivism, lawlessness, and unrestrained criminality.

Kevin Swartz, a Los Angeles County Deputy DA and former New York prosecutor, provides a grim summation:

"The ideology behind the Criminal Reform movement wants to 'destroy our civilization and way of life.' It's the only way to make sense of it."

His observation is not hyperbole—it is a reality reflected in crime statistics, policy failures, and the rising human toll of a justice system that has abandoned its fundamental purpose.

The Recidivism Crisis: A Blueprint for Anarchy

The data leaves little room for ambiguity. Jurisdictions that implement deterrence-based policies achieve greater public safety, while those that prioritize leniency fuel repeat offenses and rising crime rates. The recidivism crisis is not just a symptom of failed governance; it is a direct consequence of an ideology that refuses to acknowledge crime as an individual moral failing, instead treating it as a social construct requiring systemic absolution.

The fundamental purpose of the justice system is not rehabilitation—it is public protection. Any policy that subordinates deterrence to ideological considerations will produce only one outcome: the sustained erosion of law and order.

The Role of Law Schools: A Factory of Criminal Justice Saboteurs

Elite law schools have become ideological factories producing prosecutors who see their role not as enforcing the law but as dismantling it from within. The legal education system has systematically replaced traditional concepts of justice—deterrence, accountability, and impartiality—with an activist framework that views prosecution as a tool for social engineering rather than punishment.

Mike Romano and the Legal Corruption of Prosecution

Mike Romano, founder of the Stanford Justice Advocacy Project, embodies the academic push to use prosecution as a vehicle for ideological reform. His work on the Three Strikes Project led to the release of over 3,000 criminals serving life sentences, many of whom posed clear public safety risks. This is not legal advocacy; it is the calculated dismantling of enforcement under the pretext of humanitarian concern.

Los Angeles Deputy DA John Lewin explains:

> They're going to law schools. And the way that they sell it is that you're going to be here and you're going to "do justice," is what they call it, you're going to end up addressing mass incarceration. They sell being a prosecutor as if you're a social worker or defense attorney. Traditional prosecutors who want to put bad people away. Prosecute bad people. That's not what attracts them. So you end up getting a bunch of people who don't really want to prosecute. They want to coddle them. They want to get them out. And that's a problem.

How Elite Law Schools Have Rewritten Prosecution

- **Redefining the Prosecutor's Role:** Stanford, Harvard, and Yale now frame prosecution as a means of correcting historical injustices, producing DA candidates who see offenders as victims and justice as malleable.
- **Cultivating a Revolving Door of Crime:** Graduates indoctrinated in these programs go on to eliminate cash bail, refuse to prosecute entire categories of offenses, and prioritize racial quotas over deterrence.
- **Judicial Sabotage from Within:** Many of these graduates ascend to judgeships, where they impose radical sentencing leniency, ensuring that even the most violent offenders cycle back into communities with little consequence.

These institutions are not producing prosecutors; they are churning out activists in robes, determined to gut law enforcement and recast crime as a byproduct of societal failure rather than individual culpability.

California: A Case Study in Judicial Malfeasance

No state exemplifies the catastrophic consequences of radical criminal justice reform better than California. A once-functioning legal system has been systematically hollowed out by progressive legislation, activist judges, and ideological prosecutors who see the law as a tool for deconstruction rather than enforcement.

Radical Judicial Appointments: The Bench as a Political Weapon

A prosecutor from Oakland reveals the consequences of California's judicial appointments:

"Now have a bunch of liberal as fuck judges. And frankly, judges that should never have become judges that were appointed by Gavin Newsom. Like, all these appointees are not qualified. They all fit a liberal quota. They're not qualified. And they come in. And they're elected positions too, and because California is in the wave of progressive liberal reform, they go that way because that's what gets them their seats next time around."[23]

California's judicial system no longer operates as a check on lawlessness but as an enabler of it. Progressive judges routinely release repeat offenders, throw out sentencing enhancements, and undermine prosecutorial efforts to hold criminals accountable.

The Direct Consequences of California's Criminal Justice Policies

This clear chain of custody binds the burgeoning criminality in California to specific legislation and directives put in place significantly from 2020. These policies are not failures by measure of their objective. Quite the contrary, their consequences are so obvious and inevitable that one must conclude they are purposeful and by design. For instance, data from the California Department of Justice shows a 31% increase in violent crime rates following the implementation of these progressive policies since 2014.[24]

Not "Failures" but Intentional

California's criminal justice collapse is not an unintended consequence—it is the predictable outcome of a movement designed to deconstruct law enforcement. The architects of these policies are not incompetent; they are committed to replacing deterrence with redistribution, shifting the consequences of crime from criminals to society at large. As one Oakland prosecutor bluntly put it: "These laws aren't failing. They're doing exactly what they were meant to do."

Conclusion: Burning Down Justice in the Name of Reform

The dissection of the criminal justice reform movement reveals something far more insidious than policy failure—it is an ideological war against the foundations of order and civilization. Cloaked in the language of equity and fairness, this movement is not about justice but the systematic erosion of accountability, where criminals are absolved and victims forgotten. Crime-equity is not reform; it is an intellectual fraud designed to dismantle the institutions that shield society from chaos.

The equity cult weaponizes victimhood, not to achieve fairness, but to undermine the moral authority of the state. It replaces deterrence with grievance redistribution, casting criminality as a systemic inevitability rather than an individual choice. The result is not a more just society, but one where lawlessness is legitimized, public safety is sacrificed, and the rule of law is stripped of consequence.

A justice system that minimizes punishment does not simply fail to deter crime—it destroys the social contract. When consequences are abandoned, trust in law disintegrates, and society descends into anarchy where only the ruthless thrive. This movement does not seek balance; it seeks destruction, replacing justice with ideological rule. If it prevails, what remains will not be a fairer system, but a hollowed-out shell incapable of upholding civilization itself.

CHAPTER 5

PRISONBREAK

The battle over criminal justice policy in California has played out in courtrooms, legislatures, and activist circles for decades, but few moments were as consequential as the Supreme Court's 2011 ruling in *Brown v. Plata*. This decision, framed as a remedy for prison overcrowding, became the catalyst for a sweeping ideological shift—one that replaced the incapacitation of offenders with their reintegration, often at the expense of public safety.

The so-called "crisis of mass incarceration" provided the perfect pretext for reformers who viewed prisons not as instruments of justice but as remnants of systemic oppression. Under this banner, California systematically dismantled the legal frameworks that once ensured accountability—gutting Three Strikes laws, reclassifying felonies as misdemeanors, and eliminating cash bail. These policies were sold as progress. In reality, they have enabled a justice system that no longer deters habitual offenders but emboldens them.

This chapter dissects the aftermath of *Brown v. Plata*, detailing how the shift from crime deterrence to offender rehabilitation transformed California's justice system into an engine of recidivism and public endangerment. The erosion of California's bipartisan tough-on-crime policies—once exemplified by Three Strikes—marked a turning point in the state's trajectory. To understand how California descended into lawlessness, we must examine the calculated dismantling of deterrence and the ideological

74

revolution that prioritized the rights of criminals over the safety of its citizens.

Brown v. Plata: The Supreme Court's Decarceration Mandate

The 2011 Supreme Court ruling in *Brown v. Plata* marked a turning point in California's criminal justice system. In a narrow 5–4 decision, Justice Anthony Kennedy authored the opinion, declaring that the state's prison overcrowding constituted cruel and unusual punishment under the Eighth Amendment. At the time, California's prisons were operating at nearly 200% capacity, prompting the Court to impose a federally mandated reduction, capping the prison population at 137.5% of designed capacity—a move that necessitated the release of tens of thousands of inmates.

The ruling cited inadequate healthcare and dire living conditions, claiming that these factors contributed to unnecessary suffering and preventable deaths among inmates. The Court's decision forced the state into a precarious situation: either comply with the reduction mandate or face a potential federal takeover of the prison system. This judicial intervention, while framed as a humanitarian necessity, set into motion a series of radical policy shifts that would prioritize decarceration over deterrence and redefine California's approach to criminal justice.

Former Los Angeles District Attorney Steve Cooley recalls the crisis: "People were stacked like sardines in a gym. The Supreme Court called it unconstitutional and demanded action. What followed were a series of rash decisions."

The aftermath of *Brown v. Plata* was not a measured prison reform but an ideological opening—a springboard for policies that eroded deterrence, normalized leniency, and emboldened offenders—all under the guise of human rights and equity. The decision did not fix California's prison system; it dismantled the legal mechanisms that once maintained public safety.

The Justifications for the Ruling

By 2006, California's prison population had swelled to 173,000 inmates, nearly double the system's intended capacity. Justice Anthony Kennedy, writing for the majority in *Brown v. Plata*, cited deteriorating healthcare, high suicide rates, and unsanitary conditions as violations of prisoners' constitutional rights. The ruling also aligned with long-standing efforts by prisoner rights groups that had long sought widespread decarceration.

While the decision was framed as a necessary response to inhumane prison conditions, its consequences extended far beyond corrections facilities. It reshaped California's entire criminal justice landscape, unleashing a wave of reckless legislation that prioritized offender reintegration over public safety.

The "Crisis of Mass Incarceration"

The claim that the United States, and California in particular, suffered from mass incarceration was central to criminal justice reform activism during this period. However, the reality is more complex. During the late 20th century, California's prison population expanded largely in response to rising violent crime rates and habitual offenders cycling through the system. The campaign against mass incarceration during this time was driven more by ideology than by data, disregarding the need for deterrence and accountability as crime rates soared.

Examining the Numbers

Contrary to activist claims that nonviolent drug offenders composed the bulk of California's prison population, over 70% of inmates were serving time for violent crimes or serious felonies. Between 1980 and 2000, violent crime in California surged by 79%, leading to stricter sentencing policies such as Three Strikes, which played a significant role in the crime decline after 1994. Career criminals committed a disproportionate share of offenses, with a small percentage of repeat offenders responsible for the majority of violent and property crimes.

Political and Media Manipulation of Mass Incarceration

Reform advocates have selectively used data to exaggerate the number of inmates serving time for minor offenses. Groups like the Sentencing Project and the ACLU have promoted the idea that the U.S. imprisons far more people than necessary, ignoring the crime reduction following the implementation of tougher sentencing laws. Media narratives have also distorted the reality of Three Strikes cases, falsely portraying them as disproportionately targeting first-time offenders when, in fact, the law was designed to remove repeat violent criminals from society.

Public Opinion and Political Pressure

During the 1990s, both Republican and Democratic leaders supported tougher sentencing laws in response to widespread public demand for safer communities. However, efforts to dismantle these deterrence policies were largely driven by activist elites, often in direct opposition to the desires of communities most affected by crime. Policymakers ignored repeated warnings from law enforcement and victims' rights groups about the dangers of releasing habitual offenders and reducing sentences for violent crimes.

The campaign against mass incarceration was never about improving public safety. It was an ideological shift that redefined justice, prioritizing rehabilitation over deterrence, regardless of the consequences. The next section will explore how this ideology led to the weakening of Three Strikes and the subsequent rise in recidivism and violent crime.

The Three Strikes Law: The Origins and Intent of California's Most Effective Crime Deterrent

The Three Strikes Law, enacted in 1994, was a direct response to soaring violent crime rates and public outcry over repeat offenders terrorizing communities. Designed to keep habitual criminals off the streets, it imposed increasingly severe penalties, mandating a life sentence for those convicted of a third felony, provided at least one of the prior convictions was categorized as a serious or violent felony. As a cornerstone of California's tough-on-crime approach, the law reflected the era's demand for stringent measures and was widely lauded for its efficacy in curbing recidivism.

The catalyst for this sweeping legislation was the murder of 12-year-old Polly Klaas by Richard Allen Davis, a repeat violent offender who had repeatedly cycled through the criminal justice system. Klaas's murder galvanized bipartisan support, leading to the passage of one of the toughest sentencing laws in the nation.[1]

The Core Principles of Three Strikes

The law was designed around a simple but effective principle: if an offender had prior convictions for serious or violent felonies, their third felony conviction would result in a mandatory life sentence. The framework relied on the idea that career criminals were responsible for a disproportionate amount of crime, and by incapacitating them, public safety would improve.

- Strike One: A serious or violent felony conviction.
- Strike Two: A second felony conviction doubled the standard sentence.
- Strike Three: A third felony conviction—regardless of its classification—resulted in a mandatory 25 years to life sentence.

The Impact of Three Strikes

Los Angeles Deputy District Attorney John Lewin, who prosecuted under Three Strikes, articulates the origins and impact of the Three Strikes Law during the 1990's, highlighting the law's initial success in reducing crime through decisive action against repeat offenders:

"It was a very violent time. I started out as a prosecutor when Three Strikes was implemented, and we targeted gang members. Crime dropped because so much of it was committed by a small number of repeat offenders."

Between 1994 and 2004, violent crime in California fell by 26%, while homicides dropped by 44%. Studies confirmed that repeat felony offenders were responsible for a disproportionate share of serious crimes, and Three Strikes significantly curtailed their ability to reoffend.[2]

These statistics align with national studies on deterrence, which show that increasing the perceived cost of criminal behavior reduces recidivism. Three Strikes removed thousands of repeat offenders from circulation, crippling organized gang activity and career criminals who had previously faced minimal consequences.[3]

Despite claims that the law fueled mass incarceration, felony conviction rates declined as habitual offenders were removed from circulation.

Public support was overwhelming, with 72% of California voters approving its passage in 1994.[4]

The Effectiveness of Three Strikes

Michael Maher, a veteran of the Los Angeles County Sheriff's Department, described how Three Strikes functioned before it was weakened: "Each crime was a strike. If a guy did three residential burglaries in a day, we'd wait for the next one, and by the end of the day, he had two strikes. These were career criminals, arrested thousands of times. We finally had a tool to get them off the streets."

Lewin also highlighted how gun enhancements deterred violent crime:

> We made carrying and using guns in crimes extremely costly. The idea was that if you're going to commit a robbery, we're going to make it so prohibitive in terms of the amount of extra time you're going to get for using a gun, that you're not going to use a gun. It was very successful. If you're armed with a gun in the crime, that's an extra ten years. You fire that gun. It's twenty years. You fire that gun and cause great bodily injury or death—that's twenty-five-to-life. Just for the gun.

However, Lewin contrasts this past effectiveness with the current reality under recent reforms: "Now, there's no penalty for using a gun. So what happens is, it's gone from gangsters worried about having guns to well, now you might as well have one and use it for whatever you need, because there's no penalty for doing it." His critique underscores the critical consequences of the law's erosion—as the fear of severe penalties dissipates, the deterrent effect diminishes, encouraging rather than curbing criminal behavior.

Who Was Affected?

Contrary to activist claims that Three Strikes unfairly targeted low-level offenders, the vast majority of those sentenced under the law were violent felons:

- By 2004, 87% of third-strike offenders were convicted of violent crimes, including rape, murder, and aggravated assault.
- Only 5% of Three Strikes cases involved nonviolent crimes, and most of those offenders had previous violent convictions.
- Career criminals who had spent years in and out of the system were finally being held accountable.

The Law's Bipartisan Support

At its peak, Three Strikes had overwhelming public backing, passing with 72% voter approval in 1994. Even Democratic leaders like Governor Gray Davis supported its strict sentencing provisions, recognizing its success in curbing recidivism. Law enforcement agencies, victims' rights groups, and community organizations championed the law as a landmark policy that restored order in neighborhoods plagued by repeat offenders.

However, despite its effectiveness, Three Strikes soon became the primary target of reform activists who viewed incarceration as inherently unjust. The next section will explore how ideological shifts and legislative efforts successfully dismantled this crime-fighting tool, paving the way for the resurgence of habitual offenders in California's streets.

The Ideological and Political Undermining of Three Strikes

The ideological and political undermining of the Three Strikes Law marks a profound shift in California's criminal justice system—one driven by ideological zeal rather than empirical evidence. Despite the clear success of the law in reducing recidivism and deterring violent crime, it became a primary target for progressive activists, academics, and criminal justice reformers who framed it as a central cause of "mass incarceration." What followed was not a movement based on data-driven reform, but rather a deliberate effort to dismantle a law that prioritized public safety over ideological purity.

As John Lewin astutely observes, the public was misled by a narrative that obscured the true causes of mass incarceration: "What happened was they got sold a bill of goods, that the biggest problem in the criminal justice system is what they refer to as mass incarceration. And the problem is, they didn't look at why we have mass incarceration. You have drug use, lack of two-parent homes, lack of education—issues the DA can't fix. But instead of addressing these root causes, the focus became emptying prisons."[5] This distortion mischaracterized the law as the problem, rather than the systemic issues that fueled high incarceration rates.

The rollback of Three Strikes was not driven by genuine reform but by a calculated ideological shift, prioritizing offender rehabilitation over public safety. The weakening of deterrence-based policies has emboldened repeat offenders, led to a rise in violent crime, and undermined public confidence in the justice system. Lawmakers, heeding the voices of activists and academics, ignored the warnings of law enforcement, crime victims, and prosecutors, who understood that habitual criminals could not be rehabilitated without strong deterrents. The result has been an era of lawlessness, where violent criminals cycle through a revolving door of weak sentencing and early release programs, and entire communities suffer the consequences.

The dismantling of Three Strikes was not an isolated incident. It set the stage for a broader wave of legislation that decriminalized serious offenses, eliminated cash bail, and reduced felonies to misdemeanors. This wave of reforms, driven by ideological purity, systematically eroded deterrence-based justice in favor of a flawed and misguided narrative of systemic oppression.

The erosion of Three Strikes has had a far-reaching impact, allowing repeat offenders to escape the harsh penalties that once acted as a necessary deterrent. This shift is emblematic of a broader trend that places offender rehabilitation above the protection of public safety, with devastating results.

The Narrative Shift: From Crime Control to Criminal Advocacy

By the late 2000s, the assault on the Three Strikes Law had moved beyond policy critique into something more profound: a revisionist effort to delegitimize deterrence itself. No longer framed as a rational safeguard against career criminality, Three Strikes was rebranded as a racialized relic of a punitive justice system—one that allegedly functioned not to protect the public, but to perpetuate systemic oppression. This was not an honest debate over sentencing efficacy but an ideological project designed to erode the very foundations of a justice system predicated on retribution and incapacitation. The goal was not just to dismantle Three Strikes; it was to delegitimize the concept of punishment as a necessary function of civil society.

Misleading Statistics: The Fabrication of the "Petty Offender"

The campaign against Three Strikes relied heavily on statistical sleight of hand. Advocacy groups, led by the ACLU and The Sentencing Project, curated a small set of cases in which defendants had ostensibly received life sentences for trivial third-strike offenses—shoplifting, drug possession, minor theft. These stories became the emotional core of the reform movement, endlessly recycled in media reports and political campaigns. Yet this framing was a deliberate misrepresentation. The overwhelming majority of those sentenced under Three Strikes had long and violent criminal histories, and their final offense was merely the last in a series of serious transgressions. The activists' argument functioned like a defense attorney pleading for clemency based on a single count while ignoring the rap sheet in its entirety.

The real purpose of Three Strikes was not, as critics claimed, to incarcerate people for stealing a slice of pizza but to neutralize criminals who had demonstrated, through repeated offenses, their refusal to abide by the social contract. By obscuring this fact, reformers were not simply arguing for a fairer justice system—they were advancing the cause of criminal impunity under the pretext of compassion.

The "Mass Incarceration" Myth: A Political Construct Masquerading as Reform

In tandem with the attack on Three Strikes was the broader "mass incarceration" narrative, which framed the United States' prison population as a moral failing rather than the predictable consequence of high crime rates. Organizations such as The Sentencing Project, the ACLU, and various academic institutions pushed the idea that America imprisoned too many people, entirely sidestepping the reality that crime plummeted as incarceration increased. This was not an accidental oversight. It was a necessary omission, as acknowledging this relationship would have undermined the entire reform movement.

The prison population had grown not because of an overzealous prosecutorial system, but because decades of policy failures—from the breakdown of the family to the erosion of law enforcement's capacity to police high-crime neighborhoods—had created a vast criminal underclass. The reforms advocated by these groups were built on a faulty premise—that the prison population itself was the problem, rather than the cycles of violence perpetuated by habitual offenders. The evidence, however, suggested that harsher sentencing had indeed contributed to declining crime rates, yet these facts were sidelined in favor of an ideologically driven agenda.

The Role of Academia: Justifying Criminality as Intellectual Currency

Academia provided the ideological framework for the dismantling of Three Strikes. The movement needed not just political and legal arguments, but a moral pretext—one that could cast incarceration itself as an injustice. The most influential voice in this regard was Michelle Alexander, whose book *The New Jim Crow* became the de facto manifesto of the anti-incarceration movement. Alexander's central claim—that mass incarceration was merely a continuation of racial segregation—was unburdened by serious engagement with crime data. She did not concern herself with the reality that violent crime was concentrated in minority communities, or that black and Hispanic victims bore the brunt of the criminality that Three Strikes had helped to suppress. Instead, she repackaged criminal justice as a racial caste system, where lawbreakers were not just perpetrators but victims of a state apparatus bent on their subjugation.

This was not scholarship; it was propaganda for the judicial nullification of punishment. The transformation of criminals into victims and of punishment into oppression provided the moral scaffolding for a movement that sought not to improve public safety, but to dismantle the mechanisms that upheld it.

The Media's Role: The Silence of the Victims

The media, ever compliant with progressive orthodoxy, functioned as the public relations arm of the anti-Three Strikes movement. The script was predictable: extensive human-interest reporting on convicts who had been "wrongly" sentenced under the law, complete with sympathetic

portraits of men whose criminal pasts were carefully edited to exclude
the full scope of their offenses. Meanwhile, the victims of repeat offenders—those who had been brutalized, murdered, or otherwise destroyed
by career criminals released under soft-on-crime policies—received no
comparable coverage.

This asymmetry was not accidental. It reflected a broader ideological
commitment: to reorient the justice system away from its fundamental
purpose—protecting law-abiding citizens—and toward the rehabilitation
of those who had violated its most basic tenets. This was not reform but
inversion: the criminal as the aggrieved, the state as the oppressor, and the
victim as an inconvenient footnote.

Mike Romano and the Three Strikes Project: The Architect of Release

Among those most responsible for dismantling Three Strikes was Mike
Romano, the director of the Stanford Three Strikes Project. Romano's
work was not a measured attempt to refine sentencing laws but a deliberate effort to weaken them into irrelevance.

Proposition 36 (2012): The Backdoor Dismantling of Three Strikes

Romano's signature achievement was his advocacy for Proposition 36, the
2012 ballot measure that amended Three Strikes to require the third-strike
offense to be "serious or violent" in order to trigger a life sentence. In practical terms, this allowed thousands of career criminals to apply for resentencing, opening the floodgates for early release. The reform was pitched
as a correction of excess, a safeguard against sentencing abuses. In reality,
it created a loophole large enough to gut the law's effectiveness.

The Fallacy of the "Nonviolent" Offender

Romano's campaign rested on the fiction that Three Strikes had ensnared
an army of low-level offenders. The data said otherwise. The overwhelming majority of those affected by the law had extensive criminal histories, often involving multiple violent felonies. But because Proposition
36 focused narrowly on the third-strike offense rather than the full criminal record, a habitual criminal who had, for example, committed multiple armed robberies but whose final conviction was for a nonviolent

crime was suddenly eligible for release. The absurdity of this framework was evident, but its proponents relied on public ignorance to push it through.

Mass Release and Its Consequences

The consequences of Proposition 36 were swift and predictable. Within two years, over 2,800 felons had been released, with recidivism rates confirming what any serious observer of criminal behavior already knew: habitual criminals do not rehabilitate when given leniency; they reoffend. Romano's efforts were framed as justice reform. In reality, they amounted to a reckless gamble with public safety, one that prioritized ideological commitments over empirical realities.

Proposition 36 (2012): The Trojan Horse of Reform

The passage of Proposition 36 in 2012 marked the beginning of the systematic dismantling of California's most effective crime deterrent. The initiative, sold as a necessary correction to an "overly punitive" system, introduced a fatal loophole: a third felony conviction would now trigger a life sentence only if classified as "serious or violent." This technical adjustment was presented as a safeguard against disproportionate sentencing, but in practice, it enabled thousands of repeat offenders—many with histories of violence—to seek early release.

The distinction between "violent" and "nonviolent" third-strike offenses was an illusion. Many offenders whose final convictions were for ostensibly nonviolent crimes had extensive records of serious felonies—armed robbery, assault, home invasions—yet were granted leniency because their most recent offense did not qualify under the new standard. The public was led to believe that benign shoplifters and low-level drug offenders had been unjustly sentenced to life under the original law. The reality was starkly different: these were habitual criminals, the very individuals Three Strikes was designed to neutralize.

Within two years, more than *2,800 inmates* had been released under Proposition 36. A California Department of Corrections study found that nearly *45% of them were rearrested within three years*—many for violent crimes. Reformers dismissed these outcomes as statistical noise, but the consequences were real: repeat offenders, once removed from circulation, were now back on the streets.

The passage of Proposition 36 in 2012 represented the first major weakening of the Three Strikes Law. Though the law still allowed for life sentences in the case of serious or violent third strikes, it opened the door for thousands of repeat offenders to apply for resentencing.

Progressive Prosecutors and the Nullification of Three Strikes

Even after legislative rollbacks, some prosecutors continued to use Three Strikes to incapacitate repeat offenders. However, the rise of progressive district attorneys like George Gascón and Chesa Boudin effectively nullified the law through non-enforcement.

George Gascón: De Facto Repeal in Los Angeles

Upon taking office as Los Angeles County District Attorney, George Gascón unilaterally announced that he would no longer pursue Three Strikes enhancements. In one sweeping decree, the most consequential tool for incapacitating repeat offenders was eliminated in the nation's largest county. Gascón's rationale? That sentencing enhancements were "racist" and "ineffective." The data, of course, suggested otherwise—violent crime had steadily declined under Three Strikes and began to rise again after its rollback. But ideology trumped empiricism, and public safety was sacrificed in the process.

Chesa Boudin: Anarcho-Tyranny in San Francisco

In San Francisco, Chesa Boudin took the project a step further, ensuring that repeat offenders would not only evade sentencing enhancements but would, in many cases, avoid prosecution altogether. He refused to pursue Three Strikes charges, even in cases where offenders had committed serious violent crimes. Instead, he championed so-called "restorative justice" programs, replacing incarceration with rehabilitative alternatives that, unsurprisingly, failed to deter recidivism. His tenure was marked by an explosion in retail theft, aggravated assault, and an increase in violent offenders cycling through the system with little to no consequence.

By eliminating sentencing enhancements, progressive prosecutors achieved what activists could not through legislation—rendering Three Strikes meaningless in many jurisdictions.

The Consequences of Weakening Three Strikes

The dismantling of Three Strikes was neither an accident nor an isolated policy shift—it was the culmination of a years-long ideological campaign. Progressive legal organizations, media activists, and political operatives spent decades distorting its impact, framing it as a driver of so-called "mass incarceration," rather than as one of the most effective crime-control measures in modern history. The ultimate goal was not simply reform but the systematic erosion of deterrence-based justice, a project that has produced precisely what its critics claimed it would not: a resurgence of violent crime, emboldened repeat offenders, and a justice system increasingly unwilling to protect law-abiding citizens.

The Rise in Recidivism and Repeat Offenses

The assumption that reducing incarceration would lead to lower crime was always a fantasy, one that has unraveled in real time. Since the passage of Proposition 36 in 2012, which altered Three Strikes to require a "serious or violent" third felony to trigger a life sentence, recidivism rates among released offenders have surged.

- **Recidivism Rates:** A California Department of Corrections and Rehabilitation (CDCR) study found that 44% of offenders released under Three Strikes reform reoffended within three years—a near certainty in statistical terms.[6]
- **Violent Crime by Repeat Offenders:** According to the Los Angeles County Sheriff's Department, a significant percentage of homicides and aggravated assaults since 2014 have been committed by individuals previously incarcerated under Three Strikes but later released due to sentencing reforms.[7]

The numbers make clear what reformers refused to acknowledge: career criminals remain career criminals. The law had functioned exactly as intended—removing habitual offenders from circulation and thereby reducing crime. Its weakening has undone that success.

Surge in Violent Crime Across California

The erosion of deterrence has had measurable and devastating consequences for public safety.

- **Los Angeles County:** Homicides increased by over 50% between 2014 and 2022, coinciding with the reduction in Three Strikes sentences.
- **San Francisco:** Aggravated assaults and property crimes skyrocketed, with burglaries up 45% from 2014 to 2021, as repeat offenders faced fewer sentencing consequences.
- **Oakland:** Carjackings doubled in frequency after the weakening of sentencing laws.

District attorneys and police forces have repeatedly sounded the alarm over the clear connection between the rollback of Three Strikes and the resurgence of habitual offenders. But these concerns have been drowned out by a political climate that views incarceration as a failure rather than a necessity.

The Revolving Door: How Three Strikes Reform Opened the Floodgates

The dismantling of Three Strikes and other deterrence-based policies was not an unintended consequence—it was the explicit goal of the criminal justice reform movement. These reforms, under the pretense of addressing systemic injustice, have created a legal framework that prioritizes offenders over victims.

Jamie McBride of the LAPD Union explains the reality:

If you get convicted of a property crime and have been in prison three times before, you no longer go to state prison for a new conviction. Instead, you go to county jail for seven years. They closed many state prisons in California. They're shifting the responsibility.

What you would always hear, like back in the day, the Sheriff would say, "Hey, we have overcrowding." And so we're going to start letting people out. So they let the non-violent offenders out. Which are the property crimes. So instead of a seven-year sentence, you may get a seven-month sentence.

What followed was predictable:

- Early releases skyrocketed, overwhelming local jails that lacked the capacity to hold inmates for extended periods.
- County jails, now housing long-term state prisoners, began releasing lower-level offenders *en masse*, further exacerbating the problem.
- Repeat offenders faced increasingly shorter sentences, if any at all, reinforcing the perception that crime carried little to no consequence.

McBride succinctly puts it: "We've got people committing crimes, getting arrested, and then being released within hours, only to commit more crimes. It's a farce."

California's largest jail system, the LA County Jail, and the largest state prison system in the country, are now little more than revolving doors. The ramifications of such policies are evident in the escalating crime rates and the growing disillusionment among law enforcement officials and the public alike. The system, designed ostensibly to reduce overcrowding, has instead catalyzed a resurgence in criminal activity by failing to address the root causes of recidivism.

A System That Favors Criminals Over Victims

Lewin succinctly captures the broader shift in priorities:

"What's happened is, we have gone to a position where we care more about what's best for the criminal than we do about what's best for the victims or society."

The result of this skewed focus is a justice system that fails to uphold its primary duty: protecting the innocent and punishing the guilty. Victims, already traumatized, are forced to navigate a labyrinthine legal system that increasingly cares more for the rights of the offenders than for victims' suffering and safety.

- Career criminals are given endless second chances, regardless of their track record of violence.
- Victims are treated as afterthoughts, their suffering deemed less important than the "rehabilitative needs" of offenders.
- Police and prosecutors are shackled, unable to enforce meaningful consequences due to legislative restrictions and judicial activism.

The justice system has not merely failed to do its job—it has redefined its purpose to serve the interests of offenders rather than law-abiding citizens.

Conclusion: The Collapse of Deterrence and the Triumph of Ideology

The dismantling of Three Strikes and the broader decarceration movement were not the result of organic, data-driven reform, but a calculated ideological shift—one that prioritized offender rehabilitation over public safety, despite overwhelming evidence that habitual criminals do not rehabilitate without strict deterrents. The rollback of these laws has emboldened repeat offenders, led to a measurable increase in violent crime, and eroded trust in the justice system.

At every step, lawmakers ignored warnings from law enforcement, crime victims, and prosecutors, instead deferring to activists and academics who framed punishment as an outdated relic of systemic oppression. The result has been an era of lawlessness, where violent criminals cycle through a revolving door of weak sentencing and early release programs, and entire communities bear the consequences of elite policy failures.

But this was only the beginning. The destruction of Three Strikes was followed by a torrent of legislative malpractice—a cascade of laws that further decriminalized serious offenses, eliminated cash bail, and reduced felony charges to misdemeanors. In the years to come, reckless policies turned California into a paradise for criminals, showing how legislators, backed by activist organizations, systematically dismantled what remained of deterrence-based justice in favor of ideological purity at the expense of public safety.

CHAPTER 6

STATUTORY NEGLIGENCE

California's descent into a vortex of criminality and suffering can be traced directly to a series of legislative experiments so recklessly conceived and predictably harmful that they amount to gross negligence enshrined into law. The key catalysts of this decline—Assembly Bill 109, Proposition 47, Proposition 57, the California Racial Justice Act, and Assembly Bill 3070—represent a radical departure from policies like Three Strikes that once upheld public safety and societal stability.

These so-called reforms were crafted for a public anesthetized by a culture of guilt and fixated on racial optics. While these laws were presented as progressive, they have transformed California's once-stable communities into battle zones of chaos and destabilization. What the state's legislators and wealthy backers failed—or perhaps refused—to foresee was the inevitable surge in crime and collapse of public trust.

The failures of these policies are not isolated. They represent a broader ideological shift where criminal rights are prioritized over public safety, and statistical disparities are conflated with injustice. At the heart of these reforms lies a dangerous narrative: that all disparities in the justice system are proof of systemic racism, irrespective of actual crime rates or community consequences.

This chapter examines how these laws have systematically eroded the foundations of law and order in California. Rather than ushering in an era of fairness and safety, California's criminal justice reforms have unleashed a wave of criminality that has left the state more dangerous, unstable, and divided than at any time since the drug wars of the 1990s.

Legislative Reforms Overview Table

LEGISLATIVE REFORM	YEAR ENACTED	KEY PROVISIONS	CONSEQUENCES
AB 109 (Realignment)	2011	Reclassified offenders, moved prisoners to local jails.	Increased recidivism, early releases, public safety risk.
Proposition 47	2014	Reduced felonies to misdemeanors for theft under $950.	Surge in petty theft, reduced arrests, increased property crimes.
Proposition 57	2016	Parole for "non-violent" offenders.	Early release for violent criminals, rise in crime rates.
Racial Justice Act	2020	Allowed challenges to convictions based on racial bias.	Legal backlog, increased challenges, weakened prosecutorial power.
AB 3070	2020	Restricted peremptory challenges in jury selection.	Juror bias concerns, reduced impartiality, more acquittals or hung juries.
SB 357	2021	Decriminalized loitering for prostitution.	Increased human trafficking, organized crime activity, public safety concerns.

Figure 1: Crime Rates Before and After the Enactment of AB 109, Proposition 47, and Proposition 57. Larceny theft and auto theft rates showed marked increases after these legislative reforms.

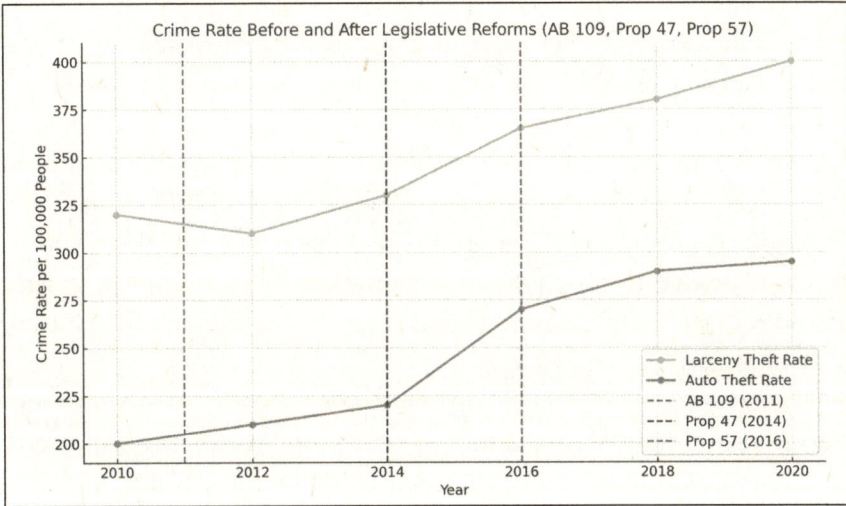

Crime Rate Before and After Legislative Reforms (AB 109, Prop 47, Prop 57)

Legend:
— Larceny Theft Rate
—●— Auto Theft Rate
--- AB 109 (2011)
--- Prop 47 (2014)
--- Prop 57 (2016)

Source: California Department of Justice, FBI Uniform Crime Reports

Assembly Bill 109 (2011): The Revolving Door of Criminality

Assembly Bill 109, cynically titled the "Public Safety Realignment Act," stands as a grotesque monument to legislative malpractice and intellectual bankruptcy. To address prison overcrowding, California's legislators orchestrated a simple solution: move the prisoners out—first to county jails but ultimately back to the streets. This was overhaul was prompted by the Supreme Court's ruling in *Brown v. Plata* (2011), which condemned the conditions in California's state prisons as cruel and unusual punishment. Former DA for LA County, Steve Cooley, explains: "AB 109, put simply, meant anyone sentenced to state prison for a non-serious or non-violent offense had to serve their sentence in the county jail. If they were convicted of a serious or violent offense, then they went to a state prison."

AB 109's fatal flaw lies in its deliberate mischaracterization of offenders. By transferring the responsibility for so-called "non-serious, non-violent" criminals from state prisons to county jails, the bill relied on euphemisms to distort the severity of crimes committed by those labeled "low-risk," a determination made solely on the basis of prisoners' most recent convictions and ignoring their broader criminal histories. A notorious example of this sleight of hand is the inclusion of offenders convicted of crimes like domestic abuse, robbery, and even forms of assault under the "non-violent" category. Many of these offenders, while not currently serving sentences for explicitly violent crimes, had long criminal histories that involved violence or threats of violence. The result was an influx of such individuals into county jails, which were never equipped to handle such an overwhelming number of offenders. This practice of reclassification is documented by a 2013 report from the Legislative Analyst's Office, which found that over half of the offenders moved under AB 109 had previously been incarcerated for violent or serious offenses, yet were now being released under a novel statutory standard of "non-serious" or "non-violent."[1]

These realignments and reclassifications resulted in dangerous individuals being funneled into communities with no significant restrictions or adequate monitoring. The state essentially converted its prison system into a revolving door for criminals, under this distorted "low-risk" framework and its disastrous results continue to be felt in the communities most affected by the ongoing crime surge.

This crisis prompted intervention from the Supreme Court, which condemned the conditions in California's state prisons as cruel and unusual punishment. Cooley explains,

The outcome was AB 109, a policy mandating that non-serious, non-violent offenders serve their sentences in county jails rather than state prisons. Cooley elaborates, "A lot of people think the scheme for reducing the prison population came from a Stanford professor whispering in Governor Brown's ear. That's how we got AB 109. AB 109, put simply, meant anyone sentenced to state prison for a non-serious or non-violent offense had to serve their sentence in the county jail. If they were convicted of a serious or violent offense, then they went to a state prison."

Recidivism

Since AB 109's passage, recidivism rates have remained alarmingly high. In 2014, a report from the Public Policy Institute of California (PPIC) found that within three years of release, 61% of offenders subjected to the "realignment" provisions of AB 109 were rearrested. Of those, 41% were convicted of a new offense.[2] Counties, lacking the resources to incarcerate offenders for the duration of their sentences, have been forced to release inmates early, leading to what can only be described as a public safety crisis.

The California Department of Corrections and Rehabilitation (CDCR) showed that offenders with significant violent histories were reclassified as non-violent due to technical definitions in AB 109, leading to early releases that exacerbated public safety risks.[3] The state's notorious crime surge is no accident—it is the direct result of AB 109's reckless policies. This predictable surge in recidivism is not a failure of oversight but an entirely foreseeable consequence of a policy that prioritizes bureaucratic convenience over justice.

Inadequate Supervision and Violent Reoffenses

AB 109 also gutted parole supervision. Before realignment, state parole officers—trained professionals with decades of experience—were responsible for monitoring released offenders. Under AB 109, that responsibility was handed over to local probation departments, which were woefully underfunded and unprepared for this massive influx of high-risk individuals. Without the financial or staffing resources to properly supervise

Figure 2: Recidivism Rates Pre-and Post-AB 109 and Proposition 47. Rearrest and reconviction rates have continued to rise after the implementation of these reforms, indicating persistent challenges in reducing repeat offenses.

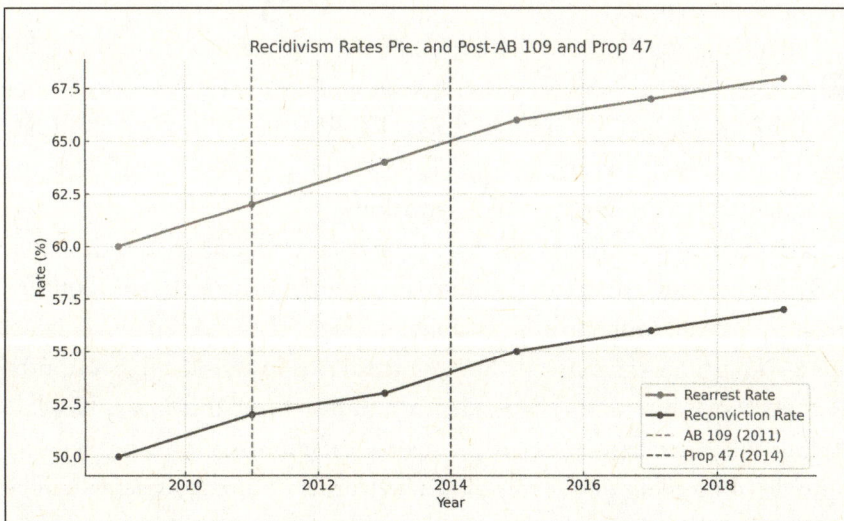

Source: Public Policy Institute of California, California Department of Corrections and Rehabilitation

offenders, AB 109 rendered California's parole system a farce. Offenders violate parole with impunity, knowing full well that the overwhelmed probation departments have neither the resources nor the will to hold them accountable. According to a *Los Angeles Times* investigation, parolees under local supervision have committed crimes ranging from assault to robbery, knowing that the state's weakened response to violations would carry little consequence.[4]

Case Study: Ike Souzer

One need only look to the case of Ike Souzer to see the dangers of this law manifest. At the age of 13, Ike Souzer fatally stabbed his mother in Garden Grove, California. In 2017, he was arrested and later convicted of voluntary manslaughter and sentenced to juvenile detention until he turned 25, which is the maximum age for juvenile detention under California law. Souzer's case drew attention because of his young age and the severity of the crime.[5]

While incarcerated, Souzer's behavior continued to attract legal attention. He was involved in multiple incidents, including attacking correctional officers and manufacturing a weapon while in jail. His history of violence made him a notable figure within the criminal justice system, and authorities labeled him as extremely dangerous. In one high-profile incident, Souzer escaped from a juvenile detention facility in 2019, only to be recaptured later.

Following Ike Souzer's release under AB 109, Souzer continued his pattern of criminal behavior. After his release into a halfway house, Souzer violated his probation multiple times. He fled the halfway house, leading to a manhunt that culminated in his capture in Mexico. This escape occurred after a series of previous violations.

His case is not an outlier; it is emblematic of the recklessness that AB 109 has engendered in California's criminal justice system. Souzer's recapture after fleeing probation violations highlights an even graver issue: under AB 109, offenders like him are treated as low-risk, subject to probationary conditions wholly inadequate to the threat they pose. His case reveals the tragic flaw in AB 109's ideological approach, one that has sacrificed public safety on the misguided belief that criminal offenders can be rehabilitated by sheer bureaucratic decree.[6]

Lack of Rehabilitation Programs

Proponents of AB 109 promised that its cornerstone would be robust rehabilitation programs. However, data from the Legislative Analyst's Office (LAO) reveals that such programs have been woefully underfunded and, in many counties, nonexistent. Despite state-level promises, counties have struggled to provide even basic rehabilitation services, and many programs intended to address drug addiction, mental health issues, and job readiness are laughably inadequate.[7]

In 2015, a report from the Center on Juvenile and Criminal Justice found that the lack of resources for rehabilitation has resulted in a paltry 9% participation rate among offenders eligible for such programs. This glaring absence of rehabilitative support has left offenders ill-prepared to reintegrate into society, virtually guaranteeing their return to criminal behavior.[8]

The so-called "realignment" does little more than funnel offenders through a system that neither rehabilitates nor punishes, releasing them back into communities without having addressed the root causes of their criminal behavior. AB 109 has, in effect, institutionalized failure—both for the criminal justice system and for the offenders themselves.

Technical Violations and Reduced Consequences

AB 109 eliminated the practice of sending parole violators back to state prison for technical violations, such as failing a drug test or missing a meeting with a parole officer. Instead, these violations now result in shorter county jail sentences or no significant consequences at all, reducing the deterrent effect and increasing non-compliance among parolees.

Proposition 47 (2014): Decriminalizing Theft and Institutionalizing Lawlessness

If AB 109 cracked open the door for lawlessness, Proposition 47 shattered it wide open. Branded as a reform to reduce prison overcrowding, Prop 47 effectively decriminalized theft and drug possession, emboldening criminals across the state, transforming California into a haven for low-level criminality

Deceptively branded as the "Safe Neighborhoods and Schools Act," Prop 47 passed with 60% voter support in 2014 and stands as one of California's most catastrophic legislative missteps. Proposition 47, passed in 2014, delivered another crippling blow. Under the banner of further reducing incarceration, it reclassified a host of felony offenses as misdemeanors. Theft under $950, previously classified as grand theft with a lower threshold of $400, was now a misdemeanor. This reform emboldened criminals, who quickly grasped the implications: their offenses would be met with little to no consequence. The effects were swift and predictable. Local law enforcement, stripped of the necessary tools to combat rising crime, found themselves scrambling as property crime skyrocketed and brazen lawlessness took root. The state's residents were left as unwilling participants in an ill-conceived social experiment.

Felony Threshold for Theft: Legalizing Petty Crime

Perhaps the most egregious provision was the increase in the felony threshold for theft, raising it from $400 to $950. While this may appear to be a mere bureaucratic adjustment, in practice, it effectively legalized petty theft. Criminals quickly learned they could steal up to nearly $1,000 worth of goods with minimal fear of serious consequences. Store owners, already under economic pressure, found themselves powerless to stop the surge in theft that Proposition 47 invited. Rather than reducing crime, the law incentivized it, creating a permissive environment for repeat offenders to operate without significant repercussions.

DNA Testing: A Devastating Loss for Law Enforcement

One of the most insidious aspects of Proposition 47 was the elimination of mandatory DNA testing for individuals convicted of these newly downgraded misdemeanors. By no longer requiring DNA collection from those convicted of drug possession or theft, law enforcement was stripped of a critical tool for solving more serious crimes. Without DNA evidence, linking repeat offenders to violent crimes such as rape or murder became far more difficult. The reduction in DNA testing severely hampered police efforts to solve cold cases, with critics pointing out that Proposition 47 had, in effect, provided a shield for more dangerous criminals to operate under the radar.

Erosion of Public Safety and Property Crime Surge

Proposition 47 was passed under the banner of justice reform but has become an emblem of criminal impunity. Far from creating safer

Figure 3: Theft Rates Before and After Proposition 47 (2013-2018). Following the passage of Proposition 47 in 2014, which reclassified certain theft offenses from felonies to misdemeanors, theft rates saw a notable increase, particularly in larceny-related crimes.

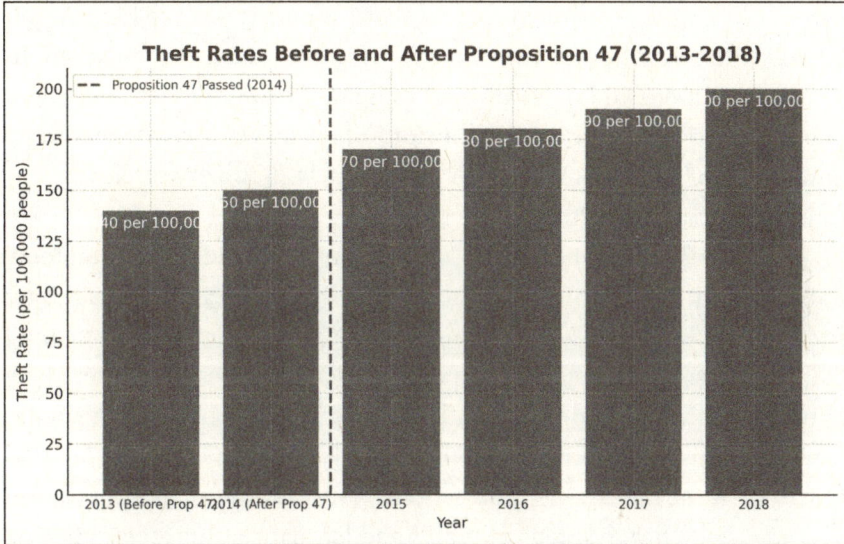

Theft Rates Before and After Proposition 47 (2013-2018)

- - Proposition 47 Passed (2014)

40 per 100,00 | 50 per 100,00 | 70 per 100,00 | 80 per 100,00 | 90 per 100,00 | 00 per 100,00

Theft Rate (per 100,000 people)

2013 (Before Prop 47) | 2014 (After Prop 47) | 2015 | 2016 | 2017 | 2018

Year

Source: Public Policy Institute of California, California Department of Justice.

neighborhoods or improving schools, the law hollowed out the state's very ability to maintain order. It did not reform crime; it institutionalized it. What was pitched as a step toward progress became, in practice, a carte blanche for lawlessness—a blueprint for the dissolution of civic norms. Criminals faced little more than a slap on the wrist, while the law-abiding were left to pick up the shattered remnants of a system designed, not to rehabilitate or deter, but to fail.[9]

In the wake of Proposition 47's passage, larceny thefts skyrocketed by approximately 9%—amounting to roughly 135 more thefts per 100,000 residents compared to other states.[10] What once were prosecutable felonies were suddenly relegated to the status of misdemeanors, trivial offenses barely worth the ink used to write the police reports. This surge in property crime can be traced directly to the reclassification of theft and drug possession offenses, which gutted any meaningful deterrent that might have kept potential offenders in check. The legal apparatus, already struggling under the weight of a deteriorating system, found itself incapacitated—stripped of its teeth by the very electorate it was designed to protect.

Local law enforcement, those on the frontlines of societal stability, were forced to contend with an escalating wave of criminal activity while being hobbled by a mandate that made their task almost Sisyphean in scope. They were asked to stop a flood with a teaspoon, as Proposition 47 had effectively bound their hands, relegating them to bystanders in a battle they were no longer allowed to fight. The inevitable result was a dramatic erosion in the quality of life for California's citizens—a wholesale unravelling of the social fabric, felt most acutely in urban centers like Los Angeles and San Francisco.

These cities, once synonymous with opportunity and innovation, now stand as grim testaments to the folly of misguided reform. From their streets come images of a society in freefall: tent encampments sprawling like metastasized tumors across public spaces, businesses shuttered by rampant theft, and a populace no longer able to rely on the most fundamental promise of governance—public safety. This breakdown in law and order, far from the trivial, "non-serious" offenses touted by Proposition 47's advocates, has shocked the world and left native Californians fleeing in droves, seeking refuge from a state that seems hellbent on legislating itself into oblivion.

What is most damning, however, is the sheer arrogance that underpinned the entire endeavor. The architects of Proposition 47 did not merely misjudge the consequences of their actions—they refused to see the obvious truth: a society without deterrence is one that invites chaos. In their haste to appear enlightened, they unleashed an experiment on the unsuspecting citizens of California, one that is eroding not just property values or business revenues but the very social contract upon which civil society depends.

Decline in Arrest Rates for Drugs and Theft

The arrest rate for theft cases did not merely decline—it collapsed, plummeting from 15% in 2013 to a pitiful 6.6% by 2022. This catastrophic failure to enforce the law reflects Proposition 47's obliteration of any meaningful deterrence. In over 90% of reported thefts, no one is arrested.[11] This is not simply a legal oversight; it is the wholesale abandonment of the rule of law. Criminals have learned that theft, once a prosecutable offense, has now become a free-for-all.

The consequences are not abstract. With law enforcement rendered powerless, criminals have grown emboldened, seizing upon the chaos. Those meant to uphold the law have been shackled by a policy that prioritizes the welfare of the offender over the safety of the victim. Proposition 47 did not fail because of a lack of enforcement; it failed by design. Its authors stripped away the very tools required to maintain public safety, leaving communities to fend for themselves in a landscape where crime is met with indifference. The victims are not statistics; they are the business owners, the families, and the citizens forced to live in a state where their government has chosen to look the other way.

The same tragic pattern repeats itself in the sphere of drug offenses. Proposition 47's reduction of penalties for drug possession was heralded as compassionate reform. The reality is anything but. Drug-related arrests dropped by 23%, not due to a sudden wave of rehabilitation but because law enforcement had its hands tied. Meanwhile, the streets of California became the tragic epicenter of open drug use and human devastation. It is not just a failure of policy; it is a moral failure. Emergency room visits for overdoses surged by 25% in the year following the law's enactment.[12]

Between April 2022 and March 2023, California witnessed the staggering deaths of 11,403 addicts on its streets—the highest toll in the nation.[13] This is not a mere statistic; it is a brutal indictment of a state that has forsaken its most vulnerable, not by refusing to help them, but by pretending that "help" meant less accountability. Proposition 47, far from reducing harm, entrenched it. This was not the result of ignorance but of calculated negligence, a policy that chose to look away as the crisis deepened.

And what of the promise that Proposition 47 would reduce recidivism? The evidence could not be clearer: 70% of those released under its provisions were re-arrested within three years.[14] This is the measure of its failure. It is not enough to say the law did not work as intended—it functioned exactly as it was designed to, with devastating precision. It reduced penalties, reduced arrests, and unleashed a tide of criminality upon the state. The devastation caused Proposition 47 is not some unforeseen consequence—it was a certainty written into the very framework of the law; and it's authors have blood on their hands.

Proposition 47 is not just a cautionary tale of policy gone wrong. It is a damning testament to what happens when ideology supplants responsibility. It is a monument to failure—crafted by those too blinded by their own agenda to see the wreckage they were creating. California's citizens have paid the price for this failure, and the cost is rising with every day that this law remains in effect.

Figure 4: Declining Arrest Rates for Theft After Proposition 47. The arrest rate for theft-related crimes, including shoplifting and petty theft, dropped significantly following the reclassification of many thefts as misdemeanors.

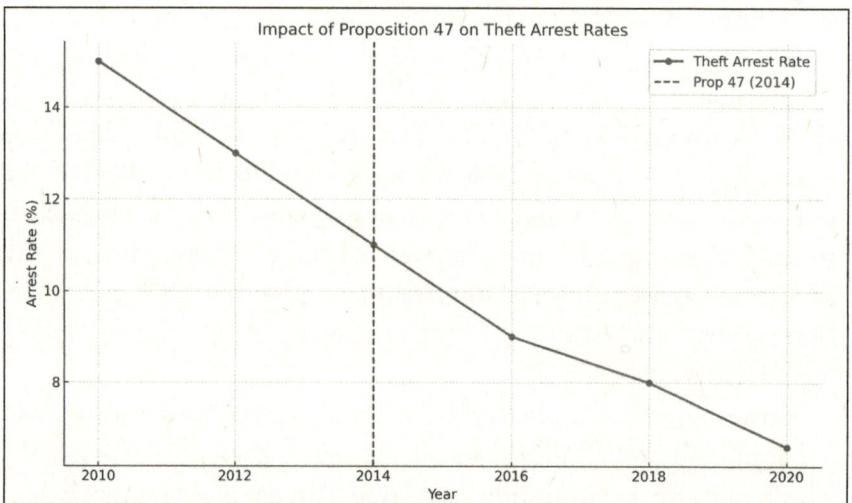

Source: California Department of Justice, Public Policy Institute of California.

Proposition 57 (2016): Releasing Violent Offenders Under the Guise of Reform

Perhaps the most egregious piece of this disastrous puzzle was Proposition 57. Passed by California voters in November 2016, Prop 57 was deceptively branded as the "Public Safety and Rehabilitation Act of 2016." On the ballot, the initiative was titled (at the discretion of Kamala Harris) the "California Parole for Non-Violent Criminals and Juvenile Court Trial Requirements Initiative." Its stated goal was to address the state's prison overcrowding by increasing parole opportunities for non-violent offenders and transferring the authority to decide whether juveniles should be tried as adults from prosecutors to judges. But beneath this veneer of reform was a law that opened the floodgates for violent criminals to be released back into society, a reckless gamble with public safety that California is still paying for.

Former prosecutor Kathleen Cady laid bare the cynicism of this narrative: "Voters hear things like 'the system's broken, there's too many people in custody, and oh my god, it's horrible. And it's all the people who are black and brown, they're being disenfranchised!' You say it enough, people start to believe it. He [Governor Jerry Brown] counted on people having that kind of guilt." This manipulation of guilt was the keystone of the policy's success, while the impact on public safety was brushed aside.

California's prison system, already notorious for overcrowding, reached a breaking point in 2006 with more than 173,000 inmates crammed into facilities designed for half that number. Federal mandates forced the state to reduce the prison population, and Proposition 57 was one in a series of legislative measures intended to address this. But it wasn't designed to reduce crime or improve public safety—it was designed to shift the burden of incarceration away from the state, regardless of the consequences for ordinary citizens.

The most damning flaw of Proposition 57 lies in its definition of "non-violent" offenses, a term twisted beyond recognition under California law. Crimes such as assault with a deadly weapon, domestic violence, and even rape by intoxication could be classified as non-violent. In fact, the entire definition of non-violent under Proposition 57 is a fraud, as all crime with the exception of twenty-three specific violent offenses listed in an obscure section of the penal code would be deemed "non-violent."[15] This legal fiction meant that offenders convicted of these heinous acts became eligible for early parole, their release justified under the guise of overcrowding relief. The tragic irony is that the law unleashed many of the very criminals it was ostensibly designed to control.

A Violent Crime Surge: Blood on the Streets

The results of Proposition 57 were not speculative or theoretical; they were immediately felt. In the years following its passage, violent crime surged across the state. Between 2019 and 2020 alone, California saw an 8.4% rise in violent crime, including a staggering increase in homicides—over

500 additional murders.[16] This is not an unfortunate side effect—it is a direct consequence of a law that prioritized the freedom of violent criminals over the safety of the public.[17]

One of the most horrific examples of Proposition 57's impact came in April 2022, with the Sacramento mass gang shooting that claimed six lives and injured twelve others. Smiley Martin, one of the suspects, had been released early due to the "good time" credits he earned under Proposition 57, despite his conviction for violent offenses. Martin, who should have been behind bars serving his sentence, was instead granted early release by a law that placed political expediency above common sense. The blood of those victims is the grim price of a law designed to empty prisons, not protect the public.[18]

Figure 5: California Crime Trends Pre- and Post-Legislative Reforms (2009-2020). The chart shows property crime and violent crime rates over time, highlighting the impact of Proposition 47 (2014) and Proposition 57 (2016). While property crime rates rose significantly after Proposition 47, violent crime rates were more stable and influenced by factors other than the reforms.

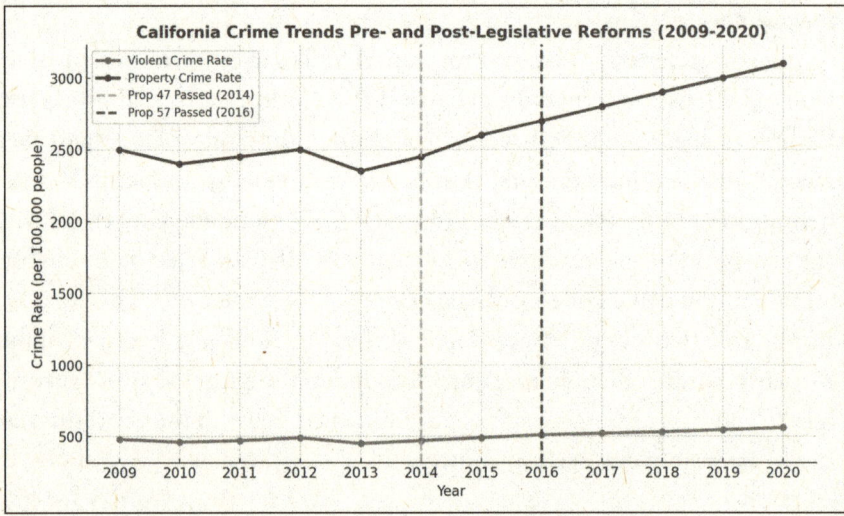

Source: Public Policy Institute of California, California Department of Justice, and FBI Uniform Crime Reporting.

Racial Justice Act (2020): When Equity Trumps Evidence

As the damage from these legislative missteps mounted, the state's criminal justice system was further weakened by the introduction of the Racial Justice Act. While earlier reforms had reduced penalties for individual crimes, the RJA opened a new front in dismantling the legal system by allowing convicted offenders to challenge their sentences based on broad claims of racial bias. The consequences were clear: a system more concerned with racial optics than accountability for violent actions.

The California Racial Justice Act (RJA) of 2020 is a glaring testament to legislative malpractice and willful statutory negligence, subverting foundational common law principles of evidence in furtherance of crime-equity deconstructionism. The RJA represents a dangerous and cynical ploy by crime-equity radicals to hijack the legal system and repurpose it as a tool for their own ethno-revolutionary, deconstructionist agenda. In the process, it has obliterated public safety and left law enforcement crippled, while transforming criminal courts into theaters of perpetual grievance and manufactured victimhood.

At its core, the RJA allows defendants to challenge convictions and sentences by alleging that racial bias—explicit or implicit—played a role in their case. This can be demonstrated through statistical disparities, racially charged language, or juror conduct perceived to be racially biased. It not only applies to future cases but also allows defendants with older convictions to retroactively challenge their sentences based on perceived racial bias.[19] This aspect alone opens the floodgates to a deluge of litigation, overwhelming courts already struggling with backlogs, diverting resources from the adjudication of new and ongoing cases, and effectively rewriting the narrative of countless prior convictions.[20]

Fraudulent Premise: Stats Not Facts

The intellectual dishonesty of the RJA lies in its foundational premise: the notion that statistical disparities in criminal charges or sentencing are inherently evidence of racial bias. This is a lazy and fundamentally dangerous assumption, one that ignores the complexities of crime, criminal behavior, and the enforcement of laws. The Act gives defense attorneys carte blanche to present racial disparities as proof of injustice, without requiring any evidence that actual racial bias influenced a case. In doing so, it warps the criminal justice system into a numbers game—where statistical outcomes, divorced from the facts of individual cases, override the bedrock principles of due process and personal responsibility.

Let's be clear: disparities in prosecution do not prove discrimination, nor do they invalidate the guilt of the defendant. Yet, under the RJA, this statistical shell game has become a de facto get-out-of-jail-free card for defense attorneys eager to exploit the porous language of the Act. It allows them to sidestep the question of the defendant's guilt entirely, and instead argue that any racial disparity in the broader system is sufficient grounds for overturning a conviction. The result is the obliteration of individual accountability and the wholesale collapse of prosecutorial authority.

The California Racial Justice Act of 2020 defines racially discriminatory language broadly and somewhat vaguely, allowing for wide-ranging interpretation. Specifically, it addresses any language or conduct that suggests racial bias during the prosecution, sentencing, or conviction process. The Act identifies several categories under which racial bias may be alleged, including:

1. **Racially Discriminatory Statements:** This includes any explicit or implicit language used by attorneys, judges, jurors, or witnesses during a trial that is deemed racially biased. These statements do not need to be overt; the Act allows challenges based on language that could imply racial bias, even if not directly articulated. Such language may be interpreted as discriminatory if it is perceived to reflect racial prejudice or reinforce negative racial stereotypes.

2. **Racial Bias in Conduct:** Beyond language, the Act also allows defendants to challenge convictions based on racial bias in the conduct of court officers, including discriminatory practices during jury selection, questioning, or other trial procedures. For instance, if jurors were excluded in a manner that suggests racial bias or if racially charged comments were made during proceedings, these actions can serve as grounds for appeal under the Act.

3. **Statistical Disparities as Evidence:** The Act goes beyond
   just verbal statements and allows challenges based on
   statistical evidence of racial disparities in sentencing,
   prosecution decisions, or jury composition. In other words,
   if statistical analysis shows that a defendant's racial group is
   disproportionately affected by a particular legal practice or
   decision, this can be cited as evidence of racial discrimination,
   even without overt racially discriminatory language being used.

This expansive definition of racially discriminatory language and conduct
is problematic because it introduces a high degree of subjectivity into the
judicial process. What constitutes "racial bias" can often be interpreted
differently depending on context, personal perspective, or prevailing social
attitudes. This creates a legal environment where almost any conviction
can be challenged on the basis of perceived racial injustice, significantly
complicating the task of ensuring finality in criminal cases.

Legal Nihilism and Retroactive Injustice
The retroactive component of the RJA is perhaps its most egregious and
dangerous aspect. It invites convicted felons—many of whom are guilty
of heinous crimes—to challenge decades-old convictions on the basis
of alleged racial bias. This provision is not just an affront to the principles of judicial finality; it is an open door to legal chaos. By reopening
settled cases, the RJA undermines the legitimacy of the entire criminal
justice process, casting doubt on the validity of convictions that have
long been upheld by the courts. This retroactive application threatens to
overwhelm an already overburdened judicial system with a flood of race-
based appeals, further delaying justice for crime victims and consuming
valuable resources that could be better spent addressing the state's rising
crime rates.

This legal nihilism is emblematic of the broader progressive agenda,
which seeks to dismantle existing systems under the pretext of "equity"
and "justice." The very notion of guilt or innocence is subordinated to an
ideological litmus test, where the racial identity of the defendant becomes
more important than the evidence of their crime. In doing so, the RJA

inverts the purpose of the criminal justice system, which is to protect society from criminals, not to protect criminals from accountability.

Paralyzing Prosecutors: The Law's Real Target

The true, if unspoken, aim of the Racial Justice Act (RJA) is not to correct racial inequities, but to dismantle the prosecutorial authority that underpins the justice system. In effect, the law has neutered the ability of prosecutors to perform their duties, reducing them to anxious functionaries, cowering in fear of accusations of racial bias. A prosecutor from Los Angeles County grimly observed, "Every case we prosecute involving a minority defendant now risks being overturned, not due to any error on our part, but because disparities exist in the data. It's a complete nightmare."

This pervasive fear of being accused of racial bias has cast a long shadow over the legal system, producing a chilling effect that is palpable in every prosecutorial decision. No longer free to pursue justice unimpeded, prosecutors must now endlessly second-guess themselves—whether to press charges, whether to seek sentencing enhancements, and even whether to take cases to trial. The looming specter of the RJA haunts every move they make. The law, written in vague and expansive terms, allows almost any prosecutorial action to be challenged on racial grounds, forcing those sworn to uphold justice into a perpetual state of defensive posturing. Prosecutors are no longer focused on securing justice for victims; instead, they are consumed by the need to avoid accusations of systemic racism. This has emboldened criminals and hamstrung law enforcement.[21]

But this paralysis is not a mere unfortunate consequence of the RJA; it is the intended result. The law's architects and the deep-pocketed donors who support them have long made their goal clear: they seek to dismantle what they perceive as a racist and oppressive justice system. Their aim is not justice or fairness; their ambition is to tear down the very institutions that protect society from anarchy.

The RJA has tied the hands of prosecutors, who now face constant, crippling threats of racial bias claims. Defense attorneys invoke the Act to challenge every stage of prosecution, leading to dismissals of charges, the dropping of sentence enhancements, and the prolonging of legal proceedings to the point of farce. Criminals, emboldened by the weakened system, exploit this dysfunction, while law enforcement struggles to maintain order. As one Deputy District Attorney from Alameda County lamented, "This law is so poorly written and so ill-conceived that it's rendered us powerless. No matter what we do, we can be accused of racial bias. And for the record, race only comes into our calculations when identification is an issue—like when two African Americans match the description of a suspect in a crime. Otherwise, it's irrelevant to us."

This isn't mere hyperbole. Prosecutors are now reduced to a permanent defensive crouch, knowing full well that any action they take could be subjected to the nebulous, and often arbitrary, standards of the RJA. In a legal system that once required evidence of guilt to convict, the burden has shifted onto the state to continually defend itself against expansive accusations of racial bias. The chilling effect this creates is particularly devastating in cases involving violent or repeat offenders—individuals who stand to benefit most from the law's loose definitions and broad scope.

Critics have rightly pointed out that the RJA is so ambiguously drafted that it has become a weapon for defense attorneys to exploit. Nearly every prosecutorial action can now be contested under the guise of racial disparity, leaving prosecutors paralyzed, unable to act decisively. This legal paralysis has, in turn, disrupted the procedural flow of justice, resulting in a system that is both inefficient and increasingly incapable of protecting the public from serious criminal threats.

Case Example: Thought Crime Jurisprudence in Antioch

The Antioch police scandal, set against the backdrop of the broader legal implications of the California Racial Justice Act (RJA), presents a vivid example of how the Act's far-reaching powers can disrupt the pursuit of justice. In 2023, the city of Antioch, located in Contra Costa County, found itself at the center of a legal storm after a scandal involving racially charged text messages sent by local police officers. This incident became a pivotal test case for the RJA and illustrated the profound effects the Act can have on criminal proceedings—effects that transcend the guilt or innocence of the defendants themselves.

The controversy erupted when text messages exchanged by several members of the Antioch Police Department—filled with racist, sexist, and homophobic content—came to light. These messages were sent in the midst of an investigation into a 2021 murder conspiracy involving four Black defendants: Eric Windom, Terryon Pugh, Keyshawn McGee, and Trent Allen. All four were charged with serious gang-related crimes, including conspiracy to commit murder and attempted murder. The case should have focused squarely on the severity of the offenses and the overwhelming evidence linking the defendants to violent activities. Instead, the focus shifted dramatically when the text messages were introduced into the defense's strategy.

Rather than addressing the defendants' actions, the defense used the existence of the offensive text messages to challenge the validity of gang enhancements that could have resulted in life sentences without parole. The text messages—though reprehensible—were unrelated to the core facts of the case, yet they became the fulcrum for dismantling the prosecution's argument. Judge David Goldstein, overseeing the case, dismissed the gang enhancements, effectively reducing the potential sentences for the defendants. These enhancements were stripped away—not because of any new exculpatory evidence or changes in the facts of the case, but because under the Racial Justice Act, ideological non sequitur is elevated to legal principle. Goldstein's decision effectively removes life without parole as a potential sentence for the accused. This ruling underscored how the RJA could be wielded to sidestep the actual criminal conduct of the defendants, prioritizing perceptions of systemic bias over the pursuit of justice.

This was not an isolated incident. In previous rulings under the RJA in Contra Costa County, another judge overturned murder convictions in a different case due to the prosecutor's use of "racially coded language" during the trial. [22]

The implications of the Antioch case are profound. By stripping away the gang enhancements, the RJA has created a legal framework where irrelevant factors—such as offensive, unrelated text messages—can derail prosecutions. This effectively grants defense attorneys the ability to shift the focus from the criminal actions of their clients to broader societal grievances about race, using the RJA as a tool to invalidate otherwise solid prosecutions.

This case reveals the deeper issues with the RJA: it creates a justice system more concerned with virtue-signaling and statistical equality than with protecting the public. The focus has shifted from determining the guilt or innocence of defendants to whether the system itself can be portrayed as racially biased. This shift allows violent criminals to evade accountability, effectively absolving them of responsibility for their actions under the guise of rectifying racial injustice.

The Antioch case is symptomatic of a larger trend in California's justice system under the RJA. In a similar 2023 decision in Contra Costa County, gang enhancements were dismissed based solely on statistical data showing that Black men were disproportionately charged with these enhancements. The dismissals were not tied to any proven racial bias in specific cases, but rather to demographic trends that had nothing to do with the crimes at hand. This approach fundamentally undermines the principle of individual responsibility in the justice system.

What this means is that criminals who commit violent acts can now evade harsher penalties by pointing to statistical disparities, regardless of their actual guilt. In this new paradigm, the justice system is put on trial—not the defendant. The Antioch case underscores how the RJA has enabled defense attorneys to litigate societal grievances under the guise of defending their clients, turning the courtroom into a battleground for ideological debates rather than a forum for justice. This is not the triumph of justice—it is its sabotage. Under this framework, the criminal is no longer held accountable for his crimes; instead, the system itself is put on trial. The RJA enables defense attorneys to litigate societal grievances under the guise of defending their clients, exploiting the politics of race to sidestep justice. [23]

Architects and Financiers of Anarchy

At the helm of the Racial Justice Act (RJA) debacle lies Ash Kalra, the Canadian-born Assemblymember from San Jose who has been the ideological architect of this legislative farce. Kalra, a former public defender with a career built on racial grievance politics, has positioned himself as the vanguard in Sacramento of a movement that prioritizes criminals over citizens. His perspective is tainted by defender of the accused, through which he views the criminal as a perpetual victim and every conviction as a potential miscarriage of justice. Kalra's worldview, devoid of any nuanced understanding of criminal behavior, personal responsibility, or socioeconomic realities, is built on the dangerously simplistic notion that all racial disparities are products of systemic oppression—irrespective of evidence to the contrary.

Kalra's legislative misadventure is not a solo endeavor. Behind him stands a predictable cast of progressive organizations—the American Civil Liberties Union (ACLU), the Ella Baker Center for Human Rights, and an empire of activist groups that have capitalized on the politics of victimhood. The ACLU, once a venerable institution defending civil liberties, has devolved into a partisan tool pushing identity politics. It cherry-picks data and exaggerates claims of systemic racism to justify its support for the RJA. The Ella Baker Center, an organization committed to dismantling the current justice system, views the RJA as a step toward a society reshaped along racial lines, where guilt or innocence takes a backseat to identity.

These organizations are not driven by a genuine desire to improve the justice system or protect the innocent. Their obsession with equity, at any cost, reflects an ideological crusade that cares little for public safety or the rule of law. The RJA, instead of tackling the real causes of crime—such as poverty, family breakdown, or lack of education—advances a distorted narrative. In Kalra's world, every racial disparity is proof of systemic racism, a falsehood that fuels their push for policies that ultimately undermine the very concept of justice.

Kalra's authorship of the RJA, supported by a formidable coalition of progressive donors and activists, epitomizes the intellectual bankruptcy of the modern left's criminal justice agenda. What they call reform is, in reality, a grotesque distortion of justice. The RJA enables defendants to challenge convictions based not on evidence of innocence but on statistical disparities that have little to do with the facts of their case. Guilt and innocence become secondary in a system where racial optics matter more than justice.

This subversion of justice has been orchestrated with ruthless efficiency by the financial and ideological forces backing the RJA. The Open Society Foundations, spearheaded by George Soros, the ACLU, and the California Public Defenders Association have executed an assault on the justice system under the guise of civil rights.[24] But their true aim is far more insidious: the dismantling of the legal structures that protect society. Cloaked in the language of equity, they have systematically eroded public safety mechanisms while portraying their efforts as noble progress.

Soros's Open Society Foundations alone committed $220 million in 2020 toward racial justice initiatives, with a substantial portion directed toward legal reforms like the RJA.[25] Soros's influence extends far beyond direct donations; his foundation has long supported movements aimed at restructuring the U.S. legal system by addressing racial inequities. Other donors, such as Patty Quillin, wife of Netflix CEO Reed Hastings, and Elizabeth Simons, daughter of hedge fund billionaire James Simons, added to this financial engine, contributing $22 million to criminal justice ballot measures and candidates aligned with the RJA's objectives.[26]

The funds from the Open Society Foundations and progressive donors were not haphazardly thrown at the cause. Instead, they were strategically allocated to grassroots movements, legislative advocacy, and direct lobbying efforts focused on racial justice reforms. Organizations like the ACLU and California Public Defenders Association played key roles in shaping the RJA. The financial backing from these sources empowered advocacy groups to craft legal frameworks, run public awareness campaigns, and apply political pressure to ensure the passage of the Act.

Lobbying for the RJA involved a combination of direct political engagement and public advocacy. Wealthy donors and the organizations they backed worked closely with key legislators in Sacramento, leveraging media and public campaigns to sway opinions. High-profile donors enlisted the expertise of political operatives and former lawmakers to navigate the intricacies of the California legislature.

A Legal System in Freefall

The Racial Justice Act is part of California's broader descent into legal anarchy, a systemic unraveling masked as reform. While past legislative

misadventures like Proposition 47 and Proposition 57 began this dangerous trend by softening penalties for serious crimes, the RJA signals an even
deeper shift: a reimagining of justice itself. These measures, rather than
addressing crime's root causes, instead hand out impunity under the guise
of "equity." By permitting convicted criminals to challenge their sentences
on the grounds of racial bias, the RJA plants the seeds for widespread
judicial paralysis, where genuine grievances are drowned out by a deluge
of spurious claims.

California, under the weight of these reckless legal experiments, is
careening into chaos. Cities like San Francisco and Los Angeles bear the
brunt of the impact, grappling with surges in crime, homelessness, and
lawlessness. The courts, already overburdened, now face the prospect of an
avalanche of appeals—most based not on factual innocence but on statistical sleight of hand. In a state desperate for justice, the RJA instead offers
judicial gamesmanship, where identity politics is wielded as a legal cudgel.

At its core, the RJA is not about righting individual wrongs; it is about
subverting the rule of law. By injecting race as a primary determinant of
guilt or innocence, the Act undermines the foundational principle that
justice should be blind. This law does not merely invite abuse—it practically demands it. The inevitable outcome is that real victims of crime are
forgotten, their suffering compounded by a system that elevates race over
responsibility.

The Act's damage extends beyond courtroom delays and overturned
sentences. It corrodes public trust in the legal system, already frayed by
years of failed reforms. As California grapples with increasing violence,
laws like the RJA embolden criminals, signaling that the consequences of
their actions can be mitigated—or erased—by manipulating racial narratives. The victims, left to fend for themselves, are reduced to mere statistics, while the architects of this disaster pat themselves on the back for
their "progress."

This is not justice. It is a betrayal of the very idea of justice, sacrificed
on the altar of political expediency. By prioritizing abstract notions of
"equity" over concrete safety concerns, the RJA embodies the regression of
law, where fairness and accountability are discarded for a fleeting sense of
moral superiority. This Act turns the legal system from a tool of protection

into an instrument of chaos, blurring the line between perpetrator and victim.

Far from addressing the structural causes of crime—education, poverty, opportunity—the RJA focuses solely on optics. It assumes that every disparity is the result of oppression, rather than considering the complex interplay of factors that lead to criminal behavior. In doing so, it ignores the real needs of disadvantaged communities, who bear the brunt of rising crime rates, and instead offers a symbolic victory that accomplishes little beyond virtue signaling.

The ultimate cost of this experiment is borne by California's citizens—those who watch, powerless, as their streets become more dangerous, their courts more ineffective, and their leaders more disconnected from reality. The RJA, sold as a step toward fairness, drags the state further away from any semblance of justice, leaving a wake of lawlessness and despair in its path. What masquerades as progress is, in truth, a profound retreat from the values that uphold the rule of law. The RJA is the embodiment of capricious law, a malleable instrument of racialized injustice that warps the purpose of the legal system to serve political ends.

In its mad dash to rectify perceived racial injustices, California has passed a law that will only create new, far more tangible injustices—ones that will be felt not by the ideologues who drafted the RJA, but by the law-abiding citizens left to suffer the consequences of this abject failure in governance. In dismantling public safety in the name of ideology, the RJA is not just misguided; it is catastrophic. By transforming racial grievance into a legal tool, it risks tearing apart the very fabric of California's justice system. This is not the future of justice—it is its undoing.

AB 3070 (2020): Jury Erosion and the Death of Impartiality

The Racial Justice Act (RJA) had already laid the groundwork for a legal system that prioritized perceived racial disparities over actual justice. Building on this framework of undermining prosecutorial authority, AB 3070 took the assault on the legal process even further by overhauling the jury selection system. While the RJA allowed convicted criminals to challenge sentences based on racial bias, AB 3070 restricted the removal of jurors, shifting the focus from a fair trial to one dictated by identity politics. Together, these laws eroded the basic principles of accountability and impartiality within California's courts.

Of the many wicked and destructive policies born from the chaotic fog of the pandemic, Assembly Bill 3070 stands as one of the most egregious. Passed by the California legislature in 2020, AB 3070 fundamentally reimagines the jury selection process through the prism of crime-equity. The law represents not merely a procedural adjustment but a contortion of the very concept of impartial adjudication.

At its core, AB 3070 severely restricts attorneys' ability to exercise peremptory challenges—a tool long used to remove jurors deemed unfit to serve. Under this law, any peremptory challenge against a member of a so-called "cognizable group" triggers a presumption of improper bias. This group includes not only categories like race, ethnicity, and gender but extends to a wide range of identities including sexual orientation, disability, *gender identity*, and even the vaguely defined "perceived membership" in these groups. To overcome this presumption, the attorney must provide clear and convincing evidence that an "objectively reasonable person" would view the exclusion as unrelated to the juror's group identity—a standard so nebulous that it invites endless litigation and subjective interpretation.

The law does not stop at merely presuming bias; it actively deems certain justifications for peremptory challenges as presumptively invalid. These include reasons like distrust of law enforcement, beliefs about discriminatory enforcement of laws, and even attire or employment fields dominated by protected groups. The result is a jury selection process that prioritizes demographic representation over the qualifications and impartiality of those selected to serve.

Veteran LA prosecutor John Lewin explains the paradigmatic shift created by AB 3070:

"It was passed in June of 2020. Nobody covered it. Middle of the pandemic. Prior to that, let's say that I have a defendant that I'm prosecuting. Doesn't matter what race they are. I have a juror who says, 'Listen, I don't like police officers. My son was prosecuted by the DA's office. I'm a member of Black Lives Matter.' I can kick them off for any one of those three things because they're race neutral. The legislature, led by I think,

Mike Romano, a professor from Stanford, went through all of the areas in California that allowed you to kick off a juror. And they basically passed a new law that said, those are no longer reasons, you cannot use them."[27]

The consequences of this legislation are far-reaching. By elevating demographic considerations above the impartiality and suitability of jurors, AB 3070 effectively turns jury selection into an exercise in identity politics. It represents a seismic shift away from a justice system rooted in the evaluation of evidence toward one where racial and social grievances overshadow the pursuit of truth.

An Oakland-based gang prosecutor offers a stark illustration of the law's impact:

"I have been told to my face before, after the jury rendered a verdict, 'I will not convict a black man.' People don't reveal their biases during jury selection because people are trying to get on juries to fuck shit up. In my county, just like in the last couple of months, they have acquit four separate murders. Some gang related and some not."

This isn't an anomaly; it's a feature of the new system—where identity tribal factionalism supersedes impartial justice, where evidence and law are subordinated to the primacy of racial solidarity.

John Lewin grimly observes, "It's made it much more difficult for us to get jurors who want to rule based on the evidence. And what we're going to get are a lot of OJ juries who are not basing their decisions on the evidence." This sentiment is echoed by a Bay Area prosecutor who laments, "It is just so sad because the juries now have an agenda. And as me, a white woman, that's problematic. And particularly in Oakland, it is the hardest to get a conviction."[28] In other words, the race of the prosecutor has become as relevant as the evidence they present—a chilling development for anyone who believes in the sanctity of a fair trial. As if this weren't enough, AB 3070 is slated to extend its reach to civil trials beginning in 2026, further entrenching this paradigm of identity-driven adjudication into the fabric of California's legal system.[29]

Consider the case of a serial rapist, repeatedly acquitted under this new regime. The prosecutor recounts:

"Went to trial for a bunch of sexual assaults, convicted of something extremely minor out on the streets very, very quickly. He gets arrested again for a parole violation. I take him to trial again for multiple sexual assaults. Jury engages in improper conduct. We remove one of the jurors who did the bad conduct, reconstituted with an alternate, and they convicted. Court of Appeals overturns that conviction and says we should not have removed that juror. And so then four years later, I have to bring all those people back, including the victim herself, to retestify. My point is, is that no matter where we turn, we are screwed. The juries didn't want to convict a black man."

AB 3070 adds further insult by preventing the removal of jurors for being "inattentive" or providing "unintelligent" or "confused answers." For prosecutors who rely heavily on the testimony of police officers, this presents a near-insurmountable obstacle. As a longtime prosecutor stated:

"How do you get a criminal conviction when you have two or three jurors sitting on a jury who openly said they have animus and bias toward police officers? What's going to happen is you're going to get more hung juries, which is a waste of taxpayer money, or worse, you're going to get criminals being acquitted, which means victims are not going to get justice."

In a further affront to common sense, Senate Bill 310, the "Right to Jury Act," which came into effect in 2020, now permits former felons to serve on juries while excluding police officers from the same duty.[30] As one prosecutor put it, "We've just gone too far." This isn't merely a contradiction; it's a calculated perversion of the very foundations of justice, where those once convicted of crimes are now entrusted with deciding the fate of others, while those sworn to uphold the law are sidelined. One wonders if, in the next act of this farce, we'll see defendants judging themselves, with prosecutors required to provide character references.

Following AB 3070's restructuring of the jury selection process, which prioritized identity politics over fair adjudication, the erosion of law and order continued with Senate Bill 357. While AB 3070 undermined the integrity of court trials by restricting peremptory challenges, SB 357 took aim at public safety on the streets. By decriminalizing loitering for prostitution, this legislation further handicapped law enforcement, giving organized crime and human trafficking syndicates more freedom to operate openly without fear of intervention.

Figure 6: Voter Sentiment vs. Real-World Outcomes. Public approval for reforms like Proposition 47 and 57 has declined as crime rates have increased, reflecting growing public concern over safety.

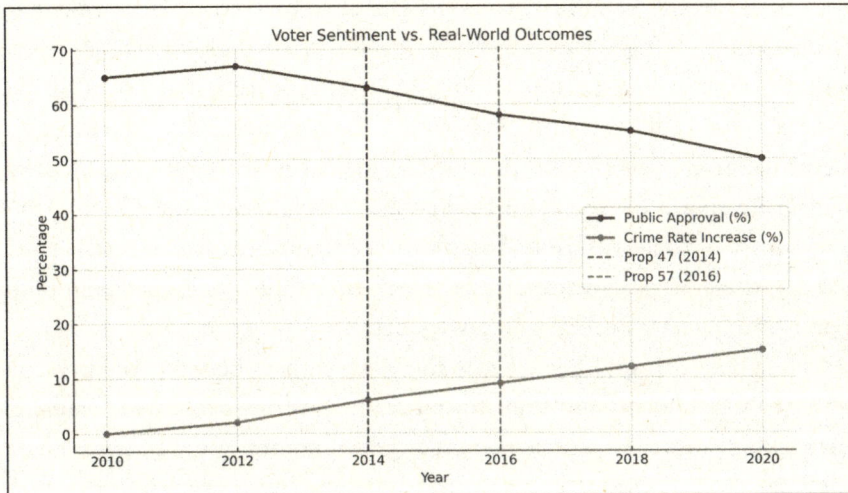

Source: Berkeley IGS Poll, Public Policy.

Conclusion

The consequences of California's judicial leniency are profound and corrosive. Policies designed to shield criminals from accountability have simultaneously shackled law enforcement and left communities to fend for themselves. As a Deputy District Attorney from the Bay Area lamented, "The crime has become much more violent because they know they can get away with it. And the cops are not doing proactive patrolling anymore because it's not to their benefit." This grim reality is the direct result of reforms that prioritize criminal rights at the expense of public safety, a trend that has left victims voiceless and neighborhoods at the mercy of unchecked criminality.

The exodus of over 120 seasoned prosecutors from the Los Angeles District Attorney's office, driven by frustration with policies that hamstring their ability to prosecute effectively, speaks to the deeper systemic collapse. Their departures, as one prosecutor noted, have led to the "dilution of prosecutorial experience," leaving a justice system ill-equipped to confront the escalating crime wave. Law enforcement officers, too, find themselves demoralized, trapped in a web of regulations that elevate the liberties of criminals over the protection of the innocent. The result is a state of paralysis, where proactive policing has all but vanished.

Yet, as Deputy DA John Lewin insightfully observed, "The people that elected them thought it was a free vote. In other words, they're all good with criminal justice reform, as long as it doesn't impact them. And it's turned out that it's impacting everybody." This is the heart of the tragedy. Reforms, crafted in the vacuum of ideological fervor and implemented with little regard for their practical consequences, are now reshaping the very fabric of society. Crime doesn't discriminate—it thrives in the gaps left by these legislative experiments, transforming once-safe neighborhoods into enclaves of fear and lawlessness.

The greatest irony, however, is the yawning gap between the perception of these reforms and their brutal reality. As one exhausted Oakland prosecutor points out, voters remain largely ignorant of the actual state of the law:

"Even my friends who are highly educated and lawyers themselves are like, 'Oh my God, that's so great. We shouldn't be charging juveniles as adults.' I'm like, 'We don't do that. We can't do that.' Again, we're back to the uneducated voter, which is 95% of California and has no idea what they are even talking about."

This pervasive disconnect between the public's well-meaning but uninformed support for reform and the real-world consequences of these policies has emboldened criminals, weakened law enforcement, and left California's citizens to bear the burden.

In the end, the California criminal justice system has been fundamentally corrupted by a misplaced prioritization of criminal rights over community safety. Judicial bias, uninformed voters, and reckless reforms have unleashed a wave of crime, leaving victims defenseless and communities crumbling under the weight of violence and fear. The social contract has been violated, replaced by a system where ideology triumphs over justice and accountability is a relic of the past.

PART II

PLUNDER AND DOMINION

CHAPTER 7

FORSAKEN

California has become the face of a modern plague, one with two relentless strains: homelessness and drug addiction. Nowhere is this more devastatingly visible than in Los Angeles, where these intertwined crises have spread like an unchecked contagion, leaving the city disfigured. Over 75,000 people live on its streets—an epidemic that grows despite billions spent in its name.

The encampments that stretch across Los Angeles are more than signs of poverty; they are markers of a deeper societal failure. Addiction, fueled by the ubiquity of fentanyl, cuts through the city like a toxic current, hollowing out lives and eroding any hope for recovery. Efforts to intervene, whether through public health programs or law enforcement, have been undermined by corruption, mismanagement, and inertia. What remains is a city paralyzed, unable to contain the spread of despair that now defines its streets.

This chapter examines how these crises have metastasized, fueled by policies that promised solutions but instead deepened the suffering. It explores the decisions that allowed this plague to flourish and questions whether Los Angeles can reclaim itself before the damage becomes irreversible.

Humanity on the Margins: The Failure of Progressivism

The crisis in Los Angeles cannot be disentangled from the ideological framework that has allowed it to fester. Progressivism, in its modern

Californian form, functions less as a coherent policy platform and more as a form of secular orthodoxy. Its adherents, convinced of the moral infallibility of their intentions, have transformed homelessness into a cause célèbre—a symbol of compassion to display rather than a problem to solve. The focus is not on alleviating suffering but on assuaging collective guilt, prioritizing appearances over outcomes.

Prosecutor John Lewin captures the grim consequences succinctly: "What we have done is we have basically said that we're going to, in essence, legalize drug use. We are going to legalize theft, and we're going to allow mentally ill, drug-addicted homeless people to live on the streets supporting themselves through theft. And it's a revolving door." This revolving door is evident in the encampments that stretch across Los Angeles, where survival is often predicated on the grim economy of narcotics, prostitution, and exploitation.

Homeless encampments have become hubs of crime and exploitation, where the line between survival and victimization blurs. LAPD officer Jamie McBride points to the harsh reality: "There's a very large portion of homeless tents being used for prostitution and narcotics, and no one talks about it." Detective Mike Maher adds another chilling dimension: "Homeless in Venice are paying tribute $25–50 a day to local street gangs. If they can't pay, they force them to sell drugs and commit other crimes. This is common amongst most homeless in Los Angeles." These makeshift shelters are not simply places of refuge; they are the epicenters of an underground economy that preys on society's most vulnerable.

The mental health crisis fuels this cycle of despair. Severe untreated psychiatric disorders leave individuals trapped in a volatile state, often spiraling into addiction or crime.[1] Instead of receiving care, many are funneled into the criminal justice system, further destabilizing an already fragile community. Gangs and criminal networks exploit this vulnerability, perpetuating cycles of violence and lawlessness. In 2023, one out of every four homicide victims in Los Angeles was homeless.[2] Murder within this population has significantly driven the city's rising homicide rates over the past three years, while drug overdoses now account for 37% of all homeless deaths.[3]

Public spaces, once symbols of civic life, have become casualties of this crisis. Parks and libraries, once bastions of community engagement, now serve as asylums for the unhoused and dens for drug use. The unchecked expansion of encampments carries devastating economic and social consequences. Businesses near these areas face rampant theft and vandalism, pushing economic activity away and deepening the instability of already strained communities.

What persists in Los Angeles is not a lack of resources but a failure of vision and courage. Policies that prioritize ideological purity over pragmatic solutions have turned homelessness into a crisis that defines the city itself. It is a humanitarian disaster born of negligence, misplaced priorities, and an unwillingness to confront the real and uncomfortable complexities of the problem.

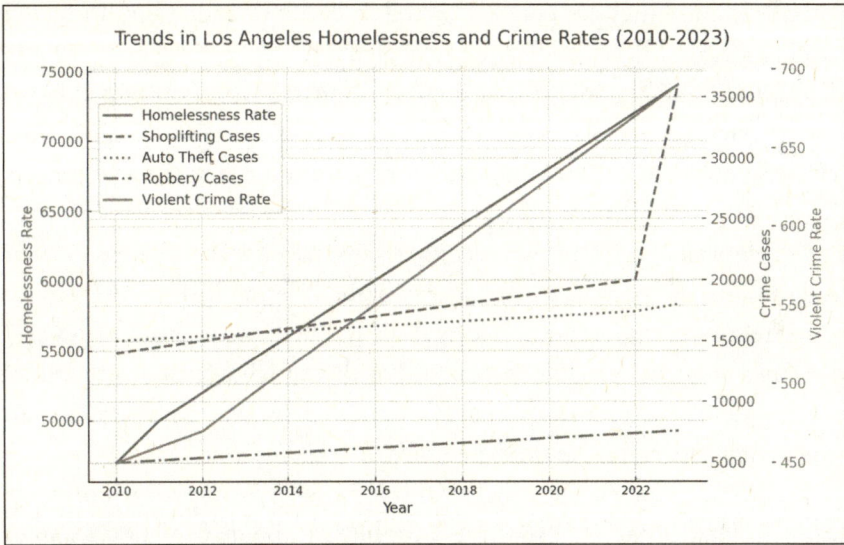

Trends in Los Angeles Homelessness and Crime Rates (2010-2023)

Los Angeles's Billion-Dollar Illusion

Los Angeles has spent over $1.3 billion in recent years to address homelessness—a staggering sum that stands as a monument to both the gravity of the crisis and the spectacular ineptitude of those tasked with solving it.[4] Far from alleviating the problem, this immense expenditure has coincided with an unrelenting surge in homelessness. The 2023 Greater Los Angeles Homeless Count reported a 9% increase in just one year, bringing the total to 75,518 individuals.[5] Over the past five years, homelessness in Los Angeles has skyrocketed by 40%, and each successive initiative seems only to underline the city's inability to grasp the scale or nature of the disaster unfolding in its streets.[6]

At the heart of this failure lies the state's unwavering faith in the "Housing First" model, a policy framework that prioritizes providing housing without requiring treatment for addiction or mental illness.[7] While this approach has shown promise in isolated cases, it is wholly inadequate for addressing the complex realities of homelessness in Los Angeles, where 75% of the homeless population suffers from severe mental illness or substance use disorders, according to the Los Angeles Homeless Services Authority (LAHSA).[8] To offer housing as a standalone solution is to misunderstand the problem entirely. These are not simply people without homes; they are people trapped in cycles of addiction, untreated psychiatric conditions, and systemic neglect.

Adding insult to injury, the cost of implementing Housing First in Los Angeles has reached absurd heights. Some supportive housing units have cost as much as $700,000 each—an astronomical figure that reflects the grotesque inefficiency of the city's bureaucracy and its collusion with private contractors.[9] This is not compassion; it is a racket, where bloated budgets line the pockets of developers while offering little in the way of actual relief to those in need. Meanwhile, public disorder proliferates and the city's residents are left to contend with the fallout: rampant crime, encampments that stretch for miles, and a crisis that feels less like an emergency and more like the new normal.

The failure is not merely logistical but moral. Los Angeles's leadership seems to view homelessness as a PR problem to be managed rather than a humanitarian disaster to be solved. The city has become adept at producing glossy press releases and high-minded rhetoric while ignoring the grim realities on the ground. Fentanyl—a cheap, lethal poison that has saturated the narcotics trade—kills with ruthless efficiency, driving overdose deaths to unprecedented levels. Yet rather than addressing the root causes of addiction, the city effectively enables it, tolerating open-air drug markets and treating law enforcement as an afterthought.

This unchecked permissiveness has not only failed to alleviate the crisis but has also emboldened those who exploit it. Homeless encampments have become hubs for organized crime, where gangs extort the vulnerable and use the streets as marketplaces for narcotics and prostitution. Public spaces that once symbolized civic life—parks, libraries, and sidewalks—have been surrendered, eroding the fabric of the city and deepening public despair.

What Los Angeles faces is not a lack of resources but a lack of will. Its leaders have chosen performative virtue over practical governance, ideological purity over common sense. Housing First, as implemented here, is a cruel misnomer: housing is not first, last, or anywhere at all for the thousands still languishing on the streets. Until the city confronts the underlying issues of addiction, mental illness, and bureaucratic bloat, the billions spent will continue to vanish into the void, leaving behind only the hollow promises of a failed system.

This is not just a crisis of policy; it is a crisis of vision, integrity, and responsibility. The question is no longer whether Los Angeles can fix its homelessness epidemic, but whether it is even capable of trying.

Bureaucracy's Failure to Deliver

Los Angeles County's strategy to combat homelessness is marred by a labyrinthine bureaucracy that significantly hampers its effectiveness. The fragmented approach involves multiple agencies operating with overlapping responsibilities and little coordination, leading to redundant services and inefficient use of resources. For instance, various departments run parallel outreach programs and emergency shelters without effective communication or strategic planning, resulting in service duplication and wasted efforts.

A substantial portion of the funds allocated for homelessness is consumed by administrative overhead rather than direct services. High salaries for executives and staff within homelessness agencies, coupled with extensive operational costs, divert funds away from essential services like housing and mental health support. For example, in some agencies, less than half of the budget directly benefits homeless individuals, with the remainder absorbed by administrative expenses.[10]

The Los Angeles Homeless Services Authority (LAHSA), the lead agency in the county's continuum of care, has faced scathing criticism for its inefficiency. Despite a budget of approximately $875 million, a recent audit revealed that LAHSA routinely paid service providers late, disrupting the delivery of critical services to the homeless population.[11]

Moreover, the county administers more than 700 contracts with over 100 community-based organizations to provide services to people experiencing homelessness or at risk of losing their homes. This complex web of contracts often leads to overlapping services and a lack of accountability, further exacerbating the inefficiencies within the system and worsening the crisis.[12]

Corruption and Mismanagement: A Crisis of Betrayal

Los Angeles's homelessness crisis is not simply the byproduct of misguided policies but a damning reflection of systemic corruption and incompetence. Those charged with alleviating suffering have instead enriched themselves, squandered resources, and allowed the city's humanitarian disaster to metastasize. This is not merely a failure of governance; it is a moral failure—a calculated abdication of responsibility that sacrifices the vulnerable on the altar of personal gain and bureaucratic inertia.

The Price of Corruption

Corruption in Los Angeles's homelessness programs is not an anomaly but a defining feature of its governance. Consider the indictment of Councilman Curren Price, who stands accused of funneling over $150,000 to his wife through developers tied to Proposition HHH-funded projects. Proposition HHH, a $1.2 billion initiative intended to create 10,000 supportive housing units, has instead become a monument to delays, spiraling costs, and political profiteering. More than six years after its passage, fewer than half of the promised units have been built, and some have come at an astonishing price of $700,000 per unit.[13]

Similarly, the fall of José Huizar, another City Councilman, lays bare the intersection of power and greed in Los Angeles. Huizar accepted over $1.5 million in bribes from developers, including a $600,000 payoff to quietly settle a sexual harassment lawsuit.[14] Huizar was sentenced to 13 years in federal prison on racketeering and tax evasion charges is emblematic of how public office in Los Angeles has been weaponized for personal enrichment, often at the expense of initiatives aimed at solving the city's most pressing crises.[15]

These scandals are not isolated incidents; they are the predictable outcome of a system in which oversight is weak, accountability is nonexistent, and personal enrichment eclipses public duty.

Bureaucratic Dysfunction: A System in Disarray

Corruption may steal headlines, but mismanagement is equally culpable for the collapse of Los Angeles's homelessness initiatives. Proposition HHH, lauded as a transformative measure, has delivered a fraction of its promised housing due to inefficiencies and bloated contracts. Meanwhile, the Los Angeles Homeless Services Authority (LAHSA), tasked with coordinating services for the homeless, has become a symbol of bureaucratic failure. Despite managing nearly $1 billion annually, LAHSA has been dogged by audits revealing late payments to service providers, poorly defined goals, and inconsistent care.[16]

Even well-intentioned programs like the Inside Safe initiative, designed to move individuals from encampments into temporary hotel accommodations, have faltered. With $250 million allocated to the program for the 2023–24 fiscal year, its results have been underwhelming.[17] By October 2024, Inside Safe had transitioned only 4% of the city's 46,000 homeless individuals into hotels, and many of those housed have since returned to the streets.[18] The program's failure to address underlying issues such as addiction and mental illness has rendered it an expensive stopgap rather than a sustainable solution.

The Human Cost

The consequences of corruption and mismanagement are borne by the city's most vulnerable. Funds that should provide shelter and services are instead funneled into inflated contracts, exorbitant administrative costs, and substandard programs. Homeless encampments grow, unchecked addiction spreads, and public spaces—parks, sidewalks, libraries—become scenes of desolation and despair.

The collapse of the Skid Row Housing Trust offers a grim illustration of these failures. Once a cornerstone of Los Angeles's housing strategy, the Trust has devolved into a cautionary tale of financial mismanagement and neglect. Audits revealed that funds intended for housing construction were routinely diverted to cover administrative costs, delaying projects and leaving tenants in unsafe, poorly maintained buildings. For the thousands of residents who depend on these units, the Trust's failures are not abstract—they are daily reminders of a system that values bureaucracy over humanity.

A System at the Brink

The corruption and dysfunction within Los Angeles's homelessness initiatives are not unfortunate side effects—they are central to the system's collapse. Programs designed to address suffering have become engines of self-enrichment, their failures compounded by bureaucratic inertia and political grandstanding.

Restoring functionality to these programs requires more than platitudes and budget increases. It demands an unflinching systemic overhaul: rigorous oversight to prevent embezzlement, transparency in contracting processes, and policies that prioritize direct services over administrative bloat. Without these changes, the billions spent will continue to vanish into a void of inefficiency and exploitation, leaving Los Angeles as a city defined not by its solutions but by its squandered potential.

This is not just a crisis of policy; it is a crisis of will. The question is not whether Los Angeles has the resources to address its homelessness epidemic but whether it has the integrity to use them effectively.

L.A. County 2023 homelessness by race and ethnicity

■ Percent of unhoused population   ■ Percent of general population

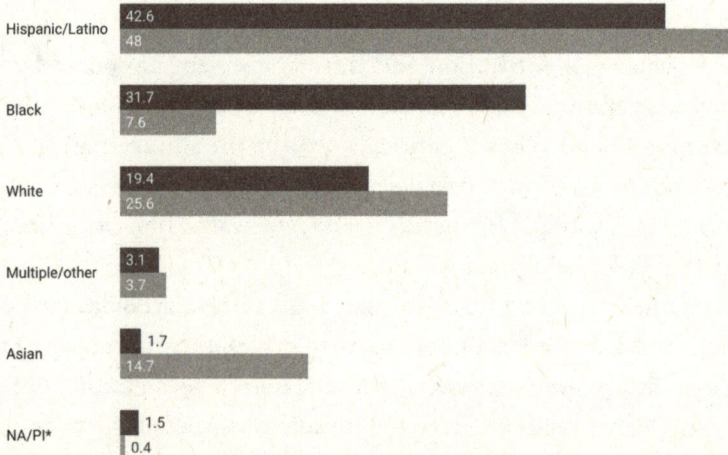

Race/Ethnicity	Percent of unhoused population	Percent of general population
Hispanic/Latino	42.6	48
Black	31.7	7.6
White	19.4	25.6
Multiple/other	3.1	3.7
Asian	1.7	14.7
NA/PI*	1.5	0.4

*Native American/Pacific Islander

Source: Los Angeles Homeless Services Authority 2023 count • Created with Datawrapper

Homelessness in Los Angeles, 2015–2023

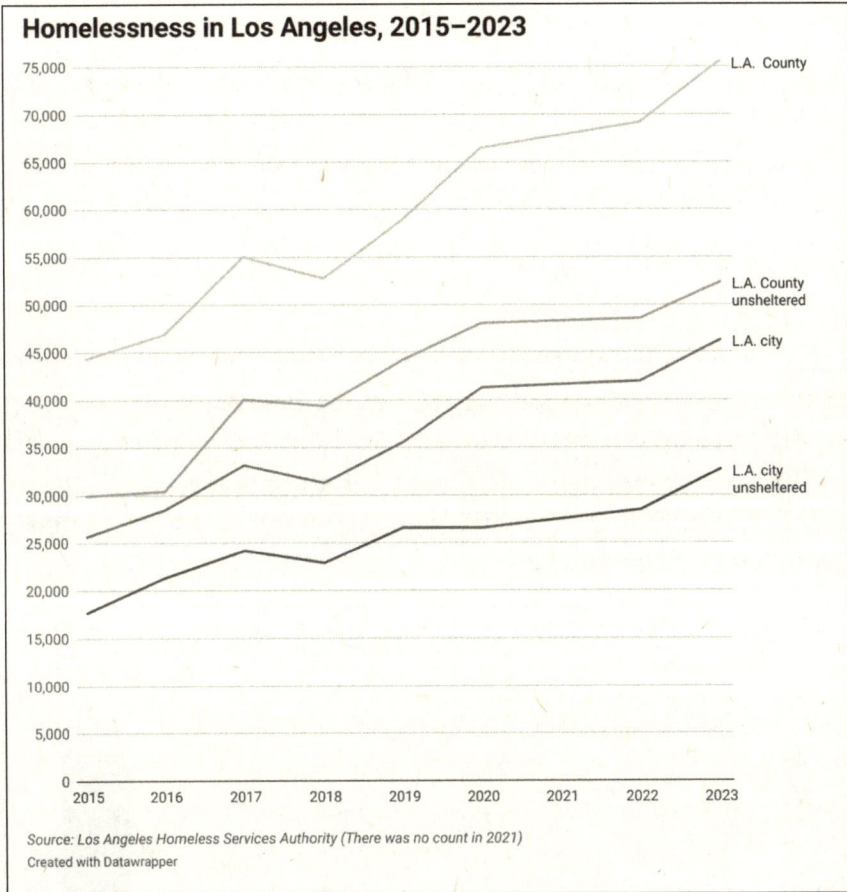

Source: Los Angeles Homeless Services Authority (There was no count in 2021)
Created with Datawrapper

The Drug Crisis: Fentanyl's Stranglehold on Los Angeles

The homelessness crisis in Los Angeles is compounded by a more insidious and lethal threat: the fentanyl epidemic. This potent synthetic opioid has infiltrated the city's narcotics trade, exacerbating urban decay and overwhelming public health resources.

Escalating Fentanyl Seizures

In 2023, the California National Guard's Counterdrug Task Force supported operations that resulted in the seizure of 62,224 pounds of fentanyl—a staggering 1,066% increase from 2021.[19] The street value of these seizures was estimated at approximately $649 million, with the amount confiscated in 2023 alone containing enough fentanyl to potentially kill the global population nearly twice over.[20] This represents a significant rise from earlier years, such as 2021, when fentanyl seizures had a street value of $64.1 million, and 2022, when the value increased to $230 million. This drastic increase in both seizures and street value highlights the growing prevalence of fentanyl in the drug market and its escalating impact on public health and law enforcement.

Surging Overdose Deaths

Despite these enforcement efforts, fentanyl-related fatalities have surged. In Los Angeles County, accidental fentanyl overdose deaths escalated from 109 in 2016 to 1,910 in 2022—a 1,652% increase.[21] Preliminary data indicates a slight decrease in drug-related overdose deaths in 2023, marking the first reduction since 2014. However, fentanyl remains a primary contributor to these fatalities.

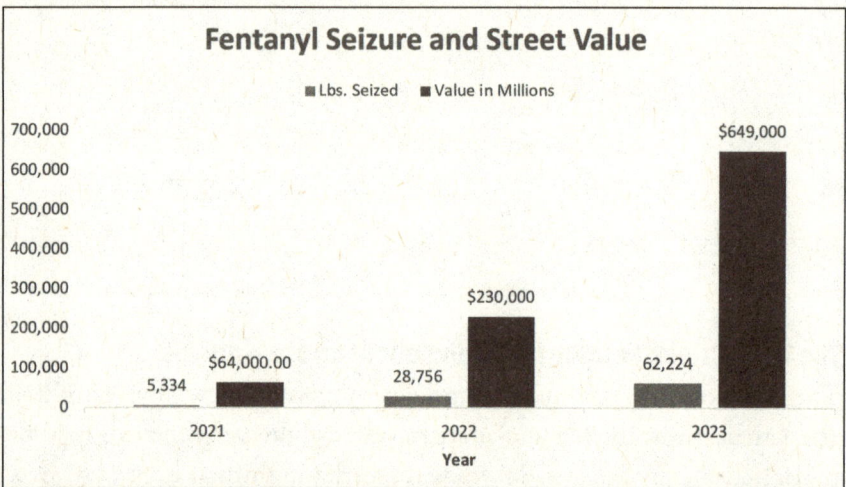

Fentanyl Seizure and Street Value

■ Lbs. Seized   ■ Value in Millions

Year	Lbs. Seized	Value in Millions
2021	5,334	$64,000.00
2022	28,756	$230,000
2023	62,224	$649,000

Pervasive Contamination of Street Drugs

Detective Sam Bailey of the Los Angeles Police Department highlights the pervasive contamination of street drugs with fentanyl: "Fentanyl is on EVERYTHING. It's like salt. They shake it on everything. It's on weed. That's why so many people are overdosing. If you're getting a pill from the street, fentanyl is in it."

Underscoring Bailey's statement and the scale of the crisis, federal authorities in 2023 seized nearly 80 million fentanyl-laced fake pills and 12,000 pounds of fentanyl powder. This widespread adulteration has created a significant public health crisis, driving a surge in overdoses and fatalities.

Sophisticated Narcotics Trade

The narcotics trade in Los Angeles has evolved into a sophisticated and expansive industry. Detective Bailey elaborates on its complexity, noting the intricate logistics required to move large quantities of narcotics: "When you talk narcotics, we're talking not just the dope trafficking and the dealing, we're talking about moving large, large quantities and weights and now we're talking a truck company, a warehouse because you have to have logistics to move that stuff. Very sophisticated operations."

Lax Enforcement and Policy Failures

The enforcement of drug laws across the state has become alarmingly lax. A Deputy District Attorney from Alameda County affirms, "We are not prosecuting drug crime. Period. Unless it's a significant amount, we're not doing it." This hands-off approach has emboldened the proliferation of fentanyl, transforming it into a virulent plague.

Devastating Human Toll

The human toll is devastating. In 2022, Los Angeles County reported over 1,000 drug-related deaths among the homeless population, with 728 linked to fentanyl. Preliminary data suggests a 15% increase in fentanyl-related deaths among the homeless from 2022 to 2023.[22]

In Los Angeles County, fentanyl has become the most common drug listed for overdose deaths in 2022, surpassing methamphetamine, and was linked to about 60% of all accidental drug or alcohol overdoses.[23] The impact of fentanyl is disproportionately severe among blacks.[24]

"Drugs are different now," as Bailey starkly observes. "I don't have to go to some apartment at the bottom half of the Jordan Downs (a housing project) to get my crack. Everybody's popping pills."

Economic Decline: The Vicious Cycle of Drug Crime

The homelessness and drug crises in Los Angeles have become economic wrecking balls, dismantling local businesses and destabilizing entire communities. Small businesses in areas besieged by homelessness and crime face mounting challenges, with many shuttering their doors under the weight of declining revenues and rising operational costs. The Los Angeles Chamber of Commerce and other business advocates have repeatedly emphasized how pervasive criminal activity, including theft and vandalism, drives down revenues and weakens the city's economic fabric. Crime doesn't merely disrupt commerce; it erodes public trust, creating a vicious cycle of fear, avoidance, and economic decline.

Reports highlight that increased crime directly undermines Americans' sense of safety, leading to reduced foot traffic for small businesses, particularly in areas with visible urban disorder. This erosion of public confidence diminishes not just the frequency of visits to local businesses but also community cohesion, as residents increasingly view these areas as unsafe and uninviting. Neighborhoods plagued by crime often see an exodus of long-time customers, further exacerbating the decline of once-thriving commercial corridors.[25]

Business owners who manage to keep their doors open are paying a steep price. Rising security costs, including private patrols and fortified storefronts, have become the norm, with many spending more on protection than rent. For these business owners, the city's abdication of basic law enforcement is not merely a failure of policy but a profound betrayal of their role as economic and social anchors in their communities.

Beyond the financial toll, crime has a corrosive effect on social trust, leaving neighborhoods fractured and unstable. Public spaces, long the lifeblood of urban life, have become no-go zones. Parks once filled with families are now overrun by drug use and encampments, and commercial areas have become hotspots for theft and intimidation, driving more businesses and residents away.

Erosion of Trust: Institutions in Doubt

At the root of this economic unraveling is a larger breakdown in trust in public institutions. Residents and business owners alike feel abandoned by a government that appears incapable—or unwilling—to uphold basic standards of safety and order. According to surveys by the *Los Angeles Times*, over 60% of Angelenos express dissatisfaction with the city's handling of crime and homelessness.[26] This collapse in trust extends beyond government agencies to law enforcement and the judicial system, creating a vacuum of authority that allows disorder to thrive.

As businesses close, customers flee, and neighborhoods deteriorate, the city faces a dangerous feedback loop where economic decline and social instability feed into one another. Rebuilding trust in institutions is not merely a matter of optics but a necessary step to break this cycle. Without decisive action to restore public order and economic stability, Los Angeles risks becoming a city defined by decay rather than opportunity.

A Blueprint for Recovery: Policies to Reverse the Crisis

Addressing Los Angeles's intertwined crises of homelessness, addiction, and urban decay requires a decisive departure from the failed policies of the past. A fundamental shift in approach is imperative—one grounded in accountability, pragmatism, and results.

Restoring Public Order

The enforcement of public order laws is essential. Allowing minor offenses such as public camping, open drug use, and vandalism to persist unchecked fosters an environment of lawlessness that accelerates urban decay. Strict enforcement of these laws can deter smaller crimes that collectively degrade public spaces and diminish quality of life. Clean, safe streets are not luxuries but prerequisites for a functioning city.

Incentivizing Private Development

Housing affordability must also be addressed through pragmatic reform. Reducing zoning regulations and streamlining the permitting process would remove significant barriers to private development, allowing for the construction of much-needed housing. Cities like Houston have demonstrated that cutting red tape can unleash private-sector innovation and investment, providing a pathway to increased housing stock without bloated government intervention.

Linking Housing to Responsibility

Los Angeles must move beyond the flawed "Housing First" model, which prioritizes shelter without addressing the underlying causes of homelessness. Housing assistance should be contingent upon participation in mandatory drug rehabilitation and mental health treatment programs. Such an approach acknowledges the reality that many individuals experiencing homelessness are grappling with addiction and severe mental illness. Providing housing without addressing these root causes is akin to treating symptoms while ignoring the disease. This policy shift promotes personal responsibility, facilitating societal reintegration rather than perpetuating dependency.

Workfare Over Welfare

Transitioning from unconditional welfare to workfare programs would further reinforce the principle of accountability. Able-bodied individuals should contribute to the economy while receiving support, reducing dependency and fostering a sense of purpose. Workfare programs not only address immediate economic needs but also help individuals rebuild their lives through structure, dignity, and community integration.

Learning from Houston and New York

Houston, Texas, offers a compelling example of what is achievable. Since 2011, the city has reduced its homeless population by over 54%, employing a pragmatic balance of "housing-first" initiatives alongside stringent enforcement of anti-camping laws.[27] Houston's emphasis on rapid rehousing, coupled with robust support services, demonstrates that compassionate policies can coexist with firm public order enforcement.

New York requires welfare recipients to engage in work-related activities as a condition of aid. This policy has resulted in decreased welfare dependency and increased employment among former homeless individuals, showcasing the efficacy of coupling aid with accountability. Los Angeles must take heed if it wishes to escape its current trajectory toward self-destruction.

Conclusion

Los Angeles stands not at a crossroads but on the precipice, teetering between reclamation and collapse. This is not merely a city in decline—it is a civic experiment unraveling, undone by a permissive drug culture, bureaucratic paralysis, and the moral abdication of its leaders. The homelessness crisis is not an isolated calamity but the logical endpoint of policies shaped by ideological fantasies rather than hard realities.

What Los Angeles faces is not just a crisis of governance but a test of its very identity as a functioning metropolis. Its current trajectory—a spiraling descent into lawlessness, disorder, and decay—is unsustainable. The city cannot survive as both a haven for unchecked criminality and a place where citizens expect safety, dignity, and opportunity.

If Los Angeles is to halt its slide toward chaos, it must reject the complacency and self-congratulatory rhetoric that have defined its governance. The solutions are not mysterious, nor are they easy. They demand a return to fundamentals: the enforcement of laws, the accountability of institutions, and the prioritization of public safety over performative moralism.

Los Angeles is not beyond saving, but its survival depends on a willingness to confront uncomfortable truths and make hard choices. The alternative is not just further decline but the transformation of a once-iconic city into a cautionary tale—a monument to squandered potential and failed leadership. The question is not whether Los Angeles can be saved, but whether it has the courage to save itself.

CHAPTER 8

RAPINE

California's crisis of governance has birthed an unsettling reality: as legitimate industries collapse under the weight of overregulation and prohibitive costs, crime has taken their place as a growth enterprise. Once the beacon of opportunity, the state now seems better suited to incubating criminal innovation than economic prosperity. Manufacturing jobs have vanished by the tens of thousands, but in their absence, theft, burglary, and organized crime have surged with alarming efficiency.

At the heart of this upheaval lies a policy framework that rewards leniency at the expense of accountability. Laws like Proposition 47, which reclassified serious offenses as minor misdemeanors, have transformed California into a haven for opportunistic crime. Criminal networks, both local and international, have seized on this permissive environment, leveraging the state's blind spots in enforcement to operate with near impunity.

This chapter examines how California's policy failures have not only fostered the proliferation of organized crime but also eroded the state's economic stability and social cohesion. From emboldened retail theft rings to sophisticated burglary networks, the consequences of these decisions ripple far beyond the immediate victims, threatening to redefine public safety and economic resilience in the state. As California grapples with its identity, one question looms large: how long can a society endure when criminality becomes its most resilient industry?

The Industrialization of Crime

California's paradoxical policy framework has given rise to an unintended yet thriving industry: crime. Over the past decade, the state has hemorrhaged approximately 157,000 manufacturing jobs, driven out by exorbitant operational costs, labyrinthine regulations, and a punitive tax regime. In the vacuum left by these vanishing industries, crime has emerged as an unlikely yet flourishing economic force, filling the void with ruthless efficiency.

This transformation has been aided, if not engineered, by the state's systematic softening of the penal code. Proposition 47, introduced under the banner of criminal justice reform, epitomizes this shift. By reclassifying a host of non-violent felonies as misdemeanors, the law effectively decriminalized offenses such as theft and burglary. Predictably, this policy has served as an open invitation to criminal enterprises, reducing the risks of apprehension and penalties while increasing the rewards of unlawful activity.

The consequences of this misguided approach have been devastating. Middle-class families, affluent neighborhoods, and small businesses find themselves on the front lines of a relentless surge in property crimes. Burglaries, armed robberies, and home invasions have become near-daily occurrences, while retail theft has ballooned to industrial proportions. These crimes are no longer isolated or opportunistic; they are calculated, organized, and methodical, reflecting a level of sophistication more commonly associated with corporate logistics than street-level crime.

This grimly ironic dynamic—where equity-driven policies have empowered criminal enterprises—underscores the broader dysfunction in California's governance. As legitimate industries are suffocated under the weight of bureaucratic inefficiency, crime flourishes as the state's most resilient and unregulated economy. The stark reality is that California's policy landscape, whether through incompetence or design, has created a fertile ground where brigandry thrives while lawful commerce withers.

What remains most striking is the state's inability—or unwillingness—to reckon with the consequences of these policies. The persistent erosion of public safety and economic stability is not merely a byproduct of poor governance; it is a symptom of a deeper ideological commitment to policies that prioritize appearances over outcomes. In a state where crime increasingly functions as an alternative economy, the need for a radical reassessment of the rule of law has never been more urgent.

As California struggles with the ramifications of its policy failures, one undeniable truth emerges: when governance falters, crime does not simply fill the void—it dominates it. The industrialization of criminality stands as both a warning and an indictment, laying bare the costs of ideological experiments untethered from reality.

Burglary Tourists

A particularly revealing aspect of California's escalating crime wave is the rise of organized burglary rings from South America, colloquially referred to as "burglary tourists." These professional, clean-cut, and black-clad ninja-like burglars are primarily from Chile, but also elsewhere in South America and exploit the U.S. visa system, entering the country under the Electronic System for Travel Authorization (ESTA) program. This program allows them to stay for up to 90 days without undergoing background checks—a loophole they continue to monetize.[1]

Detective Mike Maher, who led the LA County Sheriff's Department task force on this issue, provides a detailed account of their operations: "Four guys from Chile, organized, get their plane tickets paid for. They land in Los Angeles, stay in prearranged apartments, and use rental cars provided by a specific company. During the day, they commit vehicle burglaries, and at night, they target high-end houses." Their sophisticated operation involves disabling home security systems and shipping stolen goods back to South America, where the criminals evade U.S. legal repercussions and are hailed as heroes in their home countries.[2]

While the program is intended to streamline travel, it has become a conduit for transnational crime. Criminals exploit the ninety-day stay period to orchestrate and execute meticulously planned burglaries, then return home, only to re-enter the U.S. with ease. The recurring nature of these crimes highlights significant flaws in the enforcement and monitoring of visa regulations. The absence of mandatory background checks under the ESTA program means law enforcement is often unaware of the criminal histories of these entrants, complicating efforts to prevent such crimes.

The lack of cooperation from South American governments, particularly Chile, in providing criminal histories exacerbates the problem of burglary tourists. Without comprehensive background information, U.S. authorities struggle to identify and apprehend repeat offenders, allowing these criminals to operate with near impunity. Many of these offenders, once released on bail, abscond and fail to return for court appearances, underscoring critical weaknesses in the enforcement and monitoring of visa regulations.

In response to these systemic issues, the Orange County District Attorney has taken the extraordinary step of suing the federal government. This legal action seeks stricter enforcement of visa regulations to prevent such abuses and ensure that repeat offenders cannot easily re-enter the country to continue their criminal activities.

The economic and social impacts of these crimes are profound. For instance, Felipe Leiva Solis was linked to at least thirty burglaries in West Los Angeles, using a fake passport to open a bank account and wire stolen money back to Chile. Other notable arrests include three Chilean men apprehended with $1 million worth of stolen items in Beverly Hills. These cases highlight the high level of organization and substantial financial toll on victims, with burglaries often resulting in millions of dollars in stolen valuables annually.

These criminals use sophisticated tools, such as jamming devices, to disable home security systems. Their operations are not confined to California but span across various states, including New York, New Jersey, and Virginia. Prosecutors face significant hurdles due to the lack of criminal history records from the Chilean government, complicating efforts to prove these burglars' ties to multiple crimes. Furthermore, many criminals evade justice by using fake documents and quickly fleeing the country when caught. One notable burglary involved the theft of $1.2 million in valuables from a single residence.

The persistence of such criminal enterprises underscores a grim reality: in California, where legitimate industries struggle, crime remains a resilient enterprise. The systemic failures in visa regulation enforcement, compounded by the lack of international cooperation, have created fertile ground for these organized crime rings.

Follow-Home Robberies

Perhaps the most disturbing trend in Los Angeles is the rise of follow-home robberies, where gangs target individuals perceived to be wealthy, follow them, and stage violent home invasions or other aggressive thefts. According to NBC News, the LAPD has identified at least seventeen Los Angeles gangs involved in these "follow-home" robberies. These gangs spot potential victims leaving upscale venues and trail them home, often using social media platforms like Instagram to identify individuals flaunting luxury items.

Deputy DA John Lewin describes the operations: "Gangs from South LA are now executing a lot of these 'follow-home' robberies, following people from clubs. That's become very popular. You've got now social media where people are posting stuff on Instagram, and the gangsters go to the houses, they know people are partying. They've become a lot more sophisticated. And the internet and social media have really opened it up."

The mechanics of these robberies are both brazen and meticulous. Gang members often use spotters to identify targets with high-value items such as expensive jewelry, watches, handbags, or cars. Once a target is identified, up to five carloads of gang members may follow and swarm the victim at their residence, executing the robbery with precision and aggression. These attacks often start suddenly, leaving victims no chance to comply. The suspects employ extreme violence, such as pistol-whipping, punching, and at times, shooting victims.

The impact on victims is profound and multifaceted. Many are left traumatized, having guns pointed at them and suffering physical injuries from being tackled, kicked, beaten, punched, or pistol-whipped. The psychological scars run deep, as the safety of one's home is violated in the most invasive manner. In 2021, 165 follow-home robberies were reported. Gang-related follow-home robberies accounted for 29% of all robberies in Los Angeles in the first two months of 2024, with fifty-six incidents documented so far this year.

These crimes often escalate to violence, with thirteen victims shot during such incidents, two of whom succumbed to their injuries. The sheer audacity and frequency of these robberies underscore a broader narrative of urban danger and the erosion of public safety in Los Angeles. As gangs become more technologically savvy, leveraging social media for criminal gain, the challenge for law enforcement and the community grows increasingly complex.

Knock-Knock Burglaries

"Knock-knock" burglaries have become a notable crime trend due to their deceptive simplicity and effectiveness. Perpetrators of these crimes pose as door-to-door salespeople, maintenance workers, or utility inspectors to determine if homes are occupied before breaking in. This method allows criminals to blend seamlessly into the fabric of everyday suburban life, avoiding suspicion while they scout their targets.

NBC Los Angeles has detailed how suspects often use high-end vehicles to infiltrate affluent neighborhoods, enhancing their guise of legitimacy. This strategy leverages appearances to facilitate their illicit activities, allowing them to move through these areas with minimal detection.

Knock-knock burglars typically work in teams, employing a variety of ruses to ensure that homes are unoccupied. Once they confirm that no one is home, they break in, often targeting high-value items such as jewelry, electronics, and cash. Their methods are quick and efficient, typically involving forced entry through front doors, windows, or side entrances.

According to LAPD data, knock-knock burglaries have seen a significant increase in recent years. In 2023 alone, there were over 2,500 reported incidents, marking a 15% increase from the previous year. These crimes are not confined to any single area but are prevalent across various upscale neighborhoods, including Beverly Hills, Brentwood, and the Hollywood Hills.

One notable case involved a group of burglars who, posing as landscapers, targeted homes in the affluent neighborhood of Pacific Palisades. They used gardening tools to appear inconspicuous while casing properties. Their operation was so sophisticated that they managed to evade law enforcement for months, stealing over $1 million in goods before being apprehended.

The psychological impact on victims of knock-knock burglaries runs deep. Homeowners often report feeling violated and unsafe in their own homes, with the knowledge that their security was breached under the guise of normalcy. This type of burglary not only results in significant financial losses but also leaves lasting emotional scars.

To combat this rising trend, law enforcement agencies have stepped up community outreach and education efforts, advising residents on how to spot potential burglars and encouraging them to report suspicious activities. Security experts recommend the use of advanced home security systems, including surveillance cameras and smart locks, to deter would-be burglars. In other words, homes are becoming fortresses as the police can barely keep up with the brigands. The message is clear: you're on your own.

Retail Theft Rings

Retail theft is the most arresting and visceral manifestation of California's lawlessness, starkly highlighting the degradation affecting ordinary people and shocking visitors from across the world. Walking into a CVS in Brentwood, where deodorant is locked behind glass and toiletries require permission to retrieve, paints a bleak and pathetic picture of a city in shambles. This rampant theft spree has evolved into a veritable cottage industry, symbolizing the most visceral indictment of a failing state.

Indeed, retail theft rings have become a significant concern for law enforcement and businesses across California. Contrary to public perception, these thieves are often gang-affiliated, operating within sophisticated networks of organized crime. These crimes are multimillion-dollar operations where stolen goods are resold for profit, revealing a sophisticated network of thieves and fences. Fences are essential to the sustainability of such criminal enterprises, as they facilitate the conversion of stolen goods into cash, maintaining the flow of illicit activities.

Detective Sam Bailey describes the scale of these operations, citing a case involving a fence living in a multi-million-dollar home: "A recent case involved a fence who owned a large house in the hills. She received stolen property, lived luxuriously, and ran a wholesale business reselling these items. This operation was worth billions of dollars, just in LA County."

Retail theft rings operate with a high degree of organization and coordination. Thieves target high-value items such as electronics, designer clothing, and luxury goods. These items are then quickly transferred to fences who resell them, often online, through platforms like Amazon and eBay, or in underground markets. This organized network illustrates the complexity and scale of modern criminal operations, where traditional theft merges with digital platforms to create new challenges for law enforcement.

Incidents in California are particularly severe. According to Brian Dodge, President of the Retail Industry Leaders Association (RILA), policy decisions in the state have made it easier for criminals to avoid prosecution and recruit individuals for theft operations. California's approach to shoplifting—prosecuting incidents under $950 as misdemeanors—has inadvertently fueled the rise in organized retail crime. Misdemeanors, punishable by up to six months in county jail or a fine up to $1,000, rarely serve as a deterrent. As a result, high-profile incidents, such as the ransacking of a Nordstrom store in Los Angeles, where $60,000 to $100,000 worth of merchandise was stolen, have become more frequent and brazen.

The economic impact of these theft rings is staggering. Organized retail crime is estimated to cost the retail industry nearly $100 billion annually. This loss not only affects large retailers but also small businesses that struggle to absorb the financial hits. Los Angeles County has seen the highest rates of commercial robbery in the state. From 2019 to 2022, commercial robberies increased by 13.3%, with a notable 9.1% uptick in 2022 alone. Additionally, Los Angeles saw an 81% rise in shoplifting in 2023. California leads with an estimated $7.837 billion in annual revenue losses due to retail theft.[3]

The legislative environment in California has also contributed to the persistence of these crimes. Most thefts under $950 result in a citation with no fine or jail time. This leniency has created a low-risk, high-reward scenario for criminals, encouraging repeated offenses and the recruitment of new individuals into these operations.

The impact of retail theft rings extends beyond economic losses. These crimes contribute to a sense of insecurity and chaos across the state. The unabated frequency of such thefts invariably damage business confidence, reduce investment, and, ultimately, contribute to economic downturn in local economies. As businesses close or relocate due to the constant threat of theft, job losses and reduced economic activity follow, further destabilizing communities.

To combat the rise of organized retail crime, law enforcement agencies have been increasing their efforts to dismantle these networks. Task forces have been established to specifically address retail theft, focusing on both prevention and prosecution. However, these efforts require significant resources and coordination across multiple jurisdictions, highlighting the need for a comprehensive and sustained approach.

Retailers are investing in advanced security measures, such as surveillance technology, electronic article surveillance (EAS) tags, and employee training programs to prevent theft and improve response times. Community awareness campaigns are also being launched to educate the public on how to report suspicious activities and support local businesses in their fight against retail crime.

The rise of retail theft rings underscores the evolving nature of crime in urban areas. These networks leverage technology and exploit legal loopholes, presenting complex challenges for law enforcement and businesses. Addressing this issue requires a holistic approach that combines stringent legal measures, robust law enforcement actions, and community engagement to restore safety and economic stability to affected areas.

Organized groups are often behind significant heists, using tactics like disabling security systems and targeting high-value items like designer handbags and luxury watches. Recent data suggests an increase in burglaries by organized groups, especially from South America. Retail theft leads to higher security costs, increased insurance premiums, and higher consumer prices, burdening both businesses and consumers.

The rampant retail theft rings in California represent a visceral and damning indictment of the state's failing policies. This criminal enterprise, thriving amidst legislative leniency, demands urgent and comprehensive reforms to protect businesses, restore public safety, and reinvigorate the state's economic stability.

Flocking

Industrialized theft has reached staggering levels, as evidenced by the phenomenon known as "flocking," a burglary trend in Los Angeles mainly targeting affluent neighborhoods. The term "flocking" comes from the idea of seagulls flocking to a target, reflecting the volume and relentlessness of these burglaries, and the coordinated manner in which these thieves navigate areas to loot.

Flocking involves groups of gang members—often from rival gangs but operating under temporary ceasefire to execute the crimes—who converge on high-end neighborhoods to commit residential burglaries. Gang members often wear button-down shirts and polished shoes to blend into affluent areas. They use luxury sedans to avoid suspicion while scouting for potential target homes. Detective Mike Maher outlines the scale of these activities: "It's a huge industry. It just is. And it's over and over again. And you do it daily and daily and daily, and daily you're making tens and hundreds of thousands of dollars of cash every day."

Flocking is a methodical approach to burglary, indicative of a sophisticated understanding of both physical security measures and social behaviors. "Residential burglaries became the engine to finance the gang," Maher explains. "The thought was it's an easy crime. You sell dope in the street. The Mexicans will kill you. If you break into a house, nobody is going to hurt you. So break in the house. Not violent. Not scary. It's easy. So easy they're doing $10k-$20k a day."[4]

During a typical flocking burglary, which will usually happen mid-day during the work week, a team of burglars will stalk a house they believe to be empty, knock on the front door of the target, and if no one answers they break in. In cases where someone answers, the burglar will typically pretend to be lost and leave. Flockers look for homes that appear to have no security cameras and they will take anything easy to fence—cash, jewelry, weapons, etc.

The burglars usually select different gang members each day to avoid being noticed repeatedly in the same neighborhood. The burglaries are swift, with perpetrators aiming to be in and out quickly, often within three minutes if no audible alarm sounds.

This crime trend has permeated popular culture, with references in music and even in merchandise sold by the burglars themselves. Detective Maher notes, "There are rap singers who sing and make videos about flocking. It's become an underground lifestyle. There are flockers, professional burglars who run pop up stores down on the west side on Melrose, where they sell flocking T-shirts and hats. You know, it's a Benjamin Franklin with a tattoo and he's running with a bag of money. That's their little emblem of flocking."[5, 6]

Flocking has become such a meticulous, well-honed craft that some gangs train other gangs on how to flock, for which they're paid a consulting fee. Detective Bailey describes the Rollin' 30s, a notorious South LA gang, credited with refining the flocking technique, that trains other gangs in these methods: "They're credited with being the first ones to perfect the skill of flocking. They're cadre members now. They show up to your neighborhood. They teach your guys how to flock. They take you out on a mission. The mission is successful. You pay me a fee for training you and I'm out. And now your hood knows how to how to properly do flocking: how to scout locations, how to look the part, what car to drive, what clothes to wear, which houses to try to hit, which neighborhood, they even go down to the demographic."

Law enforcement faces significant challenges in dismantling these networks due to their sophistication and the sheer volume of crimes committed. Once again, the LAPD appears remarkably impotent in the face of this plundering and advise residents (if they can afford it) to fortify their homes with advanced surveillance systems, smart home security, and attack dogs.

Jugging

"Jugging," the ghetto term for highway robbery, is a notable crime trend in Los Angeles in which organized burglary crews target and follow individuals from banks to rob them of large withdrawals. These burglary crews are often from out-of-state, and notably linked to Houston. Detective Maher describes the prototypical jugging:

> Out of state criminals will get together, fly into Los Angeles for the day to jugg. And here's what jugging is . . . you're a couple of gangsters out of Houston. Fly into LA on cash tickets or buy one-way tickets to LA, we land in LA, we go rent a car, we take the car to the local tint shop. And for $150 bucks, the local tint shop tints all

the windows in the rental car. And now we drive to banks in Asian areas. Walnut, Diamond Bar, and we'll sit in the bank parking lot. And all they do is jugging. Jugging is waiting for the little lady in her Mercedes Banz to get out like a cartoon, carrying a bag that has dollar signs on it, out of the bank. She'll throw it in her backseat and get in her car and put her visor on and she'll start driving a Mercedes with $1 or $100,000, they don't know, in her backseat, and they're driving along and they will either take her home and do a robbery. If she's stuck in traffic, they'll run up and smash the back window and just grab it out of her back window. And they'll do that for the day, maybe two or three days. They come up, make money, get back on a plane and fly back to Houston. They'll fly into LA, do the same thing and then drive up to Fremont in San Jose, very wealthy area. They'll go jugg in San Jose and Fremont. And that's just a follow-off robbery. They just sit at the banks and wait for who's the right target. See me walking out of the bank—probably not a good target. You see her walking out of the bank carrying a bag. That's probably a business owner, that's probably a cash transaction, we'll follow her wherever she goes. And she's not going to stop us from robbing or punching or whatever it may be.[7]

The LAPD believe over 100 individuals from Houston alone have flown to Los Angeles for the purpose of engaging in jugging burglaries.

Target: Asians

The Latin and Black burglary crews, of all the types described, racially profile their victims; as such, Asians have been frequently and specifically targeted. Detective Maher describes the method: "Asians carry a lot of cash. They look for shoes on the porch. So that's an Asian house. Now we know that's a good target house. They search white pages for like a Kahn—Middle Eastern names because they own jewelry stores, watch stores. It's genius."

According, to Detective Chris Murphy of the Simi Valley PD, which is just north of Los Angeles, he is inundated with cases of "East Asian immigrant doughnut shop owners being followed home and robbed, typically by Latin burglary crews."

Likewise, small shop owners from India are also on the radar screen of these brigands as Indians are known to carry gold and are likewise easy and generally defenseless marks.

In Orange County, which has a large Asian community and where these crimes have also taken root, the District Attorney has filed hate crime enhancements on burglary crews targeting Asian homeowners.

Detective Bailey notes that gangs from South LA have been hitting East Asian families in the San Gabriel Valley, knowing that older generation Asians traditionally carry a lot of cash as they are untrustworthy of banks: "They may come from a communist country where you put your money in a bank, the government may take it or the bank may just go out of business and there goes through your life savings. Right? So you keep the money with them." In California, plunder is a double-edged sword that cuts through legal working-class immigrants from both the state government and the de facto state-sponsored brigands. Equity has a hierarchy.

Conclusion

California, in its misguided pursuit of criminal justice reform, has inadvertently fostered an environment where crime thrives unabated. The state's lenient policies have transformed it into a haven for organized theft and burglary. From the industrial-scale operations of retail theft rings to the sophisticated tactics of flocking, jugging, and targeted burglaries against Asian communities, crime has become a flourishing enterprise. This paradoxical situation, where equity policies empower criminal activities, underscores the urgent need for a radical reassessment of California's legislative and enforcement strategies. The state must confront its failures and adopt stringent measures to restore order, protect its citizens, and revive its faltering economy. In the absence of such reforms, California's descent into lawlessness will only deepen, eroding public safety and trust in governance.

CHAPTER 9

CHILD SOLDIERS

Los Angeles has become a city where children are no longer spared the brutal realities of crime but are instead enlisted into its machinery. Gangs, astute in their exploitation of a lenient legal system, have turned minors into instruments of calculated violence. These are not youthful indiscretions but deliberate acts—robberies, home invasions, even murders—committed by children who understand they face little to no real consequence.

This is not an aberration but the logical outcome of a justice system dismantled by ideology. Laws like Proposition 57, celebrated as progressive reform, have stripped away accountability, creating a permissive environment where organized crime thrives. Armed with smartphones and emboldened by their legal immunity, young recruits are dispatched into affluent neighborhoods, turning acts of delinquency into high-stakes operations.

This chapter examines how systemic failures in policy and enforcement have fostered the rise of juvenile crime, exposing the role of organized crime, legislative negligence, and societal decay in turning Los Angeles into a battleground where the most vulnerable are both victims and perpetrators.

TikTok Gangsters: Weaponizing LA's Kids

Los Angeles is under siege by a new breed of criminal: children deployed as foot soldiers in the service of gangs that have turned the city into their hunting ground. No longer confined to the traditional gang strongholds of South Central and East Los Angeles, these groups are using social media and geolocation technology to target wealthier neighborhoods with precision. What was once an opportunistic crime of proximity has now become a calculated expansion, as juveniles—armed and emboldened—move into areas where residents once believed they were insulated from street-level violence.

The shift is staggering. Children as young as ten are being drafted into the ranks of gangs like the Eight Tray Crips, receiving their first assignments before they reach middle school. These minors, shielded by laws that treat them as incapable of real criminal intent, are sent to commit robberies, carjackings, and even homicides.[1] Veteran Los Angeles law enforcement officer Detective Sam Bailey has watched this transformation unfold: "The spike in crime, particularly robberies, is actually coming from the juveniles. This is different from when I started my career. Real different," he explains. Over the past decade, juvenile gang violence has metastasized into something altogether more organized and depraved:

> Probably within the last ten years, this thing really went left and slipped off the road. There was a series of carjackings, particularly by the Eight Tray Crips, they're a very large Crip gang in South Central, just east of our city. And they were picking on victims all throughout the South Bay, this area of LA County. One of their youngest carjackers was ten. His partner was twelve. We're talking armed carjacking, so they will walk up on the victim with a firearm. Ten to twelve years old.[2]

The most chilling example of this trend came in 2022 when a teenage gang member murdered rapper PnB Rock in broad daylight at a South Los Angeles restaurant. The shooter, a boy no older than sixteen, carried out the killing, then casually fled with his father—himself a longtime gang member—before escaping to Las Vegas. This was not the rash decision of a wayward youth. It was a calculated, professional hit, executed by a child already conditioned for a life of violent crime. Bailey recounts the episode: "A kid, fifteen, sixteen years old, shot and killed someone right there on the spot, and then hopped in the car with his dad, who's from the gang. And they both go to Vegas."[3]

The Rise of Social Media-Driven Crime

Social media, once a tool for trivial entertainment, has become a command center for crime. Gangs now use TikTok, Instagram, and encrypted messaging apps to flaunt stolen goods, recruit new members, and coordinate real-time operations. Platforms originally designed for viral challenges are now hosting car theft tutorials, robbery how-tos, and direct communication between gang leaders and their juvenile enforcers. These digital gangsters have adapted to an age where crime is both performative and profitable.

Oakland, another epicenter of California's juvenile crime wave, has seen a similarly grim trajectory. Acting Oakland Police Chief Darren Allison reported 100 robberies in a single week, with fifty occurring over just one weekend.[4] The perpetrators, overwhelmingly juveniles, are emboldened by a system that refuses to hold them accountable. In Los Angeles, the same dynamic is playing out. On April 23, 2024, two minors were arrested in Los Angeles's Westchester and Playa del Rey areas in connection with over ninety car break-ins and vandalism incidents dating back to January 20, 2024. The stolen items recovered included backpacks, identification cards, and credit cards. According to the LAPD, security camera footage helped identify these juveniles, who were subsequently detained in an apartment complex. The case has been forwarded to prosecutors for a filing decision.[5]

The Systematic Recruitment of Child Soldiers

Unlike past generations of gang members who were initiated through violent rites of passage, today's recruits are absorbed into the gang lifestyle through a slow and deliberate process. Detective Bailey describes how this transformation takes place:

> Traditional recruiting happens in every gang. You grow up around that gang. And the gang members are not strangers to you. A lot of them you went to school with. Normally, a divide starts to happen between the end of elementary and the beginning of middle

school—it doesn't matter if you're Hispanic, Black, whatever. That's the time of puberty for boys. They start to get emboldened, they venture farther away from home, and gang members are already in that circle of people.

For many, joining a gang is not a decision—it is an inevitability. Some children are born into gang families, where membership is inherited. In other cases, gangs provide the stability and protection that fractured homes and failing institutions fail to offer. Detective Bailey explains: "If they don't have a strong support group at home—obviously—the gang would become the family. Some of those kids' situations, the home life is so poor that the gang does become the family. They do feed them. They do clothe them. They do house them. They do keep them away from being attacked by the other neighborhood and look after them. So they start to feel obligated."

Detective Bailey notes that in some instances, joining a gang is less a factor of domestic poverty and desperation and more a legacy obligation: "Or there's the other kid. He's born into the family. Grandpa, his father, all of his uncles and cousins. They're already members of the gang. And so that kid was doomed from the beginning. The culture exists in his house. So it's family business. So he didn't even have to jump in. He can 'legacy in.' His family put in work for the hood, and he's expected to do the same."

This generational cycle of violence is not accidental—it is cultivated. California's juvenile justice system, gutted by reforms that have eliminated meaningful consequences for young offenders, has made it possible for gangs to use children as disposable assets. Proposition 57, which ended the direct transfer of juveniles to adult courts, has only deepened the crisis, ensuring that even the most heinous crimes committed by minors will be met with little more than a bureaucratic shrug.

What is happening in Los Angeles is not a temporary surge in youth crime; it is the deliberate weaponization of juveniles as criminal operatives. These young offenders are not just misguided youth who have lost their way—they are being molded, exploited, and deployed with ruthless efficiency. The result is an unprecedented wave of organized juvenile crime, a crisis that California's leadership refuses to acknowledge, let alone confront.

Legislative Impact: The Unraveling of Juvenile Justice

California's Proposition 57 was sold as a progressive step toward rehabilitating juvenile offenders, but in practice, it has transformed the state into a haven for gang recruitment. By stripping prosecutors of their authority to directly transfer juveniles to adult courts, the law has effectively neutered the justice system's ability to impose meaningful consequences on violent youth offenders. The result? A staggering 34.3% increase in juvenile arrests from 2021 to 2022, a surge fueled not by random social decay but by a calculated adaptation of gang strategy to exploit legislative weakness.[6]

Detective Sam Bailey, who has spent years observing the mutation of street crime, is blunt about the consequences: "Yes, they are having the kids do this because they're not going to go to jail." The logic is simple. Under California's current system, juvenile offenders—even those caught committing serious felonies—are often met with little more than a citation before being returned to their parents. "Most of them are so young that they get cited and sent back home to their parents," Bailey explains. "Some do end up in court, but only after their third or fourth robbery or theft."[7] By the time they reach that threshold, many have already become fully embedded in gang culture, hardened by a system that all but ensures they will suffer no real consequences.

For California's gangs, this isn't just leniency—it's a blueprint. Proposition 57 has turned children into legally bulletproof operatives, perfect for carrying out high-risk crimes without exposing the organization to severe legal consequences. Carjackings, armed robberies, and burglaries are now being delegated to juveniles with the full knowledge that the state has little appetite for holding them accountable. What was once a deterrent—fear of serious punishment—has been replaced with a revolving door of arrests and releases, ensuring that for every child caught, another is ready to take his place.

This is not rehabilitation. This is systemic failure, weaponized by gangs and sanctioned by legislators too ideologically committed to criminal leniency to recognize the chaos they have unleashed. Until the state acknowledges that real deterrence is necessary, juvenile crime will not just persist—it will continue to escalate, reshaping California's streets into a battleground where the law no longer applies.

Societal Changes: A Generation Raised in Lawlessness

The collapse of traditional working-class stability in California has fueled the juvenile crime epidemic, creating a demographic unmoored from both economic opportunity and legal consequence. The decline of manufacturing jobs and the transition to a service-based economy have gutted pathways to stable employment for the lower socioeconomic strata, leaving a void increasingly filled by criminal enterprise. The logic is as brutal as it is predictable: where legal means of survival diminish, the underworld provides both structure and income.

Detective Bailey underscores this generational shift, describing today's juvenile offenders as smarter, more technologically adept, and less constrained by traditional gang hierarchies:

"We have the disease of the Gen Z generation. These are the teenagers you see on the street—the foot soldiers in the gang. They're smarter. They have a different worldview. They have technology in a way gang members from my generation never did. It's like the military: the more intelligence and communication you have, the better tactics you can apply on the battlefield and with more aggression. And these kids, they move differently. The society around them has changed too. Gas is up. Jobs have dried up. Some jobs that used to exist . . . they rolled up . . . factory jobs are rolled up. We're going from a manufacturing society to a service society. And the whole lower half of society—black, white, Hispanic, Asian, pick a demographic, it doesn't matter—all those kids are involved in the underworld. They have one foot in it."

Bailey's assessment is damning: for young offenders, criminality is no longer a deviation but a calculated career path—one shaped by economic displacement wrought by globalization, the financialization of the economy, and the erosion of stable working-class opportunities. With manufacturing gutted and traditional pathways to stability vanishing, crime offers both structure and profit. Compounding this is a legal system that, in its refusal to impose meaningful consequences, has abandoned these juveniles not only to gang exploitation but to their own worst impulses.

Legal Context and Impact on Prosecution

California's juvenile justice reforms, framed as humanitarian efforts to rehabilitate young offenders, have instead given gangs an invaluable recruiting tool. By dismantling mechanisms that once allowed the justice system to hold teenage criminals accountable, these policies have emboldened criminal syndicates to use minors as expendable assets. Proposition 57, a hallmark of this misguided agenda, has made it nearly impossible to prosecute juveniles as adults, stripping the legal system of its most effective deterrents.

Los Angeles District Attorney George Gascón has exemplified this shift, implementing policies that prioritize ideology over public safety. His office categorically refused to allow Deputy District Attorneys from transferring juveniles to adult court or state prisons, even in cases of extreme violence. He has also reversed many cases that had held previously held young offenders accountable. Kathleen Cady, a former prosecutor, describes this policy dereliction with stark clarity:

"He [Gascón] would never allow someone who was under eighteen, who committed a crime, to go to adult court. And children should never be prosecuted in adult court ever, period, end of sentence. So that means if a seventeen-year-old on the eve of his eighteenth birthday decides to be one of these mass murderers and go to his high school and kill twenty people, well, he's a minor, and we must treat children as children, so he could never be prosecuted in adult court."

Cady further explains the implications: "When you're prosecuted in juvenile court, juvenile court jurisdiction ends when you're twenty-five, so it doesn't matter what your crime was. When you hit twenty-five, there's no longer juvenile jurisdiction, so you get released from custody period."[8]

The consequences of such policies are visible in hard numbers. In 2022, there were just fifty-nine adult-level court dispositions for juvenile offenders in California—a staggeringly low figure for a state grappling with an explosion in juvenile crime. This near-immunity incentivizes recidivism, emboldening young offenders and reinforcing a culture where criminality is consequence-free.

Gascón's policy of outright barring his office from transferring juveniles to adult court notwithstanding the extreme or heinous nature of the case was attenuated slightly after immense public backlash. Gascón responded with a performative concession, establishing a committee—largely composed of individuals from the public defender's office—to review and decide on transfers.[9] Former Los Angeles County District Attorney Steve Cooley explained the impact of this ideological reengineering: "When he came into office, he got a deputy public defender, who is an expert in juvenile law to come over and unwind the eighty-eight cases where Jackie Lacey's office [Lacey is the former Los Angeles District Attorney preceding Gascón] had sought to transfer juvenile offenders to state prison. It was an ideological purge, not a legal decision."

By minimizing the consequences for these young offenders, the system sent a dangerously permissive signal, emboldening gang recruiters to exploit even younger children; and understanding the procedural dynamic in Los Angeles, gangs made a logical calculus: send in the kids, because the state won't touch them.

The Catastrophic Closure of Youth Prisons

California's closure of state-run youth prisons, hailed by progressives as a victory for rehabilitation, has proven to be a catastrophic miscalculation. Senate Bill 823, which transferred the responsibility of juvenile incarceration from state-run facilities to county-level programs, has produced precisely the chaos its critics predicted.

County probation departments, ill-equipped to handle serious juvenile offenders, have been inundated with cases they lack the resources or experience to manage. Instead of rehabilitating young criminals, the system now cycles them through short-term county facilities, where recidivism rates remain alarmingly high. These facilities, originally designed for minor offenses, are now housing violent offenders without the capacity to control them.

The result? Young offenders, many of them hardened by gang culture and trauma, cycle in and out of custody with no serious intervention—fueling the very crisis these reforms were supposed to solve. Juvenile detention in California is no longer a deterrent; it is a revolving door, offering offenders little more than a brief inconvenience before they return to the streets.

The Escalation of Juvenile Violence: A Failing System Exposed

California's juvenile justice system is failing on every front, and the numbers confirm it. Despite the shuttering of state-run youth detention centers under the pretense of criminal justice reform, juvenile crime is not declining—it is accelerating at an alarming rate. In Los Angeles County and beyond, youth incarceration rates are climbing, exposing the failure of a system that has abandoned deterrence in favor of ideological leniency. The *Juvenile Justice in California 2022* report by the Criminal Justice Statistics Center documents a 34.3% spike in juvenile arrests from 2021 to 2022, with a staggering 45.8% of these arrests involving felonies—a stunning reversal of the state's claims that rehabilitation policies would curb youth crime.[10] Meanwhile, adult arrests *declined by 3.8%* during the same period, underscoring the unique and growing crisis of juvenile delinquency.

The trend did not abate in 2023. Juvenile arrests spiked again—this time by 27.2%—with 50.1% of these cases classified as felonies.[11] In contrast, adult arrests saw only a 2.1% uptick, reinforcing what law enforcement officials like Sam Bailey have long warned: Juveniles, emboldened by policies that shield them from serious consequences, are fueling California's crime epidemic.[12]

This explosion in youth crime is not occurring in isolation; it mirrors the broader surge in violent offenses across the state. In 2022, violent crime increased by 6.1%, with aggravated assaults and robberies driving much of the rise.[13] The correlation between lenient juvenile policies and the spike in serious crimes is impossible to ignore. And while some officials tout minor reductions in crime in early 2023, cities like Oakland have seen record-breaking increases in violent offenses, proving that the erosion of accountability for young offenders is not merely a failure of policy—it is a blueprint for societal collapse.[14]

The Changing Face of Juvenile Crime: Who Commits, Who Suffers

Juvenile crime data reveals stark racial, ethnic, and gender disparities at every stage of the justice system. In 2022, Black and Hispanic youth were disproportionately represented, accounting for 57.1% and 48.3% of petitions filed, respectively. Black juveniles had the highest rates of felony arrests among offenders aged ten to seventeen, a reality no amount of progressive rhetoric can obscure.[15]

An equally alarming trend is the rise in violent crime among female offenders. Once a statistical anomaly in gang-related violence, young women are increasingly responsible for serious offenses. In 2022, females surpassed males in arrests for misdemeanor assault and battery (49.1% vs. 38.3%) and theft (12.3% vs. 7.5%). Even among felony arrests, a higher percentage of female offenders (53.9%) were arrested for violent crimes compared to 42.3% of males.[16]

Although males still dominate overall felony arrests (50.6% of all male juvenile arrests in 2022, compared to 31.1% for females), the escalation of violence among young women is unmistakable. The evolving landscape of juvenile crime underscores not only racial and ethnic disparities—with minorities consistently overrepresented in arrests and petition filings—but also a shifting gender dynamic, as female juvenile offenders play an increasing role in violent crime.[17,18]

Juvenile Crime by Numbers: Key Statistics

Juvenile Felony Violent Offenses

- A greater percentage of females were referred for felony violent offenses compared to males (46.2% vs. 36.5%).
- In 2022, a larger percentage of females were arrested for misdemeanor assault and battery (49.1%) and theft offenses (12.3%) than males (38.3% and 7.5%, respectively).
- Among females arrested for felonies, 53.9% were for violent offenses, compared to 42.3% for males. This shows a higher proportion of females involved in violent felonies within their specific group but does not outnumber male arrests overall.

Juvenile Felony Arrests

- In 2022, males accounted for the majority of juvenile arrests. Of the 19,574 arrests of males, 50.6% were for felonies (9,905 arrests). In contrast, there were 6,426 arrests of females, with 31.1% being for felonies (1,997 arrests).

- Males are more frequently arrested overall and for more felonies compared to females. However, within the arrested population, a higher percentage of females are involved in specific categories of offenses like felony violence and misdemeanor assault and battery.
- Black and Latino youth accounted for 80% of all felony arrests involving juveniles under age eighteen in California in 2020.

Conclusion

California's juvenile justice system has not merely failed—it has become an instrument of criminal reproduction. The state's decision to close youth detention centers, coupled with legal reforms that have stripped the system of deterrence, has ensured that juvenile crime does not just persist but flourishes. Gangs, ever attuned to the weaknesses of their environment, have filled the void, molding young offenders into efficient operatives who know that, whatever their crime, the worst they will face is a temporary citation and a return to the streets. The state has not merely tolerated this arrangement; it has enabled it.

This is not a breakdown of order—it is the calculated result of policies designed by people who mistake leniency for virtue and see consequences as cruelty. The assumption that juvenile offenders are mere victims of circumstance, rather than knowing participants in an economy of violence, has gutted the justice system of its purpose. The idea that reducing penalties would lead to fewer crimes was always a fantasy peddled by those who do not have to live with the consequences. The reality is that the young offenders who terrorize cities like Los Angeles and Oakland have rationally assessed the legal environment and concluded—correctly—that it rewards transgression.

California is not failing to address juvenile crime; it is actively manufacturing it. A legal system that refuses to punish, a political class that refuses to govern, and a social order that refuses to protect its citizens have all conspired to turn crime into a viable career path. Until deterrence is restored—until there is something to fear beyond a citation—the state will continue to produce not just criminals, but generations of them, learning early that the law does not apply to those willing to ignore it.

CHAPTER 10

WARLORDS

California is no longer merely grappling with the scourge of organized crime—it is defined by it. The state has become a territory governed as much by gang syndicates as by its elected officials, with Los Angeles standing as its most glaring example. Here, crime is no longer an aberration but a parallel system of governance, a shadow sovereignty whose reach extends from the streets to the prisons and beyond state borders to transnational trafficking networks. The designation of Los Angeles as the "Gang Capital of America" is not rhetorical flourish; it is a grim reality that reflects the failure of the state to impose order in the face of organized criminal empires.

The dominance of these gangs—led by the likes of the Mexican Mafia and MS-13—is not a spontaneous development but a direct consequence of systemic neglect, failed policies, and demographic shifts that the political class refuses to address. Unchecked illegal immigration has created isolated enclaves where the state's authority is practically nonexistent, and in the absence of governance, these communities have become breeding grounds for criminal recruitment. These are not chaotic street gangs but calculated enterprises that rival multinational corporations in their efficiency and structure, controlling not just drug trafficking but extortion, human smuggling, and violence with ruthless precision.

This chapter examines how California has become a willing accomplice in its own subjugation to gang power. From policies like

Proposition 57 that have gutted the justice system's deterrent power to the endemic corruption within the state's prison system, the narrative is one of systemic failure at every level. By dissecting the rise of California's gangs, this chapter lays bare the complicity of a political apparatus more interested in virtue-signaling than in confronting the hard truths of governance. What emerges is a portrait of a state in decline, where justice has been supplanted by the rule of criminal syndicates and the institutions designed to combat them have become instruments of their proliferation.

Enclaves of Impunity: The Recruitment Grounds for Organized Crime

California's gang crisis is not a law enforcement failure—it is the predictable result of a state that has systematically abdicated control over its own territory. The unchecked influx of illegal immigrants, far from fostering the utopian vision of diversity incessantly championed by its political class, has instead created isolated, impoverished enclaves where law enforcement exists only in theory, and governance is outsourced to the most ruthless actors willing to impose order. These are not communities in any meaningful sense; they are neglected buffer zones where the state has withdrawn, leaving behind pockets of ungoverned space that function as breeding grounds for organized crime.

For the cartels and street syndicates, these enclaves are more than hideouts—they are fertile recruiting grounds, where gangs inherit their next generation of enforcers from a population trapped in systemic marginalization. These neighborhoods do not suffer from random violence; they are carefully maintained zones of control, where the Mexican Mafia, MS-13, and other syndicates operate with the cold efficiency of corporate management. Extortion, drug trafficking, and human smuggling are not chaotic enterprises but well-structured economic systems, optimized for maximum profit and minimal disruption by law enforcement. Gangs function as the de facto power in these regions, levying taxes, settling disputes, and providing an illicit form of security in places where the state has ceased to do so.

This is not merely a law enforcement failure—it is a state-sanctioned retreat from governance itself. Gangs are no longer evading the law; they are leveraging it. The very legislative framework designed to rehabilitate offenders has instead become an asset to criminal syndicates, enabling their growth and shielding them from meaningful consequences. California's political class, too preoccupied with ideological posturing, has enabled this metastasis. The result is a state where entire urban regions function as de facto fiefdoms of organized crime, a parallel system of governance built on fear, brutality, and absolute control.

The most damning aspect of this crisis is not merely that gangs exist—it is that they thrive by exploiting the very legal system meant to suppress them. California's political class, rather than confronting the metastasizing influence of organized crime, has facilitated its spread through a blend of ideological blindness and legislative negligence. Laws like Proposition 57, ostensibly designed to reform sentencing for non-violent offenders, have in practice provided a revolving door for juvenile criminals, many of whom are groomed by gangs precisely because of their legal insulation. Meanwhile, California's prisons, far from serving as deterrents, have become corporate headquarters for these syndicates, where incarcerated gang leaders command operations with impunity. The Mexican Mafia, in particular, wields enormous power behind bars, orchestrating operations with the precision of a multinational corporation. For these gangs, incarceration is not a setback but an opportunity—a secure base from which to consolidate their control over both the streets and the state's fragmented justice system. The state has not merely failed to contain these organizations—it has institutionalized their power.

What remains is a grotesque inversion of justice: gangs are no longer evading the law; they are weaponizing it. They have learned to navigate its loopholes, exploit its leniency, and manipulate its blind spots to expand their operations with impunity. California, in its refusal to impose control, has created a power vacuum—one that has been filled not by civic institutions, but by ruthless criminal empires that now dictate the rules of entire regions. The result is a state where governance has been outsourced to organized crime, and where the citizens abandoned within these enclaves live under the dominion of syndicates that operate with a brutality the state itself is too feeble to counter.

Los Angeles: "Gang Capital of America"

California, and particularly Los Angeles County, stands as the stark epitome of a gang-infested nation. Since the 1930's, Los Angeles has been called the "gang capital of America." This is not hyperbole, but a sobering truth supported by decades of entrenched gang activity and sophisticated criminal networks that permeate the state. California's prison yards and inner-city streets have birthed some of the most murderous and destructive gangs in U.S. history. These brigands are not merely local nuisances; they are, in many cases, formidable terror organizations with transnational reach and political influence. Gangs like the Mexican Mafia and MS-13 have transcended Los Angeles barrios, metastasizing into highly organized syndicates shaping the criminal landscape both within and beyond California's borders. Indeed, gangster culture is definitively a hallmark of California's exports, created to a significant degree by California's signature imports: illegal aliens.

The numbers, though imprecise due to the state's deliberate refusal to conduct recent gang censuses, remain staggering. According to a 2010 estimate by the California Department of Justice, the state harbored approximately 300,000 gang members—nearly equivalent to the entire Army National Guard.[1,2] Likewise, there has not been a recent gang census in Los Angeles County, but the National Drug Intelligence Center within the Justice Department, estimated that in 2007, Los Angeles County harbored somewhere between 80,000 and 140,000 gang members, who were affiliated with 3,400 active street gangs.[3,4] For many residents, these figures are not just statistics but the defining reality of daily life—a cityscape fractured into fiefdoms of extortion, drug distribution, and racketeering.

This vast criminal underworld is not an amorphous swarm of violent misfits—it is structured, disciplined, and, above all, deeply entrenched. California is home to more than 6,000 distinct gangs, varying in sophistication from hyper-local cliques to transnational networks with ties to drug cartels and human trafficking syndicates.[5] The Justice Department's most recent estimates suggest that the estimated gang population nationwide stands between 750,000 and 1.4 million gang members, affiliated with at least 33,000 distinct gangs.[6] California accounts for a disproportionate share of that figure. Los Angeles, more than any other city in the nation, epitomizes this crisis, its gang problem not merely a public safety issue but a geopolitical liability.

Demographic Shifts and the Rise of Latino Gangs

Latinos overwhelmingly dominate California's gang landscape. According to the California Gang Database, the first and largest shared gang database in the U.S., in 2023 Latinos were believed to constitute 67% of the state's gang members, followed by 23% Black, 7% White, and 3% Asian.[7] These numbers are not incidental; they reflect seismic shifts that have fundamentally reshaped California's social order. Since the 1990s, mass illegal migration has swelled the state's Latino population, fostering an environment where gang culture is not only sustained but increasingly entrenched.

The state's decades-long refusal to enforce federal immigration laws has not simply enabled this crisis; it has institutionalized it. The unrestrained influx of illegal immigrants has created densely packed enclaves of poverty, where the rule of law is tenuous at best and where criminal enterprises serve as the only functioning authority. These communities—alienated from broader civic society, economically marginalized, and shielded from scrutiny by a political class beholden to "diversity" at any cost—have become the ideal recruitment pools for gangs.

This process of entrenchment is self-perpetuating. As California's public services buckle under the weight of its imported peasantry, entire neighborhoods have morphed into American favelas, where gangs provide the structure that the state refuses to impose. Within these isolated pockets, young recruits are indoctrinated early, conditioned to see crime not as a deviation but as a birthright. Social media has only accelerated this phenomenon, turning gang affiliation into a lifestyle brand, where cartel-glorifying narco-culture is celebrated in rap videos and Instagram reels.

Detective Bailey provides a stark account of this demographic transformation:

> We have an economic downturn, price of gold goes through the roof. At the same time, you sort of see the streets of LA, probably from 2000 to 2010: South Central Los Angeles, Southern Los Angeles is turning from black to brown. With all of Southern

California becoming more, much more brown. It's not just black or
white. And so the power in the streets began to change. Compton
historically was a black gang infested and rap, you know, "*Straight
Outta Compton.*" Today it's probably 80%, Latino, Hispanic.
Maybe more. Really. I mean, the whole dynamics of Los Angeles
have begun to change.

This displacement is not just a shift in numbers; it is a fundamental
restructuring of power. With the decline of Black gang influence, Latino
gangs—led by the Mexican Mafia and its affiliates—have consolidated
their hold over the region, enforcing a hierarchical, cartel-style model of
control. What has emerged is not random street violence but an organized, paramilitary-like structure that dictates the drug trade, extortion
rackets, and even local political influence.

California's gang crisis is not an accident. It is the logical consequence
of a state that has systematically eroded its own sovereignty, prioritizing ideological vanity over the basic functions of governance. The rise of
Latino gang dominance is inseparable from the state's refusal to enforce
immigration laws, its dismantling of prosecutorial power, and its obsession with "reform" at the expense of public safety.

The criminal syndicates operating out of Los Angeles are not hiding in
the shadows—they are thriving in plain sight, aided by policies that grant
them operational impunity. This is not a crisis of enforcement alone; it is
a crisis of deliberate political neglect. And unless California's leaders are
willing to acknowledge the scale of this disaster, the state's future is all but
sealed: a patchwork of gang-ruled enclaves, where the only laws that matter are the ones dictated by criminal enterprises.

Gang Crime Is Organized Crime: Corporate Strategy

California's gangs are not mindless hordes of violent criminals—they are
sophisticated, multi-tiered organizations that function with the precision
and foresight of diversified corporate enterprises. From drug trafficking
and human smuggling to large-scale burglary, extortion, and fraud, these
syndicates generate tens of billions annually, feeding a vast black-market
economy estimated to be in the hundreds of billions. The Mexican drug

cartels, acting as the primary suppliers of narcotics, ensure a steady flow of illicit revenue, while street-level gangs serve as the retail arms and tariff enforcers of this highly structured supply chain.

The public clings to an outdated caricature of gang members as reckless, uncoordinated thugs engaging in random street violence. But as Kathleen Cady, a former LA County prosecutor, explains, this assumption dangerously underestimates their strategic capabilities:

> The general public thinks gang members are crude, that they don't think much, that they're just out to wreak havoc and violence. That's not accurate. There are going to be some gang members who are like that, but the way gangs get their power is money. And they're just like any corporation. They look around at the market. The market represents all the potential victims, and they figure out where the weak spots are.

Gangs are keen observers of legal and political shifts, adapting their tactics to exploit weaknesses in California's criminal justice system with chilling efficiency. Cady continues:

> If the weak spot is that juveniles aren't being prosecuted, well, then we'll just have the juveniles commit the crime. If another weak spot is property crimes, and we can just go in and do the smash and grabs and nothing happens to us other than we get a ticket, then we'll do that. If prostitution isn't being policed anymore, then we'll just go out and use girls or boys potentially, because we can use them over and over and over again, unlike drugs, which we can only sell once. So they look at the market and they figure out, how can we make the most money?[8]

This is not disorder—it is a meticulously economic model, in which state and local policies serve as nothing more than industry variables, to be analyzed and leveraged like fluctuations in supply chains or shifts in regulatory policies. California's gangs are not surviving despite the state's policies; they are thriving because of them. Whether it's utilizing children for

violent crimes to avoid adult sentencing or capitalizing on toothless property crime laws, California gangs demonstrate a remarkable aptitude for
survival and adaptation within the legitimate political economy, adroitly
navigating the vicissitudes of California's failing justice system.

Detective Bailey dismantles the Hollywood myth of gang culture as
a collection of visible street hoods posturing on forsaken corners of Los
Angeles:

> They organize things from a distance. You'll never see them stand-
> ing on a corner with a rag hanging out their pocket. That's people's
> perception of gang membership . . . that's *Colors* [the 1988 film]. It's
> the guy sitting in a polo shirt, sipping tea at a coffee shop and he's
> running the whole thing. And you'll never see obvious, identifiable
> gang members . . . you'll never see them in public with each other.
> Because there are layers of separation between them. It's no different
> in the Mafia.

This layered approach to criminal governance mimics that of high-level
financial crime syndicates. California's gang leaders have learned that real
power does not come from street fights but from institutional infiltration, economic dominance, and legal insulation. The state, whether by
incompetence or ideological blindness, has furnished them with a *de
facto business model*—one in which the failure to enforce laws and build
a criminal justice system based on criminal justice reform, serves as a
financial boon to organized crime. This is not random criminality but a
fully developed, self-sustaining ecosystem of exploitation and violence,
in which the state's failures become assets in gang's relentless pursuit of
illicit market share.

Prisons Rule the Street

Within the California prison system exists a thriving underground economy controlled by ethno-tribal warbands, which transact billions annually
and command an army of street gangs from whom they collect "taxes" in
a manner reminiscent of a feudal lord. The state may claim dominion over
the penal system, but in reality, it is the prison gangs that rule, issuing

directives that reverberate from the yards of maximum-security facilities to the streets of Los Angeles.

As of 2023, the California Department of Corrections and Rehabilitation (CDCR) reports over 30,000 identified gang members within a prison population of 95,000.[9,10] These inmates maintain robust affiliations, exerting control over operations both inside and outside prison walls. The prison gang culture, particularly dominated by the Mexican Mafia, significantly impacts the behavior and structure of street gangs through sophisticated communication networks and alliances formed within the prison environment.

Sergeant Michael Maher (ret.), of the Los Angeles Sheriff's Department Major Crimes Bureau provides a stark explanation: "The prison system runs the streets. Because if you're caught in the street, you're going to prison. And how you are received in prison is what motivates how you behave on the street. If you disrespect people on the street, get caught by the cops—nobody cares about the cops catching you. When you go to prison, you pay your price there."

Prison is not a deterrent; it is an induction. For low-level gang members, arrest is neither a setback nor a miscalculation—it is a rite of passage, a formal step into deeper criminal entrenchment where incarceration serves as an advanced education rather than a punishment. As Detective Mike Maher explains, "putting in work for the gang" is not merely expected—it is mandatory. Arrest is a logistical inevitability, an eventuality baked into the career trajectory of organized crime. But prison is not where their power ends; it is where it consolidates.

Profits extorted from the streets do not trickle up; they flow in a regimented financial system, with prison gangs extracting "taxes" from their street-level affiliates. Inmates are not merely confined—they are governed. Their fate behind bars depends not on the justice system, but on the authority of the gang leadership inside. The Mexican Mafia and other prison syndicates adjudicate discipline, administer punishment, and enforce hierarchy with a precision the state cannot match. California's prisons are not correctional facilities in any meaningful sense—they are a parallel governance structure, adjudicating gang justice, which, in many cases, is the only justice that truly exists.

Even bitter rivals are bound to a singular order. Latino street gangs, which may slaughter each other with abandon outside, submit without question to the authority of the Mexican Mafia the moment they enter prison. The lines drawn in neighborhoods vanish behind bars. The Mexican Mafia's dominion is absolute, not only in prison but over the entirety of California's criminal underworld. They are the de facto state within a state, the unchallenged architects of the violence that spills onto the streets.

Mechanisms of Infiltration

That California's organized crime is orchestrated from inside its own prisons should be a national scandal. But, like so many grotesque realities of the state's dysfunction, it is treated with a mixture of bureaucratic indifference and quiet acceptance. The fact that convicted criminals can direct criminal enterprises from behind bars is not a failure of enforcement in theory—it is a demonstration of enforcement's nonexistence. A prison system that does not incapacitate criminals is not a prison system at all; it is a logistical hub for gang operations.

The corruption facilitating this control is not incidental—it is systemic. Prison gangs recruit and coerce staff into smuggling contraband, including drugs and cell phones, allowing uninterrupted communication with street operations. Reports from the CDCR detail the persistence of contraband phones, which serve as command terminals for cartel-affiliated bosses. From inside their cells, they issue orders, conduct business, and execute punishments.

This subjugation extends beyond bribery. Threats against the families of corrections officers are common, a silent yet effective tool that ensures compliance where money fails. Those who refuse to cooperate may find themselves marked—inside and outside the prison walls. The result is an institution compromised at every level, a fortress with its gates permanently open from within.

Recruitment in prison follows the same pattern. Young offenders who enter the system quickly fall under the control of established prison gangs, locked into a hierarchy that is impossible to escape. Detective Sam Bailey describes the structured nature of this control:

"Every gang leans to a hierarchy. There is no street organization that does not answer to a higher organized entity. . . . All the Sureños that claim to have a 13 tag on to their gang name are either actively planning taxes or actively paying taxes to a tax collector that's attached to the Mexican Mafia."

Street gangs are not independent actors; they are foot soldiers in a vast criminal enterprise directed from within prison walls. They execute the orders of incarcerated shot-callers, ensuring the uninterrupted flow of narcotics, extortion payments, and targeted violence. The relationship is symbiotic—street gangs provide manpower and revenue, while prison gangs offer protection, coordination, and an unbreakable chain of command that extends beyond the walls of any correctional facility. The financial power wielded by prison gangs is immense, with organized extortion rackets and drug distribution pipelines operating as regimented industries. Every operation, from small-time drug sales to large-scale human trafficking, feeds a sophisticated economic structure controlled by those who, ostensibly, are behind bars.

No organization embodies this dynamic more than the Mexican Mafia, the undisputed sovereign of California's Latino gang underworld. Though individual street gangs may be bitter rivals on the outside, their feuds evaporate upon entering the prison system. Once inside, they answer to a singular authority—La Eme. The Mexican Mafia does not just govern the prisons; it dictates the rules of the streets. To understand the criminal ecosystem of California, one must first understand the organization that stands at its apex.

The Mexican Mafia: The Invisible Hand of California's Underworld

The undisputed power in the California prison system is the Mexican Mafia, or La Eme, a prison gang which originated in the 1960's as a consolidated protection racket for Latino inmates, regardless of national origin. The Mexican Mafia's power stems in part from the surfeit representation of Hispanics in prison. More than any other faction within the prison system, which is segmented by race, the Mexican Mafia has established itself as the ultimate authority and indeed, judiciary, across all Hispanic gangs in California. In recent decades, the Mexican Mafia has also become a semi-proxy of the Mexican drug cartel, from whom it buys wholesale and whose affiliates on the street have exclusive narcotics distribution rights.

La Eme has a hierarchical structure, with orders and commands extending from high-ranking members in prison to associates on the streets. The Mexican Mafia commands respect through extreme violence and has a vast intelligence network. They have sympathizers in various law enforcement and government. The gang culture is deeply embedded, making it difficult for law enforcement to dismantle. Despite numerous RICO cases, the Mexican Mafia adapts and continues to operate. Their legacy spans multiple generations within the Latino community. They possess the ability to manipulate situations both within prisons and on the streets, leveraging relationships with corrupt officials and using organized crime tactics to sustain their power.

Within the prison system, La Eme enforces strict rules and commands, including issuing "green light" orders for violence against specific targets. They hold ultimate authority over their members and can direct violent actions swiftly and efficiently. This system of control and discipline extends to their operatives on the streets, ensuring cohesive operations These gangs are organized and work as a unit, under the directive brain of the Mexican Mafia. The prison gang provides orders and maintains an extensive intelligence network, ensuring swift communication and control over its operations.

La Eme's power is not merely sustained by brute force but by a sophisticated system of governance. The organization enforces a strict hierarchy, where orders flow from high-ranking members inside the prison system down to associates on the streets. Through coded messages, smuggled contraband phones, and intermediaries posing as attorneys or family members, directives are relayed with ruthless efficiency. This ensures that even when behind bars, the Mexican Mafia maintains absolute control over its operations.

Detective Bailey illustrates the nexus of Latino street gangs operating under the Mexican Mafia's dominion:

"Inglewood is predominantly a Blood city. We have Hispanic gangs, the largest Hispanic gang is Inglewood-13. They have a Mexican Mafia member on the council in prison. They pay taxes either directly to him or whoever is the tax collector that's out of custody and walking around the streets of LA County. And they organize it. The westside all pays a particular person because they split it, the South Bay Sureño gangs pay a specific one person. Even if I'm a rival. So Inglewood-13 is a rival with Linux-13. They shoot at each other all the time. But they pay one tax collector. Because they wear that 13. And so they're claiming affiliation with the Mexican Mafia, they need to pay their dues."

Even warring gangs—who engage in deadly turf battles over street corners—submit to the higher authority of La Eme. Their rivalries end at the gates of the prison system, where they fall into rank and file under a unified criminal bureaucracy that adjudicates disputes, enforces discipline, and ensures a steady stream of revenue.

Hostile Takeover: The Cartel-Backed War on Black Gangs

For decades, Los Angeles's drug trade was dominated by black gangs aligned with the Bloods and Crips. But by the early 2000s, a seismic shift occurred—the Mexican drug cartels, through their affiliates in La Eme, orchestrated a hostile takeover of the California drug market.

The method of displacement was as brutal as it was effective. Sergeant Maher describes how black gangsters who attempt to deal dope in cartel-controlled territory are swiftly, and often gruesomely, eliminated: "They are literally decapitated by the cartel proxies in or outside of prison."

Maher explains the implications for black gangs: "If you're a black gangster on the street, you're getting arrested, you're going to prison. Prisons are run by the Mexican Mafia. Just is, by the sheer numbers."[11, 12, 13, 14, 15]

The numbers alone dictate who holds power. Hispanic gangs outnumber their black counterparts both on the street and inside prison, and sheer demographic dominance has allowed them to muscle black dealers out of the narcotics trade altogether. Black gangs, recognizing that they cannot compete with the cartel-backed Mexican Mafia, are now forced to buy directly from Latino distributors.

Detective Bailey confirms this economic restructuring:

"Black gangs don't have the dope nexus outside the country, so they have to buy directly from Hispanic gangs, who are in turn getting it directly from the Mexican drug cartels." Coordination between black gangs and the cartels has some framework, though it is typically mediated through Hispanic gangs. Bailey adds, "I'm sure there are some agreements along the way, because the black gangs still do move dope. Still do move drugs, but not to the level they used to." This layered structure adds complexity to the gang-cartel relationship, making it difficult for law enforcement to target key figures directly.

Having been systematically removed from their dominant role in the drug trade, black gangs have pivoted to other forms of criminal revenue. Their new enterprises are less dangerous, more lucrative, and do not infringe on cartel-controlled turf. The rise of flocking crews—black gangs that now target affluent neighborhoods for high-end burglaries— coincides with their forced displacement from drug markets.

Instead of selling drugs in their own territory, black gangs now target middle-class and wealthy enclaves—an ironic reversal of fortunes that sees crime spilling into areas previously insulated from gang violence. They have turned to large-scale retail theft, prostitution, and fraud, diversifying their portfolio in response to Mexican cartel domination over narcotics.

This shift is not the result of any conscious strategy but a brutal market correction dictated by sheer force. The cartel-backed Mexican Mafia reigns supreme over California's criminal underworld, and those who cannot adapt do not survive.

Legacy Black Gangs: The Crips, Bloods, and Their Evolution

No discussion of Los Angeles gang history is complete without the Crips and Bloods—once grassroots community organizations that have since become entrenched criminal institutions. These groups, which emerged from the wreckage of economic and racial strife in the late 20th century, have undergone a transformation from quasi-political neighborhood militias to transnational enterprises driven by narcotics, extortion, and organized violence.

The Crips were founded in 1969 by Raymond Washington and Stanley "Tookie" Williams, originally under the guise of community self-defense. But like most utopian projects of the era, the vision quickly gave way to a brutal reality. By the late 1970s, the organization had fractured into warring sets, and Washington's murder in 1979 sealed the gang's transition into a decentralized criminal network. The Bloods, formed in response to the Crips' aggressive territorial expansion, were not so much a singular gang as a coalition of smaller groups bound by a common enemy. What began as a defensive alliance rapidly morphed into a mirror image of the Crips, locked in an endless cycle of retaliatory violence.

By the 1980s, both gangs had outgrown their original strongholds, spreading across the country through the twin engines of crack cocaine and prison consolidation. The Reagan-era drug boom provided a financial windfall that fueled expansion, with Crip and Blood factions establishing footholds in major cities well beyond Los Angeles. What had begun as an internal feud between black gangs in South Central LA metastasized into an epidemic of violence that gripped urban America.

The Crips and Bloods in the Prison Hierarchy

The street wars may have played out in public, but true power was consolidated behind bars. In California's prison system, the hierarchy among black gangs is as rigid and structured as any paramilitary organization. Detective Bailey describes how this pyramid functions:

"For black gangs, it's level between Bloods and Crips and then their hierarchies in custody, because it's a pyramid for the blacks. So you have your street gang organizations, and then you have your in-custody disruptive groups. For Crips, it's 'Blue Note' and 'CCO: Consolidated Crip Organization.' For the Bloods it's 'BL: Bloodline' and 'United Blood Nation.' And then at the top pyramid you have 'BGF: Black Guerrilla Family.'"

At the pinnacle of this structure sits the Black Guerrilla Family (BGF), a radically ideological entity that transcends the gangland feuds of its subordinates. Unlike the Crips and Bloods, who still engage in internecine warfare, the BGF is focused on a singular target: the state itself. Their animus is not toward rival gangs, but toward the government and its functionaries, particularly law enforcement and correctional officers. "At the top of that pyramid, they are revolutionaries. They're so far off the top that Bloods and Crips stuff doesn't matter. Their enemy is the government. So that's why they're so violent in custody, because they hate cops. They hate the COs (correctional officers)."

The Black Guerrilla Family: The Revolutionary Criminal Vanguard

Unlike its prison counterparts, the Black Guerrilla Family (BGF) is not merely a gang—it is an insurrectionary movement with a criminal arm. Founded in 1966 by George Jackson, a militant Marxist-Leninist, the BGF is unique in that it views crime as a means to an ideological end. Unlike the profit-driven motives of the Mexican Mafia or Aryan Brotherhood, the BGF envisions itself as the vanguard of an armed revolutionary struggle against the U.S. government.

Jackson, who was radicalized while incarcerated, viewed the American prison system as an extension of state oppression and sought to weaponize black inmates into political foot soldiers. Under his influence, the BGF adopted a strict militarized structure, enforcing ideological indoctrination alongside gang discipline. The gang was deeply influenced by the Black Power movement, aligning itself with groups like the Black Panther Party, Weather Underground, and other revolutionary organizations.

While Jackson himself was killed in a failed prison escape in 1971, his ideology endured. The BGF remains one of the most politically charged gangs in the U.S. prison system, its members espousing a blend of black nationalism, Marxism, and militant anti-government rhetoric. Unlike the Mexican Mafia or Aryan Brotherhood, which primarily focus on expanding their economic enterprises, the BGF's primary enemy is the state itself.

"Their closest representation of government is the guy wearing a badge and walking a tear," says Bailey. "So they gas those guys, they scare those guys, they hit them with bone."

Violence against correctional officers is not just a byproduct of criminal activity—it is part of the BGF's ideological doctrine. Their stringent organizational structure, commitment to an anti-government cause, and willingness to employ extreme violence make them one of the most dangerous prison gangs in America.

The BGF's Legacy: Ideology Meets Organized Crime

While the Mexican Mafia dominates the drug trade and exerts direct control over Latino gangs, the Black Guerrilla Family occupies a different, but no less influential, niche in California's criminal underworld. They are less visible but equally entrenched, wielding political ideology as both a recruitment tool and a justification for extreme violence.

The BGF operates both within and outside the prison system, maintaining strongholds in California, Maryland, and other states with high black inmate populations. Though they lack the economic muscle of the Mexican Mafia, their ideological fervor and highly structured hierarchy make them a persistent and dangerous force.

Unlike the Crips and Bloods, whose wars are rooted in territory and profit, the BGF's struggle is one of revolution—a criminal organization that views itself not as a gang, but as an army at war with the state itself.

Conclusion

California's gang crisis is not merely a problem of crime—it is a crisis of governance, an indictment of a state that has abdicated its most fundamental responsibilities. From the sprawling influence of the Mexican Mafia to the ideological militancy of the Black Guerrilla Family, organized crime has entrenched itself not just in the streets, but in the very institutions meant to suppress it. What was once a fight against lawlessness has become something darker: a war between rival governments—one criminal, one nominally legitimate—with the former often proving more disciplined, more brutal, and, crucially, more effective.

As this chapter has laid bare, California's gang apparatus does not operate in the shadows—it thrives in plain sight, exploiting a justice system that has chosen to accommodate rather than confront it. The state's refusal to enforce immigration laws has seeded vast enclaves where gangs flourish unchecked. Prison reform efforts, far from neutralizing gang leadership, have instead emboldened it, creating a system where the most hardened criminals govern from their cells with impunity. Law enforcement, underfunded and politically shackled, is left to wage an asymmetric war against syndicates whose operational discipline rivals that of multinational corporations.

Any serious effort to dismantle California's gang infrastructure requires not just reform, but rupture. The state prison system must be reclaimed from the inside, stripped of the corruption and bureaucratic rot that has allowed organized crime to dictate its own terms. Prisoners must come to fear the prison itself, not merely the internal justice meted out by gangs. This fear must be instilled through a zero-tolerance approach to corruption, beginning with immediate investigations and removals of corrupt prison staff. A rigorous system of background checks and continuous monitoring will ensure integrity and accountability among prison employees.

For inmates, especially gang leaders and high-ranking members, strict solitary confinement must be enforced to sever communication lines with their networks. Advanced surveillance systems will monitor all inmate activities and communications, utilizing contraband detection technology to prevent the smuggling of cell phones and drugs. Prison must no longer be a command center—it must become a dead end.

The prison system is so broken and the inmates so empowered, the state must necessarily look to its past for radical but warranted solutions. Public hangings in the prison yard for gang-related crimes within the prison system will serve as a stark deterrent, signaling an unyielding stance against organized crime. Expedited trials and executions for severe offenses will reinforce the severity of the state's resolve and commitment to the people. Additionally, reinstating hard labor programs will ensure that inmates contribute to society while serving their sentences, reducing the idle time that leads to further criminal plotting.

Legislative and judicial reforms must be pursued aggressively. Stringent laws facilitating the prosecution of gang activities, both inside and outside prison walls, are essential. Harsher sentencing for gang-related crimes and an expedited judicial process will ensure swift and decisive action against perpetrators. Collaboration between federal, state, and local law enforcement agencies must be strengthened to create a unified front against gang activity, sharing intelligence and resources to dismantle gang networks comprehensively. Specialized task forces will target and eliminate gang influence in specific hotspots across California. The notion that gang members, particularly juveniles, are merely victims of circumstance must be discarded; they are foot soldiers in an ongoing war, and the state must respond accordingly. The laws must be rewritten to reflect this reality, ensuring that violent offenders are permanently removed from the communities they terrorize.

Beyond enforcement, California must confront the cultural entrenchment that has turned gang life into a multi-generational inheritance.
The normalization of criminality in certain communities has created an
unbroken cycle of recruitment, radicalization, and reinvestment in violence. Reversing this will require not just police action but an ideological
counteroffensive—one that reasserts the primacy of law, national identity,
and the non-negotiable terms of citizenship.

For too long, California has treated the gang crisis as a problem to be
managed rather than eradicated. This is not a battle that can be fought
with half-measures. The state must decide whether it will reclaim its sovereignty or continue its slow drift into a failed state status, where the only
functioning authority belongs to those who enforce their will with blood
and terror.

The prisoners must no longer fear only the justice of their own underworld—they must fear the full, unrelenting force of state justice. They
must fear prison not as a mere inconvenience, but as an abyss from which
there is no return. They must come to understand, with absolute certainty,
that the era of accommodation is over, and that the will of the people—
unyielding, implacable—demands the eradication of their reign of terror.
The law must not merely contain them; it must break them, with enforcement that is swift, severe, and utterly inescapable.

CHAPTER 11

CARTELIZATION

The infiltration of Mexican drug cartels into California represents an unparalleled breach of U.S. national security. These cartels have transcended the realm of organized crime, evolving into quasi-sovereign entities that exert influence over vast territories with the sophistication of proto-states. No longer confined to drug trafficking, their reach extends into human smuggling, financial crime, and political subversion, fundamentally reshaping California's social, economic, and security landscape.

Bolstered by corruption within the Mexican government and facilitated by porous U.S. borders, the cartels operate with impunity, exploiting legal loopholes and a compromised justice system. Their operations generate billions annually, funding an empire that rivals multinational corporations in scope and efficiency. In many regions, they have imposed their own governance, exacting taxes, enforcing their own brand of law, and supplanting state authority.

This chapter examines the cartels' expansion, their economic and geopolitical influence, and the systemic failures that have enabled their rise. The crisis is no longer one of crime alone—it is an existential threat to U.S. sovereignty.

Quasi-Sovereign Empires: The Cartels' Rise to Power

Mexico's cartels are no longer mere criminal organizations; they are quasi-sovereign entities whose operations blur the lines between organized crime, terrorism, and governance. These cartels wield extraordinary power, not only through their staggering financial scale and enterprise diversification but also through their ability to project influence across borders and manipulate political systems. Unlike conventional criminal syndicates, these organizations have ascended to a level of geopolitical significance, rivaling historical entities such as the Barbary Pirates, the East India Company, and the Knights Templar in their capacity to challenge state sovereignty.

Operating as proto-states, the cartels have effectively established their own form of suzerainty. Within vast swathes of Mexico, they function as de facto rulers, imposing taxes, delivering "justice," and enforcing law through violence. This control extends into the United States, where their influence permeates communities, corrupts officials, and destabilizes public safety. Far from existing in isolation, the cartels operate with tacit support from elements within the Mexican government and elite, who either fear retribution or profit from complicity. This interdependence grants the cartels a veneer of legitimacy, enabling them to operate with near-impunity on both sides of the border.

To fully comprehend the gravity of this crisis, one must abandon the conventional lens of organized crime and view the cartels as geopolitical actors reshaping power dynamics on both local and national levels. They are not just adversaries of law enforcement but systemic threats to sovereignty, wielding their economic, political, and cultural influence with calculated precision. In their rise, the cartels expose the vulnerabilities of state institutions, exploiting gaps in governance and creating an enduring challenge to the traditional concept of nation-state authority. Addressing this unprecedented crisis demands a recognition of its true nature: the cartels are no longer simply a criminal nuisance—they are a parallel power structure, and their unchecked rise is nothing short of a national security catastrophe.

Historical Precedents: Cartel Proto-States

Throughout history, powerful non-state actors have risen to challenge the authority of states, exploiting gaps in governance to establish quasi-sovereign control over trade, territory, and populations. The Mexican drug cartels, with their immense economic influence, paramilitary capabilities, and transnational reach, evoke striking parallels to such historical entities as the Barbary Pirates, the East India Company, and the Knights Templar. These comparisons illuminate the unprecedented scope of the cartels' power and offer critical lessons in understanding—and countering—their modern dominance.

The Thread of Sovereignty

At the heart of these historical analogies is the concept of quasi-sovereignty, wherein non-state actors accumulate power rivaling that of formal governments. The Barbary Pirates, who terrorized Mediterranean trade routes from the 16th to 19th centuries, exemplify this phenomenon. Operating under the nominal protection of North African states and the Ottoman Empire, they exercised maritime suzerainty, extorting tribute and ransoms from European powers. Their unchecked control mirrors the cartels' domination of drug routes and human trafficking corridors between Mexico and the United States. Like the Barbary Pirates, who forced European nations into humiliating concessions, cartels extract economic and political leverage from the chaos they control, profiting massively from their grip on illicit trade.

The East India Company offers another instructive parallel. Initially established as a trading enterprise, it evolved into a quasi-governmental power, maintaining its own army, conducting diplomacy, and controlling vast resources. Mexican cartels operate with similar corporate-like sophistication, blending economic dominance with paramilitary force. They enforce their own laws, tax local economies, and supplant state authority, creating a shadow state whose operations seamlessly integrate violence with governance.

Economic Power and Innovation

Historically, proto-states or non-state entities have often matched or outpaced established states in their financial ingenuity; the cartels are no exception. The Knights Templar, a medieval military order, amassed enormous wealth and created financial systems that prefigured modern banking. Their ability to manage and move vast sums of money across borders resonates with the cartels' sophisticated money-laundering operations. Employing shell companies, real estate investments, and legitimate remittance channels, cartels funnel billions of dollars through financial systems while evading detection.

The cartels' economic dominance also mirrors the strategies of mafia organizations like the Sicilian Mafia and the Yakuza, which infiltrated legitimate businesses to create parallel economies. Similarly, cartels operate at the intersection of legality and criminality, blending illicit drug trafficking and human smuggling with investments in agriculture, construction, and other legitimate industries. By controlling both the underworld and elements of the legitimate economy, they entrench themselves in local and international systems, rendering their operations extraordinarily difficult to disrupt.

Challenging State Authority

Perhaps the most critical historical parallel is the cartels' ability to erode and supplant state authority. The Barbary Pirates humiliated European powers by forcing them into treaties and tribute payments, while the East India Company effectively dictated British foreign policy in India. The Knights Templar, at the height of their influence, posed such a threat to established power structures that their suppression became a geopolitical necessity.

Today, Mexican drug cartels wield comparable influence. They shape U.S. border and drug policies through corruption and intimidation, while effectively governing regions of Mexico where state institutions have failed. Their seamless cross-border operations and ability to maintain international networks highlight the unprecedented scale of their challenge to modern state sovereignty. They not only exploit weak governance but also actively undermine it, creating vacuums of authority that they are uniquely positioned to fill.

Cartelization: California and Beyond

The landscape of drug trafficking and organized crime in the United States has undergone a dramatic transformation, with Mexican drug cartels emerging as paramount criminal forces that extend their influence far beyond the southern border. Los Angeles, in particular, has become a critical hub for the import and distribution of synthetic narcotics, primarily fentanyl and methamphetamine, into the United States.

The production chain of these high-margin drugs begins in Mexico, where low-cost facilities manufacture them using chemical precursors primarily sourced from China. This international connection highlights the global dimensions of cartel operations. Beijing's capital controls create significant demand for U.S. dollars, enticing legitimate businesses to supply upstream materials to the cartels, which possess substantial cash reserves. The intertwining of Mexican and Chinese economic interests in this illicit trade exemplifies the global dimensions of cartel operations.

Within California's criminal economy, the cartels are the dominant market drivers. They wield a supra-ethnic dominion over Latino gangs—an army perhaps as large as 200,000 soldiers across the state. The tendrils of cartel influence extend deep into the country, touching every state and even the most isolated enclaves, such as Indian reservations in Montana.

Beyond California, the cartels have established strategic hubs for the U.S. market in major cities like Phoenix, Houston, Chicago, and Miami. These geographically and logistically strategic locations reflect significant gang presence and large immigrant populations, providing the cartels with both the manpower and the cover they need to operate effectively.

Tom Homan, the current Border Czar and former Acting Director of U.S. Immigration and Customs Enforcement in the Trump Administration, provides a striking perspective on the cartels' operations. Homan insists that they should be thought of as "Fortune 500 companies," highlighting their sophisticated business models, revenue projections, and operational strategies.[1] However, unlike the Fortune 500, the cartels exercise quasi-state authority over Mexican territory and project power—indeed suzerainty—over the U.S. southern border, one of the world's most important trade corridors, through which $2 billion passes daily.

The cartels' control exerted over the U.S.-Mexico border is near-absolute, as Homan starkly portrays: "The cartels totally own the border. Every single migrant who has crossed the border has paid the cartels. It is impossible to cross the border without paying the cartels. The cartels will kill anyone who crosses the border without cartel sanction and payment."

This geopolitical leverage has significant economic implications. Migrants reportedly pay between $4,000 and $20,000 each for passage into the United States. Since the advent of the Biden-Harris administration in 2021, U.S. Customs and Border Protection (CBP) has reported over 7.8 million encounters at the Southwest border. Based on these figures, the *New York Times* reports that the cartels are earning an estimated $13 billion a year from smuggling migrants alone.[2]

This massive influx of funds further entrenches the cartels' power, financing their other criminal enterprises and solidifying their status as proto-state actors both within Mexico and beyond its borders. The situation is further complicated by what Homan refers to as "got aways"— individuals who evade interception by U.S. Border Patrol. Homan expresses particular concern about the estimated 2 million "got aways," an unprecedented number that potentially represents a significant security threat.

These "got aways" are not merely statistics; they represent a clear and present danger to national security. As Homan explains, these individuals are knowingly evading interception by U.S. Border Patrol, forfeiting the opportunity to be processed and potentially receive government benefits. Their deliberate avoidance of being tracked, printed, and scanned suggests a criminal intent that goes beyond the typical motivations of illegal border crossers. Homan argues that this cohort creates "a real and abiding terror threat on the U.S. homeland."

The threat is compounded by the nature of those crossing the border. Homan chillingly highlights, "The vast majority of 'minors' coming across the border are single males in their late teens. 'Unaccompanied minors' are not minors. They are gangsters."[3] This revelation adds another layer of complexity to the already dire situation, suggesting that the cartels are not just facilitating illegal border crossings but potentially importing a ready-made criminal workforce.

Local gangs play a crucial role in the cartels' operations within the United States. As both enforcers and distributors, these gangs provide the cartels with the manpower needed to enforce their will and distribute their products. Detective Sam Bailey, a gang investigator for the Inglewood PD, explains the structure: "You have guys that are on the ground here that belong to those cartels and in return they're the wholesale guy that deals directly with the local gangs. Your largest Hispanic gangs are the ones that get the dope and then it's broken down from there and shipped to wherever their subsidiary. A lot of that dope comes into California and don't even stop here. It just keeps going."

This corporate-like structure allows for efficient distribution across the country, with California often serving as a transitory point rather than the final destination for many shipments.

The impact of this highly organized drug trade on public health is severe. The Los Angeles County Department of Public Health reports a 58% increase in fentanyl-related deaths in the past year, underscoring the deadly consequences of the cartels' operations. Fentanyl, a synthetic opioid approximately fifty to 100 times more potent than morphine and thirty to fifty times more potent than heroin, has become the cartels' flagship narcotic due to its high profitability and recurring revenue potential.

Beyond drug trafficking, the cartels have aggressively expanded their criminal portfolio, with kidnapping for ransom emerging as an increasingly lucrative enterprise. According to Detective Jamie McBride of the LAPD, cartel operatives are no longer limiting their targets to individuals involved in the drug trade but are systematically preying on both random civilians and high-profile figures. Their strategy is simple: terrorize communities, extract wealth, and exert control. McBride details this chilling development: "The drug cartels are doing a lot more kidnap-for-ransom. They're doing this in LA and San Diego. . . . They'll go after random people, people of status, they go after their family. Say you've got a big business chain—these guys will get somebody to kidnap someone from the CEO's family."[4]

The rise of Mexican drug cartels to quasi-state actors presents an unparalleled challenge to American sovereignty and national security. Their transnational networks do not merely traffic narcotics; they erode the very foundations of governance, undermine border integrity, and dissolve social cohesion. The economic and human toll—manifested through drug proliferation, human trafficking, and the systemic corruption of institutions—strikes at the core of American stability.

This crisis does not lend itself to half-measures. The unchecked metastasis of cartel power demands not just policy adjustments but a fundamental shift in strategy. What is required is a reassertion of state authority through uncompromising border enforcement, a revival of aggressive law enforcement tactics, and a commitment to dismantling these organizations at their root. The scale of the threat necessitates a response akin to the military campaigns that eradicated the Barbary Pirates in the early 19th century—forceful, unrelenting, and decisive.

Narco-Industrial Complex

Paradigm Shift in Mexico

The evolution of Mexican drug cartels from localized smuggling operations into transnational criminal conglomerates represents a fundamental restructuring of organized crime. This transformation, catalyzed by the geopolitical shifts of the late 1980s and early 1990s, has not only reconfigured the global narcotics trade but also poses unprecedented challenges for governments.

The pivotal moment came in 1989 when U.S. authorities successfully intercepted a twenty-one ton shipment of cocaine in Los Angeles, leading to the collapse of the Guadalajara Cartel. This event, coupled with the dismantling of Caribbean trafficking routes, created a power vacuum that emerging Mexican organizations swiftly exploited. Groups like the Sinaloa Cartel and the Gulf Cartel, previously subordinate to Colombian suppliers, seized the opportunity to control the entire supply chain, from production to distribution.

Modern cartels now operate with a level of complexity that often exceeds that of legitimate multinational corporations. The Sinaloa Cartel, for instance, employs a decentralized structure with semi-autonomous "plaza bosses" overseeing specific territories. This model allows for rapid decision-making and adaptability to local conditions while maintaining overall strategic coherence. According to a 2023 DEA intelligence report, the Sinaloa Cartel operates in at least fifty countries, with a particularly strong presence in Australia, where it controls an estimated 60% of the cocaine market.[5]

The organizational sophistication of these cartels is evident in their logistical operations. In 2022, authorities uncovered a Sinaloa Cartel-operated underground rail system spanning 1.3 kilometers beneath the U.S.-Mexico border. This tunnel, equipped with ventilation, lighting, and an electric cart system, could move an estimated 300 kilograms of narcotics daily.[6] Such infrastructure projects require significant engineering expertise and financial resources, highlighting the cartels' ability to rival legitimate construction firms.

Cartel diversification extends far beyond the commerce of illicit commodities. The Jalisco New Generation Cartel (CJNG), for example, has established a significant presence in Mexico's avocado industry. A 2024 report by the Mexican Institute for Competitiveness estimated that the CJNG extorts up to 30% of avocado farmers in Michoacán, generating annual revenues of approximately $150 million from this sector alone.[7] This infiltration of legitimate agriculture not only provides a means of money laundering but also grants the cartel significant influence over local economies and politics.

Mexican drug cartels have adeptly expanded their operations into the digital realm, employing sophisticated cyber tactics to enhance their criminal enterprises. They have been known to recruit skilled hackers to develop malware targeting financial institutions, exemplified by the Bandidos gang's creation of ATM malware that exploited vulnerabilities in Mexico's interbanking system to illicitly extract funds.[8] Additionally, cartels utilize the dark web to source synthetic opioids, such as fentanyl, from international suppliers, notably in China, and employ cryptocurrencies like Bitcoin to launder illicit proceeds, thereby obscuring financial trails and evading law enforcement scrutiny.[9] Their cyber activities extend to intelligence gathering and psychological operations; cartels have deployed spyware to monitor and intimidate adversaries, including journalists and rival factions, and have leveraged social media platforms and online gaming communities to recruit new members and propagate their influence.[10] This strategic integration of cyber capabilities not only amplifies their operational efficiency but also poses a significant and evolving threat to national and international security frameworks.

The cartels' influence extends into governance structures, particularly in rural areas with limited state presence. In regions where state authority is tenuous, Mexican drug cartels have increasingly assumed quasi-governmental roles, providing services and exerting control over local communities. For instance, during the COVID-19 pandemic, cartels distributed food and essential supplies to residents in areas under their influence, a move interpreted as an effort to bolster local support and legitimacy.[11] Additionally, in the state of Michoacán, groups like La Familia Michoacana have not only engaged in criminal activities but have also taken on roles such as extorting "taxes" from businesses, funding community projects, controlling petty crime, and settling local disputes, effectively acting as a parallel state.[12]

These actions underscore the complex relationship between criminal organizations and local populations, where cartels fill vacuums left by weak governmental institutions, thereby challenging traditional notions of state sovereignty and governance. The Sinaloa Cartel has been reported to collude with government officials to undermine rival cartels, thereby consolidating its power and influence. Such dynamics have led to situations where cartels not only manage illicit activities but also impose order, adjudicate disputes, and provide services within the communities they dominate. This usurpation of state functions by criminal organizations challenges traditional notions of sovereignty and governance, highlighting the complex interplay between illicit power structures and formal political institutions.

This narco-industrial complex presents formidable challenges to traditional law enforcement approaches. Standard interdiction tactics often prove ineffective against organizations with the resources to quickly adapt their routes and methods. For instance, following the increased use of maritime patrols in the Gulf of Mexico, the Gulf Cartel responded by developing semi-submersible vessels capable of transporting up to ten tons of cocaine. These vessels, first detected in 2020, are estimated to have a 70% success rate in evading detection.[13]

The rise of this narco-industrial complex signifies a fundamental shift in regional power dynamics. As these cartels grow in sophistication and reach, they increasingly challenge state authority, creating parallel governance structures that undermine official institutions. This paradigm shift necessitates a reevaluation of traditional anti-narcotics strategies, as methods effective against simpler criminal organizations falter when confronted with these adaptive, resilient, and highly efficient narco-empires.

Drug Trafficking: Lifeblood of Cartel Empires

Mexican drug cartels operate with the precision and efficiency of vertically integrated multinational corporations, controlling every stage of the drug trade from raw material acquisition to street-level distribution. Their dominance extends from the remote fields where illicit crops are cultivated to the urban markets where their products are sold, ensuring that no aspect of the supply chain escapes their control.

This operational model is built upon a foundation of agricultural production, with the cartels either overseeing or directly managing vast plantations of marijuana, opium poppies, and coca plants across Mexico and parts of South America. These raw materials fuel a global narcotics empire, but the real transformation occurs in clandestine laboratories, where cartels have mastered the synthesis of increasingly potent and profitable drugs.

Synthetic opioids, particularly fentanyl, have revolutionized the illicit drug market, allowing cartels to scale production without the constraints of traditional agriculture. Unlike plant-based narcotics, fentanyl is entirely synthesized from chemical precursors, primarily sourced from China, which enables rapid manufacturing in makeshift labs scattered across Mexico's rugged interior. The process is so hazardous that workers must wear respirators and protective gear to avoid fatal exposure. The shift from crop-dependent production to lab-based synthesis has reshaped the geography of cartel operations, decentralizing manufacturing and expanding their workforce to include former farmers who now churn out synthetic opioids rather than tending fields. The advent of fentanyl and other synthetics has been nothing short of a revolution in the industry.

The transportation of narcotics across international borders is a testament to the cartels' ingenuity and adaptability. Their methods range from crude yet effective smuggling techniques to high-tech innovations. Submarines and semi-submersible vessels evade maritime patrols, drones slip past heavily guarded border checkpoints, and sophisticated tunnel networks—some stretching for miles—are outfitted with ventilation systems, lighting, and rail tracks to ensure seamless movement of product. When stealth is required, drugs are expertly concealed within legitimate cargo shipments, hidden among agricultural produce or electronics, making detection difficult even for the most vigilant authorities.

Cartels have also embraced digital technology to streamline operations and evade law enforcement. Encrypted communication platforms and custom-built secure networks facilitate coordination with near impunity. Social media and encrypted messaging apps serve as marketing channels for illicit substances, allowing cartels to bypass traditional distribution networks. Meanwhile, blockchain technology and cryptocurrency exchanges provide a discreet financial infrastructure, enabling the seamless movement of billions of dollars without triggering red flags in the formal banking system.

The scale of these operations is staggering. Mexican cartels now dominate the production and distribution of heroin and methamphetamine in the United States. With respect to fentanyl production, the Sinaloa and Jalisco New Generation cartels are the primary suppliers controlling inflows into the U.S. market. Cocaine remains a cornerstone of the narco-empires, sourced from Colombia and distributed globally. Even as marijuana legalization has diminished demand for illicit cannabis in some markets, cartels continue to move vast quantities across the border, demonstrating a remarkable ability to pivot in response to shifting market conditions and evolving legal landscapes.

This operational sophistication has yielded astronomical profits. Estimates suggest the cartels' earnings from narcotics trafficking may exceed $50 billion annually.[14] In 2021 alone, the cartels made an estimated $13 billion just from human trafficking and smuggling.[15] But these profits are not just measured in dollars—they are soaked in blood. Since 2006, when the Mexican government launched its war against the cartels, more than 431,000 homicides have been recorded, while an additional 79,000 people have simply vanished, presumed casualties of cartel brutality.[16,17] The human toll is incalculable, a ledger of devastation where every dollar earned is shadowed by suffering, terror, and loss.

In the United States, fentanyl has emerged as the deadliest drug crisis in modern history. Unlike heroin or cocaine, fentanyl is frequently laced into other substances, often without the user's knowledge, resulting in mass overdoses. The sheer potency of the drug—fifty times stronger than heroin—has made even minimal exposure lethal, driving an unprecedented public health catastrophe.

As law enforcement agencies on both sides of the border struggle to contain this hydra-headed threat, the cartels continue to adapt and evolve. Their operations have become so deeply entrenched in the economic and social fabric of Mexico that disentangling legitimate business from criminal enterprise is often impossible. The challenge facing authorities is not just one of law enforcement, but of dismantling an alternative economic system that has taken root in the shadows.

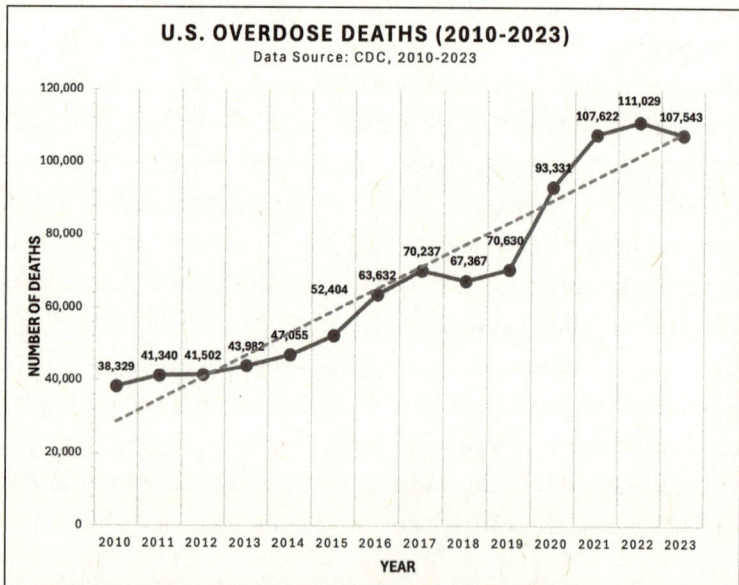

U.S. OVERDOSE DEATHS (2010-2023)
Data Source: CDC, 2010-2023

Human Trafficking and Slavery

In the shadow of America's collapsing border enforcement, Mexican cartels have industrialized human trafficking, transforming it into a billion-dollar enterprise that now rivals their narcotics trade. This is not merely an expansion of criminal operations but a fundamental shift in the nature of cartel strategy. The same organizations that flood U.S. streets with fentanyl and violence have resurrected one of humanity's oldest evils—the mass commodification of human beings.

By commoditizing human beings at scale, the cartels have effectively resurrected the chattel slave trade, creating a perverse synergy with their established narcotics trafficking networks. This strategic pivot has significantly amplified the cartel's geopolitical significance and international footprint, demonstrating an unprecedented level of power projection into the United States.

Perhaps the most damning aspect of this crisis is not the brutality of the cartels—whose savagery is well-documented—but the complicity of the Biden administration. The Biden-Harris administration's policies have not merely failed to address human trafficking—they have actively encouraged its business model. By dismantling border enforcement and halting deportations, the administration has turned the U.S. into a de facto partner in the cartel slave trade. Every single illegal border crossing enriches cartel networks, as migrants must pay between $4,000 and $20,000 per head to cross cartel-controlled smuggling routes.[18] Failure to pay results in rape, mutilation, or execution. The Biden administration's refusal to secure the border not only enabled modern slavery but ensured its continued expansion.

Industrialized Slavery: A Business Model

Cartels have refined human trafficking into a methodical, vertically integrated operation, mirroring the efficiency of multinational logistics firms. Their business model follows a three-stage process: recruitment, transportation, and exploitation.

- **Recruitment:** Cartel operatives target vulnerable populations globally, exploiting economic desperation and social marginalization. On TikTok, WhatsApp, and Facebook, the cartels deploy sophisticated social media campaigns and manipulate personal networks, offering false promises of employment or education. These deceptions are meticulously tailored to specific socioeconomic vulnerabilities, creating an inescapable trap for victims across continents.

- **Transportation:** Once under cartel control, victims are treated as inventory. Leveraging the cartels' well-established drug smuggling routes, they moving human cargo across borders with chilling efficiency. Victims endure harrowing journeys, often crammed into hidden vehicle compartments or forced through treacherous terrains. The use of falsified documents and corrupt officials facilitates this movement, exploiting gaps in international border security and immigration policies.

- **Exploitation:** Upon arrival in destination countries, trafficked individuals are funneled into forced labor, cartel-controlled prostitution rings, or debt servitude. Victims are stripped of identification and subject to severe abuse across various sectors. The global demand for cheap labor has even led to trafficking victims working in technology and manufacturing sectors. Cartels maintain control through relentless intimidation and violence, ensuring victims' silence and compliance.

The scale of these operations is staggering, with cartels collaborating with local criminal organizations and corrupt officials worldwide. They have created vast networks that span from rural communities to major cities across multiple countries, utilizing safe houses, forged documents, and bribery to evade law enforcement.

California: A Sanctuary for Cartel Traffickers

California, by virtue of both geography and policy, has become the premier stronghold for cartel-driven human trafficking in the United States. Its porous border, sanctuary laws, and vast underground economy provide an almost frictionless environment for exploitation. From the agricultural fields of the Central Valley to illicit brothels operating within the shadows of major cities, trafficked individuals exist in plain sight—hidden not by secrecy but by willful political negligence.

Sex trafficking victims in the U.S. report being forced to service as many as fifty men per day, with cartel enforcers using torture to ensure obedience. The traffickers, well aware of California's weak enforcement mechanisms and ideological resistance to immigration crackdowns, exploit legal loopholes to operate with near impunity.[19] The staggering scale of this modern-day slave trade reflects not only a failure of immigration enforcement but an abdication of state authority itself.

The National Human Trafficking Hotline reports that California consistently leads the nation in human trafficking cases, with victims as young as twelve being sold repeatedly. Migrants who endure the perilous journey north often find themselves trapped in debt bondage, working in conditions indistinguishable from slavery. For many, escape is impossible—cartel enforcers keep them compliant through a combination of psychological terror, physical violence, and threats against their families back home.

State law enforcement, bound by political constraints and deprived of meaningful federal cooperation, remains largely powerless to combat the crisis. Until California acknowledges the extent of cartel influence and abandons policies that effectively shield traffickers, the state will continue to serve as America's primary hub for one of the most depraved industries in human history.

The Statistics of Slavery
The magnitude of cartel-driven human trafficking is both staggering and deeply unsettling. While precise figures are elusive due to the clandestine nature of these operations, available data offers a harrowing snapshot:

- **Victims Trafficked Annually:** Estimates suggest that between 14,500 and 17,500 individuals are trafficked into the United States each year. A significant proportion of these victims are undocumented immigrants, making them particularly vulnerable to exploitation.[20]
- **Unaccompanied Minors:** Since 2021, nearly 540,000 unaccompanied children have been taken into federal custody

at the U.S. border. Alarmingly, reports indicate that the
government has lost track of over 320,000 of these children,
raising concerns about their safety and potential exploitation.[21]

- **Exploitation of Migrant Children:** Studies indicate that
  a significant number of unaccompanied migrant children,
  perhaps 60%, fall prey to cartels, who exploit them through
  forced labor, child pornography, and drug trafficking.[22]

State-Sanctioned Slavery: The Biden Administration's Complicity

Despite this humanitarian catastrophe, the Biden administration has not
merely failed to act—it has actively facilitated the largest human trafficking operation in modern American history. Through deliberate policy
choices, including the systematic dismantling of border enforcement and
the mass release of illegal migrants into the interior, the U.S. government has become a willing accomplice to the cartel slave trade. Every
unaccompanied minor lost, every woman raped in cartel-controlled stash
houses, and every trafficked laborer working under duress is the direct
consequence of an administration that prioritizes ideological open-border
policies over the most basic human rights. This is not negligence—it is
complicity on a scale that defies precedent.

The cartels' industrial-scale human trafficking operation is not just
a humanitarian catastrophe—it is a financial juggernaut, fueling their
broader criminal empire with staggering profits. This trade in human
misery has become a central pillar of their economic model, rivaling
even the narcotics trade in profitability. Every smuggled migrant, every
trafficked woman, and every enslaved child represents another revenue
stream that strengthens cartel power, funds their paramilitary operations,
and extends their grip on both sides of the border. With each passing
year, this enterprise deepens their war chest, allowing them to buy more
weapons, corrupt more officials, and tighten their stranglehold over
entire regions. The U.S. government's refusal to crack down on this modern slave trade has not only emboldened the cartels but has also cemented
their status as the most powerful transnational criminal syndicates in the
Western Hemisphere.

CARTEL REVENUE BREAKDOWN BY SOURCE (BILLION $)

Other:
$5B (8%)

Money Laundering:
$15B (25%)

Drug Trafficking:
$25B (42%)

Extortion:
$2B (3%)

Human Trafficking
$13B (22%)

- Drug Trafficking
- Human Trafficking
- Extortion
- Money Laundering
- Other Criminal Activities

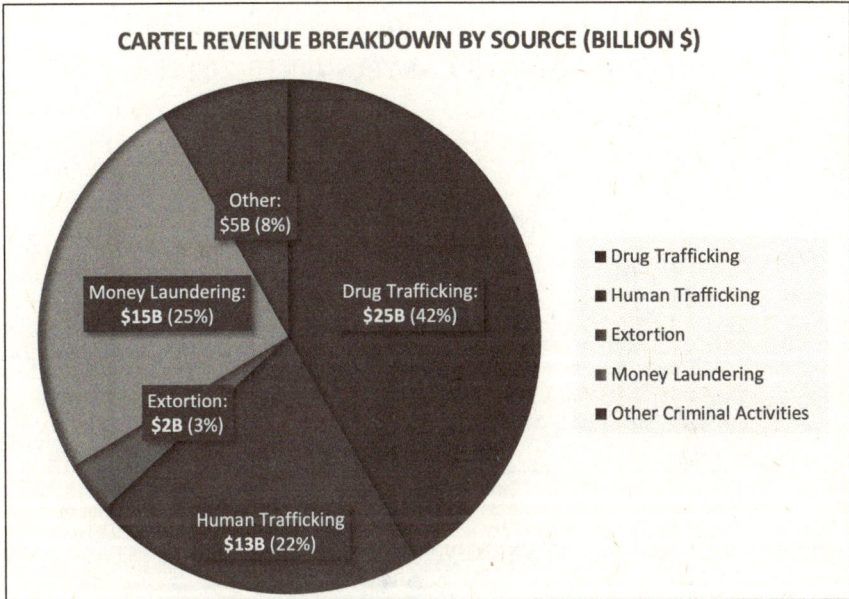

Financial Empire of the Cartels

The financial might of Mexican drug cartels represents a staggering example of illicit wealth accumulation on a global scale. Their revenue streams, diversified across multiple criminal enterprises, have reached proportions that rival legitimate multinational corporations, underscoring the immense challenge faced by law enforcement and policymakers in combating these organizations.

At the core of cartel finances lies their drug trafficking operations, estimated to generate between $20 and $30 billion annually. This figure, however, likely understates the true scale of their narcotics trade, given the clandestine nature of these activities and the constantly evolving market dynamics. The profit margins in this sector are nothing short of astronomical, particularly when it comes to synthetic drugs like fentanyl.

Fentanyl exemplifies the cartels' ruthless business acumen. With production costs as low as $1,000 to $3,000 per kilogram, cartels can sell this synthetic opioid for $10,000 to $30,000 per kilogram at wholesale prices. When distributed at the street level, often disguised as or mixed with other substances, the profit margins can exceed an astonishing 200,000%.[23] This economic incentive has driven cartels to flood markets with synthetic

ANNUAL REVENUE AND NET INCOME OF MEXICAN DRUG CARTELS (2010-2023)

■ REVENUE (USD BILLIONS) ■ NET INCOME (USD BILLIONS)

A bar chart titled "Annual Revenue and Net Income of Mexican Drug Cartels (2010-2023)". The vertical axis is labeled "USD BILLIONS" ranging from 0 to 70. The horizontal axis is labeled "YEAR" with values from 2010 to 2023. Each year shows two bars, revenue and net income:

Year	Revenue (USD Billions)	Net Income (USD Billions)
2010	35	28
2011	37	30
2012	39	31
2013	41	33
2014	43	34
2015	45	36
2016	47	37
2017	49	39
2018	51	40
2019	53	42
2020	55	44
2021	57	46
2022	59	47
2023	61	49

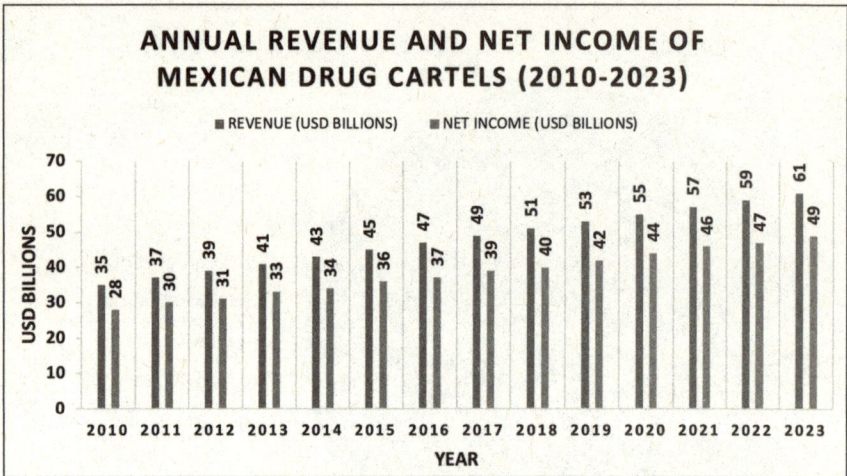

opioids, contributing significantly to the ongoing overdose crisis in the United States and beyond.

The economics of other narcotics are similarly profitable, if not quite as extreme. Cocaine, for instance, purchased from Colombian suppliers at around $1,000 per kilogram, can fetch between $30,000 to $60,000 per kilogram on U.S. streets, yielding profit margins upwards of 1,000%.[24] Methamphetamine, manufactured at a cost of $1,500 to $7,000 per kilogram, can retail for as much as $800 per gram, resulting in profits of 500% or more.[25]

However, drug trafficking is no longer the sole pillar of cartel finances. Human trafficking and smuggling operations have emerged as a significant revenue source, estimated to generate around $13 billion annually.[26] Migrants may pay between $5,000 and $15,000 each to be smuggled across borders, while victims of sex trafficking or forced labor can be sold for $30,000 to $100,000, depending on various factors.[27] The low operational costs of these activities ensure high profit margins, making human trafficking an increasingly attractive business line for cartels.

Extortion practices further bolster cartel coffers, with estimates ranging from $300 million to $2 billion annually generated through "taxing" local businesses, farmers, and migrants.[28] This practice not only provides direct revenue but also reinforces the cartels' territorial control and influence over local economies.

The sophistication of cartel financial operations extends to money laundering, a critical component of their business model. Estimates suggest that between $10 billion to $25 billion are laundered annually through various means. One notable method involves exploiting legitimate remittance services. By breaking large sums into smaller transactions, a practice known as "structuring," cartels can move vast amounts of money under the guise of ordinary remittances. In 2021, remittances to Mexico reached a record $51.6 billion, with authorities estimating that around 7.5% of these transfers might be linked to cartel activities.[29]

This infiltration of legitimate financial systems poses a significant challenge to regulators and law enforcement. The sheer volume of transactions makes it difficult to distinguish between legal remittances and laundered funds. Moreover, cartels have diversified their money laundering tactics, establishing shell companies, investing in real estate and construction projects, and integrating illicit funds into the legitimate economy.

The financial prowess of Mexican cartels extends beyond North America. Organizations like the Jalisco Cartel have expanded their reach into global markets, including Australia and Europe, particularly with synthetic drugs. This international expansion not only diversifies their revenue sources but also complicates efforts to combat their operations on a global scale.

The staggering profits generated by these criminal enterprises underscore the limitations of traditional law enforcement approaches. The economic incentives are simply too great, and the potential losses from interdiction too small, to significantly impact cartel operations through seizures and arrests alone. This financial reality necessitates a more comprehensive strategy that addresses the economic foundations of cartel power, including targeting their money laundering operations, disrupting their legitimate business fronts, and addressing the socioeconomic conditions that make their criminal enterprises so profitable.[30]

Moreover, the cartels' financial sophistication highlights the need for enhanced international cooperation in tracking and seizing illicit funds. As these organizations continue to exploit gaps in global financial systems, a coordinated response that involves financial institutions, regulatory bodies, and law enforcement agencies across multiple jurisdictions becomes increasingly crucial.

The economic might of Mexican drug cartels represents not just a law enforcement challenge but a fundamental threat to economic stability, public health, and national security across multiple countries. Addressing this threat will require innovative approaches that go beyond traditional drug interdiction efforts, focusing instead on dismantling the complex financial networks that sustain and grow these criminal empires.

Money Laundering

The vast sums generated by Mexican drug cartels through their illicit activities necessitate an equally sophisticated system to integrate these funds into the legitimate economy. This process of money laundering represents not merely an ancillary function of cartel operations, but a critical pillar that sustains and expands their criminal empires. Estimates suggest that between $10 billion to $25 billion are laundered annually, a figure that underscores the staggering scale of this financial sleight of hand.

At the heart of the cartels' money laundering strategy lies a deceptively simple yet remarkably effective tactic: the exploitation of legitimate remittance services. Companies such as Western Union and MoneyGram, which serve as vital lifelines for millions of Mexican migrants sending money home to their families, have unwittingly become conduits for the cartels' illicit wealth. This method, known as "structuring," involves breaking down large sums into a multitude of smaller transactions, each innocuous enough to evade regulatory scrutiny.

The ingenuity of this approach lies in its camouflage. By blending their transactions with the billions of dollars in legitimate remittances sent annually, cartels create a needle-in-a-haystack scenario for financial regulators. The sheer volume of legitimate transfers provides perfect cover for illicit funds, making detection a Herculean task for even the most vigilant authorities.

The COVID-19 pandemic, with its disruption of traditional cash smuggling routes, has only accelerated the cartels' pivot towards this method. In 2021, remittances to Mexico reached an unprecedented $51.6 billion, a record that should be cause for celebration but instead raises alarming questions. Authorities estimate that approximately 7.5% of these remittances might be linked to cartel activities, amounting to billions in laundered funds flowing freely across borders.[31]

However, remittance exploitation represents only one facet of the cartels' money laundering arsenal. These criminal organizations have demonstrated a remarkable ability to infiltrate and manipulate legitimate business sectors. Shell companies, often operating under the guise of innocuous enterprises, serve as fronts for laundering operations. The real estate and construction industries, with their high-value transactions and complex financial structures, provide fertile ground for integrating illicit funds into the legitimate economy.

This diversification of laundering methods creates a labyrinthine challenge for financial regulators and law enforcement agencies. Each sector penetrated by cartel money adds another layer of complexity to the task of tracing and confiscating illicit assets. The result is a financial ecosystem where the boundaries between legitimate and criminal enterprises become increasingly blurred.

The implications of this sophisticated money laundering apparatus extend far beyond the realm of drug trafficking. By successfully integrating their illicit profits into legitimate economic systems, cartels gain a veneer of respectability and influence that transcends their criminal origins. This financial integration allows them to exert influence over legitimate businesses, corrupt public officials, and even shape local and regional economies.

Moreover, the success of these laundering operations provides cartels with a robust financial infrastructure that can weather law enforcement efforts. Even when drug shipments are intercepted or high-ranking members arrested, the laundered funds ensure a continuous flow of capital to sustain and rebuild their operations.

Addressing this aspect of cartel operations presents a unique set of challenges. Traditional law enforcement approaches, focused on drug interdiction and arrests, often fall short in combating these sophisticated financial networks. The task requires a multifaceted approach involving international cooperation, enhanced financial regulations, and innovative tracking technologies.

However, any efforts to combat cartel money laundering must grapple with a fundamental dilemma: how to target illicit financial flows without disrupting the legitimate remittance systems that millions of families depend on. The intertwining of criminal and legitimate financial activities creates a complex web that defies simple solutions.

As cartels continue to refine and expand their money laundering capabilities, they not only secure their own operations but also pose a growing threat to the integrity of global financial systems. The ability to move and legitimize vast sums of illicit money gives these criminal organizations a degree of economic power that rivals many legitimate multinational corporations. This financial might translates into political influence, societal impact, and a resilience that traditional law enforcement methods struggle to counter.

MAJOR MEXICAN DRUG CARTELS	
CARTEL	**DESCRIPTION**
Sinaloa Cartel	One of the oldest and most influential, formerly led by Joaquín "El Chapo" Guzmán.
Jalisco New Generation Cartel (CJNG)	Splintered from Sinaloa in 2010, known for rapid expansion and violent confrontations.
Beltrán-Leyva Organization (BLO)	Formed in 2008, operates throughout Mexico with ties to other cartels.
Los Zetas	Known for being technologically advanced and violent, has splintered into rival wings.
Guerreros Unidos (GU)	Based in southwestern Mexico, involved in the heroin trade.
Gulf Cartel	Based in northeast Mexico, has splintered into various factions.
Juárez Cartel	Long-standing rival of Sinaloa, based in Chihuahua.
La Familia Michoacána (LFM)	Formed in the 1980s, weakened and fragmented in recent years.
Los Rojos	Splinter group of BLO, involved in kidnapping and extortion.

The battle against cartel money laundering, therefore, is not merely a matter of financial regulation or law enforcement. It is a crucial front in the larger war against the corrosive influence of organized crime on global society. As these criminal empires continue to evolve their financial tactics, the international community faces an ongoing challenge to develop equally sophisticated and adaptive strategies to combat this pernicious aspect of the narco-economy.

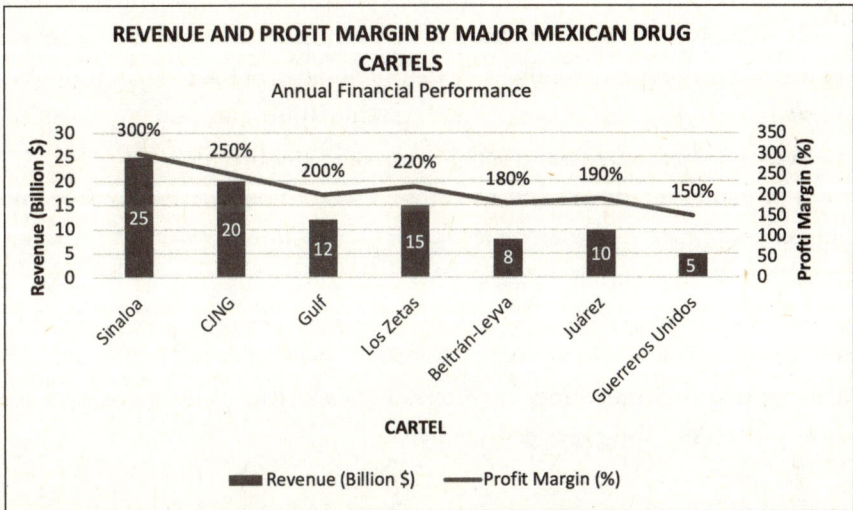

REVENUE AND PROFIT MARGIN BY MAJOR MEXICAN DRUG CARTELS
Annual Financial Performance

Revenue (Billion $): Sinaloa 25, CJNG 20, Gulf 12, Los Zetas 15, Beltrán-Leyva 8, Juárez 10, Guerreros Unidos 5

Profit Margin (%): Sinaloa 300%, CJNG 250%, Gulf 200%, Los Zetas 220%, Beltrán-Leyva 180%, Juárez 190%, Guerreros Unidos 150%

Legend: Revenue (Billion $) — Profit Margin (%)

Suzerainty of the Cartels: A New Power Paradigm

The ascendancy of Mexican drug cartels to positions of quasi-sovereign power represents a paradigm shift in our understanding of geopolitical influence and control. These organizations have transcended their origins as mere criminal enterprises to become formidable actors on the international stage, wielding influence that challenges traditional notions of state sovereignty and regional hegemony.

To comprehend the full scope of cartel power, we must expand our analytical framework beyond conventional criminology and into the realm of international relations theory. The concept of suzerainty, traditionally used to describe relationships between states, provides a compelling lens through which to view the cartels' multifaceted dominion.

In international relations and strategic theory, suzerainty describes a situation where a dominant state (the suzerain) allows a subordinate state (the vassal) to govern itself internally while retaining control over its external affairs. This concept, often implying a relationship more symbolic than legal, aptly characterizes the complex influence cartels exert over regions in Mexico and across the U.S.-Mexico border.

Edward Luttwak's concept of "geopolitical suzerainty" is particularly relevant in this context. Luttwak, a renowned military historian and strategic analyst, developed this idea to explain how powerful entities can dictate terms to weaker ones through economic, political, cultural, and military means, without resorting to formal colonization or direct governance. His work, particularly "The Grand Strategy of the Roman Empire," provides insights into how strategic manipulation and power projection can achieve dominance, mirroring the cartels' modus operandi.

The economic dimension of cartel suzerainty is particularly striking. These organizations have created a parallel economic system that intertwines with and often overshadows legitimate commerce. In regions under their sway, cartels effectively control labor markets, dictate terms of trade, and influence investment patterns. Their economic reach extends far beyond drug trafficking, encompassing industries as diverse as agriculture, real estate, and even technology.

For instance, the Sinaloa Cartel's operations within the United States exemplify this economic suzerainty. Their ability to seamlessly integrate into the U.S. financial system, exploiting global networks for money laundering and legitimate investments, underscores their power and autonomy. The cartel's sophisticated financial maneuvers, as detailed in recent federal indictments, reveal an organization operating with the complexity and global reach of a multinational corporation, yet unconstrained by legal and regulatory frameworks.

The political and social control exerted by cartels further cements their quasi-suzerain status. In many regions of Mexico, and increasingly in parts of the United States, cartels have filled the vacuum left by weak or absent state institutions. They impose their own forms of governance, including taxation, law enforcement, and even social services. This parallel state structure not only undermines the legitimacy of official governments but also creates a population dependent on cartel largesse for basic needs and economic opportunities.

The cartels' power is not only rooted in their capacity for violence but also in their ability to corrupt and co-opt local and federal authorities, manipulate economies, and exert social control. They use their vast profits to pay off judges, officers, and politicians, and coerce officials into cooperation. This system of corruption and coercion flourished during the PRI's rule in Mexico, allowing cartels to cultivate an extensive network of corrupt officials that continues to facilitate their operations.

The strategic and security implications of cartel suzerainty pose profound challenges to traditional state-centric models of international relations. These organizations operate across borders with impunity, leveraging violence, corruption, and economic coercion to achieve their objectives. Their ability to compromise law enforcement, judiciary systems, and political structures on both sides of the U.S.-Mexico border represents a form of soft power projection that rivals that of many sovereign states.

The pervasive influence of cartels has forced a recalibration of U.S. foreign and domestic policy. The allocation of vast resources to combat drug trafficking, the militarization of border regions, and the reshaping of international cooperation frameworks all attest to the de facto recognition of cartel power. This responsive posture inadvertently reinforces the cartels' status as quasi-suzerain entities, capable of compelling policy shifts in the world's most powerful nation.

Moreover, the cartels' suzerainty extends into the realm of cultural influence. Through a combination of intimidation, propaganda, and the glamorization of narco-culture, these organizations have shaped social norms and values in ways that facilitate their operations and recruitment. This cultural dimension of their power further blurs the lines between criminal enterprise and quasi-state actor.

The concept of cartel suzerainty challenges us to rethink our approaches to combating transnational organized crime. Traditional law enforcement strategies, focused on interdiction and arrests, have proven inadequate against entities that operate with state-like sophistication and resilience. Addressing this threat requires a multifaceted approach that combines economic, political, and cultural strategies to undermine the foundations of cartel power. Their ability to exert economic, political, and social control across borders, often surpassing the influence of legitimate state actors, demands a reevaluation of our conceptual frameworks for understanding international relations and security. As these organizations continue to evolve and expand their reach, the international community faces the daunting challenge of developing new paradigms and strategies to counter this unconventional but increasingly dominant form of power.

Conclusion

The ascendance of Mexican drug cartels from mere criminal syndicates into transnational warlord enterprises is not merely a troubling development—it is an indictment of the feebleness, corruption, and moral cowardice of the modern state. The cartels have not seized power in a vacuum; they have been granted it through the deliberate incompetence and willing paralysis of governments too craven, too bureaucratically decadent, and too ideologically hobbled to defend their own borders, institutions, and people.

No longer content with the narcotics trade, these organizations have metastasized into economic and political behemoths, their reach extending into human trafficking, resource extraction, extortion economies, and political corruption on both sides of the U.S.-Mexico border. They operate with the ruthless efficiency of multinational corporations and the impunity of medieval warlords, while the very governments tasked with confronting them engage in ritualistic posturing and token enforcement measures, doing just enough to appear engaged but never enough to actually win.

The most damning indictment of all, however, is not simply the failure to dismantle these criminal empires but the unforgivable complicity of the American government in their rise. Through its refusal to enforce border security, through its systematic dismantling of deportation policies, and through its fanatical commitment to open-border ideology, the Biden administration has functionally subsidized cartel expansion. Each unguarded mile of border, each unvetted migrant processed and released, represents another financial windfall for the very warlords America pretends to be fighting.

The reality of the cartel insurgency is not merely economic or political—it is existential. These organizations have become de facto sovereign entities, governing swaths of Mexico and increasingly dictating the conditions under which America's borderlands operate. The notion that these cartels are mere "criminal organizations" is a fantasy for bureaucrats and journalists who still imagine this crisis can be solved through well-funded DEA task forces and diplomatic handshakes.

This is not crime. This is war. Yet, instead of waging it, the United States accommodates the enemy. It builds intelligence-sharing agreements with the very Mexican officials whose pockets are lined with cartel money. It prosecutes cartel operatives only to release them in grotesque prisoner exchanges. It allows cartel financiers to operate openly in real estate markets, shell corporations, and wire transfer networks—all in the name of "due process" and regulatory complexity.

Meanwhile, the cartels themselves do not suffer from such illusions. They do not respect borders; they overrun them. They do not recognize laws; they impose their own. They do not ask for permission; they buy it. They are not beholden to the moral niceties of the liberal state, and so they triumph over it.

If the cartels were operating under a flag, if their leaders wore uniforms and paraded before an assembled government, the response would be immediate. Drones would rain fire upon them, financial institutions would be seized, and military operations would be launched to eradicate them. Instead, America treats them as mere criminals to be managed, an inconvenience rather than an existential challenge to its sovereignty.

The solution is not another study, not another summit, not another hollow press conference about "regional cooperation." The solution is war, waged with the full force of state power—militarized border enforcement, targeted extrajudicial elimination of cartel leadership, complete asset seizure, and the uncompromising eradication of cartel-affiliated gangs within the United States. The alternative is not peace. The alternative is the continued abdication of sovereignty to the most vicious, depraved, and strategically adept criminal syndicates in modern history.

CHAPTER 12

ATAVISM

The violence perpetuated by Mexican drug cartels and their affiliated gangs transcends mere strategic necessity. Their brutality, so extreme and unrelenting, seems to draw from a primordial lineage, harking back to a distant past steeped in ritualistic savagery and the thanato-theism. As the Mexican drug cartels continue to exert a shadowy suzerainty over much of the United States—most notably California—the urgency to scrutinize their wanton methods and seemingly preternatural impulse for evil becomes starkly apparent and relevant to this analysis.

As cartel operatives spill across a border that their organizations effectively control, Mexican-style narco violence seeps into American cities. This infiltration brings with it the same brutality and terror tactics that have long characterized their operations in Mexico. This cross-border proliferation of violence is not merely a criminal import, but a cultural and historical phenomenon demanding critical scrutiny and contextualization.

This chapter posits an anthropological theory: the extreme violence of the Mexican drug cartels is not merely strategic brutality but a form of cultural atavism—the regression to a primordial ethos in which ritualized violence and thanatological mysticism serve as mechanisms of physical and spiritual power. The cartels' macabre spectacles of mutilation, dismemberment, and public executions echo the sacrificial rites of pre-Columbian Mesoamerican civilizations, including the Mexica (Aztec), Mixtec, Olmec, and Maya, whose societies were structured around religiously sanctioned

terror. This continuity suggests that rather than being aberrant, cartel violence is an embedded cultural expression—an ancestral inheritance reconstituted in contemporary form. Understanding the historical and spiritual
roots of this phenomenon demands a deeper examination of pre-Columbian practices and their survival in modern narco-ritualism.

Historical and Demographic Context

Latin America—particularly Mexico and Central America—bears the
imprint of a unique historical synthesis. The Spanish conquest did not
annihilate the indigenous civilizations it encountered; rather, it fused
them with the European invaders, creating a hybrid Spanish-Indian caste
known as the Mestizos, who today constitute the majority in these regions.
This fusion was not merely genetic but deeply cultural, as indigenous traditions, both visible and subterranean, persisted beneath the veneer of
Catholicism imposed by the Spanish crown. Mexico's national flag, with
its emblematic depiction of an eagle devouring a serpent—an allusion to
the Aztec founding of Tenochtitlán—stands as an enduring testament to
this dual heritage.

Yet this syncretism is not merely historical pageantry; it continues to
shape Mexico's spiritual and social fabric, often in ways that blur the line
between reverence and something far more primeval. Nowhere is this
more apparent than in *Día de los Muertos*, where Catholic and indigenous
traditions merge into an elaborate communion with the dead, a ritual
celebration whose pre-Hispanic antecedents stretch back to the Maya and
Mexica. But the persistence of ancestral rites does not always take benign
form. The same undercurrents of death veneration, mysticism, and sacrificial spectacle that once defined Mesoamerican societies have resurfaced
in the brutal rituals of modern cartels. In their world, mutilation, public
executions, and necromantic symbolism are not merely instruments of
terror; they are deeply rooted in the atavistic remnants of a belief system
where violence is sacred, blood is currency, and death is not an end, but
a form of dominion. To understand cartel violence in its full context, one
must recognize it not as mere criminality, but as the reanimation of a cultural inheritance long thought extinct—a resurrection of the specters of
Mexico's past.

Origins: Aztecan and Mayan Ritualistic Violence

Human Sacrifice: Blood as Divine Currency
Ritualized violence in Aztec society was not a mere act of devotion but a calculated assertion of power, where theology and statecraft were indistinguishable. Public sacrifice functioned as both **cosmic maintenance and political subjugation**, a spectacle designed to cement the authority of the ruling elite while binding the population in a shared metaphysical terror. These orchestrated executions—gruesome, theatrical, and methodically staged—ensured that both the conquered and the subjugated understood their place within the imperial order. To witness captives ascending the temple steps, only to be cast down as mutilated husks, was to absorb an unmistakable lesson: resistance was futile, and sovereignty belonged to those who controlled the apparatus of death.

This synthesis of violence, governance, and mythology finds an eerie parallel in the modus operandi of modern Mexican drug cartels, whose savagery is not an aberration but an evolutionary permutation of a deep-seated cultural logic. The public display of dismembered corpses hanging from bridges, the ritualized executions filmed and disseminated for mass consumption, and the near-religious invocation of Santa Muerte and folk saints—all mirror the Aztec synthesis of fear, divinity, and control. Just as the Mexica priesthood justified mass sacrifice as the price of cosmic order, the cartels employ violence not as an impulsive act of brutality but as a carefully choreographed assertion of sovereignty over the lawless spaces they inhabit. In both cases, the act of killing transcends its immediate victims; it becomes an instrument of systemic domination, a language through which power is expressed and legitimacy is enforced.

Nowhere is this continuum of violence more evident than in California, where cartel influence—sanctified by state-level policies that shield them from immigration enforcement—has transformed parts of the state into narco-colonies. The same brutality that once secured Aztec hegemony now manifests in the operational logic of cartel rule: economic tribute through extortion, psychological submission through public mutilation, and the collapse of state authority in regions where their presence becomes unchallenged. The Mexican cartels do not merely bring organized crime northward; they bring an entire governing model, one that replaces legal structures with the atavistic order of ritualized terror, just as their predecessors did centuries ago. California, through its self-imposed legal and political paralysis, has welcomed this regression into primordial rule, allowing its criminal underworld to be governed not by the state, but by a force more ancient, more ruthless, and ultimately, more effective in securing loyalty through fear.

To the Mexica—better known as the Aztecs—human sacrifice was neither aberration nor merely spectacle; it was a civic duty, a theological necessity, and an inescapable function of governance. It was not enough to rule by force; the state ruled by fear consecrated into faith, a belief system in which the gods did not merely require devotion but demanded the flesh of the living.

Aztec society was structured around an understanding that existence itself was precarious—an eternal struggle against cosmic collapse. Their principal deity was the Sun, the god *Huitzilopochtli*, who waged an unending battle against darkness, and to falter in feeding him the blood he required to wage this cosmic dual was to risk the destruction of the world. This was not metaphor. This was state policy. The sun would rise because men were cut open, their hearts torn from their chests, and their skulls stacked in great racks as proof that the social order had been preserved.

The scale was staggering. At its peak, 250,000 people—approximately 1% of the population under Aztec control—were sacrificed each year.[1] In 1487, during the consecration of the Templo Mayor, chroniclers recorded 84,000 deaths over four days, a figure so vast that even if exaggerated, it suggests a system of mass execution so routine that the true number is hardly relevant.[2] Victims were led to the top of temple pyramids, where priests, using razor-sharp obsidian blades, sliced open their chests, extracted the still-beating heart, and cast the corpse down the steps. The remains were not wasted; skulls were cleaned and mounted, bones repurposed into tools, and the flesh distributed for ritual meals. The dish pozole, now made with pork, was once prepared with human meat—an eerie continuity acknowledged by the Spanish, who noted the unsettling resemblance in taste.[3]

Ritualistic violence in Aztec society was not mere religious observance; it was a calculated instrument of governance. Public executions—performed with an almost theatrical precision—were designed to inspire both awe and submission, reinforcing the omnipotence of the ruling elite. Human sacrifice functioned as a mechanism of cosmic maintenance and political subjugation, binding the people in a shared belief that survival itself depended on a steady offering of blood. These displays were as much about consolidating power over tributary states as they were about appeasing the gods. To witness a procession of captives ascending the temple steps, only to be cast down as lifeless husks, was to be reminded of the futility of resistance. In this way, ritualized slaughter was both a metaphysical necessity and a brutal form of social control, ensuring the obedience of the conquered and the unchallenged dominance of the priestly-military order.

One of the most gruesome festivals was *Tlacaxipehualiztli*, "The Festival of the Flaying of Men," during which priests skinned men alive to mimic maize shedding its husk. The victims' skins were dyed yellow to resemble the hue of the Aztec's staple crop, and then donned by dancing priests.[4,5]

Echoes of Ritualistic Violence: From Tenochtitlán to the Cartel-State

The sacrificial altars of Tenochtitlán may have long crumbled, but the grim logic that once fueled them persists in the modern narco-state. The Aztec theology of bloodletting, terror, and divine appeasement was not simply a set of religious superstitions—it was an entire system of governance, a method by which elites exerted control through ritualized brutality. Nowhere is this legacy more grotesquely evident than in the modern Mexican cartels, whose own acts of ritualistic horror—dismemberment, public executions, and ceremonial killings—are chillingly reminiscent of their ancient predecessors. In California, where cartel influence has metastasized under the permissive veil of sanctuary laws, this atavistic savagery has begun to carve its own reality, one in which the lines between civilization and barbarism blur with alarming speed.

Child Sacrifice: The Ultimate Tribute

If human sacrifice formed the foundation of Aztec religious order, then child sacrifice was its most extreme and macabre expression. To appease *Tlaloc*, the god of rain and fertility, children—selected for their purity— were marched up the temple steps, their screams transmuted into pleas for divine mercy. The priests, wielding obsidian blades, cut open their small bodies, offering still-beating hearts as gifts to a deity that demanded suffering as supplication. Other ceremonies saw children drowned in sacred lakes or buried alive in ritual pits, their tears believed to summon the seasonal rains. The more they suffered, the more powerful the sacrifice.

This logic—that power is asserted through the calculated annihilation of the innocent—has not vanished with time. The modern cartels, in their grotesque mimicry of these ancient rites, have institutionalized child sacrifice in a new form. Whether through the mass trafficking of children across the U.S. border, where they are sold into sex slavery and forced labor, or through the deliberate recruitment of young sicarios, who are brutalized into killers before they reach adolescence, the underlying principle remains intact: the suffering of the weak fuels the machinery of dominance. In cartel strongholds, boys are given machetes before they reach puberty, their initiation rites requiring them to sever the limbs of captives as proof of their loyalty. In California, these same organizations operate with near impunity, trafficking minors through sanctuary corridors with the tacit blessing of a legal system that has chosen to prioritize political ideology over the lives of the vulnerable.

Ritualistic Warfare: The Resurrection of the Flower Wars

The Aztecs did not fight for conquest alone; they fought for the harvest of human flesh. Their "Flower Wars"—ritualized battles staged with neighboring states—were not about territorial expansion but about securing a constant supply of sacrificial victims. The captives were not executed in the heat of battle but were instead saved for the ceremonial blade, their deaths meticulously staged to reinforce both political control and divine favor. These staged conflicts were not deviations from war but rather war itself, reimagined as a never-ending, cyclical necessity to sustain an empire that thrived on terror.[6,7]

The Mexican cartels, whether knowingly or not, have resurrected this philosophy of perpetual war. Their skirmishes with rival factions are less about material gains and more about demonstrations of dominance, the public nature of their killings designed not simply to eliminate enemies but to send a message to the living. Bodies hung from bridges, beheadings filmed for mass consumption, and mass graves unearthed in cartel-controlled territories—all of these echo the same psychological warfare employed by the Aztec priesthood. In places like California, where cartel factions have embedded themselves within criminal networks, the Flower War logic is visible in the indiscriminate brutality inflicted upon their rivals, upon those who refuse to pay tribute, upon communities that resist their influence.

This transformation of California into a narco-colony, where cartel enforcers operate in tandem with a legal system that refuses to acknowledge their presence, marks a haunting return to a form of rule that predates the very concept of Western governance.

Bloodletting and the Economy of Fear

For the Maya, bloodletting was a divine transaction, a belief that the gods demanded nourishment in the form of spilled human essence.[8] Mayan rulers cut themselves with stingray spines, bled onto ritual papers, and burned the blood as an offering—not merely as religious acts but as statements of authority. To endure the pain of self-mutilation was to prove one's legitimacy; to bleed before the people was to confirm one's place at the apex of the social order.[9]

Human sacrifices, though not as widespread or as frequent as among the Aztecs, did occur in Mayan society, particularly during significant calendrical events and in times of crisis. These sacrifices were often conducted in cenotes, natural sinkholes regarded as sacred portals to the underworld. Victims, typically captives from warfare, were offered to appease the gods and ensure the prosperity and stability of Mayan society. The blood of these sacrifices was believed to nourish the gods, securing their benevolence and the continuation of natural cycles critical for agriculture and societal well-being.[10]

These sacrificial practices served not only as religious acts but also as potent political tools. They reinforced the social hierarchy, with the ruling class asserting their divine mandate through the orchestration of such spectacles. The public nature of these sacrifices served to unify the community through shared religious experiences, while simultaneously intimidating potential adversaries and maintaining social order.[11]

The modern cartel elite—those who control Mexico's drug empire and its incursions into California—engage in their own grotesque form of ritual bloodletting. While the ancient Maya rulers bled themselves, cartel lords outsource their pain onto others. Their subordinates, their enemies, and even their own recruits are subjected to ordeals of violence that serve as modern initiations into the empire of organized crime. Torture is not merely a means to an end but a rite of passage, a demonstration of loyalty, an assertion of dominance. Those who fail the test—those who scream too soon, who falter before the knife—are disposed of. In a chilling inversion of the ancient Mayan customs, the modern narco-priesthood does not sacrifice itself for legitimacy but sacrifices others to consolidate its power.

Resurrecting Ritual Violence: Cartel Brutality as Atavistic Continuity

The grotesque violence of Mexico's drug cartels is not merely a symptom of organized crime—it is the resurgence of a ritualized order that finds its antecedents in the sacrificial economies of pre-Columbian civilizations. Unlike the hierarchical structures of European and American mafias, which rely on discretion and backroom dealings, the Mexican cartels operate through the theater of terror, their violence not only functional but symbolic, orchestrated to communicate power through fear. The methods they employ—beheadings, dismemberments, public displays of corpses, and ceremonial executions—suggest not a modern criminal enterprise alone but a deep-seated cultural atavism, an inheritance of Mesoamerican systems of governance, where terror and tribute were inextricably linked.

The Revival of Death Spectacles

The most extreme forms of cartel violence are not merely tactical or punitive—they are performative, designed to instill awe and submission in the observer. In the same way that the Aztec priesthood mounted the skulls of their victims onto *tzompantli* (skull racks) to demonstrate the power of the state, cartel enforcers now hang bodies from bridges, dismember rivals in public squares, and post execution videos as both warning and spectacle. The case of Santiago Meza López, known as "El Pozolero" (The Stewmaker), who confessed to dissolving at least 300 bodies in acid at the behest of the Tijuana Cartel, mirrors the ceremonial dismemberments practiced by the Aztecs, where victims were torn apart to be "offered" to multiple deities. The ritualistic destruction of the body—whether through dissolution, decapitation, or immolation—suggests a continuity in the spiritual grammar of violence, one where the annihilation of the victim serves not only a practical end but a metaphysical one.[12]

Beyond the mere pragmatism of killing, the cartels engage in practices that suggest a fusion of criminal brutality and religious zealotry. Many sicarios (hitmen) are adherents of Santa Muerte, the narco-saint of death, whose veneration eerily resembles the human sacrifice cults of the past. Cartel members have been known to perform ritual bloodlettings before executions, invoke supernatural protection through ceremonial offerings, and engage in Santería practices to "bless" their killing sprees. Unlike traditional mafia organizations, which thrive on omertà (secrecy), the cartels revel in a sacrificial economy of violence, broadcasting their killings as a means of consolidating territorial and psychological dominance.

Symbolic Violence: Terror as Governance

The public nature of cartel executions is not an aberration of criminality but a return to a more archaic form of governance. Just as the Aztecs transformed sacrifice into a public ritual, where thousands would gather to witness the flaying, burning, and decapitation of captives, the cartels have revived the practice of ritualized warfare, where the spectacle of death serves both as punishment and reaffirmation of power. In cartel-controlled territories, mass executions function as both warning and tribute, compelling submission through acts of calculated savagery.

The hanging of mutilated bodies from overpasses, the abandonment of dismembered corpses in mass graves, and the ritual execution of defectors serve not just to eliminate enemies but to recreate the psychological landscape of Mesoamerican warfare, where captives were paraded through the streets before being sacrificed atop temple pyramids. The cartels' use of social media to disseminate beheading videos, often accompanied by chants, invocations, and symbolic gestures, further underscores the fusion of atavistic ritual and modern technological propaganda.

Unlike the European Mafia, which relies on silence, or the Colombian cartels, which operated under a strict profit-driven ethos, Mexican narco-violence resembles something closer to a death cult—one that has adopted the political theology of Mesoamerican warlords, fusing economic domination with ritualized terror. In this neo-tribal system, the cartels no longer exist simply as criminal organizations but as shadow governments, wielding terror as both currency and decree.

Cultural Atavism and the Cartel Phenomenon

Anthropological and Sociological Insights

Cultural atavism—the tendency of societies to revert to earlier patterns of behavior and social organization—offers a compelling framework for understanding the ritualistic violence of Mexican drug cartels. Anthropologists have long observed that in times of social, economic, or political instability, societies often resurrect archaic structures of power as a means of restoring control. In Mexico, the cartels' publicly staged executions, ceremonial mutilations, and supernatural justifications for violence are not merely tools of intimidation but echoes of pre-Columbian modes of governance, in which rule was predicated on terror, sacrificial spectacle, and the invocation of mystical forces.[13]

British anthropologist Edward Tylor's theory of "survivals" describes how cultural remnants persist beyond their original function, often re-emerging in moments of crisis.[14] The cartels' fixation on decapitation, flaying, and corpse desecration is not an aberration but a cultural survival—an unconscious inheritance of Mesoamerican rule, in which power was expressed through the public display of butchered bodies. These acts function as both propaganda and social control, terrifying rivals while reinforcing the quasi-religious authority of cartel warlords.

The persistence of these atavistic traits is not purely reactionary; they are embedded within the very fabric of Mexican cultural history. While much of the country's Spanish Catholic veneer outwardly rejected indigenous ritualistic violence, elements of it survived beneath the surface, subtly woven into spiritual practices, folk traditions, and even state violence. The resurgence of these ancient practices within cartel warfare is not just opportunism—it is a cultural reawakening of power through bloodletting.

Violence as a Form of Social and Political Order

Anthropologists have long contended that violence is not merely the absence of order—it is an alternative system of governance. In societies where state authority collapses, power defaults to those who can enforce it through spectacle, terror, and ritual.[15] The cartels, filling the vacuum left by a failing Mexican state, do not just employ violence as a tool of enforcement; they deify it, creating a parallel order in which brutality is sacralized, much like the theocratic warlords of Mesoamerican antiquity.

Cartel rule is governed by a hierarchy of death, in which public executions server multiple functions:

- **Initiation and Loyalty-Binding:** New recruits must often participate in ritual killings, much like warriors in Aztec and Mayan military cults.
- **Sacred Violence:** Killings are infused with supernatural meaning, mirroring pre-Columbian sacrifices that sustained cosmic balance.
- **Symbolic Dominance:** Corpses are staged in deliberate patterns—bodies flayed, hearts removed, remains suspended from bridges—serving the same terroristic function as the pyramidal displays of sacrificial victims in Tenochtitlán.

Sociologist Pierre Bourdieu's concept of symbolic violence is particularly relevant here. Cartel killings are not just executions; they are messages—engrained into the collective psyche through public displays of suffering.[16] Just as the Aztecs orchestrated mass sacrifices to intimidate subject populations, the cartels wield ritualized murder as an instrument of social control, ensuring submission through collective trauma.[17]

History offers abundant parallels to this atavistic regression in times of crisis. The rise of fascist movements in the early 20th century, for instance, saw entire societies regress into ritualized political violence, sacrificing individuals for the supposed purification of the state.[18] Similarly, religious fundamentalism often marks a return to theocratic bloodshed as a response to modernity's perceived decadence.[19] Mexican cartels embody a comparable regression—an abandonment of the bureaucratic order for a warlordism predicated on cruelty, devotion, and spectacle.[20,21,22]

Cartel Occultism: The Religious Basis for Extreme Violence

E. Richard Sorenson's concept of *pre-conquest consciousness* offers a compelling lens through which to analyze the persistence of ritualistic violence and occult traditions within modern Mexican society. Unlike the post-Enlightenment, rationalist framework that defines Western legal and moral structures, *pre-conquest consciousness* operates through a visceral, experiential mode of cognition, where reality is shaped by communal rituals, spiritual forces, and a sacralized understanding of violence. Within this framework, the ceremonial bloodletting and sacrificial rites of Mesoamerican civilizations were not mere expressions of brutality but fundamental mechanisms for maintaining cosmic order. These deeply embedded cultural memories, rather than being extinguished by conquest and colonization, have resurfaced in the underworld of contemporary organized crime. The narco-rituals of cartels, the veneration of Santa Muerte, and the mystical justifications for extreme violence reflect a latent but enduring epistemology—one where power, death, and transcendence remain intertwined in a sacred continuum beyond the constraints of modern juridical structures.[23]

Indeed, consider the veneration of Santa Muerte, the skeletal "Saint of Death," whose shrines fill cartel safehouses, adorned with offerings of tobacco, alcohol, and human remains. Santa Muerte is a modern incarnation of Mictecacihuatl, the Aztec goddess of the underworld, worshipped to ensure victory in battle and protection in the afterlife. The Narcosantuario of Jesús Malverde, the so-called "Narco-Saint," serves a similar function—a blend of Catholic ritual and indigenous mysticism, reinforcing the belief that divine favor justifies criminal enterprise.[24,25]

Anthropologist Ioan Grillo has documented how cartels employ brujos (sorcerers) and santeros (priests) to sanctify weapons, curse enemies, and "bless" executions. These rituals often involve animal sacrifice, human effigies, and blood offerings, replicating Mesoamerican rites meant to bind warriors to their gods.[26] This is not mere superstition—it is a calculated attempt to sacralize violence, legitimizing cartel killings as both an economic necessity and a cosmic duty.

Former El Paso deputy police chief Robert Almonte, an expert on narcotics and occult practices, observes:

"Narcos and gangs hold a profound belief in the power of prayer. They
are convinced that supernatural entities will shield them regardless of their
actions—a notion that dangerously emboldens traffickers, who genuinely
believe they can commit heinous acts and still secure a place in heaven."[27]

This belief system is expanding at an alarming rate, with estimates of
over 12 million adherents in Mexico and the U.S. Santa Muerte shrines
are increasingly discovered in cartel-controlled stash houses, often alongside human remains used in sacrificial rites. In 2010, a trafficker placed a
severed head next to the tomb of legendary cartel leader Arturo Beltrán
Leyva, an apparent offering to Santa Muerte.

The Catholic Church has condemned Santa Muerte as "blasphemous
and Satanic," with Pope Francis denouncing its worship as one of the
world's fastest-growing "religious" movements. Despite this, cartel devotion to death saints continues to spread, reinforcing the notion that cartel
rule is not merely criminal but quasi-religious, transforming violence into
an article of faith.

Altars to Santa Muerte can be found in private homes, with larger
statues standing in public squares in Mexico's impoverished areas.
Additionally, a Santa Muerte sanctuary boasting numerous life-sized effigies resides in an industrial zone of Las Vegas. Occasionally, these altars
exhibit bundles of cash offerings considered inviolable. Rival narcos—
including those from the infamous MS-13 gang—avoid tampering with
the money out of fear of inciting the saint's wrath, according to law
enforcement officials.

Many brutal murders, such as beheadings and human sacrifices committed by Mexican drug gangs, are in the name of Santa Muerte. In a
2016 interview, Edgar, a sicario for the Juarez Cartel, detailed his worship
practices, revealing to documentary filmmakers that he would pray to the
saint before each assassination to ensure success. "I actually sacrifice people for my Santa Muerte," stated Edgar, then twenty-six. "I kill for orders,
but I converse with her and say, 'Hey, I have a job. Just make it successful;
this life is yours.'" Edgar claimed to have executed sixty individuals on
behalf of the Juarez Cartel.[28]

The Santa Muerte cult's origins trace back to colonial-era Mexico, where worshippers venerated the folk deity clandestinely due to a Catholic Church ban. The cult re-emerged forcefully in the 1940s and surged again in 2001 when Queta Romero, a street vendor, established an outdoor shrine to Santa Muerte in Tepito, one of Mexico City's most violent districts. The shrine drew thousands of worshippers, including women seeking the saint's intervention against their husbands' mistresses.

In January 2010, a trafficker placed a severed head next to the tomb of legendary cartel leader Arturo Beltran Leyva, which is adorned with Santa Muerte paraphernalia. Experts suggested the severed head was an offering to Santa Muerte. Authorities have reported a few Santa Muerte-inspired murders on the U.S. side of the border, including a 2010 beheading in Chandler, Arizona.[29] In Cook County, Chicago, prosecutors recorded thirteen Santa Muerte-linked murders between 2009 and 2011 by cartel hit squads.[30] One such crew had Santa Muerte stickers on their vehicles, tattoos on their bodies, altars in their homes, and Santa bands for their cash.[31]

In these practices, the cartels draw a direct line to their Mesoamerican heritage, not as mere homage but as a strategic invocation of ancient power. The blend of ritualistic killings, Santería, and the worship of death saints like Santa Muerte underscores a form of cultural atavism that perpetuates the legacy of historical religious practices. This continuity of ancient rites within modern criminal operations illustrates how deeply embedded these cultural elements remain, influencing the extreme and unusual brutality of Mexico's cartels.

The Persistence of Ritualistic Violence

What we see in the ritualized violence of Mexican cartels is not mere brutality, but a cultural and historical continuity—a return to archaic models of governance, in which death is both spectacle and sacrament. The beheadings, the dismemberments, the ritual sacrifices—these are not aberrations, but echoes of a past in which rule was enforced through bloodletting and divine terror.

Just as the Aztecs once offered thousands of human hearts to their gods, so too do modern cartels spill blood to assert dominion over their criminal fiefdoms. The invocation of Santa Muerte, Malverde, and pre-Columbian ritualism is not incidental—it is a deliberate assertion of an ancient social order in the face of modern chaos.

The collapse of Mexico's state authority has not produced a lawless vacuum, but a return to a more primal form of sovereignty—one in which power is defined not by constitutions, but by the monopoly on terror. Cartel violence is a modern expression of an ancient truth: when institutions fail, men turn to the gods of death, and order is written in blood.

Comparative Analysis with Other Organized Crime

Unlike Mexican cartels, traditional organized crime syndicates—the Italian Mafia, Russian Bratva, and Japanese Yakuza—function within cultural contexts that emphasize discretion, secrecy, and economic longevity. Their violence is measured, used sparingly to maintain order within their ranks or eliminate threats, but rarely as a public performance of dominance.

In *Mafias on the Move*, Federico Varese details how these organizations prioritize stealth over spectacle, operating within a framework that ensures long-term survival rather than immediate terror.[32] Similarly, Mark Bowden's *Killing Pablo* describes how the Colombian cartels, despite their notoriety, engaged in strategically targeted violence—assassinations of rivals, bombings designed to eliminate obstacles to business, but never the grotesque theater of terror that defines Mexico's cartels. Pablo Escobar's brutality was legendary, but even he did not employ the ritualized, sacrificial violence that is common in cartel operations.[33]

This is the crucial distinction: Mexican cartels do not merely use violence; they weaponize spectacle. Their brutality is not just strategic—it is ceremonial, deeply embedded in a cultural logic of power that traces back to pre-Columbian civilizations. While the Sicilian Mafia kills in whispers, the cartels kill in proclamations, ensuring that their executions are not only seen but absorbed as acts of submission, ritual, and governance.

The ritualized and symbolic nature of cartel violence is an outlier in global organized crime. It is not simply about controlling territory or eliminating competitors; it is a reassertion of a historical mode of rule, one where terror was not a means to an end but an instrument of social cohesion and divine affirmation. This form of cultural atavism—where ancient traditions resurface in response to contemporary crises—has no real equivalent in other organized crime contexts. The cartels, in this sense, are not just criminal networks; they are the inheritors of a much older, more brutal lineage of rule—one that has outlived empires and nations and shows no sign of fading.

California: Narco-Colony—The Return of Pre-Columbian Violence

Cartel dominance in Mexico is not an isolated crisis—it is a geopolitical contagion that has spread northward, facilitated by California's weak governance, sanctuary policies, and institutional corruption. What was once the western frontier of American civilization, a beacon of prosperity and order, has now devolved into a battleground where the cartel warlords exercise de facto sovereignty. California is no longer merely a hub for cartel operations; it is an occupied territory, where cartel influence has metastasized beyond the narcotics trade and into the very fabric of the state's governance, economy, and criminal underworld. Through a mix of coercion, corruption, and institutional infiltration, California has, in effect, become an extension of the Mexican narco-state.

The cartels do not simply bring crime to California—they bring an entire governing model, one rooted in a form of ritualized terror that is both an instrument of control and a symbolic assertion of power. This model, forged in the tribal warfare of pre-Columbian Mesoamerica, reintroduces an atavistic intensity of violence that stands in stark contrast to the rule of law that once defined the state. The sheer brutality of cartel violence—the public beheadings, the mutilations, the bodies left as warnings—bears a disturbing resemblance to the sacrificial terror once employed by the Aztec priest-kings. The message is the same: submission or annihilation.

California as the Cartel's Tributary State

Sanctuary policies, coupled with the federal government's abdication of border security, have not only allowed the cartels to infiltrate California—they have effectively invited them. The state's refusal to cooperate with federal immigration enforcement, combined with its permissive stance toward illicit economies, has provided the perfect breeding ground for cartel expansion. From the fentanyl trade flooding the streets of Los Angeles and San Francisco to human trafficking networks operating with impunity, California has become a vital outpost in the cartels' empire, a staging ground for further incursions into the United States.

Cartels now dictate the rules of engagement in vast swaths of California's underworld, from the Emerald Triangle's black market cannabis farms—where armed cartel enforcers intimidate and murder local growers—to the drug corridors running through the Central Valley. Entire communities, particularly in rural and agricultural regions, have become dependent on the narco-economy, either through direct involvement or through the extortion and taxation mechanisms that mimic the Aztec tribute system.

Conclusion

The theory that Mexican cartel violence is not an aberration but a resurgence of deep-seated cultural atavism from pre-Columbian Mesoamerica reframes the nature of the crisis spilling across the U.S.-Mexico border. The ritualized brutality—beheadings, dismemberments, and sacrificial executions—does not merely serve strategic ends; it mirrors the ceremonial bloodshed of the Aztecs and Maya, where terror was governance, violence was currency, and death was an instrument of dominion. What we see today in cartel-controlled territories is not simply organized crime—it is a system of rule, a resurrected form of political violence that has transcended time, conquest, and even nation-states.

This atavistic continuity is no longer confined to Mexico. California, through its sanctuary policies, porous border enforcement, and institutionalized complacency, has allowed this parallel order to take root on American soil. The Golden State, once a beacon of prosperity and law, now harbors a criminal class that wields power in a manner indistinguishable from the warlords of Mesoamerican history. The mass graves found in remote regions, the dismembered bodies left as warnings in cartel-occupied towns, and the narco-economy fueling entire industries—these are not the isolated actions of underground syndicates. They are the signs of a foreign system of power embedding itself into the American landscape.

The failure to recognize this historical continuity has crippled any meaningful response. Viewing cartel violence purely as a law enforcement issue, as though it were merely a criminal enterprise rather than a governing model, ensures failure. The cartel state is not a deviation from Mexico's past—it is its extension. And California, by allowing this imported governance model to metastasize, has become a testing ground for the erosion of American sovereignty. Without a radical reassessment of this threat—one that accounts for the ideological, historical, and mythological dimensions of cartel power—California will continue its descent from a functioning state into a narco-colony, where blood, fear, and submission dictate the terms of order.

PART III

SILENT CONQUEST

CHAPTER 13

TREASON BY NEGLIGENCE

A nation that refuses to defend its borders is no longer a nation—it is a landmass governed by inertia, awaiting its dissolution. This is not a question of ideology but of first principles, understood from antiquity to modernity. Sovereignty is not a philosophical abstraction; it is a hard boundary, the line between order and anarchy, between self-rule and subjugation. And yet, under the Biden-Harris administration, this most fundamental prerogative of statehood has not been eroded by invasion or conquest, but by deliberate abdication. The collapse of the southern border is not a policy failure but the most brazen betrayal of the constitutional order in modern American history—a dereliction so sweeping that it constitutes treason by willful neglect.

This is not the treason of spies or saboteurs, but a quieter, more insidious betrayal—the kind committed not by foreign adversaries, but by those entrusted with the nation's survival. The administration's refusal to enforce immigration law has led to the unimpeded influx of at least eight million illegal migrants—a demographic tidal wave that eclipses the scale of most military invasions. Under Kamala Harris, the "Border Czar," and Homeland Security Secretary Alejandro Mayorkas, immigration enforcement has been reduced to a pantomime. Laws are ignored, resources are squandered, and sovereignty is ceded, not in dramatic defeats, but in daily, grinding surrender.

The consequences are not theoretical; they are manifest: cartel-controlled human trafficking networks operate with impunity, fentanyl pours into American cities, and violent criminals cross unchecked—all with the silent endorsement of an administration that has chosen political expediency over national survival. This is not incompetence—incompetence would imply an effort, however misguided. This is intentional.

A republic cannot long survive when those charged with its defense surrender its borders as a matter of policy. What we are witnessing is not the accidental unraveling of a nation, but its deliberate unmaking. This chapter will examine the legal, historical, and philosophical dimensions of treason, arguing that the Biden administration's actions—or, more precisely, its studied inaction—constitute an existential attack on the American nation.

Legal Framework for Treason in the United States

The United States Constitution, in Article III, Section 3, defines treason as follows: "Treason against the United States shall consist only in levying War against them, or in adhering to their Enemies, giving them Aid and Comfort."[1]

This language is deliberately narrow, designed by the framers to prevent the misuse of treason charges, which in English history had often been employed as a tool of political oppression. Historically, courts have applied this definition conservatively, reserving treason charges for direct acts of war or collusion with declared enemies.[2]

However, modern threats do not conform to 18th-century expectations. The framers could not have anticipated a world in which non-state actors—terrorist networks, transnational cartels, and criminal empires—exerted the kind of power once reserved for nation-states. The legal framework governing treason, designed for traditional warfare, is ill-equipped to address asymmetric threats—entities that do not bear a flag, but nonetheless wage war on the republic.

Mexican drug cartels, for all practical purposes, function as hostile paramilitary organizations. They exert territorial control, enforce their own legal codes, wage open warfare against both the Mexican and U.S. governments, and deploy tactical operations that resemble insurgency rather than crime. If treason is defined as giving "aid and comfort" to enemies of the United States, then a government that facilitates cartel expansion, weakens border security, and allows cartel operatives to flourish within U.S. territory must be held accountable under the highest constitutional scrutiny.

Expanding the Definition of "Enemy"

Traditional legal interpretations of "enemy" under Article III, Section 3 have historically been confined to foreign nations engaged in declared wars. But this rigid framework fails to account for modern asymmetric threats—terrorist networks, transnational criminal organizations, and cartel regimes that operate as de facto states, wielding military, political, and economic influence.

Measured by sheer body count, Mexican drug cartels have inflicted more casualties on American civilians than any foreign adversary in modern history. Their tactics, reach, and ability to destabilize the United States far exceed those of conventional belligerents. They do not simply traffic narcotics—they engage in targeted assassinations, coordinate cross-border incursions, and systematically poison the American population through fentanyl distribution. By any functional measure, they meet the criteria of a hostile entity actively waging war on U.S. sovereignty.

Furthermore, the cartels are not merely organized crime syndicates; they are territorial powers that exert sovereign-like control over multiple Mexican states and dictate passage across the U.S.-Mexico border. They do not operate within the constraints of a criminal network—they function as quasi-state actors, establishing shadow governments, levying "taxes" on businesses and residents, and enforcing laws through extrajudicial executions.

This distinction is not theoretical. Cartels are fundamentally different from groups like the Italian Mafia, Russian Bratva, or Japanese Yakuza. They do not seek to avoid confrontation with the state; they actively challenge it. Their influence is not limited to economic exploitation but extends to territorial occupation, direct engagement with government forces, and infiltration of legal institutions.

Cartels systematically assassinate politicians, journalists, and law enforcement officers who oppose their rule.

They control vast swathes of Mexico, collecting tribute and dictating governance in ways indistinguishable from insurgent forces.

They possess military-grade weaponry, armored vehicles, and personnel trained in warfare—outgunning many official armed forces.

Perhaps most damningly, cartels are responsible for the mass trafficking of fentanyl—a substance so lethal that it qualifies as a weapon of mass destruction in all but name. The Biden administration's failure to secure the border has enabled these organizations to expand their operations deep into American territory, embedding their networks within U.S. cities.

This is not neglect—it is complicity. By refusing to secure the border, the administration is not merely allowing cartel activity; it is facilitating it. It is aiding and abetting forces that actively undermine national sovereignty, devastate communities, and inflict large-scale destruction.

If a government knowingly allows hostile actors to infiltrate and flourish within its borders, how does that not constitute "giving aid and comfort" to an enemy of the state?

Levying War through Non-Enforcement

The argument that an administration has "levied war" against the United States by inaction may seem unconventional, yet modern conflict is not always waged through formal military confrontations. Warfare today is often fought through indirect means—cyber attacks, economic destabilization, demographic shifts, and the erosion of national security.

The deliberate refusal to enforce border security, allowing millions of undocumented migrants—some linked to cartels, gangs, and terror networks—to enter the country, constitutes a form of asymmetric warfare. By knowingly creating the conditions under which the nation is weakened from within, the administration is passively engaging in an act that directly undermines U.S. sovereignty.

This is not hyperbole. A porous border is not just a lapse in security—it is a structural attack on the integrity of the nation-state. The sheer scale of illegal migration and cartel infiltration transforms what might be classified as policy failure into an active dismantling of the United States as a sovereign entity.

The Guarantee Clause: Securing the Nation against Invasion

The Guarantee Clause of the U.S. Constitution (Article IV, Section 4) obliges the federal government to protect states from invasion. While the framers envisioned military threats, contemporary legal scholars have expanded this to include non-military incursions that threaten national security, such as the mass state-sanctioned illegal immigration currently destabilizing the U.S. border.[3] This modern "invasion," often accompanied by drug cartels and human traffickers, undermines sovereignty and community stability.

In *New York v. United States* (1992), the Supreme Court recognized the federal government's constitutional responsibility to protect states.[4] Although the case concerned the disposal of radioactive waste, the ruling affirmed the government's duty under the Guarantee Clause to intervene when state security is threatened. This principle applies equally to today's border crisis, where criminal elements exploit weakened borders, destabilizing communities across the nation. The federal government's failure to secure the southern border represents not merely a lapse in policy but a fundamental breach of its constitutional duty to protect the states from invasion, both in spirit and in law.

Take Care Clause: Constitutional Obligation to Execute the Law

The Take Care Clause of the U.S. Constitution (Article II, Section 3) mandates that the President "shall take Care that the Laws be faithfully executed." This clause imposes a duty upon the President to ensure that federal laws are implemented as enacted by Congress. The Immigration and Nationality Act (INA) requires the detention of individuals entering the United States without proper documentation. The Biden administration's policies allowing for the release of illegal alien migrants into the interior constitutes a failure to uphold this statutory mandate.

As noted by Judge T. Kent Wetherell, this dereliction effectively replaces statutory law with the administration's own policy, an unconstitutional overreach that usurps Congress's legislative authority. Judge Wetherell likened the administration's approach to posting a "Come In, We're Open" sign at the southern border, suggesting an invitation to lawlessness and a significant constitutional violation.[5]

Legal scholars have debated the extent of executive discretion under the Take Care Clause. While the President possesses some latitude in enforcing laws, this discretion is not absolute. The Congressional Research Service notes that the Take Care Clause imposes a duty on the President to comply with and execute clear statutory directives as enacted by Congress.[6] Therefore, policies that effectively replace statutory law with administrative preferences may overstep constitutional boundaries, undermining the separation of powers by encroaching upon Congress's legislative authority.

Jeffrey H. Anderson, in *City Journal*, underscores that Biden's refusal to enforce the INA is not just a policy failure, but a direct violation of the Constitution. By prioritizing political considerations over the rule of law, Biden has substituted his administration's policy for the immigration law established by Congress. This abdication of constitutional duty meets the threshold for impeachment by undermining Congress's exclusive legislative authority and eroding the foundational principle of separation of powers.[7]

By ignoring the INA, Biden has abandoned the executive's core function, and in doing so, has opened the door to impeachment for his refusal to "faithfully execute" the laws of the United States. This deliberate inaction, favoring politically motivated agendas over statutory obligations, undermines the constitutional framework and the separation of powers that underpin American governance.

Federal Responsibility for Immigration Enforcement: *Arizona v. United States*

Immigration enforcement has long been the exclusive prerogative of the federal government, a principle emphatically reinforced by the Supreme Court in *Arizona v. United States*, 567 U.S. 387 (2012).[8] In this landmark case, the Court invalidated significant provisions of an Arizona law aimed at regulating immigration, holding that control over immigration falls squarely within federal jurisdiction. By failing to secure the southern border and permitting mass migration, the federal government is abdicating its constitutionally mandated duty to regulate immigration, a clear violation of its exclusive authority.

The Court's decision in *Arizona v. United States* underscores the preemption of state efforts to legislate in matters of immigration, reiterating the federal government's overarching responsibility to secure national borders.[9] The Biden-Harris administration's refusal to enforce immigration laws thus constitutes a clear dereliction constitutional enforcement duties.

Migrant Protection Protocols and Federal Negligence: *Texas v. Biden*
The legal battle over the Migrant Protection Protocols (MPP), also known as the "Remain in Mexico" policy, further underscores the administration's negligence. In *Texas v. Biden*, states argued that the Biden-Harris administration's rescission of the MPP exacerbated illegal immigration, leading to security risks along the southern border. The Fifth Circuit Court of Appeals ruled that the administration's termination of this program violated federal law, highlighting the government's failure to implement effective border control policies.[10]

The significance of this case lies in its clear assertion that immigration policies are essential to national security, and that the executive's refusal to enforce them is a violation of its legal duty. The administration's reckless abandonment of border security measures like the MPP is a gross dereliction of its responsibilities.

Gross Negligence and Dereliction of Duty: A Constitutional Crisis
Gross negligence represents a severe departure from the expected standard of care, particularly when it shows reckless disregard for the safety, rights, and well-being of others. In the case of governmental officials, such negligence becomes actionable when it results in constitutional violations. The Biden-Harris administration's failure to secure the southern border is not simply a policy misstep but a constitutional breach that meets, and arguably exceeds, this threshold of gross negligence.

Constitutional Obligations
Under Article II, Section 3, the President is constitutionally required to "take Care that the Laws be faithfully executed." Additionally, Article IV, Section 4—the Guarantee Clause—mandates that the federal government protect states from invasion.[11] Unauthorized mass migration, facilitated

by transnational criminal organizations, could reasonably fall within this broad interpretation of "invasion." The administration's inaction in the face of such a crisis not only violates statutory mandates but also undermines fundamental constitutional duties.

Legal Obligations and Dereliction of Duty

The federal government is legally obligated to protect the United States from foreign threats, including unauthorized mass migration. The Immigration and Nationality Act (INA) provides a statutory framework for border enforcement, mandating the detention and removal of unauthorized entrants.[12] By dismantling effective border control measures—such as terminating the "Remain in Mexico" policy—and by refusing to enforce the law, the administration has clearly breached its legal responsibilities. This deliberate failure to act constitutes gross negligence as it directly endangers the nation's security.

Statutory Mandates

The Immigration and Nationality Act (INA), as a core statutory mandate, requires the detention and removal of unauthorized entrants.[13] The administration's decision to terminate critical border policies, coupled with non-enforcement directives that limit ICE and Border Patrol operations, constitutes a breach of the duty of care. This policy shift has facilitated a surge in illegal entries, empowered criminal organizations, and left the southern border dangerously vulnerable.[14]

Foreseeable Harm

The harm caused by these non-enforcement policies was not only foreseeable but also preventable. The administration was fully aware of the risks posed by its border policies—ranging from increased violent crime to drug trafficking and widespread social disorder—yet it pursued these policies despite the clear evidence of impending harm. The administration's actions thus reflect reckless disregard, with the resulting increase in crime and social instability directly linked to its refusal to enforce immigration laws and secure the border.

Causation and Foreseeability

A critical element in establishing gross negligence is demonstrating that the harm caused was both foreseeable and avoidable. The Biden-Harris administration was well aware of the risks associated with its lax border policies. The unchecked influx of migrants, including individuals with criminal backgrounds and ties to hostile entities, has led to a documented rise in violent crimes, drug overdoses, and a breakdown in social order. These consequences were not accidental; they were entirely foreseeable and preventable had the administration adhered to its statutory and constitutional responsibilities.

Comparative Negligence Doctrine

In tort law, the Comparative Negligence Doctrine allows for liability to be apportioned based on the degree of fault. Applying this principle to the federal government's failure to secure the border, one could argue that the administration bears the lion's share of responsibility for the ongoing border crisis. While state policies or local enforcement actions may have played a role, the federal government's gross negligence in dismantling border controls and refusing to enforce the law is the primary cause of the damage wrought by illegal immigration, criminal activities, and the national security risks currently facing the United States.[15]

The Biden-Harris administration's handling of border security is not just an example of failed policy—it represents gross negligence and a dereliction of constitutional duty. By ignoring statutory and constitutional mandates, the administration has recklessly endangered the well-being of American citizens. The foreseeable harm caused by these policies is severe, including the empowerment of criminal organizations, the erosion of public safety, and a deterioration of national sovereignty. The administration's actions have not only undermined the rule of law but also placed the security of the United States at profound risk.

Negligence as Betrayal: Lessons from History and Philosophy

The Biden administration's failure to secure the southern border is not a mere lapse in policy—it represents a far more insidious form of governance failure. When those entrusted with power neglect their primary duties, such negligence becomes a betrayal of the very foundations of the state. History is replete with examples where such failures, whether through inaction or passive complicity, catalyzed the collapse of civilizations. From Cicero's Rome to the Court of Charles I, and through the philosophical reflections of thinkers like Aristotle, John Locke, and Edmund Burke, we find a consistent warning: the most dangerous betrayal is often not the dagger in the back, but the slow rot from within, caused by negligence and dereliction of duty.

Cicero's Rome: The Consequences of Political Inaction

Cicero, one of Rome's most eloquent statesmen, understood that neglect in governance was as dangerous as outright conspiracy. In his *Orations Against Catiline*, Cicero condemned the Roman Senate's failure to act decisively against the internal threat posed by Catiline's conspiracy. Catiline sought to overthrow the Republic, yet the Senate hesitated, paralyzed by indifference and fear. Cicero's oratory did more than expose a traitor; it revealed the deep rot of inaction within Rome's ruling class. The Senate's passivity, Cicero argued, was a betrayal of the Republic itself—one that would hasten its demise.[16]

The Roman Senate's failure to act decisively mirrors contemporary governance failures. Today, the federal government's refusal to enforce border security despite clear and escalating threats—drug cartels, human trafficking, and illegal migration—parallels the inaction that allowed Rome to crumble from within. Just as the Senate's negligence enabled Rome's enemies to gather strength, so too does the current administration's passive stance embolden criminal elements to operate with impunity. In both cases, inaction undermines the integrity of the state, betraying its core duty to protect its citizens.

Aristotle's Polis and the Moral Obligation of Governance

Aristotle's political philosophy is built on the idea that the state (the polis) exists to enable its citizens to achieve their highest potential. A well-functioning state must prioritize justice, security, and the common good. For Aristotle, leaders who fail to uphold these principles are not merely incompetent; they are morally culpable for the state's decline. Governance is not simply about maintaining order—it is about actively promoting the flourishing of its citizens. Neglect, in this sense, is not just a dereliction of duty but a betrayal of the moral purpose of the state.

This concept applies to the contemporary border crisis. By failing to protect the southern border, the state abdicates its fundamental obligation to ensure the safety and well-being of its people. In Aristotle's framework, such negligence undermines the polis, creating conditions where injustice thrives, and societal harmony disintegrates. Criminal cartels and human traffickers, much like the destabilizing forces in ancient Greece, exploit this governmental vacuum, further eroding the state's capacity to fulfill its moral duty.

Locke and the Social Contract: Breach of Trust

John Locke's *Second Treatise of Government* provides a robust framework for understanding why the state's failure to protect its citizens constitutes a profound breach of trust. According to Locke, the government exists to protect the life, liberty, and property of its citizens. The social contract is built upon this premise: citizens surrender certain freedoms in exchange for the security that the government provides. When a government fails to meet this obligation—particularly by failing to protect its citizens from external threats—it violates the social contract and forfeits its legitimacy.[17]

The unchecked flow of illegal migrants, criminal organizations, and narcotics across the southern border represents a direct violation of the social contract. The Biden administration's failure to enforce immigration laws and secure the border jeopardizes the safety, property, and well-being of American citizens. Locke would argue that such negligence not only erodes public trust but fundamentally undermines the government's claim to legitimate authority. When the state abandons its protective role, it breaks the very covenant upon which its power is founded.

Negligence as Treason: The Crucible of Charles I

The execution of King Charles I during the English Civil War serves as a compelling historical example of how neglecting one's sovereign duties can rise to the level of treason. While Charles is often remembered for his abuses of power and his authoritarian tendencies, his downfall was equally the result of his failure to effectively manage the unrest within his king-dom. By refusing to adequately address the grievances of Parliament and his subjects, Charles allowed internal disorder to fester, ultimately leading to civil war and the collapse of the monarchy.[18]

Charles was not executed solely for overreach; he was condemned for his negligence in leadership. His inability to secure the stability of the monarchy in the face of mounting crises, including his failure to meaning-fully engage with Parliament, made him complicit in the kingdom's disin-tegration.[19] This negligence became a form of betrayal—one that invited domestic chaos and rendered his authority untenable.

The parallels to the current U.S. border crisis are striking. Just as Charles I neglected his responsibility to address growing internal instabil-ity, the Biden-Harris administration's failure to secure the southern bor-der represents a dangerous abdication of its constitutional duty. National security, like the stability of Charles's monarchy, is predicated on main-taining order and addressing clear threats. The administration's deliberate inaction in the face of escalating border crises—marked by unchecked migration and the rise of criminal cartels—jeopardizes the stability of the nation, much as Charles's negligence endangered his kingdom.

In both cases, neglect is not merely a failure of governance but a pro-found betrayal of the sovereign duty to protect the state. King Charles's refusal to heed the political and social fractures of his time led directly to his trial and execution in 1649, setting a precedent for how neglect in leadership can become treasonous. His downfall demonstrates that gover-nance is not merely about wielding power; it requires a proactive defense of the state's integrity. Failing to act decisively when the survival of the nation is at stake amounts to an abdication of sovereignty itself.

The Biden-Harris administration's current neglect of border security mir-rors Charles I's failure to address the unrest within England. Criminal activi-ties and unchecked migration across the U.S. southern border are the mod-ern equivalent of the internal disorder that plagued Charles's reign. In both cases, the consequences of neglect are not theoretical; they manifest in real-time threats to national stability. Like Charles, the administration's refusal to fulfill its protective responsibilities risks a profound collapse of order—one that can only be viewed as a betrayal of the state's most fundamental duties.

The historical record is clear: when rulers fail to address domestic disorder, when they neglect the security of the state, their negligence can rise to the level of treason. The lessons from King Charles I's execution resonate with the current border crisis, underscoring the dangerous consequences of inaction in governance.

Burke and the Moral Duty of Leadership

Edmund Burke, in his *Reflections on the Revolution in France*, emphasized the moral responsibility of leaders to protect and preserve the institutions that sustain society. For Burke, leadership was not just about wielding power; it was about safeguarding the social order against decay. Neglecting this responsibility, especially in the face of clear threats, is a profound betrayal of the trust placed in leaders by the people.[20]

Burke's warning applies directly to the current border crisis. By failing to secure the border, the administration is neglecting its most basic duty to protect the nation from external threats. This dereliction of duty is not just a policy failure; it is a moral failure, one that threatens the integrity of the state itself.[21] Much like the French revolutionaries who tore down the institutions meant to protect the people, the administration's failure to act decisively in the face of a border crisis is a betrayal of its sacred trust.

Executive Accountability: Lessons from Andrew Johnson's Impeachment

The impeachment of President Andrew Johnson in 1868 stands as a pivotal example of how a president's failure to execute the law can lead to serious constitutional consequences. Although the formal charges against Johnson revolved around his violation of the Tenure of Office Act, the underlying issue was far broader: Johnson's refusal to enforce federal Reconstruction laws, specifically those designed to protect the civil rights of freed slaves and maintain order in the post-Civil War South. His neglect was seen as a deliberate undermining of the nation's effort to rebuild, and it was this broader context of executive negligence that motivated Congress to act.[22]

Johnson's impeachment serves as a critical reminder that a president's responsibility extends beyond merely following statutes—it encompasses the duty to faithfully execute laws that preserve the nation's welfare and security. By refusing to uphold these laws, Johnson breached his constitutional obligations, jeopardizing the fragile peace of a nation emerging from civil conflict. Congress viewed this negligence as a constitutional violation severe enough to warrant his removal from office.

This precedent has modern implications. The Biden-Harris administration's failure to secure the U.S. southern border—despite clear legal obligations under the Immigration and Nationality Act—represents a similar kind of executive negligence. Immigration law, much like Reconstruction law, is designed to safeguard national security and the rule of law. By selectively neglecting their duty to enforce these laws, the administration not only undermines the statutory framework but also risks destabilizing the country's social and political fabric.

Johnson's impeachment illustrates that gross negligence, particularly when it endangers national stability, can rise to the level of an impeachable offense. His refusal to enforce laws crucial to the integrity of the nation drew Congress's ire not merely as a violation of a specific statute but as a profound betrayal of the executive's duty to protect and uphold the law. The lesson is clear: when a president's actions (or inactions) threaten the security and constitutional order of the country, the mechanisms for accountability—impeachment being the ultimate one—must come into play.

In this light, the Biden-Harris administration's ongoing failure to enforce immigration laws represents more than a mere policy disagreement. Like Johnson's dereliction during Reconstruction, it raises serious questions about constitutional accountability. The administration's negligence in addressing the border crisis, despite the clear and present dangers posed by criminal cartels and unchecked migration, mirrors the failure of past leaders who neglected their duties in times of national crisis.

The impeachment of Andrew Johnson thus serves not only as a historical event but as a constitutional precedent. It underscores that gross negligence in executing federal law, especially when it imperils national security and civil order, can and should be grounds for serious scrutiny, and potentially, for impeachment. As in Johnson's time, the refusal to uphold federal law in today's context is not merely a political misstep—it is a constitutional failure with profound consequences for the nation's stability and security.

Federal Negligence and the Collapse of California

The crisis created by the Biden administration's willful negligence and dereliction of duty to protect the border, has metastasized across American
cities and fundamentally undermined millions of Americans' quality of
life and their pursuit of happiness. None more so than California has
borne the brunt of this administrative betrayal. The state now functions as
the primary cartel staging ground in the United States:

- Los Angeles and San Diego serve as major hubs for cartel
  operations, with cartel-linked fentanyl overdoses reaching
  unprecedented levels.
- Sanctuary policies shield cartel operatives from federal
  prosecution, ensuring that their networks remain intact.
- Illegal marijuana grow operations in Northern California
  are now dominated by cartel affiliates, running labor camps
  indistinguishable from those in cartel-controlled Mexico.

This is not merely a failure of federal leadership; it is a collapse of governance at every level. The same patterns that allowed cartels to seize control
of Mexican territory are now observable in California. The state, once an
economic and cultural powerhouse, is descending into a neo-feudal order,
where lawlessness is tolerated, criminals are protected, and sovereignty is
an afterthought.

The Biden administration's betrayal is not an abstract legal argument—
it is a lived reality, evident in the degradation of cities like San Francisco,
Los Angeles, and Fresno, where cartel activity is indistinguishable from
that south of the border.

Conclusion

The Biden-Harris administration's failure to secure the southern border
represents not merely a policy misstep but an existential threat to the very
foundations of sovereignty, rule of law, and national security. The implications of this dereliction extend far beyond the immediate crisis—it erodes
the essential pillars of governance, setting dangerous precedents that reverberate through the fabric of the state. When the government willingly

neglects its duty to enforce the law, public trust is eroded, legal institutions are undermined, and the cohesion necessary for a stable society begins to unravel.

At its core, this negligence compromises the nation's sovereignty—an inviolable principle enshrined in both international law and the U.S. Constitution. By failing to control its borders, the federal government weakens the integrity of the state and opens the door to external and internal threats, empowering transnational criminal organizations and exacerbating public safety concerns. Crime, public health risks, and the overextension of public resources become inevitable consequences of this unchecked influx, creating a strain on communities that threatens the welfare of American citizens.

Internationally, the erosion of border security signals weakness, emboldening adversaries and undermining the United States' standing in global affairs. A nation that cannot defend its own borders invites challenges to its authority, both from within and beyond, diminishing its influence and credibility on the world stage.

Negligence in governance, particularly in the domain of national security, amounts to a profound betrayal of constitutional duty and ethical responsibility. The administration's failure to uphold its obligations under the Guarantee Clause and the Immigration and Nationality Act presents a compelling case for treason by negligence. As history has demonstrated—from the fall of the Roman Republic to the collapse of the Confederacy—the abdication of sovereign responsibilities by leaders, whether by malice or neglect, inevitably leads to national decline.

Philosophers such as Locke, Burke, and Aristotle have long warned of the perils of weak leadership and the moral duty of the state to protect its citizens. These failures are not theoretical—they manifest in real-world consequences that threaten the stability and continuity of the state. When a government fails to secure the social contract, when it neglects the protection of its people, it forfeits the moral and legal legitimacy to rule.

The administration's mishandling of border security represents a stark case of gross negligence, perhaps rising to the level of treason. While the argument for treason may challenge traditional legal interpretations, it is an essential exploration in light of the unprecedented scale of the crisis.

More concretely, the charge of gross negligence is irrefutable, supported by statutory obligations, legal precedents, and the clear foreseeability of the harm caused.

The Biden-Harris administration's failure to act has not only weakened the nation's borders but also exposed its citizens to escalating dangers, underscoring the urgent need for accountability at the highest levels of governance. The stakes could not be higher, for the path forward will determine whether the American experiment continues to thrive or succumbs to the errors of history.

CHAPTER 14

ETHNIC CLEANSING

Ethnic cleansing is often imagined as something crude and brutal—machetes in the night, mass graves, forced marches through barren landscapes. But history tells a more unsettling story. The most effective demographic reconfigurations have rarely been executed through overt violence alone; more often, they have been coldly bureaucratic, methodical, and justified under the banner of progress. The Biden-Harris administration's immigration policies fit this mold with unnerving precision. What is being carried out under the guise of compassion and inclusion is, in reality, a calculated strategy to transform the demographic and political fabric of the United States.

This is not a mismanaged border crisis. It is state-engineered displacement. The arrival of over 12 million illegal migrants since 2021 is not an accident, nor a humanitarian inevitability—it is the product of deliberate policy choices designed to erode national cohesion, dilute the existing electorate, and establish an unchallengeable political hegemony. The blueprint is not new. From Stalin's forced relocations to the Chinese Communist Party's demographic engineering in Xinjiang, history is rife with regimes using population shifts as instruments of power. The key difference is that in America, the process has been repackaged as social justice, and its consequences are no less profound.

This chapter dissects the ideological and strategic motives behind the administration's demographic agenda, placing it within the broader historical context of state-led population engineering. It examines how mass immigration—once a tool of national development—has been weaponized as a mechanism for political entrenchment, with California serving as a grim case study in the corrosive effects of such policies. It interrogates the legal, ethical, and constitutional implications of this grand demographic experiment and argues that the transformation being inflicted upon the United States is not a passive shift, but an act of deliberate, systemic displacement—one that demands urgent scrutiny before the nation is rendered unrecognizable.

Historical Precedents: Strategic Manipulation of Demographics

The Partition of India (1947): Ethnic Homogenization by Design

The partition of India in 1947 presents a harrowing example of demographic engineering on a colossal scale. The partition was sanitized as migration and often depicted as an inevitable outcome of decolonization—a chaotic and tragic unraveling of the British Empire's final threads. However, this interpretation obscures the deliberate machinations that led to one of the largest forced migrations in human history. The decision to divide India along religious lines was not a reluctant concession to on-the-ground realities but a calculated move to create ethnically homogeneous states that would be easier to control and govern post-independence.[1]

This redrawing of borders was not a benign or neutral act; it was an exercise in demographic engineering on a massive scale. The British administrators, keen to avoid the complexities of a multicultural and multi-religious state, opted instead for a "clean break"—a euphemism for the violent uprooting of millions. The human toll was staggering: nearly 14 million people were displaced, and over a million perished in the accompanying violence.[2]

The parallels with current U.S. immigration policies, while less overtly violent, are no less significant. The Biden-Harris administration's approach can be seen as a form of social reengineering, designed to alter the demographic makeup of the nation in ways that may benefit certain political objectives. Just as the British sought to create a more manageable post-colonial landscape, the current policies appear to be reshaping the

American electorate in ways that could have long-term consequences for national identity and stability.

Stalin's Deportations: The Instrumentalization of Ethnicity

Joseph Stalin's forced deportations were not merely acts of repression; they were strategic tools in the Soviet leader's arsenal to forge a homogenized and pliant state. Entire ethnic groups, from the Chechens to the Crimean Tatars, were uprooted and scattered across the vast Soviet Union—not as punishment for collective guilt but as a means of diluting potential sources of dissent and resistance.

Stalin's approach to demographic manipulation was sophisticated in its brutality. By dispersing these groups, he sought not only to break their spirit but to erase their identities, replacing them with a new, Soviet identity—one that was loyal, malleable, and devoid of any pre-existing cultural or ethnic allegiances. The deportations were accompanied by a campaign of terror, ensuring that those who survived would be too cowed to resist the new order.[3]

This historical precedent finds a disturbing echo in contemporary U.S. policies that, while far less draconian, nonetheless aim to manipulate demographic realities to achieve political ends. The Biden-Harris administration's relaxation of immigration controls and enforcement represent as an attempt to dilute the influence of certain demographic groups by encouraging the influx of populations more likely to support specific political agendas. Just as Stalin used deportation to fragment and control, modern policies appear to be subtly shifting the demographic landscape to consolidate political power.

Contemporary Parallels

China's Xinxiang Policy: A Modern Ethnic Cleansing

The Chinese Communist Party's (CCP) campaign in Xinjiang is perhaps the most chilling contemporary example of state-sponsored ethnic cleansing. Under the guise of combating extremism and promoting stability, the CCP has embarked on a systematic effort to eradicate the Uyghur identity and assimilate this Muslim minority into the Han Chinese mainstream.

The tools of this campaign—mass internment, forced labor, and coercive birth control—are designed to weaken and eventually erase the Uyghur culture. Over a million Uyghurs have been detained in CCP reeducation camps, where they are subjected to political indoctrination and stripped of their cultural and religious identities. Simultaneously, the Chinese government has encouraged the resettlement of Han Chinese into Xinjiang, further altering the region's demographic balance.[4]

The international community has rightly condemned these actions as ethnic cleansing, recognizing in them the same sinister intent that drove Stalin's purges and the horrors of partition. The parallels to Biden immigration policies, though less extreme, are nonetheless significant. Both involve the deliberate use of state power to alter demographic realities in pursuit of broader political objectives. The Biden-Harris administration's policies, which facilitate the influx of disparate, pliant, and encumbered migrants, can be seen as a means of reshaping the American cultural and political landscape—much like the CCP's efforts to transform Xinjiang. While the methods differ, the underlying strategy of using demographic engineering as a tool of statecraft and to achieve political consolidation reveals a chilling and ineluctable similarity.

This demographic shift is not a side effect but a deliberate strategy to weaken the cultural and political influence of minority groups. By incentivizing Han Chinese migration into these regions, the CCP is not only consolidating control but also diluting the presence and power of non-Han populations.

The comparison to U.S. immigration policies becomes clear when one considers the potential for these policies to similarly alter the demographic and political landscape of the United States. The Biden-Harris administration's approach to immigration could be seen as an effort to reshape key electoral battlegrounds, much as the BRI reshapes strategic regions in China. Both are examples of how state power can be used to engineer demographic outcomes that serve broader political goals.

European Migration Crisis: Demographic Transformation and Social Fragmentation

The European Migration Crisis of 2015 was not simply an exodus of displaced people; it was a profound and calculated maneuver to reshape the cultural and political landscape of Europe. Beneath the veneer of humanitarian rhetoric lies a deeper, more disturbing agenda—one that seeks to erode the concept of the nation-state and replace it with a homogenized, controllable populace. This is not the result of mismanagement or naïve benevolence, but of a deliberate strategy by political elites who regard national identities as obstacles to their broader vision of a global order.

Germany, which once epitomized order and stability, has become a case study in the consequences of such demographic engineering. The foreign-born population has surged from 6.7% in 1990 to over 19% by 2022, a change that has not merely altered the demographic makeup but has frayed the very social fabric of the nation.[5] This transformation was not an unintended consequence; it was the intended outcome of policies designed to dilute the concept of a cohesive national identity. In a society where multiple, often conflicting, identities vie for recognition, the idea of a unified national ethos becomes untenable. The fragmentation we see today is not the byproduct of poor policy but the fulfillment of its true purpose: to create a populace that is easier to govern because it is less capable of unified resistance.

In the United Kingdom, the consequences have taken on a more overtly Orwellian character. The imposition of diversity has led to a regime where free speech is no longer a right but a privilege granted by the state—one that can be revoked at will. The rise of speech controls and punitive measures against dissent is a clear indication that the state no longer serves its citizens but seeks to control them.[6] This is a society where the apparatus of government, once a protector of civil liberties, has been weaponized to enforce ideological conformity. Orwell warned of a world where language itself becomes a tool of oppression, and in modern Britain, we see this chilling vision coming to life.[7] The criminalization of speech is not about protecting minorities or fostering inclusion; it is about consolidating power and silencing those who dare to question the demographic revolution imposed upon them.

France, a nation once defined by its cultural cohesion, now finds itself grappling with the consequences of policies that have radically altered its social landscape. The Muslim population has risen from 2% in 1960 to 10% in 2009—a demographic shift that has not only strained the nation's resources but has challenged the very notion of what it means to be French.[8] The tensions and divisions that have emerged are not the unfortunate side effects of a well-intentioned policy; they are the logical outcome of a deliberate strategy to weaken the nation-state. The elites who push these policies are not interested in preserving French identity; they are committed to dissolving it in favor of a new, more pliable order. This is not just a change in population; it is a change in power dynamics, where the traditional structures of authority and identity are dismantled to make way for a more centralized, authoritarian regime.

The Orwellian implications of these developments cannot be over-stated. What we are witnessing is the slow but deliberate erosion of the freedoms and identities that have defined Europe for centuries. The rise of surveillance states, the suppression of dissent, and the enforcement of ideological conformity are not isolated phenomena—they are the symptoms of a broader shift towards totalitarianism. Orwell's dystopian vision was one where power was not just exercised but perpetuated for its own sake, and in modern Europe, we see this vision becoming a reality. The elites who drive these changes are not interested in serving the people; they are interested in controlling them. By fragmenting societies and erod-ing national identities, they create a populace that is easier to govern, less capable of resistance, and more dependent on the state for its sense of self.

The parallels between Europe's trajectory and emerging trends in the United States are not coincidental. The same strategies of demographic engineering, speech control, and cultural dilution are being employed across the Atlantic, with similarly troubling implications. The lessons of Europe are clear: when a society is stripped of its identity and subjected to constant surveillance and ideological enforcement, it becomes ripe for authoritarian rule. The crisis in Europe is not just a crisis of migration; it is a crisis of civilization, where the very concepts of freedom, identity, and nationhood are being systematically dismantled in the name of a new, more controlled order.

Venezuelan Migration Crisis: Demographic Manipulation as Political Strategy

Venezuela's ongoing political and economic crisis has led to the displace-ment of millions of Venezuelans, creating one of the largest migration flows in the world. Neighboring countries in Latin America, such as Colombia, Brazil, and Peru, have experienced significant demographic changes as a result. The Venezuelan government has been accused of using migration as a tool to weaken political opposition by encouraging the emigration of dissidents and opposition supporters. This has led to a "brain drain" and a shift in the country's demographic composition.[9] The Venezuelan migration crisis offers a modern example of how demographic manipulation can be used to achieve political objectives, both within the country of origin and in the host countries. In the U.S. context, this case study can be used to illustrate how immigration policies may be designed to alter the demographic and political landscape in specific regions or states, raising questions about their impact on national security under the Immigration and Nationality Act (INA).

Legal Dimensions

International Law: The Inadequacy of Current Frameworks

The legal dimensions surrounding crimes against humanity and ethnic cleansing are, by design, grounded in the overt and the observable—acts of violence that shock the conscience of the world and demand a response. The Rome Statute of the International Criminal Court (ICC) stands as a testament to this focus, enumerating crimes against humanity to include such horrors as forced deportations, massacres, and other gross violations of human rights.[10] Yet, in its rigorous emphasis on visible atrocities, international law reveals a profound inadequacy: it is ill-equipped to address the more insidious forms of demographic manipulation that, while devoid of physical violence, can achieve outcomes no less devastating.

The legal frameworks that currently exist, such as the Rome Statute, hinge on the ability to demonstrate clear intent—intent to eliminate, displace, or destroy a particular group. Ethnic cleansing, as it is traditionally understood, involves a manifest intent, often brutal in its execution. But when the instruments of demographic change are cloaked in the language of policy—subtle, bureaucratic, and ostensibly benign—the challenge of proving such intent becomes infinitely more complex. Yet, the absence of overt violence does not negate the severity of the outcome. If a policy can be shown to intentionally produce specific demographic results, to systematically reshape the population of a nation to the detriment of its existing cultural or ethnic groups, then it enters the murky waters where the legal definitions of crimes against humanity must be re-examined.

This is not merely a theoretical exercise. Consider the implications of U.S. immigration policies that, under the guise of humanitarianism or economic necessity, appear to be deliberately designed to alter the demographic composition of the nation. Such policies, though bloodless, can be coercive in their impact, subtly but inexorably transforming the cultural and ethnic landscape of a country. The question, then, is whether these non-violent acts of demographic engineering could, or should, be scrutinized under the same legal frameworks that condemn more overt forms of ethnic cleansing.

The Genocide Convention offers another pertinent lens through which to view these issues. Genocide, as defined by the Convention, involves acts committed with the intent to destroy, in whole or in part, a national, ethnical, racial, or religious group.[11] The definition is broad enough to encompass not just the physical annihilation of a people but also actions that aim to erase their cultural or ethnic identity. Whether non-violent methods—such as those that achieve demographic shifts through policy rather than force—should fall under the purview of genocide is a question of grave urgency. If a policy's design is to dilute or fundamentally alter the presence of a particular group within a territory, does it not serve the same function as more violent methods?

The applicability of these legal frameworks to U.S. immigration policies hinges on the critical issue of intent. It is not enough to demonstrate that demographic changes have occurred; the challenge lies in proving that these changes were the intended outcome of the policies in question. Herein lies the crux of the legal dilemma: how does one prove intent when the mechanisms of change are wrapped in the legitimacy of statecraft, when they are enacted not with guns or machetes but with pens and executive orders?

This raises profound questions about the very nature of crimes against humanity and ethnic cleansing in the modern world. If the intent behind a policy is to reshape the demographic makeup of a nation—to displace one group in favor of another, to erode the cultural identity of a people—does it not warrant the same level of scrutiny, the same condemnation, as more traditional forms of ethnic cleansing? The tools may have changed, but the outcomes are disturbingly similar: the alteration of a population, the erosion of cultural identities, and the reconfiguration of national character. The time has come to expand our understanding of these crimes to include the subtler, more sophisticated forms of demographic engineering that, while less visible, are no less destructive.

In this context, the limitations of current international legal frameworks become glaringly apparent. As the world grapples with new forms of power and control, where demographic shifts are orchestrated not by warlords but by politicians, the law must evolve to address these new realities.

U.S. Domestic Law: Constitutional Challenges

The constitutional landscape in the United States offers a complex and, at times, labyrinthine terrain for challenging immigration policies that appear to be designed to reshape the nation's demographic and political makeup. At the heart of these challenges lies the Equal Protection Clause of the Fourteenth Amendment, a pillar of American constitutional law that mandates no state shall "deny to any person within its jurisdiction the equal protection of the laws." This clause, born out of the post-Civil War era to protect the rights of freed slaves, has since become a bedrock for contesting discriminatory practices across a wide range of contexts.

In the realm of immigration, the Equal Protection Clause serves as a potential fulcrum for legal arguments against policies that disproportionately impact specific demographic groups. The critical question here is one of intent: are these policies merely the byproducts of broader immigration trends, or are they, in fact, instruments of political engineering, designed to dilute the influence of native-born citizens by altering the electorate? If the latter can be substantiated, then these policies could be construed as a violation of the Equal Protection Clause—an affront to the very principle that the law must treat all individuals with fairness and impartiality.

However, proving discriminatory intent in the context of immigration policy is no small task. The Biden-Harris administration, like its predecessors, has framed its immigration stance in the language of humanitarian concern and economic necessity. Yet, if it were to be demonstrated that these policies are deliberately crafted to shift the demographic composition of the electorate—thereby diminishing the political power of certain groups—then the Equal Protection Clause could be invoked to challenge these practices. The argument would hinge on substantiating that these policies are not simply benign responses to global pressures but are instead calculated efforts to reshape the electorate in a manner that serves specific political ends. This would strike at the core of what it means to have a representative democracy, where the government is not permitted to engineer the electorate to secure its own power.

Beyond the Equal Protection Clause, the Guarantee Clause (Article IV, Section 4) of the Constitution offers another, albeit less explored, avenue for challenging the demographic shifts brought about by mass immigration. The Guarantee Clause obliges the federal government to protect each state against invasion, a term traditionally associated with military incursions.[12] However, the concept of "invasion" need not be confined to armed attacks; it can, and arguably should, be interpreted to include any mass movement that threatens the stability and security of the nation.

The idea of mass, unregulated immigration as a form of demographic invasion is not without constitutional merit. If the federal government's policies are seen as facilitating an influx that significantly alters the demographic makeup of the country—thereby undermining the sovereignty and security of individual states—then it could be argued that the federal government has failed in its constitutional duty to protect the states from such incursions. The fact that a hostile quasi-state power—the Mexican drug cartels—have been instrumental in this invasion by their control of migrant flows across the U.S. southern border, substantiates the claim that the invasion is indeed militarized. This interpretation would demand a rethinking of the Guarantee Clause, broadening its scope to address the realities of the 21st century, where threats to a nation's stability can emerge not just from foreign armies but also from transnational syndicates and uncontrolled demographic shifts that erode the foundational structures of society.

The ethical and constitutional implications of such arguments are profound. They challenge not only the current administration's policies but also the very principles of democratic governance and national sovereignty. If it is accepted that the federal government has a duty to protect the states from demographic changes that threaten their stability, then the scope of the Guarantee Clause would be significantly expanded, potentially reshaping the constitutional landscape in ways that could have far-reaching consequences for immigration policy and beyond.

California: A Case Study in Demographic Engineering

California serves as a stark case study of what may lie ahead for the nation. Once a competitive two-party state, California has transformed into a Democratic stronghold, a shift that correlates closely with changing immigration patterns. In 1990, California's foreign-born population stood at 21.7%. By 2019, it had risen to 26.7%, significantly higher than the national average of 13.7%.[13]

This demographic shift has had profound political consequences. In 1994, California passed Proposition 187, which sought to deny public services to illegal immigrants.[14] However, subsequent court challenges and demographic changes led to its eventual repeal. Since then, California has implemented a series of immigrant-friendly policies, including:

- The California DREAM Act (2011), providing state financial aid to illegal immigrant students[15]
- The Trust Act (2014), limiting cooperation between local law enforcement and federal immigration authorities[16]
- The sanctuary state law (2017), further restricting state and local cooperation with federal immigration enforcement[17]

California's demographic transformation has effectively created a one-party state. The Republican Party, unable to adapt to these changes, has been rendered almost irrelevant in state politics.

These policies have cemented Democratic control in California, with the party holding supermajorities in both state legislative chambers and every statewide office. The state's experience demonstrates how demographic change, coupled with strategic policy decisions, can fundamentally alter the political landscape.

Vice President Kamala Harris, a former California Attorney General and U.S. Senator, has been a proponent of these policies. Her support for sanctuary laws and opposition to strict immigration enforcement reflects an ideological continuity with the state's approach.[18]

California's experience demonstrates how strategic demographic changes, facilitated by specific policies, can lead to lasting political realignment. The state's trajectory offers a microcosmic view of what might occur nationally under similar immigration policies, highlighting the potential for one-party dominance and the marginalization of dissenting voices.

Conclusion

The Biden-Harris administration's immigration policies, when viewed through the lens of historical precedents, reveal a deeply unsettling pattern of demographic manipulation akin to some of the most egregious examples in modern history. What is presented as humanitarianism carries with it the unmistakable intent to reshape the demographic and political landscape of the United States, much like the strategies employed by authoritarian regimes to consolidate power through the reconfiguration of populations.

These policies, which subtly erode cultural identities and weaken national cohesion, are not merely unintended consequences—they appear to be deliberate efforts to engineer a new electorate that aligns with specific political objectives. The implications of such actions challenge the very foundations of democratic governance and raise significant ethical and legal concerns that current frameworks are ill-prepared to address. The manipulation of demographics, while less overtly violent than historical atrocities, carries the same potential for destabilization and social fragmentation.

The United States now stands at a critical juncture, where the decisions made regarding immigration will have profound and lasting effects on the nation's identity and future. The lessons of history serve as a stark warning: demographic engineering, when used as a tool of statecraft, often leads to the erosion of freedom, the suppression of dissent, and the rise of authoritarian control. It is imperative to recognize the dangers inherent in these policies and to safeguard the nation's commitment to justice, equality, and democratic principles. The future of the Republic depends on a clear-eyed understanding of these issues and a steadfast refusal to allow the manipulation of its population for political ends.

CHAPTER 15

REPLACEMENTS

Few forces in history have reshaped civilizations as swiftly and irreversibly as mass migration. It is the silent engine of collapse, unmaking nations not through conquest or revolution, but through a slow erasure of sovereignty and culture. Under the Biden-Harris administration, this transformation has accelerated into something resembling a controlled demolition. More than 7.2 million illegal aliens have entered the United States since 2021—an influx so vast and so rapid that it has no historical parallel outside wartime population displacements. This is not a policy failure. *It is policy by design.*

The numbers alone are staggering. In just three years, illegal immigration has swelled the U.S. population by 2.2%—an increase almost as large as the entire city of New York.[1] But these are not the turn-of-the-century immigrants who arrived legally, determined to assimilate into the American ethos. They are economic migrants from the developing world, many with no cultural, historical, or civic ties to the nation they now inhabit. Their arrival has placed unprecedented strain on public resources, fractured social cohesion, and distorted democratic representation. Yet rather than enforcing the law, the federal government has weaponized the justice system to shield and prioritize illegal aliens over its own citizens, ensuring that this demographic shift continues unchecked. And why? Raw, unadulterated power—the same demographic engineering that cemented California as a one-party state and hastened its collapse into failure.

This chapter dissects the scale and consequences of this deliberate dismantling of America by the Traitor Joe Biden, a man who governs for his party at the existential expense of his people. It lays bare the economic, social, and environmental toll of mass illegal immigration, the calculated legal subversions that sustain it, and the neurological basis for the deepening social fracture it breeds. Drawing both from historical precedents and contemporaneous parallels—from the collapse of the Western Roman Empire to Europe's unraveling under unchecked migration—it argues that without immediate and decisive corrective action, the United States will not merely transform; it will cease to exist as the nation it once was.

Historical Context and Precedents

Migration has long determined the fate of civilizations, serving as both a catalyst for growth and harbinger of decline. As the United States grapples with an unprecedented influx of illegal immigrants, we stand at a crossroads, one that demand a clear-eyed assessment of historical precedents and their implications for the nation's future. This analysis is not an academic exercise—it is an urgent reckoning with the consequences of demographic upheaval.

The Great Wave vs. The Biden-Harris Deluge

The Great Wave of European immigration (c. 1880–1920) is often heralded as a watershed moment in American history, but its comparison to today's border crisis exposes a chasm, not a parallel. Over that forty-year period, approximately 20 million immigrants arrived in the United States, representing about 14.7% of the population.[2] While this earlier wave was larger in relative terms, crucial distinctions set today's migration crisis apart, each magnifying its potential for societal rupture:

- **Timeframe:** The Great Wave unfolded over four decades, allowing for gradual absorption and assimilation. The current surge, a veritable human tsunami, has inundated our nation in just a few years, overwhelming institutions and communities with a rapidity that defies adaptation.

- **Legal Status:** The vast majority of Great Wave immigrants arrived through legal channels, subject to stringent vetting and assimilation pressures. Today's influx consists primarily of illegal entrants, a population that by definition has circumvented the legal framework, complicating integration and overloading public services.
- **Cultural Distance:** Many Great Wave immigrants shared foundational cultural with American society—Judeo-Christian traditions, European legal systems, common ancestries, and Western civic norms—making assimilation feasible. Today's migrants often hail from regions with starkly different worldviews, widening the chasm to the point of fracture.
- **Economic Context:** The Great Wave coincided with America's industrial boom, when an insatiable demand for labor absorbed vast numbers of workers. In contrast, today's post-industrial, automated economy offers fewer low-skilled jobs, fueling economic strain and social resentment.
- **Policy Framework:** The Great Wave was met with national policies designed to foster integration, including mandatory English-language education and Americanization programs. Today, multiculturalism dictates policy, actively discouraging assimilation and fostering the emergence of insular, unassimilated enclaves.

The Fall of Rome: A Process, Not an Event

History is replete with cautionary tales of great civilizations brought low by uncontrolled migration. The Western Roman Empire stands as perhaps the starkest example, offering a chilling parallel to the United States today.

Between 376 and 476 AD, an estimated 750,000 to 1 million Germanic and Hunnic migrants breached Roman borders, constituting roughly 10% of the empire's population.[3] This mass influx, occurring over a century, overwhelmed Rome's ability to enforce its laws, maintain social cohesion, and defense its frontiers.

America's crisis is far more acute. In just *three years*, up to 12 million illegal aliens—nearly 4% of the U.S. population—have entered the country.

Edward Gibbon's seminal *The Decline and Fall of the Roman Empire* describes the Gothic invasion in terms that eerily echo today's border crisis:

"The Goths burst forth into the region of the lower Danube, and with little or no resistance, traversed the wide country of Thrace. Pillaging, burning, and destroying, they arrived under the walls of Constantinople, and were with difficulty repelled from its gates. From Thrace they hastened with rapid fury to the shores of the Adriatic, and the populous country of Italy was laid waste."[4]

While today's crisis does not resemble the large-scale battlefield invasions of antiquity, the violence accompanying mass illegal migration is undeniable. The American Southwest has become a battleground of cartel warfare, with drug syndicates controlling smuggling routes and profiting from human trafficking. Border towns are overwhelmed by crime, gang activity, and a fentanyl epidemic that has killed hundreds of thousands of Americans—a modern equivalent of Rome's inability to contain the destabilizing forces it allowed inside its borders.

The broader parallels in governance failure are inescapable. Rome's ruling class, much like America's modern elite, failed to secure its frontiers, relied on appeasement rather than enforcement, and ultimately ceded control over its own territorial integrity. The United States is now following the same trajectory—not in a single catastrophic event, but through a slow-motion collapse engineered by its own leadership.

The Tang Dynasty's Cosmopolitan Folly

China's Tang Dynasty (618–907 CE) offers another instructive parallel. At its height, the Chang'an was the world's most cosmopolitan city, home to over a million people, including significant populations of Persians, Arabs, and Turks. This diversity initially strengthened the empire—until it didn't.[5]

The An Lushan Rebellion (755–763 CE), led by a general of mixed foreign ancestry, nearly toppled the Tang Dynasty. Ethnic tensions and the ambitions of unassimilated minorities fueled a conflict that resulted in thirteen-to-sixteen million deaths, or 15–40% of the empire's population.[6]

The modern lesson is unmistakable. The idea that limitless diversity is an unqualified strength is a tautology, not a truth. Failing to assimilate large immigrant populations creates internal fractures that, in moments of crisis, can be weaponized by foreign or domestic actors—a risk the United States ignores at its peril.

The Ottoman Millet System: Multiculturalism's Progenitor

The Ottoman Empire's *millet* system offers a striking historical precedent for America's modern multiculturalism. The Ottomans managed their vast empire by allowing religious minorities to maintain their own legal systems and cultural practices. While this worked for a time, by the 19th century, it had created deeply entrenched parallel societies with competing loyalties.

These enclaves, nominally part of the empire, undermined national unity and ultimately accelerated Ottoman decline. By the empire's final century, these fissures made it incapable of responding to either internal reform or external threats.[7]

This dynamic is now unfolding in the United States. Immigrant communities with strong ties to their countries of origin often resist assimilation, creating parallel societies that function outside of American civic norms. The proliferation of sanctuary cities, which defy federal immigration law, is a modern manifestation of this phenomenon. These jurisdictions operate beyond the authority of national governance, eroding the very notion of a unified nation-state.

The Verdict of History

Across civilizations—from Rome to China to the Ottomans—the lesson is clear: unassimilated mass migration is not an expansion of national strength but a slow, grinding dissolution of the nation itself.

The Biden administration has embraced demographic transformation as governing doctrine, pushing the nation to its breaking point. If history is any guide, the outcome will not be mere transformation—it will be dissolution.

The Contemporary Forewarning: Europe Engulfed

More recent European experiences offer urgent warnings about the consequences of mass immigration and failed integration.

Sweden, once celebrated for its open-border policies, has been transformed into a cautionary tale. Crime, social unrest, and ethnic enclaves have replaced the utopian visions of multicultural harmony, according to an investigative report by Swedish Television's program *Uppdrag Granskning*. This report analyzed 843 district court cases over a five-year period. While the findings are based on court data, 58% of suspects in public rape cases are of foreign origin—a figure that soars to 85% in certain areas, such as Stockholm's subway system.[8] Far from the social model it once touted, Sweden now finds itself grappling with an imported crime wave and a fraying national identity. The once-orderly Nordic society now faces bombings, clan-based violence, and an overwhelmed welfare state—all direct consequences of a reckless immigration policy that prioritized ideology over reality.

France, too, provides a stark cautionary tale. The country's decades-long struggle to integrate its North African immigrant population has produced deepening social fractures. The 2005 banlieue riots, driven by second-generation immigrants, exposed the myth that time alone resolves cultural and economic disparities.[9] These tensions have only escalated, as evidenced by the violent unrest of June 2023, sparked by the police shooting of a teenager of Algerian descent.[10] France's experience underscores a critical truth: immigration challenges do not fade with time—they metastasize. The failures of one generation compound into the next, producing a permanent underclass alienated from the nation it inhabits yet unwilling to leave.

The United Kingdom offers yet another dire warning, particularly in the realm of security. The 2005 London bombings, carried out by British-born sons of Pakistani immigrants, shattered the illusion that a British passport equates to British identity.[11] This act of homegrown terrorism exposed the grim consequences of unchecked multiculturalism: communities that remain insular, unassimilated, and, in some cases, openly hostile to their host nation.

London itself now stands as a monument to demographic upheaval and cultural displacement. Once the proud capital of an empire, it has been transformed into a fragmented metropolis where English is often a minority language and traditional British values are steadily eroded. The city's rapid demographic shift has not merely altered its cultural landscape—it has birthed parallel societies where the bonds of national unity have frayed. In neighborhoods where Sharia courts operate and ethnic enclaves enforce their own rules, the very concept of Britain as a cohesive nation-state is dissolving.

The transformation of London—from an English metropole to a fractured, crime-ridden, multicultural experiment—offers a grim portent for other Western nations. The lesson is undeniable: unassimilated mass migration does not enrich a society; it fractures it.

Economic Toll of Demographic Inversion

The economic ramifications of the ongoing demographic shift are staggering, presenting a fiscal challenge of unprecedented magnitude. A comprehensive report by the Federation for American Immigration Reform (FAIR) lays bare the financial burden: as of 2023, illegal immigration costs U.S. taxpayers $150.7 billion annually—a sum greater than the Gross Domestic Product (GDP) of approximately eighty countries, including Kenya, Guatemala, and Bulgaria.[12,13] This figure represents a $35 billion increase since 2017, a startling reflection of the accelerating nature of the crisis.

This cost is derived by subtracting the $32 billion in tax revenue paid by illegal aliens from the gross negative economic impact of $182 billion.[14] The disparity is impossible to ignore: illegal aliens, on average, contribute just one-sixth of the public costs they impose. Many pay no income tax at all, while others even benefit from refundable tax credits—an absurd consequence of policies that incentivize unlawful migration rather than deter it.

The Individual Taxpayer's Burden

The aggregate figures are alarming, but the burden on individual Americans is equally damning. Each illegal alien or U.S.-born child of illegal aliens imposes an annual cost of $8,776 on public resources. The average American taxpayer is forced to contribute an additional $1,156 per year to sustain this growing population—a de facto surcharge on lawful citizenship.[15]

Moreover, a significant portion of illegal aliens' earnings do not even remain within the United States to circulate in the local economy. Instead, billions are siphoned out of the country through remittances, draining capital from struggling American communities and sending it overseas.[16]

The Soaring Costs of Public Services

Illegal immigration is no longer just an economic strain—it is a fiscal catastrophe, overwhelming national infrastructure. Federal expenditures tied to illegal immigration have ballooned to $66.4 billion—a 45% increase since 2017.[17] This spending is concentrated in key public sectors:

- **Education:** $6.6 billion
- **Medical Care:** $23.1 billion
- **Justice Enforcement:** $25.1 billion
- **Welfare Programs:** $11.6 billion

At the state and local level, where the burden is most acutely felt, the costs have risen to $115.6 billion—a 30% increase since 2017.[18] These figures include:

- **Education:** $73.2 billion
- **Medical Care:** $18.6 billion
- **Justice Enforcement:** $21.8 billion
- **Welfare Programs:** $2 billion

Border states and major urban centers, already grappling with skyrocketing costs of living, bear the brunt of this financial strain. Texas, at the epicenter of this demographic shift, was forced to allocate $850 million to border security in 2021 alone—diverting resources from education, healthcare, and infrastructure to cover a crisis that the federal government refuses to address.[19]

Meanwhile, in Los Angeles County, the financial burden on each household to support illegal aliens has surged to $2,340 per year—an involuntary tax on lawful residents struggling to afford basic necessities in one of the nation's most expensive cities.[20]

The Wage War against American Workers

Beyond government spending, illegal immigration has profound implications for the American labor market. Harvard economist George Borjas, in his seminal study of the 1980 Mariel boatlift, found that an influx of just 125,000 Cuban refugees into Miami depressed wages for low-skilled native workers by 10–30% for several years.[21] The lesson is clear: mass immigration—particularly of low-skilled, non-assimilating workers—undercuts wages and destroys economic mobility for America's working class.

Today's migration crisis dwarfs the Mariel boatlift. With an annual influx of 4 million illegal entrants, the effect on the American workforce—particularly in construction, manufacturing, and service industries—is far more devastating. Blue-collar workers, already struggling under inflation and declining job security, are now competing against a relentless flood of foreign labor willing to work for lower wages, often under illegal conditions.

Environmental Degradation: The Hidden Cost of Mass Migration

The environmental toll of mass illegal immigration is a critical, yet often deliberately obfuscated facet of this national crisis. Millions of unauthorized entrants strain America's natural resources, urban infrastructure, and fragile ecosystems, with regions like Southern California bearing the brunt of this anthropogenic onslaught.

Water Scarcity: A Looming Crisis

Los Angeles epitomizes the environmental fallout. The city's water resources, already precarious due to recurring droughts, now face intensified demand from a swelling illegal population. Projections from the California Department of Water Resources paint a grim picture: by 2030, an additional 5.5 million acre-feet of water will be needed annually to sustain unrestrained population growth.[22] This impending crisis threatens to drain aquifers, overwhelm water distribution systems, and push the region beyond limits.

Urban Sprawl and Air Pollution: The Environmental Regression

The consequences extend beyond water. Relentless urban sprawl, driven by uncontrolled migration and skyrocketing housing demand, is rapidly erasing green spaces, fragmenting ecosystems, and driving air pollution to unprecedented levels.

The South Coast Air Quality Management District warns that Los Angeles Basin's population surge has negated decades of progress in reducing vehicle emissions.[23] As a result, air quality is deteriorating, public health is worsening, and California's environmental leadership has crumbled into a cautionary tale of ecological collapse.

While real estate developers reap windfall profits, lawful residents pay the price through deteriorating air quality, vanishing open spaces, and a suffocating increase in urban density. Fragile ecosystems are bulldozed for endless housing developments, and worsening traffic congestion blankets city streets in a permanent haze of pollutants.

The Third-Worldization of American Cities

As urban landscapes struggle to accommodate this unchecked demographic surge, they increasingly resemble the overpopulated, environmentally compromised cities of the developing world. This transformation is not merely aesthetic—it fundamentally alters the character of American cities and imposes unsustainable environmental pressures on regions ill-equipped to handle such explosive growth.

Illegal immigration also imports environmentally destructive practices from less developed regions. Illegal dumping, unregulated waste disposal, and the unchecked exploitation of public lands for makeshift housing encampments have turned once-thriving areas into deteriorating wastelands, placing immense burdens on ecosystems and public resources.

The Traffic Nightmare

Population growth has also worsened traffic congestion to crisis levels. According to the Texas A&M Transportation Institute's Urban Mobility Report, Los Angeles drivers endure the worst traffic in the nation, wasting an average of 119 hours per year in gridlock.[24] This paralysis, directly exacerbated by rapid migration-driven population expansion, not only erodes quality of life but intensifies air pollution and carbon emissions, undermining even the most aggressive climate policies.

The Infrastructure Strain

Beyond traffic, public infrastructure is buckling under the weight of mass migration. Schools, hospitals, and emergency services are overwhelmed. A comprehensive analysis by the Center for Immigration Studies quantifies this burden at $116 billion annually, with education and healthcare alone accounting for the largest expenditures.[25]

- **Overcrowded schools** struggle with an exploding student population.
- **Emergency rooms are overrun**, delaying care for American citizens.
- **Public services collapse** under the weight of unsustainable demand.

Arizona: The Water Crisis Nobody Talks About

Arizona, a state on the front lines of the illegal immigration crisis, is already facing an environmental catastrophe. The Arizona Department of Water Resources reports groundwater levels in some border regions have plummeted by over 100 feet in recent decades. This precipitous decline, driven by unchecked population growth and skyrocketing water consumption, threatens the long-term viability of entire communities. If this trend continues, the United States may soon face a new class of environmental refugees—within its own borders.[26]

The Verdict: Immigration and Environmental Destruction

The environmental impact of mass illegal migration transcends political ideologies. Unchecked population growth is inherently unsustainable, and the evidence is overwhelming:

- Water resources are being depleted at unsustainable rates.
- Air pollution and urban congestion are reversing decades of progress.

- America's cities are transforming into sprawling, unlivable metropolises.
- Infrastructure is collapsing under the weight of imported overpopulation.

If true conservation and sustainability remain priorities, then addressing the environmental devastation caused by mass illegal immigration must be at the center of policy discussions. The cost of inaction is nothing less than ecological collapse.

Census Distortion: How Illegal Immigration Corrupts Representation

The presence of millions of illegal aliens in the United States does not merely strain resources and challenge the rule of law—it distorts the very foundation of American democracy. By inflating census counts and congressional apportionment, mass illegal immigration quietly but profoundly shifts political power, overriding the will of lawful citizens and rewarding states that refuse to enforce immigration laws. California stands as the epicenter of this democratic erosion, benefiting enormously from a system that prioritizes numbers over legitimacy.

The Census Loophole: How Illegal Aliens Reshape Political Power

The U.S. Constitution mandates that the decennial census count all "persons" residing in the country, regardless of legal status—a provision intended to ensure fair representation. Yet in the era of mass illegal immigration, this provision has transformed into a mechanism for distorting democracy itself.

According to the Center for Immigration Studies, the 2020 Census counted approximately 22.1 million noncitizens, including an estimated 11.35 million illegal aliens.[27] This is no minor statistical footnote—it represents a population larger than 44 individual states, wielding enormous influence over congressional representation, federal funding, and the Electoral College.

California: The Model for Electoral Manipulation

California, with an estimated 2.2 million illegal aliens as of 2016, stands as the starkest example of how illegal immigration distorts representative democracy. Illegal aliens comprise approximately 6% of California's total population, artificially inflating its census count and its representation in Congress.[28]

But this isn't just about adding numbers—it's about altering the weight of votes themselves. A citizen in a California district heavily populated by illegal aliens has more influence per vote in Congress than a citizen in a district with fewer illegal aliens. This de facto weighted voting system, never intended by the Founding Fathers, violates the spirit of "one person, one vote"—giving sanctuary states an outsized role in shaping national policy.

The Electoral College Distortion: Noncitizens Shaping Presidential Elections

The census distortion does not stop at Congress—it also warps the Electoral College. Because Electoral College votes are tied to congressional representation, California's inflated numbers translate into additional presidential election influence.

This means that, while illegal aliens cannot legally vote, their mere presence skews the political landscape, ensuring that sanctuary states wield disproportionate power in determining the nation's leadership.

The Financial Incentive: How the Census Rewards Lawlessness

Beyond political influence, inflated census counts unlock billions in federal funding, which is allocated based on population size. California, with its artificially boosted population, receives a disproportionate share of federal resources, effectively rewarding the state for ignoring immigration laws.

This perverse incentive structure ensures that states benefit financially from illegal immigration while states that enforce the law are penalized with diminished representation and federal funding.

The Indirect Political Influence of Illegal Immigration

Even without the right to vote, illegal aliens reshape the political landscape in profound and overlooked ways. Their sheer presence accelerates demographic shifts, influencing the political leanings of naturalized citizens and second-generation immigrants.

- Politicians in high-illegal-immigration districts gravitate toward pro-illegal immigration policies—not just to appeal to sympathetic voters, but because their district's entire representation depends on maintaining and growing this population.
- Sanctuary policies, expanded public benefits, and resistance to immigration enforcement are all byproducts of this demographic reality.
- As a result, the votes of lawful citizens in states with low illegal alien populations are effectively diluted, granting them less representation per capita than those in states that have embraced mass illegal migration.

Cui Bono? A Partisan Advantage

A study by the Government Accountability Institute suggests that counting illegal aliens for apportionment has disproportionately benefited the Democratic Party. The seats redistributed due to noncitizen counts have overwhelmingly gone to Democrat-leaning states and districts, potentially altering the balance of power in closely divided Congresses.

The Consequences: A Feedback Loop of Lawlessness

This distortion of representation is more than a partisan advantage—it is a direct assault on the legitimacy of American democracy. When the foundational principle of "one person, one vote" is undermined, it erodes public trust in electoral fairness and creates a self-reinforcing loop:

1. Census counts illegal aliens, inflating representation for sanctuary states.
2. Sanctuary states gain more seats in Congress and more Electoral College votes.
3. These states push policies that attract even more illegal aliens, further inflating their representation.
4. States that enforce immigration law lose representation and resources, weakening their national influence.

In other words, once the distortion is entrenched, it only grows.

The Rise of Parallel Societies

In the tragic annals of America's decline, few indicators are as stark as linguistic fragmentation. What was once a unified nation bound by a shared language and cultural framework is now fracturing into isolated enclaves—a modern Tower of Babel, engineered through political malfeasance and systemic dereliction.

The Los Angeles Unified School District (LAUSD) exemplifies this dissolution. Within its crumbling bureaucratic walls, over ninety languages are spoken, and nearly 150,000 students are classified as English learners.[29] This is not diversity—it is division. It is not multiculturalism; it is tribalism. The state's educational institutions have not fostered integration but entrenched linguistic orphanhood, where students become fluent in neither their parents' language nor the lingua franca of their adopted land—trapped in a liminal space between cultures and identities.

The absurdity of this situation reaches Kafkaesque proportions in our courts, as one LA County prosecutor recounts:

> I'm starting to see more and more cases with defendants from so deep within Mexico and Central America that they don't even speak Spanish. I have a defendant who requires a Nahuatl translator and another requiring a Mixtec interpreter. The Nahuatl translator doesn't even speak English, so a Spanish interpreter is translating English into Spanish for the Nahuatl interpreter, and the Nahuatl interpreter translates that into Nahuatl for the defendant.

This is not justice; it is a farce. Our institutions have become not just inefficient but fundamentally incoherent. This is not merely a failure of immigration policy—it is a failure of logic, reason, and basic governance.

We have imported a subclass of individuals not merely unassimilated but unassimilable. They are strangers not only to our language but to modernity itself, a permanent peasantry stultified even by the benighted standards of failed states.

These newcomers, as the anecdote makes clear, have not integrated into Mexican society in half a millennium. The notion that they'll seamlessly meld into the American tapestry and an Anglo-based system is a delusion of the highest order.

Yet, intoxicated by the prospects of entrenched and abiding political power, our leaders propose fast-tracking these foreign philistines into positions of civic responsibility—even military service.[30] This is not assimilation; it is national suicide.

Linguistic Balkanization: A Wrecking Ball to National Cohesion

The Balkanization of language does not simply create communication barriers—it destroys national unity. It fosters insular, ghettoized enclaves, ensuring that imported populations never assimilate and remain permanently dependent on the political class that traffics in ethnic loyalties rather than national interests.

The fiscal burden is equally grotesque. Every government interaction now requires an army of translators, each a parasitic drain on municipal budgets. We are, in effect, subsidizing our own disintegration, paying to dismantle our own cultural and linguistic heritage.

This is not a temporary adjustment period—it is a permanent condition. A 2015 Pew Research Center study found that 61% of Hispanic immigrants in the U.S. for over 20 years still struggle with English.[31] This is not assimilation—it is the birth of linguistic enclaves that will persist for generations.

The America emerging from this linguistic maelstrom will be unrecognizable—a land where basic communication is impossible, where national identity dissolves into incoherent tribalism. "E Pluribus Unum" will become a bitter joke, a cruel mockery of a unity long since shattered.

Precedents: The Historical Warnings America Ignores

The Austro-Hungarian Empire: A Nation Torn Apart by Ethnic Fragmentation

The Austro-Hungarian Empire, a multi-ethnic and multi-linguistic state, serves as a cautionary tale. This empire, a patchwork of distinct languages and cultures, was governed under a dual monarchy. The absence of a unifying language policy and the nationalistic ambitions of various ethnic factions fueled fragmentation, leading to political instability and the empire's disintegration following the First World War. The lesson is stark: a common language is the most fundamental bulwark against fractious ethnic nationalism and the erosion of the polity.[32]

Yugoslavia: When Multiculturalism Becomes a Death Sentence

Yugoslavia's descent into violent conflict in the 1990s, culminating in its catastrophic breakup, presents a grimmer tableau. Formed after World War I, Yugoslavia was a federation of republics, each with its own dominant language and ethnic group; historical grievances and nationalist aspirations weighed heavily on the system. The federal structure failed to effectively manage these differences, igniting brutal civil wars. The lesson from Yugoslavia is harsh and clear: unchecked linguistic and ethnic divisions, without a unifying framework and identity, breeds bloody and catastrophic consequences.[33]

The Lesson for America

These historical warnings cannot be ignored. Unchecked ethno-linguistic diversity breeds discord, disunity, and, eventually, dissolution.

Without a common language, national identity collapses, and with it, the ability to govern as a single nation. America, once the melting pot of the world, is now a boiling cauldron of competing tribes—each speaking its own tongue, loyal to its own enclave, and indifferent to the concept of a unified nation.

Unless this linguistic disintegration is halted, America will follow the path of Austria-Hungary, Yugoslavia, and every other failed experiment in multicultural empire-building.

The choice is stark and urgent: restore national unity through linguistic cohesion, or watch the republic dissolve into the abyss.

Protecting Criminal Aliens Over Citizens

In a startling erosion of the rule of law, our justice system has been systematically subverted to prioritize the interests of illegal aliens over the safety and well-being of American citizens. This perversion of justice, most egregious in major urban centers and "sanctuary" jurisdictions, has created a two-tiered system that mocks the fundamental principle of equality under the law, undermining the very foundations of our civic order.

The Sanctuary System: A Judicial Conspiracy against Americans

A prosecutor from Los Angeles County, speaking on condition of anonymity due to fear of professional repercussions, reveals a disturbing trend underscoring the endemic malfeasance within the California justice system: "For lower level crime/misdemeanors, illegal alien criminals will get an 'immigration friendly' plea offer."[34] This unconscionable practice often results in charges being reduced from deportable offenses to lesser crimes, allowing illegal aliens to evade the consequences of their actions and remain within our borders—a Damoclean sword perpetually hanging over our communities.

The prosecutor elaborates on this perverse system: "ICE looks at different convictions differently. They will not deport for convictions unless those convictions are crimes of moral turpitude. For instance, if an illegal alien is charged with petty theft, the DA will offer an 'immigration friendly' plea deal. They'll reduce the charge from petty theft to 'trespassing' because it's more DHS/Immigration friendly. Trespass—the feds say no big deal, versus shoplifting, which they will take into account for deportation. DAs are actively preventing this. A non-immigrant citizen would never get that offer."[35]

The situation in Los Angeles, under the aegis of District Attorney George Gascón, serves as a chilling case study in the abdication of responsibility by those sworn to uphold the law. Gascón has implemented policies that actively shield illegal aliens who commit crimes from the full force of the law. As former District Attorney Steve Cooley explains, his voice tinged with disbelief:

"Gascón has actually created policies to protect illegal aliens who happen to be caught up in the criminal justice system. He has policies that ensure the DDAs (deputy DAs) can't notify immigration authorities. In other instances, their immigration status can't really be a factor in the case. The policy is basically to protect illegal immigrants from the consequences of their acts. Because sometimes when an illegal immigrant commits a crime, they're supposed to be deported. By law. But Gascón protects them by making sure that that doesn't get out. Even though it's a public record."[36]

Cooley further elucidates the extent of this policy: "All I know is it became the policy of virtually all law enforcement agencies and the county sheriff cannot refer individuals whom they suspect of being illegal aliens to ICE. And Gascón made sure his deputy DAs couldn't do it." This deliberate obstruction of justice extends beyond the courtroom, as Cooley notes: "Police may end up knowing the legal status of these criminals but they're prohibited by state law from notifying ICE. Jail authorities who determine that someone in their custody is in this country illegally cannot notify ICE. And certainly it's a policy adopted by a lot of law enforcement agencies in response to public pressure."

The National Scope of the Betrayal

This systematic undermining of justice is not confined to Los Angeles. The same prosecutor notes, with palpable frustration, "In NYC there is a policy in place to shield illegal alien criminals from referral to ICE. This is a policy in most large 'blue state' cities."[37] Such policies represent a betrayal of the social contract between government and citizens, prioritizing the interests of lawbreakers over law-abiding Americans.

The Destruction of Local-Federal Cooperation

The erosion of cooperation between local law enforcement and federal immigration authorities represents a stark departure from past practices, as Detective Mike Maher, a veteran of the Los Angeles County Sherriff's Department, reveals:

> Three decades ago, we had clear coordination with federal authorities. The Mira Loma jail in LA County served as a federal detention center. During arrests, we routinely asked about national origin, and this information was part of the standard booking process. There was transparent coordination between local jails and immigration authorities. Today, this system has been completely dismantled. Not only is there no coordination, but we're explicitly prohibited from even inquiring about immigration status. This ban extends

to situations where such information could benefit the individual, such as obtaining consular assistance. It's a complete reversal that hamstrings our ability to enforce the law effectively or even provide appropriate assistance.[38]

This systematic dismantling of cooperation between local and federal authorities not only hampers law enforcement efforts but also creates a dangerous environment where illegal aliens can potentially exploit the system, knowing that their immigration status is off-limits to local law enforcement. The shift from a system of coordination to one of enforced ignorance represents a troubling trend in our approach to public safety and national security.

The legal landscape has been further complicated by recent court decisions. A veteran prosecutor from Alameda County, speaking on condition of anonymity, elucidates the convoluted legal reasoning now plaguing the justice system:

> There's also a law, a case that came down, that says we have to consider immigration consequences. It doesn't specify how we are to consider it, but it mandates that it must be considered. This has led to significant confusion. Defense attorneys interpret it as meaning we must consider it to the defendant's benefit. It raises serious equal protection issues. We're essentially being told to give a benefit to someone here illegally, while a legal resident like "Joe White" would face harsher sentencing for the same offense. It's a perversion of justice that defies common sense.

The same prosecutor reveals an even more troubling trend: "Yes. I've had defense attorneys on violent sex cases, go above my head, because they think they'll get a better deal from up above to not get deported." This shocking revelation underscores the extent to which the system has been corrupted, with even the most heinous criminals benefiting from this perverse prioritization of immigration status over public safety.

This legal quagmire not only complicates the prosecution of crimes but also raises serious questions about the equal application of the law. It creates a perverse incentive structure that rewards lawbreaking and penalizes citizenship, fundamentally altering the relationship between the state and its citizens.

The directive issued by Gascón perhaps stands as the most egregious example of this sovereignty erosion. It explicitly orders prosecutors to avoid filing criminal charges against illegal immigrants to prevent deportation. Under this directive, prosecutors must consider the immigration status of suspects when making charging decisions, effectively creating a two-tiered justice system that places the interests of illegal aliens above the safety of American citizens.

This policy goes so far as to encourage alternatives to criminal convictions, such as diversion programs, specifically to help illegal immigrants avoid deportation. Such an approach not only undermines the rule of law but also sends an unequivocal message that Los Angeles—and by extension, other sanctuary cities—are safe havens for criminal aliens.

Law Enforcement Impotence: Criminal Aliens as Protected Classes

The deleterious effects of these policies extend to law enforcement, hamstringing those on the front lines of public safety. LAPD Union Director and veteran detective Jamie McBride laments:

"We can't do anything when it comes to immigration, we can't check someone's status, we can't do anything. So I talk to guys on the street and they say that the good majority of the gangsters they stop are illegals. They stop them numerous times and nothing happens."

This frustration echoes throughout law enforcement agencies, as officers find themselves increasingly powerless to protect their communities from criminal aliens who exploit these sanctuary policies.

The Ultimate Insanity: Arming Illegal Aliens

In a move that defies logic and undermines national security, the Los Angeles Police Department has taken this perversion of justice to new heights by requesting federal permission to arm illegal aliens who will be granted police powers. This follows a 2022 state law allowing non-citizens under DACA to become police officers, though it currently does not permit them to be armed.

LAPD Chief Michael Moore, in an act of stunning irresponsibility, is actively lobbying the Department of Justice to change rules to allow arming these individuals. Moore argues that DACA recipients are "responsible, tax-paying individuals" who can contribute as armed officers. This dangerous proposition not only blurs the line between legal and illegal residents but also potentially puts weapons in the hands of individuals whose very presence in the country is a violation of federal law.

From Local to Federal: The Open-Borders Coup

The ramifications of these policies extend beyond local jurisdictions. At the federal level, proposals such as those by Illinois Senator Dick Durbin to allow illegal aliens to join the U.S. military, and Senator Tammy Duckworth's bill suggesting granting citizenship to undocumented individuals who serve honorably in the military, further illustrate the extent to which our national institutions are being compromised.[39]

This systematic undermining of law enforcement and the justice system represents nothing less than a slow-motion coup against the rule of law, a dismantling of the very foundations of our civil society. It creates a perverse incentive structure that rewards lawbreaking and penalizes citizenship, fundamentally altering the relationship between the state and its citizens.

Penalizing Citizenship

The message sent by these policies is clear: in the eyes of many of our elected officials and law enforcement leaders, American citizenship is no longer a privileged status that confers rights and protections, but rather a burden that subjects one to stricter application of the law. This inversion of justice not only endangers public safety but also erodes the very concept of national sovereignty and citizenship.

The consequences of these policies are far-reaching and potentially catastrophic. By creating a protected class of illegal aliens who are shielded from the full consequences of their criminal actions, we are effectively incentivizing further illegal immigration and criminal behavior. This not only puts law-abiding citizens at risk but also undermines the integrity of our entire legal system.

Moreover, the refusal to cooperate with federal immigration authorities creates dangerous blind spots in our national security apparatus. As criminal aliens move freely between jurisdictions, taking advantage of sanctuary policies, the ability of law enforcement to track and apprehend dangerous individuals is severely compromised.

Conclusion: California—A Nation Unmade

California was not lost to incompetence but to design. Mass migration, criminal impunity, and political manipulation have turned it from a powerhouse into a failed state.

Its leaders flooded the electorate with the dependent and the desperate, securing power while shattering the middle-class. Crime became normalized—MS-13 dumps bodies in parks, fentanyl floods the streets, and law enforcement is ordered to stand down. The state protects illegal criminals while abandoning its citizens.

Worse, California has rigged the system itself. By counting millions of illegal residents in the census, it inflates its congressional power, robbing law-abiding states. This demographic gerrymandering rewards lawlessness with control, making California's decline a national contagion.

This is what happens when leaders abandon their own civilization—when they dismantle borders, erase law, and gamble with the demographics of a nation. California is not the future.

It is the warning. And America is next.

PART IV

RULERS OF RUIN

CHAPTER 16

ARSONISTS

The deliberate collapse of California's criminal justice system did not happen overnight, nor was it the result of mere negligence. It is the product of an ideological coup waged from within, orchestrated by district attorneys who have abandoned their duty to prosecute crime in favor of a radical experiment in social engineering. District Attorneys George Gascón in Los Angeles and Pamela Price in Alameda County are not reformers; they are saboteurs, leveraging the immense power of prosecutorial discretion to dismantle the legal infrastructure that once safeguarded public order.

These figures, bankrolled by George Soros and his network of political financiers, have transformed their offices into laboratories of criminal impunity. Their policies—abolition of cash bail, refusal to charge violent offenders, and the systematic dismantling of sentencing enhancements—have institutionalized lawlessness. The state's legal apparatus, once a bulwark against disorder, now functions as a sieve, ensuring that criminals are swiftly recycled back onto the streets while victims are left to fend for themselves.

This chapter dissects the methodical erosion of justice under the guise of "equity," revealing how the very institutions designed to uphold the law have been weaponized against it. Gascón and Price are not simply failing in their roles; they are succeeding in a far more insidious objective: the deconstruction of law and order itself. If left unchecked, their tenure will mark the final unraveling of California's already fraying social contract, where justice is no longer blind—only absent.

The Subversion of Prosecutorial Power

The Misunderstood Reach of District Attorneys

The power wielded by district attorneys is profound, yet often misunderstood by the public. County-level district attorneys, often seen as local figures, are actually the linchpins of law enforcement in major metropolitan areas. These offices have the ability to reshape entire cities, from how crimes are prosecuted to how sentencing is applied. In a metropolis like Los Angeles, home to over ten million people, the DA's decisions ripple through the entire legal and civic landscape. District attorneys decide not only who will be charged with crimes but also how justice is distributed within their jurisdiction. The discretion they hold—to prosecute or not, to seek maximum sentencing or leniency—shapes public safety far beyond individual cases.

District attorneys have the unilateral power to:

- **Decide Charging Policies:** They determine whether to bring charges and what specific charges to file, including the ability to decline prosecution for certain offenses.
- **Influence Sentencing:** Through plea bargains and sentencing recommendations, they significantly affect the penalties defendants face.
- **Set Office-Wide Policies:** They establish guidelines and directives that all prosecutors in their office must follow.
- **Interact with Law Enforcement:** They collaborate with police departments, influencing how laws are enforced.

This concentration of power means that a district attorney's philosophy and policies can have profound impacts on crime rates, incarceration levels, and community safety.

Why Purchase Prosecutors?

The rise of progressive prosecutors like Gascón and Price is not the natural drift of political currents but the engineered outcome of a meticulously calculated campaign to institutionalize radicalism in America's largest jurisdictions. This is not organic evolution—it is a deliberate subversion of the justice system, orchestrated to erode the pillars of public order and replace them with a revolution waged in plain view.

The Soros Dollars

At the center of this project is George Soros, whose network of political action committees (PACs) has funneled over $40 million into district attorney races across the United States since 2015.[1] These Soros-backed prosecutors now hold jurisdiction over 72 million Americans, overseeing twenty-five of the fifty most populous cities and counties in the nation.[2]

Gascón and Price are not merely beneficiaries of Soros's largesse; they are the handpicked agents of a larger project to weaken American law enforcement and dismantle traditional prosecutorial practices. Gascón's campaign alone received $2.25 million from Soros-affiliated PACs, allowing him to overwhelm any serious opposition in Los Angeles.[3]

Jamie McBride of the LA Police Protective League observes, "What we see is it's very well-funded and obviously everyone knows about George Soros. . . . And they're literally changing the landscape. Just having one person in a position like that changes the landscape in the county."

John Lewin adds a personal dimension reflecting on the Soros cash flow: "A guy like George Soros and the groups that he supports are doing tremendous damage. And listen, I'm Jewish. I'm very proud of being Jewish. So, anyone who's gonna say that it's some antisemitic trope is full of shit. You know, I'm a proud supporter of Israel. And I can't stand George Soros. I don't dislike George Soros because he's Jewish. I dislike George Soros because he is single-handedly trying to destroy the fabric of America. And doing a pretty good job at it."

Opaque Motives

As a veteran of an elite LA County Sheriff's crime unit—now running one of many thriving private security firms in California, where the demand for private policing is at an all-time high—remarked: "[Gascón] is a failed cop and a failed DA, and he's failed everywhere he's gone. But he keeps winning. He's highly funded, with the Soros backing. And the Soros machine . . . do you know where a lot of their investment goes? Private security. It's genius. It's genius."

This insight, corroborated independently by a former head of federal security for LAX and one of the top traders in global finance, suggests an unsettling alignment of interests—though such claims must be approached with necessary caution. The Soros Family Office, operating through a labyrinthine structure of private placements, offshore special purpose vehicles (SPVs), and 501(c)(3)s, ensures a deliberate opacity. Public records offer only a faint glimpse into this sprawling apparatus, shielding its financial maneuvers and political ambitions from meaningful scrutiny. What we observe, then, is merely the surface—those actions too visible or too large to fully conceal. The real question, however, concerns the far greater portion of the iceberg beneath the waterline, invisible to public inquiry and thus insulated from accountability. The true scope of this financial and political architecture likely extends far deeper into the darker recesses of capital markets and influence peddling than anything the public can grasp—raising profound questions about the scale and intent of this elusive operation.

Arbitraging Justice

Stanley Druckenmiller, who worked closely with Soros at the Quantum Fund, once remarked, "George taught me that when you have tremendous conviction on a trade, you have to go for the jugular. It takes courage to be a pig."[4] This illustrates Soros's strategy: a calculated exploitation of market distortions and volatility, where chaos is not simply weathered but harnessed as an asset. Soros himself has noted that "arbitrage is an opportunity to profit by recognizing that the prevailing view in the market is distorted."[5] His infamous bet against the British pound in 1992, which earned him over a billion dollars in a single day, exemplifies this ruthless precision. Soros built his career on identifying and exploiting discrepancies between perception and reality, turning chaos into profit.

This acumen for financial engineering raises a disquieting question: Could Soros's funding of policies that foster social unrest be a form of synthetic arbitrage, in which one asset—public law enforcement—is deliberately undermined to create demand for another—private security? Or to the avail of other asset classes entirely?

The logic is chillingly efficient and reptilian. Policies that weaken public safety lead to a depreciation of urban real estate, creating a prime acquisition window for institutional investors like BlackRock to accumulate assets at significantly deflated prices. As instability rises, insurance markets adjust with elevated premiums, amplifying profitability for insurers who capitalize on the heightened risk environment. Meanwhile, firms entrenched in the security and surveillance sector, experience surging demand as cities prioritize private protection over public enforcement. In this context, volatility is no longer a market aberration but an engineered asset—a deliberate manipulation of civic disorder, where the erosion of public structures becomes a lucrative investment opportunity for those who correctly identify and time the arbitrage.

The financial calculus is methodical and demonically cynical: drive down real estate values through orchestrated destabilization, acquire distressed assets at a discount, and hedge the downside risk by investing in security and surveillance enterprises tasked with managing the disorder. As the market corrects, these devalued assets can be liquidated at significant margins, leaving the broader public to contend with hollowed-out neighborhoods and drained municipal coffers. In this framework, crime itself becomes commodified—a mechanism for capital extraction, where societal breakdown is transformed into an exploitable asset class.

Though speculative, the theory of Soros investing in private security gains credibility when considering his allies, like Pierre Omidyar, co-founder of eBay. Omidyar, much like Soros, has funded initiatives that weaken public law enforcement under the guise of reform. Yet, in 2020, it was revealed that Omidyar had also invested in Bond, a New York-based security technology company marketed as an Uber-like service for the wealthy, providing elite bodyguards on demand.[6,7] This dual investment strategy—weakening public law enforcement while backing private security services for elites—raises unsettling questions about who truly benefits from these so-called criminal justice reforms.

The Calculated Investment

What is clear, however, is that Soros's financial influence was never about elevating the most qualified candidates or engaging in a genuine debate over justice reform. It was an investment in a revolutionary ideology aimed at dismantling the structures of law and order across the country.

In Gascón's case, the $2.25 million from Soros-affiliated PACs allowed him to flood Los Angeles with campaign ads, suffocating meaningful opposition and ensuring his election without a thorough examination of the radical agenda he intended to implement. His victory was not about fixing a broken system; it was about replacing a functioning system with a destabilizing agenda aimed at dismantling the achievements of his predecessors, such as Steve Cooley and Jackie Lacey.

For Soros, this was never about reform; it was a strategic investment in revolution by other means. The broader implications of these political investments point to a reshaping of the criminal justice landscape that could ultimately serve private interests. While direct evidence of specific portfolio allocations is proprietary and elusive, the convergence of these actions with escalating societal instability suggests a far more calculated agenda. It is the deliberate exploitation of disorder, where the boundaries between public crisis and private gain blur, creating opportunities for those prepared to profit from the ruins.

Money Well Spent

The financial influence exerted by George Soros and his network is not a haphazard byproduct of philanthropic endeavors, but a meticulously engineered strategy to secure asymmetric political and judicial influence at a fraction of the capital that such leverage would typically command. With relatively modest financial commitments—when measured against the scale of Soros's vast portfolio—his investments in local district attorney races deliver an extraordinary return on investment. This approach functions as a high-efficiency capital allocation strategy, akin to private equity targeting undervalued assets. Soros's method resembles the "Moneyball" principle in baseball: leveraging data-driven insights to acquire low-cost political assets that yield disproportionately large dividends in the form of prosecutorial discretion and policymaking authority. By strategically directing resources to these local races, Soros maximizes political leverage with minimal expenditure, reshaping the judicial landscape through calculated, high-impact interventions.

Soros-backed candidates consistently outspend their opponents by margins of five or six to one. Between 2018 and 2021 alone, Soros funneled $13 million into just ten district attorney races, often covering up to 90% of the campaign funding for his handpicked candidates, ensuring their ascension and the implementation of his broader agenda.[8]

Los Angeles Fallout

The returns on this investment have been as staggering as the fallout has been catastrophic. Returning to the statistics outlined in chapter 6, we see that since George Gascón's election in Los Angeles in 2020, homicides have surged by 33.9%, robberies by 17.7%, aggravated assaults by 18.8%, and motor vehicle thefts by a 34.7%. Meanwhile, *arrests have plummeted* by 20.8%, and shooting victims have skyrocketed by a shocking 64.5%.[9] Between 2022 and 2023 alone, homicides in Los Angeles County rose by a staggering 9.23%, while grand theft auto surged by 7.56%.[10] The year-over-year numbers for 2021 and 2022 underscore the grim narrative: robberies up 23.6%, aggravated assaults up 13.53%, and burglaries spiking by an appalling 34.6%.[11]

These are not mere statistics; they are the markers of a city in free-fall, where criminality is emboldened and unfettered by a justice system joyfully castrated by the revolutionary ideology of George Soros and his political vassals. Civic decay is no longer speculative; it has become the inevitable outcome of policies designed to dismantle the mechanisms that once held crime at bay and public order in place.

As of March 2024, the situation in Los Angeles continues to deteriorate. Robberies have risen 9.5% over the previous year, while homicides have surged an astonishing 28.1%.[12] The rise in "smash-and-grab" thefts has been one of the clearest manifestations of this unchecked lawlessness. While statistics don't always separate these brazen acts from general shoplifting, the trend is unmistakable. In 2020, Los Angeles saw 14,714 reported incidents of shoplifting—a troubling figure in its own right. By 2023, that number had skyrocketed to 34,303, an increase of 133%.[13]

The Human Toll

This epidemic of theft, both across Los Angeles County and the state at large, is more than a wave of criminality—it is the starkest indicator of a broader collapse of law and order. While retailers, small businesses, and working-class Californians are forced to bear the brunt of a disintegrating justice system—one that has ceased to function as a deterrent—the architects of this ideological experiment remain entirely insulated from its real-world consequences. For the ordinary Californian, the stakes are existential: shattered livelihoods, mounting fear, and neighborhoods steadily slipping into chaos. Yet, for the elites funding this societal revolution there is no such reckoning. Shielded behind walls of private security and cushioned by their wealth, they exist in a parallel world, detached from the very chaos they have unleashed upon the public.

As crime continues to surge, the gulf between these two realities becomes ever more pronounced. For the average citizen, the streets are no longer safe, businesses face relentless looting, and public spaces descend into lawlessness, all while those responsible for enabling these conditions retreat behind gates, out of sight and reach. LAPD Interim Chief Dominic Choi captured the despair of those on the frontlines, noting, "Robberies continue to plague us as a crime problem."[14] But it is not just robberies; it is the collapse of deterrence, the dissolution of trust in institutions, and the creation of an environment where lawlessness thrives unchecked.

For the small business owners and families on the ground, this is not an ideological battleground—it is their livelihood and security at stake. As they shoulder the economic and social costs of this ideological experiment, the very notion of justice becomes a distant echo, as the privileged few who engineered this collapse remain comfortably removed from its most brutal consequences.

Oakland's Fallout

Oakland, the largest city in Alameda County, like its decaying counterpart to the south, Los Angeles, has descended into a lawless wasteland under the reckless stewardship of District Attorney Pamela Price. In just the first quarter of 2023, violent crime exploded by 21%, with robberies leaping an astonishing 38%.[15] Price's deliberate refusal to prosecute repeat offenders, combined with the wholesale abandonment of sentencing enhancements, has turned Oakland into a criminal's playground, where the notion of consequence has been systematically erased. This surge in lawlessness is not the unfortunate result of mere incompetence but the predictable outcome of ideologically motivated policies that strip the city of its last vestiges of order. Oakland now dangles on the precipice of full-blown collapse, while Price, undeterred by the wreckage she has wrought, forges ahead in her ideological crusade, oblivious—or perhaps indifferent—to the carnage in her wake.

Burn It All Down

To suggest that these policies are simply "misguided" would be to grant them an unearned indulgence. In truth, they are deliberate acts of social engineering designed to upend the existing order. Every prosecutor and law enforcement officer interviewed for this report echoed the same grim refrain: George Gascón, Pamela Price, and their cadre of ideological backers are not here to fix the system—they are here to dismantle it. Cloaked in the sanctimonious language of social justice, their agenda is not reform but demolition. "They want to burn down the system," was the consensus across the board, and the wreckage piling up in their wake stands as proof of their success.

Intellectually stunted though they be (a point made clear speaking to their colleagues), Gascón and Price are not naïve idealists chasing a misguided utopia. Their project is a calculated dismantling of the institutions that once protected society from descending into lawlessness. This strategy was never about enhancing public safety; it was about shifting the entire framework of justice away from accountability and toward the unchecked decriminalization of crime. In their vision, the moral equilibrium of society has been inverted: the criminal is the victim, and the system—previously tasked with upholding order—has become the oppressor. What we are witnessing is not a well-intentioned attempt to create a more just society but the calculated acceleration of societal decay on the road to anarchy, paved by crime-equity.

The broader implications of this cynical arbitrage of public safety are still emerging, but one fact remains indisputable: the financial backing of George Soros and his network of purchased prosecutors is not merely a political experiment—it is the systematic dismantling of public law enforcement, with chaos, disorder, and lawlessness as the inevitable outcomes. What we are observing is not just a local failure, but a strategic coup of the criminal justice system, transforming it from a force for deterrence into an enabler of crime.

Statistics may tell one part of the story, but for the residents of Oakland and Los Angeles, the reality is far more visceral. For those whose lives are now dictated by fear, whose streets are not patrolled by law enforcement but left to lawlessness, Gascón and Price are not the heralds of progress—they are the architects of California's most rapid descent into chaos in living memory. As their ideological agenda grinds forward, the very essence of justice is being eroded, leaving behind a broken system where safety and order are distant ideals, and the damage may well be beyond repair.

The cost of this ideological experiment is not measured in political capital but in human suffering, financial devastation, and the erosion of basic security. For the people on the ground, the collapse of justice is not an abstract debate—it is a lived catastrophe. The very institutions once designed to uphold order and protect the innocent have been dismantled beyond recognition. Left in their wake is a society grappling with fear, chaos, and a justice system gutted to the core, forcing Californians to contend with the grim reality that what was lost may never fully return.

Gascón's Los Angeles: A Crime-Equity Laboratory

George Gascón's policies, enacted with minimal public input and devoid of legislative oversight, rapidly recalibrated prosecutorial priorities under the banner of crime-equity—a liberationist framework that seeks to reinterpret criminal justice through the lens of historical oppression and systemic inequities. Far from being incremental reforms, these changes signaled a dramatic, ideologically driven shift away from traditional justice toward a system that privileges decarceration and rehabilitation, even at the expense of public safety.

Made in San Francisco: Gascón's Radical and Incompetent Origins

Gascón's rise to power in Los Angeles was not the product of grassroots democratic demand, but rather the culmination of a national upheaval, fueled by well-organized and heavily funded activist networks. Veteran prosecutor John Lewin correctly observed, "George Gascón was absolutely elected because of George Floyd. 100%."[16] The widespread social unrest following Floyd's death provided fertile ground for a candidate who promised sweeping changes—however disruptive and poorly conceived those changes might be. In this moment of national turmoil, Gascón, with the financial backing of George Soros's political machine, capitalized on a wave of emotion rather than reasoned debate over the true consequences of his policies.

As former San Francisco District Attorney—appointed by Gavin Newsom, then mayor, following Kamala Harris's election to state attorney general—Gascón was no stranger to controversy. The increase in violent crime in San Francisco under his tenure from 2011 to 2019, including rape and aggravated assault, was an alarming trend that foreshadowed what was to come in Los Angeles. Yet, these statistics failed to impede his ambitions. Armed with over $2 million from Soros-affiliated PACs, Gascón's campaign overwhelmed any serious opposition. "He really came down to LA to run for DA," said former LA District Attorney Steve Cooley, "because he knew the Soros money would come to him."[17] In this sense, his ascension was not a triumph of democratic engagement but the result of a well-financed and ideologically charged movement that sought not merely to reform but to transform the role of the prosecutor into something altogether unrecognizable.

John Lewin offers a scathing assessment of Gascón the man: "He is a terrible problem. He's inexperienced. He's incompetent. He's disgraceful. And he's corrupt. He's not bright, he doesn't understand even basic legal things. And he's implemented horrendous policies."[18] Gascón, by his own admission, attended an unaccredited law school and had minimal courtroom experience prior to becoming the chief of the largest prosecutorial office in the nation. Steve Cooley doesn't mince words either in his personal assessment: "I think he is an out-of-control sociopath, he probably has been most of his life and career, even when he was with LAPD."

Ideological Agendas and Policy Overhauls

Gascón wasted no time in dismantling the foundations of Los Angeles's criminal justice system. On his very first day, he enacted a series of special directives that obliterated longstanding prosecutorial standards, with no legislative oversight or public accountability. These policies, framed through the distorted lens of crime-equity, stripped away key prosecutorial tools and redefined public safety. The impact has been profound and catastrophic—visible in the escalating crime rates and the breakdown of law and order. The deconstructionist intent of these policies is clear, leaving the city to grapple with the consequences of this ideological overhaul.

His directives read like a checklist of radical reforms aimed at decarceration by any means necessary.

Gascón Policy Directives in Detail

Upon taking office, George Gascón implemented a series of special directives that radically altered the criminal justice system in Los Angeles. Each directive, cloaked in the rhetoric of equity and reform, had severe and far-reaching consequences for public safety and community order.

Special Directive 20–06: The Elimination of Cash Bail

Overview:

Gascón's decision to abolish cash bail for a wide range of offenses was framed as a pursuit of economic justice, aiming to reduce the disproportionate burden on poorer defendants. However, this policy ignored the critical issue of public safety. By eliminating financial accountability, it created an environment where even serious offenders were released without significant deterrent, often endangering the very communities Gascón claimed to protect.

Consequences:

The impact of this directive was immediate and calamitous. By 2022, Los Angeles saw a marked rise in key crime metrics—burglaries increased by 34%, robberies by 23.6%, and aggravated assaults by 13.53%.[19] Veteran prosecutor Kathleen Cady highlighted the flaw in this logic: "Gascón believes bail hurts poor people, it doesn't hurt rich people. It's not fair. So we shouldn't be asking for bail really ever unless it's a violent felony." Yet, as Cady chillingly notes, "Residential burglary on its own is not a violent felony—it's only a violent felony if someone is home. So, under this directive, if your home is burglarized while you're away, it's not considered a violent felony, and DAs were instructed not to request bail. And if they had asked for bail, they had to go in at the next court appearance and say, 'we're asking that bail be reduced or not set so that the guy can get released.'"

Gascón has defended his stance, stating that: "Money bail is as unjust as it is unsafe. It allows wealthy people who are dangerous to purchase their freedom while those without means who pose no risk to public safety languish in jail awaiting trial. There is no evidence that cash bail provides a sufficient incentive necessary for people to return to court."[20] Yet the practical outcome has been the release of dangerous individuals back into the community, often to reoffend. This disconnect between ideology and reality has disproportionately harmed the very minority communities the policy purports to uplift, leaving many victims without justice. As one prosecutor put it, "Gascón is so focused on justice for defendants, but what about justice for their victims, many of whom are Black and brown as well? Where is the justice for them? We are making them victims of the criminal justice system yet again."[21]

Special Directive 20–07: Decriminalization of Misdemeanors

Overview:
Under this directive, thirteen misdemeanors—ranging from resisting arrest to drug possession—were effectively decriminalized. Gascón justified this move as an effort to reduce the so-called criminalization of poverty and minor offenses. However, this experiment in "reform" failed to anticipate the profound disruption it would cause in maintaining community standards and public order.

Consequences:
The fallout was immediate. Los Angeles, already teetering under the weight of its crime issues, saw quality-of-life offenses skyrocket. In areas like Venice Beach and Downtown Los Angeles, public urination, aggressive panhandling, and open drug use became daily occurrences. Residents and business owners found themselves abandoned to navigate the chaos as law enforcement was left powerless to address the escalating disorder.

Jamie McBride of the LAPD Union articulated the absurdity of the situation: "If you downgrade crimes into misdemeanors in a city like LA, they rarely get prosecuted, and if they are, it's always a plea bargain to probation or something meaningless. Under this no-bail regime, *nobody* is going to jail. So you have people committing crimes, getting arrested, and going right back to commit more crimes within hours. It's a big joke."

Former Los Angeles County District Attorney Steve Cooley pointed out the absurdity of the directive: "Gascón orders Deputy DAs not to file certain misdemeanors, the very types of offenses that maintain community peace and quality of life. In seventy-eight out of the eighty-eight cities in LA County, there are no city prosecutors, meaning the County DA historically prosecutes those misdemeanors. The vacuum in prosecution has devastated the quality of life in these cities."

In essence, under Gascón policy, these crimes have been decriminalized and the state penal code upended.

Kathy Cady elaborated on the misguided rationale behind the directive: "The belief is that prosecuting misdemeanors disadvantages the poor, so many of these offenses, like trespassing, are no longer charged." This leniency has emboldened habitual offenders, who now face few, if any, consequences. John Lewin captures the growing frustration: "We see them all the time—offenders with 20 prior convictions for theft, on probation for two more, and now with another charge. And we're told prison won't help them. But when someone repeatedly violates the laws of society, there comes a point when incarceration becomes the only option. George Gascón doesn't want to incarcerate anybody."

The result has been a system in which crime, particularly at the lower levels, is effectively sanctioned. The absence of real consequences has fostered an environment where offenders have little incentive to change their behavior.

Special Directive 20–08: Abolishing Sentencing Enhancements

Overview:
Perhaps the most damaging of Gascón's reforms, Special Directive 20–08 eliminated sentencing enhancements for crimes involving gang violence, the use of firearms, and repeat offenders under California's Three Strikes Law. Prosecutors were even instructed to retroactively dismiss enhancements in ongoing cases.

Consequences:

The directive gutted one of the most effective deterrents against violent crime. Gang-related allegations plummeted by 99%, and gun-related charges fell by 63%, not due to a reduction in crime, but because of Gascón's refusal to prosecute these enhancements. Kathy Cady, a veteran prosecutor, captured the absurdity of the situation: "DAs were ordered to ask judges to dismiss allegations of great bodily injury, gang involvement, and weapons charges, regardless of the facts of the case."

By stripping prosecutors of the tools needed to pursue adequate sentences for dangerous offenders, Gascón's policies have directly contributed to the rise in violent crime. The numbers speak for themselves: gang-related allegations dropped from 2,200 cases to just thirty, a 99% decline.[22] This isn't evidence of safer streets, but of a justice system retreating from its fundamental responsibilities.

John Lewin bluntly stated, "He will not EVER file gang allegations." This shift in priorities has made it clear that Los Angeles, under Gascón's leadership, has entered an era where the pursuit of leniency for offenders is prioritized over public safety.[23]

In California, sentencing enhancements have historically been used to target the most dangerous offenders, imposing additional penalties for crimes involving firearms, gang activity, or repeat offenses. Far from punitive excess, these enhancements served to incapacitate criminals who posed a clear and present threat to public safety. The California Policy Lab revealed that since 2015, 40% of individual prison admissions involved sentencing enhancements, which, on average, extended sentences by 1.9 years. By eliminating them in the name of equity, Gascón has effectively given violent offenders a green light to operate without fear of meaningful reprisal.

As one Deputy DA from Alameda County explained, "Using a gun in a robbery could add three, four, or ten years to a sentence. If you fired the gun and caused injury, it would be twenty-five years to life. Those enhancements are still legally available, but they're no longer being used." Under Gascón, the filing of gang and firearm enhancements in Los Angeles has dropped dramatically, with gang-related enhancements falling from 688 cases in the first half of 2012 to just seventy-seven in 2021—a 90% decrease.

This decline, far from heralding progress, has directly contributed to a rise in violent crime, as offenders realize they face fewer consequences. These decisions, demonstrably negligent, reflect the core tenets of crime-equity: a redistribution of suffering, designed to balance societal inequalities by dismantling traditional deterrents.

Law Enforcement Perspectives: Inside the System

Mike Maher, a thirty-three-year veteran of the LA County Sheriff's Department and Detective Team Sergeant overseeing the Major Crimes Bureau, underscores the consequences of jettisoning enhancements, including bail:

"It's crazy to me. Soft-on-crime policies are a travesty. Ten years ago, when we formed our team, gang members shooting each other would get minimal sentences, but residential burglars would get ten years. Gang enhancements, bail enhancements—these were critical. A twenty-year-old guy in government housing, driving a $100,000 Mercedes, arrested during a home invasion robbery—his bail would be $20,000 or $40,000, easily paid in cash. Judges used to enact bail enhancements requiring proof of cash sources, setting high bail to keep these guys locked up. Now, those bail enhancements are deemed unfair. So you have people walking in with an envelope of $50,000 cash, laughing because they know they'll be out in hours."[24]

"And while they're out [waiting for a future court date], what are they doing? $50,000 a day. They're just replenishing the money and rolling and rolling, rolling," Maher remarks, highlighting the insidious cycle of crime perpetuated by these policies.

Special Directive 20–09: Juvenile Justice Reforms

Overview:

Gascón's directive forbidding the prosecution of juveniles as adults, regardless of the severity of their crimes, aimed to promote rehabilitation over punishment. However, it removed a crucial deterrent against serious juvenile offenses, ignoring the reality that some crimes warrant adult-level consequences.

Consequences:

Without the threat of adult sentencing, violent crime among juveniles escalated, particularly within gang-affiliated youth. The directive stripped prosecutors of the ability to seek meaningful penalties, even in cases involving heinous crimes. The result: emboldened young offenders who now face little more than a temporary slap on the wrist, no matter how serious their offenses. The directive ignored the reality of juvenile involvement in serious crimes and the necessity of prosecutorial discretion in extreme cases.

Special Directive 20–11: Ending the Death Penalty

Overview:

Gascón unilaterally ended the pursuit of the death penalty, even in the most egregious cases. This was a direct contradiction of both California law and the will of voters who had reaffirmed capital punishment through the ballot box.

Consequences:

This decision was met with outrage from victims' families and law enforcement. For many, the death penalty represents the only fitting justice for the most heinous crimes. By refusing to even consider this option, Gascón not only disregarded the legal framework but demonstrated a profound lack of empathy for those devastated by the actions of violent criminals.

Systemic Shifts in Parole Hearing Protocols

John Lewin highlights a significant policy change that has fundamentally altered the role of the DA's office in parole hearings: "When Gascón took office, one of his first policies was that we cannot appear at those lifer hearings unless we are supporting parole."

Previously, victims attending parole hearings would have a prosecutor present to discuss the inmate's history in prison and guide them through the process. This support provided a semblance of balance, allowing victims to make their impact statements with a sense of advocacy. The absence of this support leaves victims to fend for themselves in a process increasingly skewed towards offender rehabilitation.

This stark reversal not only strips victims of essential prosecutorial support but also epitomizes a broader, insidious shift towards a system more fixated on liberating offenders than upholding justice for their victims. Lewin continues, "We had a unit that attended these parole hearings with victims' families, primarily to oppose parole. Essentially, we've abandoned all these victims."

Former Deputy DA for LA County Kathleen Cady describes the immediate consequences for victims cruelly abandoned under this policy at a critical moment in the justice process:

> Victims, who would be going to a parole hearing before Gascón came in, would have a prosecutor who would have discussed the inmate's history in prison, what to expect to hear at a parole hearing. You know, kind of this is how it'll go. And I'll be there, I'll walk you through it, and you'll be able to make your impact statement. The day that Gascón was elected, and he issued all of his policies, one of his policies is that we will no longer attend parole hearings. So that afternoon DAs were calling victims for parole hearings for the next day saying, "I know I've been telling you for months that I'll be there with you tomorrow, but I'm not allowed to anymore, you're going to have to do it on your own."[25]

A Revolution Agenda: Day One

Steve Cooley provides a stark distillation of Gascón's basic tenets and radical—indeed revolution-inspired—agenda:

> He wants to decarcerate. He wants to have sentences be the minimum. He never wants a juvenile to ever be sentenced to state prison. He wants to prosecute law enforcement just to satisfy some of his constituents like Black Lives Matter. And so he's brought a number of filings that should not ever been filed, but he's satisfying constituents. You don't do that as a DA, follow the law and evaluate the evidence you do professionally. You have standards, you have values. You do not pick a target and then file on them.

He's basically decided he wants to go after law enforcement. It's just a weird phenomenon.[26,27,28]

The Devastating Fallout

The immediate repercussions of Gascón's policies were both profound and catastrophic. In protest, over 120 experienced prosecutors—many with expertise in complex criminal litigation—fled the DA's office. Their exodus did not merely represent a loss of institutional knowledge but a collapse in the office's ability to function effectively. The vacuum left behind was filled by a cadre of ideologically aligned but woefully inexperienced attorneys whose chief qualification seemed to be their unwavering allegiance to Gascón's radical agenda. This ideological realignment has crippled the office, leaving it incapable of grappling with the escalating crime rates that have followed.

The numbers tell a grim story: over 10,000 cases now languish in a backlog, choking the capacity of the District Attorney's Office to dispense justice in any meaningful way. As veteran prosecutor John Lewin scathingly remarked, "He doesn't follow the law. He's running his office like a mafia don, retaliating against anyone who disagrees." This analogy captures not just Gascón's administrative style but his broader approach to governance: wielding power ruthlessly and rewarding loyalty over competence, with little regard for the legal consequences.

As pointed out by one LA County prosecutor, speaking on condition of anonymity: "The vast majority of LA prosecutors are not in alignment with Gascón's equity agenda." Gascón's limited legal experience and poor policy implementation exacerbate the issue—he has never practiced as a lawyer or tried a case. As such, Gascón "does not know how to implement policies in a responsible way," the same prosecutor opines.[29]

More troubling still is the impact on the neighborhoods already buckling under the weight of multiple crises. Los Angeles, a city already grappling with skyrocketing homelessness, widespread addiction, and untreated mental health issues, found itself further destabilized by a justice system that had all but abdicated its role. Gascón's directives effectively decriminalized a host of quality-of-life offenses—vandalism, aggressive panhandling, public intoxication, and shoplifting among them—leaving law enforcement handcuffed in their ability to maintain public order.

This laissez-faire approach to low-level crime, couched in the rhetoric of social justice, ignored a fundamental truth about human behavior: that disorder begets disorder. As the prosecution of minor offenses vanished, so too did the community's sense of safety and cohesion. The neighborhoods most affected were often those least able to endure it—working-class and minority communities already on the front lines of the city's social and economic crises. These communities were not merely neglected; they were abandoned, left to bear the brunt of Gascón's ideological experiment.

Gascón has consistently framed his policies as efforts to rectify injustices against minority communities, claiming to champion the rights of the marginalized. However, as with many ideologically driven agendas, the reality on the ground tells a different story. By weakening the prosecution of gang-related violence and firearm offenses, Gascón has disproportionately harmed the very communities he claims to protect. In many of the city's minority neighborhoods, violent crime has surged, while law enforcement struggles to maintain order in the face of reduced prosecutorial support. As one prosecutor pointedly noted, "Gascón is so focused on justice for Black and brown defendants, but the victims and their families are also Black and brown. Where is the justice for them?"

Far from promoting equity, Gascón's policies have emboldened criminals while leaving victims—many of whom come from the same minority communities—abandoned by a justice system that seems to prioritize ideology over their safety and well-being.

Between 2020 and 2022, the homeless population in Los Angeles swelled by 13%, with no corresponding increase in resources to manage the complex intersection of homelessness, addiction, and mental health. This was not simply a failure of housing policy—it was a failure of public safety. Gascón's directives effectively severed the link between crime and consequence, further emboldening those who prey on the vulnerable. Crimes deeply intertwined with homelessness—public intoxication, property theft, and drug-related offenses—went unaddressed, creating an environment in which law-abiding citizens were left to navigate a city increasingly defined by chaos.

In this context, Gascón's policies must be seen for what they truly are: not the well-meaning reforms of a progressive prosecutor, but a calculated dismantling of public safety, carried out in the name of equity. The collateral damage—the erosion of public trust, the degradation of community life, and the abandonment of the rule of law—is no accident, but the inevitable outcome of a system that prioritizes ideology over pragmatism, and offenders over victims.

By unmooring criminal justice from accountability, Gascón has made a mockery of the very ideals he claims to uphold, leaving Los Angeles to reckon with the human and social costs of his ideological crusade.

Gascón's Commissars: The Radical Vanguard of Los Angeles's Criminal Justice Overhaul

In George Gascón's reshaping of Los Angeles's criminal justice system, three key figures have emerged as the intellectual and ideological driving force behind his far-reaching reforms: Tiffiny Blacknell, Joseph Iniguez, and Alisa Blair. These individuals form the core of Gascón's inner circle, each playing a pivotal role in executing his radical vision of decarceration and de-prosecution, all under the banner of "equity" and "justice reform."

Far from being mere bureaucrats, these figures are revolutionaries within the system—advocates not for reform as traditionally understood, but for a fundamental overhaul of the structures designed to maintain public safety. Their influence extends beyond policy, shaping the very philosophy of law enforcement in Los Angeles, often at the expense of both victims and public safety.

Tiffiny Blacknell: Chief of Staff and Crime-Equity Apostle

Tiffiny Blacknell, Gascón's Chief of Staff, is perhaps the most vocal and ideologically committed member of this inner circle. Her radical credentials were laid bare when she proudly admitted to participating in the 1992 Rodney King riots, describing herself as a looter during the unrest. For Blacknell, this was not an aberration but a formative experience that has deeply informed her approach to criminal justice. In a 2020 Facebook post, Blacknell wrote in reference to the devastating riots, "When the opportunity arose, we took some shit. It was one of the most formative moments of my life."[30]

A former public defender and fierce critic of law enforcement, Blacknell has played a critical role in pushing Gascón's agenda to eliminate prosecutorial tools such as sentencing enhancements. She views such measures as emblematic of an oppressive system that disproportionately harms marginalized communities. Her public statements during the 2020 Black Lives Matter riots further solidified her stance; she dismissed concerns about looting and destruction in Santa Monica and the Westside with disdain, telling critics: "Cry me a river!"—a crystalized confession of crime-equity mores, and a sharp reflection of her broader belief that the criminal justice system itself is the true source of violence, not the acts it seeks to prevent or punish.[31] In her view, the destruction wrought by looters during those protests was trivial compared to the larger ideological battle. "Don't text me SHIT about Whole Foods in West Hollywood and your beloved Santa Monica," she wrote on Facebook. In this sense, Blacknell is the personification of retributive crime-equity jurisprudence.

Beyond her radical rhetoric, Blacknell has been a lightning rod for controversy in her legal career. One particularly egregious instance occurred in 2020 when she negotiated a "sweetheart" plea deal in a gang murder case, doing so behind the backs of the prosecutor and the victim's family. Her willingness to circumvent the justice system for the sake of ideological purity is emblematic of the broader issue at play in Gascón's office.[32]

Moreover, Blacknell's opposition to the very concept of incarceration further illustrates the extremes of her worldview. She has repeatedly asserted that "prison is obsolete" and has called for the nation to "reimagine America without it." This isn't just empty rhetoric; it informs the policies coming from Gascón's office, which prioritizes decarceration above all, regardless of the consequences for public safety.

For former LA District Attorney Steve Cooley, Blacknell represents a venomous force within the Los Angeles justice system and spares no words in his rebuke:

"She is a hate-filled racist. A hate-filled racist who hates the system for whatever reason. She refers to her daughter as 'my little revolutionary' on her Facebook page. She wears shirts that are anti-police, one of which, the most famous of which is emblazoned with the words 'the police are trying to kill me.' She is a complete, unadulterated hate-filled racist who wants to help destroy the system."[33,34]

Joseph Iniguez: Chief Deputy District Attorney and Architect of Radical Leniency

Joseph Iniguez, Gascón's Chief Deputy District Attorney, has become the chief architect behind some of the most controversial aspects of Gascón's tenure. His rapid rise to power within the DA's office is notable not just for his lack of prosecutorial experience, but for his deep ideological commitment to transforming the criminal justice system from within.

Iniguez's rise to the second-in-command position of the DA's office would be improbable in any other era, given his profoundly unconventional resume. A former criminal defense attorney, Iniguez is not just a participant in Gascón's overhaul of prosecutorial norms; he is its staunch architect. His deep alignment with progressive, anti-law enforcement ideologies can be traced through his legal career and public statements.

Iniguez's influence is most apparent in his role in eliminating sentencing enhancements—critical tools that had been used to impose additional penalties on repeat offenders and those involved in gang or firearm-related crimes. His actions have led to a dramatic reduction in the prosecution of such cases, with critics warning that this has allowed dangerous offenders, including violent gang members, to avoid significant jail time.

Iniguez's radical vision extends beyond adult offenders. He has been instrumental in ensuring that juveniles, no matter the severity of their crimes, are shielded from adult prosecution. One particularly egregious example involved a seventeen-year-old gang member who fatally stabbed a rival but was tried as a juvenile under Iniguez's direction, securing a far more lenient sentence—a guaranteed release by the age of twenty-five. This decision sparked outrage, as it underscored the administration's unwillingness to impose serious consequences on even the most violent young offenders.

Iniguez's personal behavior has also raised questions about his commitment to the law he claims to be reforming. In December 2021, he was arrested for allegedly obstructing a police officer during a traffic stop.

While this incident might have been career-ending for others, Iniguez faced no substantial consequences, raising concerns about the double standards within Gascón's administration. His continued rise within the DA's office, despite such controversies, suggests that ideological alignment with Gascón's agenda is valued more than legal or ethical consistency.

Alisa Blair: Special Prosecutor for Juvenile Justice Reform and Patron of LA's Child Soldiers

Alisa Blair, appointed as Special Prosecutor for Juvenile Justice Reform, represents the cutting edge of Gascón's vision to overhaul the prosecution of young offenders. A former public defender, Blair's approach to juvenile justice is grounded in the belief that even the most violent juvenile offenders should be spared the consequences of adult prosecution.

Blair has effectively dismantled the practice of trying minors as adults, even in cases involving murder, armed robbery, or sexual assault. Under her leadership, the prosecution of juveniles has shifted away from accountability and toward rehabilitation, regardless of the severity of their crimes. One of the most notorious cases under her watch involved a sixteen-year-old gang member who fatally shot a rival but was tried as a juvenile, ensuring a sentence that would allow for release by age twenty-five. This case, emblematic of Blair's ideology, has fueled growing concern that her policies are prioritizing offenders at the expense of public safety.

The rise in juvenile crime, particularly gang-related violence, has been linked to Blair's policies, as young offenders increasingly operate with the understanding that they will face minimal consequences for their actions. Critics argue that this leniency has not only emboldened youth crime but has also undermined the public's faith in the justice system. Blair, however, remains steadfast in her commitment to what she calls "restorative justice," a philosophy that seeks to heal rather than punish, even when the victims of violent crime are left without justice.

Blacknell, Iniguez, and Blair, each in their own sphere, have transformed the Los Angeles District Attorney's Office into a laboratory for radical criminal justice reform. Their collective influence has shifted the focus away from traditional notions of justice—where consequences serve as deterrents—and toward an ideology that prioritizes decarceration and offender rehabilitation above all.

While these policies have been hailed as progressive by some, the practical consequences have been devastating for public safety. Crime rates have risen, particularly violent and gang-related offenses, and the DA's office has been criticized for failing to protect victims and communities from the fallout of these reforms. The ideology driving Gascón's administration, executed by his inner circle, may be framed as reform, but for many in Los Angeles, it feels more like abandonment.

A Gascón Case Study: The Hannah Tubbs Travesty

Among the many grotesque misadventures in George Gascón's tenure as District Attorney, the case of Hannah Tubbs stands out as an egregious monument to the perils of ideological absolutism masquerading as justice. This is not merely a failure of governance; it is a cautionary tale of how blindly applied "reform" can lead to the systematic dismantling of accountability, leaving victims in its wake while emboldening predators to mock the very system designed to restrain them.

In 2014, a then seventeen-year-old Tubbs—called James, at the time—stalked and sexually assaulted a ten-year-old girl in the bathroom of a Denny's in Palmdale, California. Tubbs grabbed the child by throat, locked her in a stall, and vaginally molested her. The girl managed to escape and Tubbs fled California. In 2019, Tubbs was arrested in Idaho on unrelated charges and subsequently linked to the 2014 attack by DNA evidence. After his arrest, Tubbs began identifying as trans female in order to get placed with juvenile girls while awaiting trial.[35]

Under Gascón's sweeping and uncompromising policy against transferring juvenile defendants to adult court, Los Angeles County prosecutors were compelled to try Tubbs as a juvenile. This despite Tubbs being twenty-five at the time of trial, and only a few days shy of his eighteenth birthday at the time of the assault. Gascón nevertheless refused to try Tubbs as an adult and consequently he was sentenced to two years in a juvenile detention facility, housed with the teenage female prisoners. Moreover, under this same policy, Tubbs was spared from having to register as sex offender.

Later, jailhouse phone recordings surfaced of Tubbs laughing about how he had gamed the system, expressing no remorse for the crime.[36] When the inevitable backlash arrived, Los Angeles County Supervisor Kathryn Barger was among the first to point out the glaring absurdity of the case, stating: "This is an outrageous abuse of our justice system." The presiding judge, Mario Barrera, also found his hands tied, bound by the constraints of a DA's office that had deliberately refused to seek an adult trial for Tubbs, even in the face of overwhelming evidence and public safety concerns.[37]

Tubbs's victim released a statement that addressed the inadequate sentence, which stated in part: "Not only do I have to live with that awful memory for the rest of my life, but I'm also given no true justice as to what happened to me."[38]

Gascón later admitted that the outcome was "unsatisfactory" but maintained that his policies were sound.[39] However, the Tubbs case underscores the perils of rigid, ideologically driven policies that fail to account for the nuances of individual cases and the imperative of public safety. This speaks to a broader truth: Gascón, like so many architects of misguided reform, is unable to recognize when his doctrine fails because the doctrine itself has become more important than its results.

This case, in its entirety, is the direct consequence of Gascón's refusal to engage with the complexities of justice. His rigid adherence to a juvenile leniency doctrine, without exception or common sense, allowed a predatory adult to escape the full weight of the law. What was supposed to be a system protecting the vulnerable became, under his stewardship, a mechanism of exploitation, where dangerous offenders like Tubbs could laugh in the face of justice.

What we see in the Tubbs case is not an isolated incident but the inevitable outcome of a system governed by slogans rather than sense. Gascón's refusal to transfer the case to adult court was not an oversight; it was a conscious decision to place ideology above reality. Tubbs, a convicted sexual predator, became the unholy beneficiary of policies designed to shield rather than punish. And in that decision, Gascón revealed the true weakness of his entire prosecutorial project: a justice system that cannot differentiate between those in need of reform and those who exploit it is not a system at all. It is chaos masquerading as compassion.

As a coda to this grotesque episode, Tubbs would later be charged with murder in a separate case in Kern County, for which he received a fifteen year sentence.[40]

Pamela Price's Oakland: "Auntie Pam's" Criminal Playground

Pamela Price's tenure as Alameda County District Attorney is nothing short of a cautionary tale for anyone who believes that ideology alone can reshape a justice system without disastrous consequences. Her arrival in Oakland's prosecutorial office, like a twisted mirror of George Gascón's Los Angeles experiment, has left the city in the grips of a crime surge that feels less like a temporary blip and more like a systemic unraveling. Price's policies—eschewing prosecution, gutting sentencing enhancements, and offering a free pass to repeat offenders—have done nothing but enable lawlessness, transforming Oakland into a dystopian stage for unchecked criminal behavior.

The numbers, though cold, are brutal in their clarity. In the first three months of 2023, violent crime in Oakland soared by 21%, robberies spiked by 38%, and car thefts shot up by 45%. These aren't mere statistical fluctuations; they are the result of an office where punishment is seen as an outdated concept and the enforcement of law a relic of an oppressive past. This is not criminal justice reform—it's abdication. According to an Alameda County deputy district attorney, speaking under the condition of anonymity, "Our crime is through the roof. And that's due to the fact that our district attorney, she's a raging psychopath. She's not even liberal. She's so far past liberal. She's chaos." [41,42]

That chaos is reflected not just in the streets of Oakland, where citizens now live with the constant threat of violence, but also in the very institution Price commands. Over 20 experienced prosecutors have fled her office, unwilling to be complicit in this ideological vandalism. Those who remain find themselves grappling with cases that languish in the system, delayed by inexperience and indifference, while the criminals they prosecute become emboldened by a justice system that has lost its way.

This is no hyperbole. Price's policies—refusal to prosecute repeat offenders, eliminating sentencing enhancements, and avoiding "special circumstances" charges in murder cases—have emboldened criminals, transforming

Oakland into a city under siege. Price's commitment to criminal justice reform is, in essence, a refusal to impose any meaningful deterrent against criminal behavior. The results have been predictable: rising lawlessness, eroded public safety, and a profound loss of trust in the judicial system.

Alameda County's Parallel Decline

Under Price's leadership, Oakland has become a playground for criminals emboldened by lenient policies and the absence of prosecutorial oversight. The most damaging aspect is the selective prosecution—where decisions are made not on the basis of justice but on political allegiance. Price has dropped charges or reduced sentences in serious cases, leaving the public to pay the price.

The DA's office has become a political battlefield, with over twenty experienced prosecutors departing in frustration, leaving behind a skeleton crew of ideological enforcers. In such an environment, justice is secondary, and the pursuit of a political agenda has become the primary goal. As Cooley noted, "These people don't care about the law. They care about power, and they're willing to sacrifice public safety to get it."

A Deputy DA from Oakland adds, "In Alameda County, everybody gets out on bail. I mean, a judge let somebody out the other day, who had stabbed somebody, and then got out and stabbed another person. And they let that person out. Like, it's just crazy."

A Criminal's Ally: "Auntie Pam"

Perhaps the most damning indictment of Price's tenure comes from the very criminals she's supposed to prosecute. Within Oakland's jail system, Pamela Price is affectionately known as "Auntie Pam" among defendants—a nickname that speaks volumes about the camaraderie between her office and the repeat offenders it refuses to hold accountable. As one deputy DA recounted: "The defendants refer to my district attorney as 'Auntie Pam,' because she gets them out. I've listened to jail calls where they're like, 'Yeah, we're gonna go with Pam!'" This grotesque inversion of the prosecutor's role—a supposed enforcer of the law reduced to an ally of those who flout it—reflects the total abdication of responsibility that has come to define Price's administration.

Price's leniency towards offenders has, by design, minimized the consequences of criminal behavior. Her refusal to apply sentencing enhancements—including in cases involving gang violence and firearm offenses—has undercut any notion of accountability. This dovetails with her policy of avoiding "special circumstances" charges in murder cases, which would typically preclude parole for the most heinous offenders. Under her leadership, even the possibility of life without parole—a measure meant for the most egregious crimes—has been all but eliminated.

This approach is not limited to Los Angeles. In Oakland, DA Pamela Price has consistently refused to authorize special circumstances on gun-related cases, deeming enhancements too harsh, particularly for minority offenders.

An Alameda County prosecutor working gang homicides summarized the resulting absurdity:

"Pamela Price has not authorized special circumstances on any case that has come before her at this point, because it unduly affects minorities. So no gun enhancement. In my county, if I were to go up to you, in a liquor store, point a gun to your head, and say, 'Give me your wallet!' it would be treated the same as if I went up to you punched you in the face and said, 'Give me your wallet.' If I shoot the gun in the air, it would also be treated the same as me punching you in the face. If I were to point a gun at your head in a liquor store and demand your wallet, it would be treated the same as if I punched you and said, 'Give me your wallet.'"

Internal Turmoil and Loss of Expertise

The consequences of Price's ideological zealotry extend beyond the streets and into the inner workings of the Alameda County DA's office, which has been hollowed out by a mass exodus of talent. Over twenty seasoned prosecutors have left, unable or unwilling to operate within the chaos that Price has imposed. Some have been placed on administrative leave for opposing her policies during the election. According to the same anonymous deputy DA, "We are losing our most seasoned attorneys, the ones who handle complex homicides and sexual assault cases. Their replacements lack the experience needed to navigate these challenging prosecutions."

The loss of expertise is staggering—over twenty prosecutors gone, with more expected to follow.

The depletion of seasoned legal minds has left the DA's office woefully unequipped to handle complex cases. Price's replacement hires, ideologically aligned but lacking in experience, are ill-prepared to handle serious criminal prosecutions. The ripple effect is clear: cases are delayed, backlogged, or dismissed, and the public suffers the consequences.

Avoidance of Accountability

Despite the spiraling crime rates, Price has largely avoided media scrutiny. She has refused interviews, restricted access to staff meetings, and limited transparency regarding the implementation and outcomes of her policies. Her refusal to engage with the media undermines any possibility of constructive dialogue about how to address Oakland's worsening public safety crisis. Instead of facing accountability, Price has chosen opacity—shielding her office from criticism while Oakland's residents are left to fend for themselves.

This reluctance to face scrutiny is symptomatic of a broader disdain for accountability that pervades her administration. As one prosecutor noted, "I have no doubt in my mind that the current elected district attorney wants to purely burn this place down. Every act she has taken, has done that."[43] It's a statement that, unfortunately, resonates with the facts on the ground. Price's policies—whether fueled by naïveté or willful negligence—have created an environment where crime thrives, offenders are emboldened, and victims are forgotten.

A City Under Siege

The numbers are undeniable. Violent crime in Oakland has increased by 11% year-to-date. Robberies surged by 34% in the first three months of 2023 alone. As public trust in law enforcement collapses, criminals operate with impunity, confident that Price's office will shield them from meaningful consequences. This lawlessness has reached the point where over twenty prosecutors—including those with decades of experience—have either left or been forced out. Meanwhile, Oakland's streets remain gripped by fear and uncertainty.

What's worse, the residents of Oakland—many of them from the very communities Price claims to protect—are bearing the brunt of this crisis. As violent crime spirals out of control, the promises of social justice have devolved into empty rhetoric. Price's refusal to uphold basic legal standards has left minority neighborhoods more vulnerable than ever, with black and brown families facing the daily threat of violence, robberies, and lawlessness that Price's policies have directly enabled.

Pamela Price's Oakland is a city where justice has been reduced to empty rhetoric. The "reform" she champions has delivered not equity but chaos, not protection but exposure. If her tenure proves anything, it is that the blind application of ideology, without respect for the complexities of law and order, leads not to progress but to collapse.

A Price Case Study: The Jasper Wu Tragedy (2021)

In a society ostensibly governed by law and reason, the murder of a child should be an unspeakable aberration—a breach in the social contract so grievous that it elicits a swift, unrelenting pursuit of justice. Yet under Pamela Price's tenure, even the murder of two-year-old Jasper Wu has been absorbed into the bureaucratic wasteland of "equitable" prosecution, where victims are lost in a fog of ideological posturing, and the very notion of accountability is deconstructed to the point of absurdity. In "Auntie Pam's" Oakland, justice is less about the crime and more about the identity of the criminal—a hallmark of the crime-equity revolution.

In November 2021, Jasper Wu was seated in the back of his family's car on Interstate 880 when a stray bullet from a gang-related shootout struck his head, killing him instantly. The suspects, with criminal records that should have guaranteed lengthy incarceration, were eventually apprehended nearly a year later. Under the administration of former District Attorney Nancy O'Malley, the gang members responsible for Jasper's death—Trevor Green and Ivory Bivens—were charged with murder and sentencing enhancements that would have precluded any possibility of parole.[44] It was, by all appearances, a path toward appropriate justice for a horrifying crime.

But 2022 brought Pamela Price to power, and with her came the systematic dismantling of accountability. Upon reviewing the case, Price dropped the special circumstance enhancements, effectively ensuring that Green and Bivens could be eligible for parole.[45] The prospect of real punishment, let alone the death penalty, vanished as quickly as Price's commitment to anything resembling justice. This decision—steeped in the rhetoric of "criminal justice reform"—did not just defy the gravity of the crime. It signaled a chilling indifference to the sanctity of a child's life, all in service of political posturing.

Now, because of their age and Price's leniency, Green and Bivens will be eligible to apply for parole after twenty-five years—or sooner—under California's youth offender parole laws.[46] They fall neatly into the category Price has championed: offenders under twenty-five, rebranded as misunderstood youth, who deserve "second chances" no matter the crime. Jasper's murder, in Price's worldview, seems an unfortunate byproduct of social inequities rather than an unforgivable act deserving lifelong punishment.

Adding insult to injury, Price's revisions didn't stop at dropping the enhancements. She also erased the criminal strikes from the record—strikes that should have doubled the prison sentences of these habitual offenders.[47] Green's robbery conviction in 2020 and Bivens' carjacking conviction in 2015—both serious felonies—were wiped from relevance, all in the name of Price's platform to "stop over-criminalizing our youth."[48] While that phrase may market well in California's progressive milieu, its indiscriminate application to violent gang members is not justice. It is a dereliction of duty that betrays the very concept of proportional punishment.

Pamela Price's actions align perfectly with her campaign promises, but in the realm of violent crime, these promises amount to little more than a surrender to chaos. The case of Jasper Wu reveals the dark underbelly of Price's administration: where rehabilitative justice, designed for low-level offenders, is recklessly applied to violent criminals. In this environment, accountability is not just weakened; it is eviscerated, leaving the public to suffer the consequences.

As Green and Bivens remain in custody awaiting trial, the specter of Price's policies looms large. There is no date for justice on the horizon, and growing concern surrounds whether Jasper's family will ever see a punishment befitting the crime. Price's refusal to apply sentencing enhancements, especially in a case involving gang violence and the death of a child, raises the terrifying prospect that these men—guilty of taking an innocent life—might one day walk free, their sentences neutered by ideology.

What Price has exposed, more clearly than any critic could, is the central flaw of her entire prosecutorial philosophy: the utter rejection of proportional justice. Under Price, crime is not treated as a moral breach but as a sociological inconvenience to be mitigated. The result is not the rule of law but the rule of identity politics, where the suffering of victims is overshadowed by the rights of criminals. In the case of Jasper Wu, this twisted approach has led to the grotesque reality where his killers may spend less time behind bars than their crime would demand.

Jasper's murder should have been a reckoning—a moment of clarity for a justice system on the brink of collapse. Instead, it has become a stark reminder of how ideology, once untethered from reason, can pervert even the most basic functions of the state. What should have been a straightforward prosecution of child murder has been reduced to a bureaucratic exercise in appeasement. And as long as this system prevails, the innocent—like Jasper—will always be the first to suffer.

The Corruption of Justice: A System in Decay

The decay within the offices of George Gascón and Pamela Price goes beyond ideological overreach; it is a deep and pervasive ethical collapse, turning the very machinery of justice into a political weapon. This is not a disagreement over reform but a dismantling of the ethical standards that should underpin any functioning legal system. As John Lewin, a seasoned prosecutor, sharply noted, "He put out a bunch of policies that some have been determined to be absolutely illegal. . . . He doesn't have the right to break the law."

Gascón's administration has been marked not only by controversial policies but by systemic retaliation against those who dare to challenge his methods. Experienced prosecutors have been replaced by ideological loyalists, many with no prosecutorial background. As one Deputy DA observed, "He has stacked our resentencing unit . . . they're going around resentencing some of the worst people out there, and we don't even know it because they don't tell us." This ideological reshuffling isn't reform—it's a subversion of justice, where dangerous criminals are quietly released, and the public remains uninformed.

In Alameda County, Pamela Price's office mirrors this same degradation. Allegations of selective prosecution have emerged, with decisions apparently driven more by political ideology than legal merits. Prosecutors who oppose her policies are not merely sidelined but placed on administrative leave, fostering an environment where dissent is punished, and loyalty to a political agenda is rewarded. This corrosive practice dismantles public trust and undermines the integrity of the justice system itself.

Ethical Erosion and Retaliation

The financial and legal consequences of Gascón's policies are staggering. With sixteen lawsuits filed against him by his own deputies and eleven civil service actions pending, the DA's office has become mired in a swamp of retaliatory legal battles. These lawsuits, combined with settlements, are bleeding public funds at an alarming rate, with projections of $1 million a month in costs.

The situation in Alameda County is equally dire. Price's refusal to prosecute certain crimes and her ideological stance on decimating sentencing enhancements has left Oakland spiraling into chaos. The policies themselves may be deeply flawed, but the real danger lies in how dissent is handled—through intimidation and retaliation, rather than dialogue and debate. The mass exodus of seasoned prosecutors in both offices has left the justice system gutted, unable to function effectively while facing surging crime rates.

Case Fixing and Political Favoritism

Even more alarming are the accusations of case fixing in both counties. Steve Cooley has pointed to the involvement of Tiffiny Blacknell, Gascón's Chief of Staff, in manipulating cases to benefit political allies. "She's been involved in two situations where she was trying to fix a case . . . but they don't investigate because she's high up in the DA's office," Cooley remarked. This manipulation strikes at the core of the justice system's integrity, reducing it to a political tool rather than a means of protecting society.

The allegations don't stop there. Gascón has been accused of filing politically motivated cases against law enforcement officers in Torrance, despite evidence that the charges were based on laws that didn't exist at the time of the alleged offenses. As Lewin described it, "He's paying a special prosecutor $2 million to go after officers based on law that wasn't the law at the time. This isn't just incompetence; it's corrupt."[49] These actions create a chilling effect, where law enforcement is targeted for political gain while real criminals evade justice.

A Culture of Corruption

The corruption within Gascón and Price's administrations runs deeper than just case manipulation or retaliation. It reveals a culture of impunity and political favoritism, where the law is not just bent but broken to serve ideological ends. The system that should be ensuring accountability has been hijacked, leaving dangerous offenders free while the innocent are left vulnerable.

In Los Angeles, this ethical decay has manifested through resignations and retaliatory lawsuits, with Gascón openly disregarding legal norms. As Lewin warned, "There are twenty lawsuits left, including mine, where he's going to lose. The DA's budget will be out $100 million. Because in the end, he doesn't care."[50,51,52]

A Broken System

What is happening in Los Angeles and Alameda County is not reform—it's corruption on a systemic level. The law has been subverted, justice has been weaponized, and the integrity of the system has been shattered. The corruption in Gascón's and Price's administrations is not just a local issue; it is a harbinger of what happens when ideology trumps justice.

As Steve Cooley so aptly put it: "They don't care about the law. They care about power." And the public, in turn, is paying the price for this corrupt pursuit of power, with justice becoming little more than a casualty in their ideological war. The damage inflicted may be irreparable, leaving cities like Los Angeles and Oakland in a state of perpetual decay, where politics has replaced principle, and lawlessness has taken the place of law.

Conclusion

The unfolding crises in Los Angeles and Oakland are symptomatic of a deeper, more systemic threat to the rule of law. These are not isolated events but rather part of a broader erosion of justice and public safety driven by a radical ideological experiment. The prioritization of criminal "equity" over accountability has not just undermined the justice system but has actively contributed to the decay of societal order. Both George Gascón and Pamela Price, in their respective roles as district attorneys, have abandoned the principles of justice, replacing them with ideological dogma that elevates the rights of criminals at the expense of the victims they have harmed.

In Los Angeles, Gascón's policies—such as the elimination of cash bail, the refusal to prosecute certain misdemeanors, and the dismantling of sentencing enhancements—have systematically removed key prosecutorial tools designed to maintain public safety. Price, following a similar path in Alameda County, has turned Oakland into a criminal playground where even the most violent offenders can expect leniency, often without the fear of significant consequences. The result is clear: violent crime has spiked, property crime has surged, and communities are gripped by fear.

The financial cost is also staggering, with millions of taxpayer dollars being funneled into legal battles, settlements, and lawsuits—particularly in Los Angeles, where Gascón faces multiple legal actions from his own staff. The social cost is most grievous: communities that were once safe are now dangerous, public trust in the legal system has eroded, and victims—often from the very minority groups that these so-called reforms are supposed to protect—are left with little recourse.

These policies have not simply failed—they have succeeded in precisely the way their architects intended. By dismantling the basic structures of accountability, they have emboldened offenders and hollowed out the institutions meant to protect us. What remains is a landscape of unchecked violence, property crime, and fear, where victims are abandoned, and justice is a hollow promise. The unraveling of order is not an unintended consequence; it is the design. As one prosecutor warns: "They want to burn the system down. They're shameless about it. I mean right in front of you, they tell you that by what they say and what they do and by their actions."

The chaos that now engulfs our cities was no accident. It is the inevitable outcome of policies designed not to balance justice but to tip the scales toward criminality. "Reforms" enacted under the banner of equity, specifically crime-equity, have had their intended effect of redistributing pain and suffering to the disfavored class and people. The wholesale abandonment of public safety that these policies represent was obvious at their inception.

CHAPTER 17

BLACK AND BLUE

Few things are more corrosive to a society than the systematic dismantling of its institutions under the guise of moral reckoning. The past decade has witnessed the transformation of law enforcement from an essential pillar of stability into a scapegoat for every societal ill, condemned not for what it does wrong, but for what it represents. The policing crisis in America is not rooted in misconduct alone—it is the byproduct of a culture war that demands not reform, but unconditional surrender.

At the heart of this upheaval lies the weaponization of martyrdom, where figures like George Floyd transcend their individual histories and become avatars of a revolution untethered from reality. The circumstances of their deaths—no longer tragic, but strategic—are repurposed to serve ideological agendas that cast the police not as fallible enforcers of law, but as systemic oppressors in an existential struggle. The result is not merely protest but purgation, a ritualistic expulsion of authority itself, where justice is no longer sought but preordained.

This chapter explores the consequences of this paradigm shift: a law enforcement apparatus paralyzed by political cowardice, a public discourse governed by binary moralism, and a society teetering on the brink of ungovernability. The very institutions designed to uphold order have been forced into retreat, hollowed out by demoralization, institutional betrayal, and the relentless assault of an ideology that sees law itself as an instrument of tyranny. What remains is a nation unmoored, where chaos is rebranded as justice, and the guardians of civilization are left to watch it burn.

George Floyd: Revolutionary Martyr

In the pantheon of modern American martyrs, George Floyd occupies a peculiar position—more symbol than man, more flashpoint than cause. His death on a Minneapolis street in May 2020 unleashed not just a torrent of righteous anger, but a cultural and political tsunami that swept away old certainties and left a new, fractured landscape in its wake. But while the collective cries of "I can't breathe" echoed across cities and continents, something far more insidious was happening within the institutions charged with maintaining law and order: a crisis of morale, unprecedented in its depth and scope.

The mythologizing of Floyd as a revolutionary martyr did not merely give birth to a movement; it redefined the very terms under which policing, prosecution, and public safety were discussed. The backlash, swift and unrelenting, manifested not only in the protests and riots that followed but in the electoral victories of figures like George Gascón, whose ascension to the position of Los Angeles Country District Attorney was, as veteran prosecutor John Lewin bluntly observed, "100% because of George Floyd."[1] The political landscape, never immune to grandstanding, had now fully surrendered to the absolutism of ideology, where complex realities were reduced to binary positions.

Catalyst for Chaos

Floyd's death occurred at a moment of perfect historical confluence—during a global pandemic that had already frayed the social fabric, and amidst a populace locked down and simmering with resentment and angst. As Detective Mike Maher of the LA County Sheriff's Department wryly noted, "That George Floyd thing was such a catalyst. The timing on that, right? During COVID. It was a farce. Really the timing was perfect for them . . . It accelerated this sort of decimation."[2] It was the convergence of crises, an opportunity seized by activists and opportunists alike, to redraw the lines of public discourse on policing.

But what followed was not a sober reckoning with systemic issues, but an orgy of chaos. Protests were no longer about justice; they became, as Maher suggests, "highly organized" performances of rage, funded by interests far removed from the communities supposedly in mourning. McBride recounts how during the riots, "individuals came from another state with a bag full of $70k, $80k, $90,000. And they're like, 'Oh, we came to buy a new car.' That's not what they're doing. They're here to pay the anarchist-type people to cause all this chaos." He continues, "It was highly organized. . . . We can all keep pointing to George Soros because he is the root of a lot of it, but there are other organizations out there funding this. . . . We saw all kinds of wild shit during the riots that was being funded. They had professional rioters and anarchists come into the city."

"There was nobody in Los Angeles rioting for George Floyd," Maher observes. "They were mostly paid performers. It was just well-organized." In his view, the street-level reality was far different from the narrative that flooded the airwaves—"Even the gangsters in the streets of LA weren't happy. To pretend that the criminal street gang element had sympathy for George Floyd is ridiculous. George Floyd was a scumbag, drug addict, violent criminal." A truth that few dared to voice amid the sanctification of a man whose record mattered less than the image his death projected.

The question must be asked: was this truly a revolution, or simply a well-choreographed riot for political gain?

The Election of Gascón: A Triumph of Narrative Over Competence

If Floyd's death was the catalyst, then the political ascension of figures like George Gascón was the revolution's direct consequence. As Lewin points out, Gascón's victory was directly tied to the George Floyd moment. "It was enough with George Floyd for Gascón to get elected," Lewin notes, underscoring the shift from competence to ideology in the realm of criminal justice.[3]

Gascón, whose platform embraced the rhetoric of Black Lives Matter and defunding the police, capitalized on the chaos to ride a wave of discontent straight into the DA's office.

But what did his election signal to those on the front lines of law enforcement? Morale, already tenuous, was shattered. Cops and prosecutors alike found themselves under siege, not only from criminals, but from a public that had turned against them, spurred on by the very officials sworn to uphold the law. "The 2020 Anti-Police movement has just decimated police departments," McBride observes. "Nobody wants to be a police officer anymore. Instead of us picking the cream of the crop, now we're asking for illegals to join the police department."[4]

The disillusionment was palpable. In Los Angeles, the same city that had weathered the 1992 riots with a renewed sense of purpose, 2020 left nothing but despair. "I was here during the '92 riots," McBride continues. "And the '92 riots were very contained. . . . What we saw in 2020 was a lot more organization." What had once been localized outbursts of violence had now metastasized into a sprawling, leaderless movement, with no clear demands other than the destruction of the old order.

The Cost of Canonization

George Floyd may have been elevated to the status of revolutionary martyr, but the consequences of his canonization have been profound and far-reaching. In the wake of his death, law enforcement has been left demoralized, the public has grown increasingly disillusioned, and the criminal justice system itself teeters on the edge of collapse. As Lewin, Maher, and McBride have made clear, the chaos unleashed by Floyd's death was no accident—it was the product of a perfect storm, a moment seized by those more interested in burning down the system than reforming it.

But as the ashes of 2020 settle, one thing becomes abundantly clear: the crisis of morale that has gripped America's cops and prosecutors is not merely a passing phase. It is the direct result of a society that, in its rush to sanctify a symbol, has forgotten the very real consequences for those tasked with maintaining the rule of law. The reverberations of Floyd's canonization have not only emboldened criminals but stripped police of their authority. As one Bay Area prosecutor aptly notes, "These movements did play a role, because now people are not afraid of the police. And because police aren't going to do anything the second you whip out your camera, because with all due respect, your camera does not capture their training . . . their experience and what they're trained to do."

The reality is as stark as it is dangerous. The mere presence of a smart-phone has neutered law enforcement, turning every interaction into a potential career-ending spectacle. Where the public once afforded officers the benefit of the doubt, they are now reframed as unwitting actors in a contrived moral theater, cast as villains in a narrative indifferent to nuance. The result? A law enforcement apparatus that hesitates at critical moments, second-guessing itself out of fear of the next viral video, while criminals, emboldened by the absence of consequences, operate with impunity. The demoralization of the police is not a side effect; it is the intended outcome of a movement that seeks to undermine authority under the pretense of reform.

This is not a temporary discontent but a systemic failure—a society in the throes of a profound and dangerous shift in values. What was once respect for law and order has been replaced by cynicism and distrust, and the criminal justice system itself now stands on the precipice of collapse.

Kamala Harris and the Moral Bankruptcy of Opportunism in 2020

To scrutinize Kamala Harris's political conduct during the seismic events of 2020 is to witness the very erosion of principle that defines the modern political class. In the wake of George Floyd's death, the rise of Black Lives Matter (BLM), and the fervent calls to defund the police, Harris did not so much lead as she followed—keenly attuned to the winds of public sentiment, yet unable or unwilling to commit to anything beyond rhetorical gestures. What emerges from her response is a portrait of political opportunism, symptomatic of a broader societal decay, where leadership is replaced by the performative dance of moral posturing.

The Expediency of Outrage

Floyd's death was a moment that demanded moral clarity. But for Harris, it provided something more advantageous: a platform from which to project outrage without the inconvenience of accountability. She swiftly condemned Floyd's killing, labeling it a "modern-day lynching" and an "act of hate," offering rhetoric that resonated with the collective anguish of the moment.[5] Yet beneath the veneer of righteous indignation lay the cold calculus of political survival.

Harris's impassioned speech on the Senate floor, during which she called Floyd's death "torture," certainly struck a chord and positioned her as a vocal advocate for police reform.[6] Yet, it remains remarkable for its strategic lack of engagement with her own past as a law enforcer. As California Attorney General from 2011 to 2017, Harris had a record that was notably at odds with the fervor of the anti-police movement. Under her leadership, California law enforcement faced repeated calls for greater transparency, particularly concerning police misconduct.[7] Her office was known to resist independent oversight of police shootings—a stance that would be anathema to the activists she now courted.[8] In calling Floyd's death an act of systemic racism, Harris deftly sidestepped her role in upholding that system, offering moral absolution to herself while aligning with the politically expedient narrative of the hour.[9]

This duplicity did not go unnoticed by those with a keener sense of history. Harris's embrace of Floyd's martyrdom, while rhetorically potent, was ultimately hollow—a performance for a public increasingly unable or unwilling to confront the contradictions of its leaders.

Embracing BLM: Performative Solidarity and Calculated Ambiguity

Harris's opportunism extended into her engagement with the Black Lives Matter movement, which she praised with the fervor of a convert, despite her past reluctance to align herself with its more radical demands. In 2020, BLM had become not just a movement but a cultural force, one that could not be ignored by any Democrat with national ambitions. And so, Harris embraced it fully, declaring that "nothing that we have achieved that has been about progress has come without a fight, and so I always am going to interpret these protests as an essential component of evolution in our country—as an essential component or mark of a real democracy."[10] Yet for all her proclamations of solidarity, Harris remained notably silent on the more incendiary aspects of the protests—particularly the violence and destruction that swept through cities like Portland and Seattle. "I actually believe that 'Black Lives Matter' has been the most significant agent for change within the criminal justice system," Harris said during the NAACP's national convention in 2020.[11]

Her support of BLM was the epitome of performative solidarity: loud in rhetoric but evasive in substance. Harris positioned herself as a defender of the downtrodden without engaging with the uncomfortable realities of law enforcement and the need for meaningful reform. When rioters set fire to public buildings or when anarchists laid siege to police precincts, Harris offered no critique, no rebuke. Indeed, Harris promoted a fund to bail out violent protesters during the 2020 riots. In a message posted on both Facebook and Twitter, Harris wrote: "If you're able to, chip in now to the Minnesota Freedom Fund to help post bail for those protesting on the ground in Minnesota."[12] Two months later, the local Fox affiliate in Minneapolis reported "among those bailed out by the Minnesota Freedom Fund (MFF) is a suspect who shot at police, a woman accused of killing a friend, and a twice convicted sex offender, according to court records reviewed by the FOX 9 Investigators."[13]

It was as if the chaos that followed Floyd's death was merely an unfortunate backdrop to her political ascension, rather than a moment requiring real leadership. This selective silence—her refusal to speak against the excesses of the protests—exemplifies Harris's moral flexibility. She was willing to endorse the broad strokes of the movement but unwilling to confront its darker manifestations. In doing so, Harris mirrored a society increasingly captivated by slogans but bereft of solutions.

Defund the Police: Hemming, Hawing, and Evasion

Perhaps nothing reveals Kamala Harris's finely tuned sense of political self-preservation more than her handling of the "defund the police" movement. In the summer of 2020, as protests surged and the far left clamored to dismantle police departments, Harris found herself walking a perilous tightrope. On one side was her branding as a tough-on-crime prosecutor, a role that had often placed her at odds with the very communities now calling for radical reform. On the other was the rising demand from the far-left base, whose cries for defunding the police became the rallying call of the moment. In characteristic fashion, Harris opted for ambiguity, offering a position so nebulous that it could be interpreted in any direction.

Appearing on *The View* in June 2020, Harris called for a "reimagining" of public safety—words that were as vague as they were politically expedient.

She spoke of "investing in communities" and "reexamining law enforcement resources," advocating for the redirection of funds toward mental health, education, and housing.[14] While this gave a nod to the demands for reform, it allowed her to sidestep fully endorsing the radical push to defund the police entirely. In an interview on a Los Angeles radio show, Harris said, "When we're talking about policing, I think we have to redirect resources."[15] Her rhetoric was calibrated to convey support for change without committing to anything specific—Harris's political hallmark.

In another interview on *Good Morning America*, Harris praised Los Angeles Mayor Eric Garcetti's decision to slash $150 million from the city's police budget to fund social services.[16] Yet, even here, she carefully hedged her bets, clarifying that the decision did not mean "getting rid" of the police. It was a performance of pragmatism, positioning herself as both an ally to the movement for reform and a voice of reason to moderates who remained wary of such radical shifts in policy. As with much of Harris's rhetoric during this period, it was a calculated evasion—designed to appeal broadly while committing to nothing of substance.

Harris's political contortionism was far from accidental. Her ambition lay in performing the delicate, and ultimately impossible, task of satisfying two irreconcilable factions: signaling sufficient progressivism to appease the radical left, while simultaneously reassuring the moderates and centrists, ever eager to be reminded of her prosecutorial credentials. This was not an exercise in conviction but in careful calibration—an artful dance of political hedging that allowed her to avoid risk at all costs. Yet, in the pursuit of offending no one, she succeeded in pleasing no one. The far left, demanding ideological purity, saw her as a figure of frustrating equivocation, while law enforcement and the more conservative electorate recognized her reformist language for what it was: hollow, vacuous, and noncommittal.

What Harris framed as pragmatic moderation was, in reality, a textbook example of cynical opportunism. Her reluctance to take a decisive stand, particularly on the "defund the police" movement, reflected not sophistication, but the shallow maneuvering of a politician unwilling to tether herself to any substantive position. This evasion, cloaked in the language of "nuance," mirrored the broader collapse of leadership in the post-Floyd era, where the very idea of law enforcement—once the bedrock of civic order—was gradually abandoned. Harris, ever adept at reading the political winds, opted to placate a volatile political climate at the expense of the very institutions she once aligned herself with, institutions now left to flounder amidst public scorn and political betrayal.

The demoralization within the ranks of law enforcement was no longer an incidental effect—it had become an institutional crisis, a slow unraveling exacerbated by the calculated indifference of political leaders like Harris. Once viewed as the stalwart defenders of civil society, police officers now found themselves stranded between the shrill demands of ideological purity and the deafening silence of their supposed advocates. Harris's equivocation on defunding the police was emblematic of this broader abandonment—a collapse of public trust that went hand in hand with the erosion of political support. Her unwillingness to commit to either side was not mere indecision; it was a glaring symptom of a deeper and more corrosive shift, in which the very notion of public order was sacrificed on the altar of political expediency.[17]

What was framed as pragmatic, even noble, restraint was in fact a capitulation to the loudest voices at the expense of those tasked with safeguarding society. Harris's refusal to stand firm on the role of law enforcement did not merely signify a tactical evasion; it signaled the larger failure of an entire political class to defend the institutions that underpin order. Officers, once champions of public safety, were recast as symbols of an outdated order, their authority systematically undermined by those who once relied on their service. In Harris's ambiguity, one finds not simply a politician's hedging, but a harbinger of the profound rift between society and the very institutions it depends on for stability. Her lack of clarity wasn't just a misstep—it was the opening act of a wider collapse in the social contract, in which the guardians of order were sacrificed to the demands of political expediency, leaving law enforcement adrift in an increasingly chaotic landscape.

The George Floyd Justice in Policing Act of 2021: Hollow Reform and the Politics of Narrative

Kamala Harris's political opportunism reached its apex in the form of the George Floyd Justice in Policing Act, co-sponsored with Senator Cory

Booker and introduced by Rep. Karen Bass and Rep. Jerrold Nadler.[18] Touted as a bold, transformative response to the events of 2020, the Act was in truth little more than a concession to the anti-police sentiment that had surged in the wake of George Floyd's death. Far from a genuine effort to reform the criminal justice system, this legislation reflected Harris's adeptness at navigating the volatile political climate—offering superficial solutions to appease activists while subtly undermining the very foundations of effective policing.

The Act's provisions—banning chokeholds and creating a national database for police misconduct—were symbolic gestures aimed more at satisfying the radical elements of her base than addressing the real challenges faced by law enforcement. Most alarmingly, it sought to limit qualified immunity, a doctrine that protects officers from personal liability in civil lawsuits, and which is essential for enabling police to perform their duties without fear of frivolous litigation. Stripping this protection would not only expose officers to endless lawsuits but would also paralyze their ability to act decisively in life-and-death situations.[19] For Harris, the Act's failure to engage with the complexities of qualified immunity was no oversight—it was a calculated political maneuver designed to placate those who view law enforcement as the problem rather than the solution.

Harris's support for the George Floyd Justice in Policing Act was not a principled stand for justice, but a cynical capitulation to the loudest voices in the room. The Act was designed not to strengthen law enforcement but to weaken it—ensuring that police officers would face greater scrutiny and legal jeopardy, while criminals would be emboldened by a system increasingly hostile to those tasked with upholding the law. By advocating for reforms that made policing more difficult, Harris signaled her willingness to sacrifice public safety for political gain.

Assault on Qualified Immunity: Undermining Police Authority

The most egregious aspect of the Act was its assault on qualified immunity, the legal shield that allows officers to perform their duties without the constant fear of personal lawsuits. This doctrine ensures that officers, when acting within the bounds of their training and legal authority, are protected from civil liability unless they violate clearly established constitutional rights. By attempting to erode this protection, Harris and her allies sought to make it easier to hold officers personally accountable for split-second decisions made in dangerous, high-pressure situations.

For those unfamiliar with the realities of policing, the removal of qualified immunity may seem like a reasonable step toward accountability. But for those who understand the stakes, it is nothing short of a disaster. Without this protection, officers would be forced to second-guess every decision they make, knowing that even a justified use of force could result in personal financial ruin. The consequence of this would be a police force that is hesitant, reactive, and ultimately ineffective—officers paralyzed by the fear of litigation rather than focused on protecting the public.

Harris's willingness to support the erosion of qualified immunity demonstrates a profound disregard for the realities of law enforcement. It is easy to pontificate about reform from the safety of political office, but it is officers who must face the consequences of such misguided policies on the streets. By undermining qualified immunity, Harris has not only jeopardized the safety of police officers but has also emboldened criminals who know that officers are now operating with one hand tied behind their backs.

Lowering the Threshold for Prosecuting Cops

The Act also proposed lowering the standard for prosecuting officers, shifting the legal requirement from "willfulness" to "recklessness." While this may sound like a technical adjustment, its implications are profound. By lowering the threshold for criminal charges, the Act makes it significantly easier to prosecute officers for actions taken in the heat of the moment. This change fails to account for the split-second decisions that officers must make, often in situations of extreme danger and uncertainty.

In advocating for this lowered standard, Harris further demonstrated her willingness to sacrifice the integrity of law enforcement for political expediency. Officers already operate under intense scrutiny, and the threat of prosecution for actions that may later be deemed "reckless" would have a chilling effect on proactive policing. This, in turn, would embolden criminal activity, as officers would understandably become more reluctant to intervene in dangerous situations for fear of legal repercussions.

This provision, like much of the George Floyd Justice in Policing Act, reveals Harris's disconnect from the realities of policing. It is one thing to call for accountability; it is quite another to create a system where officers are prosecuted for doing their jobs under extraordinarily difficult circumstances. The Act, far from delivering justice, instead threatens to dismantle the very foundations of law and order by making it easier to punish those who stand on the front lines.

The National Police Misconduct Registry: Federal Tracking of Police Officers

Another cornerstone of the Act was the establishment of a National Police Misconduct Registry, ostensibly designed to track officers with records of misconduct and prevent them from moving between departments. While this idea plays well to the public's desire for greater accountability, it raises significant concerns about fairness and due process. Without rigorous standards for what constitutes reportable misconduct, the registry risks becoming a repository of unsubstantiated accusations—effectively blacklisting officers based on minor infractions or politically motivated complaints.

Harris's endorsement of this registry once again reveals her preference for optics over substance. Rather than addressing the root causes of police misconduct, the registry serves as a tool for public relations—offering the illusion of transparency without grappling with the complexities of due process. The danger here is clear: officers, even those falsely accused or cleared of wrongdoing, could see their careers destroyed by a system more interested in placating activists than in delivering justice.

A Politician for the Moment, Not the Movement

Kamala Harris's response to the events of 2020 reveals not a leader driven by principle, but a politician adept at navigating the shifting currents of public opinion. Her actions—whether in condemning George Floyd's death, embracing BLM, or equivocating on Defund the Police—were not the product of a coherent vision but of political expediency. She was a politician for the moment, not the movement.

Harris's opportunism is emblematic of the broader collapse of moral and political leadership in an era defined by crisis. In a year when the country demanded clarity, she offered only ambiguity. In a moment that called for courage, she provided only calculated evasion. And as law enforcement morale crumbled and societal chaos grew, Harris continued to play her role in the spectacle, a product of a political system that rewards rhetoric over reality.

In the end, Kamala Harris's 2020 was not a year of principled leadership but of moral bankruptcy. It was a year in which her opportunism, far from being an aberration, became a reflection of the broader decay in public life. And as the rule of law eroded and the streets burned, Harris remained, as ever, on the right side of public opinion—though never on the right side of history.

A Predictable (and Intended) Crisis of Morale in Law Enforcement

The deterioration of morale among police officers and prosecutors in California—and indeed, across the United States—is neither accidental nor the result of socioeconomic forces. Rather, it is the logical endpoint of a calculated, ideological crusade to dismantle traditional pillars of law enforcement. This is not an unintended consequence of reform, but its explicit goal. So-called "criminal justice reformers" have worked tirelessly to discredit law enforcement, casting it as the very embodiment of institutional racism and relics of an alleged white supremacy framework. What passes for reform today is in fact cultural vandalism—a calculated assault on the structures of justice under the guise of a warped concept of equity.

Behind the rallying cry of equity lies a more cynical motive: revenge. "Reform" has become little more than code for collective punishment against an institution that dare uphold a functioning society. The vision propounded by these ideologues is not a genuine attempt to right wrongs but a grotesque reimagining of justice, where vengeance masquerades as fairness and law enforcement is viewed not as the guardian of civil order, but as its most sinister oppressor.

Prosecutorial Burnout and Dilution

The idealism that once defined the careers of police officers and prosecutors has been methodically corroded by those who view these professions through a lens of historical grievance. As a prosecutor from Alameda

County lamented: "This job used to be one of the most fun things ever, because you get to do the right thing and help people. It has turned into the most demoralizing thing you could ever imagine. People have no respect for cops. People have no respect for law enforcement, including prosecutors."

John Lewin, a seasoned prosecutor in Los Angeles, offers an even starker view of the collapse: "Morale is the lowest I've seen in 30 years. One of the problems is that we've lost 20% or 25% of our people. So everybody is having to work much, much harder. Gascón, instead of promoting quality people, he brings in public defenders who he then promotes. The DAs that they want to hire are those with defense attorney mentality."[20,21]

Lewin's words reveal a truth too bitter for many to confront: the collapse underway is not just one of morale, but of professional standards themselves. The District Attorney's office, once the bastion of impartial legal rigor, is now being infiltrated by foot soldiers of ideology. Competence has been sacrificed on the altar of political expediency. This is a deliberate subversion of meritocracy; Gascón prefers commissars over competent prosecutors.

A System Unravels: The Celebration of Criminality

What Lewin observes in Los Angeles is symptomatic of a larger, nationwide phenomenon—the slow and deliberate unraveling of the justice system, replaced by a regime in which political allegiance trumps ability, and justice is reframed as a battleground of power politics. This transformation is no accident. It is the logical result of a worldview that sees law enforcement not as a necessary protector of public order but as a symptom of systemic oppression. In this ideological climate, crime is no longer something to be deterred, but to be reframed as a form of resistance against an oppressive state. Criminality is reimagined not as a social ill, but as a response to historical wrongs—a symptom of oppression and a celebration of narrative victimhood.

The effects are catastrophic. Prosecutors, demoralized and overworked, leave in droves, only to be replaced by ideological zealots who view their role not as protectors of the public, but as agents of a new order where the law must be bent to fit a political narrative. As Lewin mourns: "Do I think that we're hiring the same quality of lawyers as what Steve Cooley or Jackie Lacey hired? Absolutely not."

A prosecutor in Los Angeles recounts the recruiting process at Gascón's DA's office:

"In the second round, there were two interviewers. One was an executive brought on by Gascón, the other was a seasoned prosecutor who has been with the office for decades prior to Gascón's election. The executive asked, 'What do you dislike about George Gascón?' This question was a trap. Applicants who answered this question earnestly were not invited back for a third round. The third round included George Gascón and his second and third in command. The interview lasted approximately 5 minutes. They asked the same basic questions as in the first interview, but also asked, 'Which special directive of Gascón is your favorite?' I named the first one that came to mind and parroted back the reasoning Gascón has given in the past as the explanation for why I supported it. Many applicants who made it to the third round were not offered the job because they failed to convince Mr. Gascón that they were drinking the Kool-Aid."

The Shrinking Ranks and Rising Danger

Law enforcement is suffering from an acute and alarming decline. The Los Angeles Police Department (LAPD), once an emblem of professional policing, is hemorrhaging officers at an unsustainable rate, reflecting the broader collapse in morale. Detective Jamie McBride captures the devastation: "The 2020 Anti-Police movement has decimated police departments." Far from exaggeration, the numbers paint a grim picture. Retirements are up 45%, resignations have skyrocketed, and recruitment efforts have plummeted. The LAPD is now at its smallest size in six years, with just 9,600 officers—its lowest number since 2017. Nearly 20% of positions lie vacant, a reflection of how demoralized the force has become.[22]

Detective Mike Maher adds that the 2020 George Floyd protests created the "perfect storm," exacerbating an already fragile situation. What had been a slow erosion of public trust in law enforcement was accelerated into a full-blown crisis of legitimacy. Officers now face relentless scrutiny in an environment where every action is second-guessed, and the authority they once commanded has been hollowed out by political and public disdain. The prevalence of cameras, as Maher notes, does little to capture the nuance of their training or the complexity of their work under pressure.

The psychological toll on those who remain in the profession is staggering. Forced overtime and burnout have become the norm, and the very idea of entering law enforcement has become anathema to a generation raised on a diet of anti-police narratives. This has had a cascading effect on recruitment, with agencies across the state, including the LAPD, becoming so desperate they've lowered hiring standards. In some cases, the LAPD has hired individuals with criminal gang affiliations, merely transferring them to desk jobs rather than firing them outright.

Marcus Barbour, president of the Santa Clara County Deputy Sheriffs Association, emphasizes the human cost of these staffing shortages: "Our department's sworn staffing is down 34%, and if you're not assessing staffing issues as to whether a location is a good place to work, you are completely missing the target as to what actual sheriff deputies believe." Deputies, Barbour explains, are forced to work overtime just to minimally staff patrol and court divisions. "Our deputies are tired, they are missing quality time at home with their families. It's about personal time for them, not the median salary posted on some website's chart."[23]

The ripple effects of these shortages are immense. As Craig Lally, president of the Los Angeles Police Protective League, notes: "Historic low police staffing levels have led to dangerous officer safety situations, slow 911 emergency response times, and mandatory overtime that equates to low officer morale."[24] The cumulative strain on officers means the system is not merely struggling—it is on the brink of collapse.

The Broader Societal Consequences: A Collapse of Legitimacy

The decay in law enforcement and prosecutorial standards is not just a crisis of morale; it is a crisis of legitimacy. The public's faith in these institutions has crumbled under the weight of sustained ideological attacks that have succeeded in not just demoralizing the officers and prosecutors who uphold the law, but in undermining the very concept of authority itself. This is not an unfortunate consequence of external pressures, but a calculated outcome of the ideological war being waged against law enforcement.

The Los Angeles Police Department, once targeted as a bastion of systemic racism, now boasts a workforce that is approximately 70–75% minority and female. Lewin captures this bitter irony: "Your typical officer on the street is Hispanic, many of them women, yet they are vilified just like everyone else. So, I think a lot of them are very frustrated, just like everybody else, by the fact that they get no respect. George Gascón has done that." [25,26] Diversity has done little to shield officers from the hostility that has become entrenched in the public psyche.

As resources dwindle, and experienced officers leave, those who remain are forced to do more with less.[27] The institutional capacity to maintain order is eroding in real time. The result is a fractured system where public safety is rapidly deteriorating, and communities are left vulnerable to rising crime. The decline of law enforcement personnel coincides with an increase in crime rates—an inevitable consequence of a system under siege from within and without.

In the end, the tragedy is not just the demoralization of police officers and prosecutors; it is the collapse of an entire system designed to safeguard society. As these institutions falter, so too does the very fabric of civil order. Law enforcement and justice are no longer seen as impartial forces for the common good, but as battlegrounds for ideological warfare. If the current trajectory continues, we will witness not only the disintegration of morale but of civil society itself.

The moral and professional erosion of police forces and district attorneys' offices across California is not the result of unfortunate socioeconomic trends—it is the outcome of a deliberate strategy to dismantle law and order. Those who celebrate this as a victory over "oppressive" institutions will soon realize that their triumph comes at the expense of the very communities they claim to protect. Without faith in law enforcement, justice becomes a hollow concept, and society itself risks unraveling.

DACA Cops: The New Face of the LAPD

In the ever-deepening saga of the collapse of law enforcement, we arrive at the latest absurdity: the graduation of DACA recipients—"Dreamers"—into the ranks of the Los Angeles Police Department. In a move that would be laughable were it not so dangerous, California now allows non-citizens, individuals protected from deportation but who do not hold legal residency, to police its streets. In one stroke, the state has stripped the badge of its final pretense of authority, turning the LAPD into a social experiment in political virtue signaling, all while the very notion of public safety is left to rot.

This ideological insanity is not confined to California. Colorado, too, has embraced this policy, allowing DACA recipients not only to serve as police officers, but to carry firearms—at least during their shifts. Without the policy change, these officers would have to leave their guns at the station when their shift ends. This staggering contradiction highlights the blurred lines between legality and law enforcement in a system that no longer knows where it stands. What message does it send when the people tasked with enforcing the law live in a gray area themselves?

Directed Demise Is Policy

The decision to allow DACA recipients to serve as police officers represents the latest step in a long march toward the erosion of law enforcement standards. Under the guise of inclusivity, this policy undermines the credibility of the very institution it claims to diversify. These individuals, who are neither citizens nor legal residents, are now expected to uphold and enforce the laws of a nation they have no formal legal standing in—a perverse reversal of logic that would be farcical if it weren't putting lives at risk.

What's more, as Maher so incisively observes, the new wave of academy graduates lacks not only the legal grounding but the physical and psychological resilience that policing once demanded. "If 90 out of 100 are Hispanics that are five foot two carrying a backpack, who have never shot a firearm in their life, who've never fought in their life . . . it's part of the directed demise," Maher warns. In this new era, size, strength, and experience—qualities that once defined law enforcement—are being replaced by politically convenient optics.[28]

The inclusion of DACA recipients in the force epitomizes this directed demise. These officers, prohibited from owning firearms in their personal lives, must lock up their guns at the station after work. This begs the question: what kind of authority can they project when they can't even possess the very tools of their trade off-duty? The LAPD's embrace of this farcical policy only serves to highlight the ideological drift that has rendered the department a shell of its former self.

Danger from Within

The impact of these policy changes goes far beyond morale; it strikes at the heart of public trust in law enforcement. McBride's account of a DACA recruit linked to gang activity reveals the potential for corruption and incompetence that such policies invite. A female DACA recipient, still in the police academy, was discovered to be connected to Florencia 13 gang members, one of Los Angeles's most notorious criminal organizations. The connection came to light after her vehicle, registered in her name, was used in a shootout with an off-duty LAPD detective. And yet, this woman had been handed a badge and a gun, tasked with enforcing the law.

This is not an isolated incident but part of a larger pattern in which the standards of recruitment are continually lowered to accommodate political agendas. As McBride puts it, "These are the people we're hiring. And, you know what? How much of a background can you possibly do on these people?" When the force begins hiring individuals with ties to violent gangs, it's not just a recruitment problem—it's a public safety crisis in the making.

Worse still, as McBride highlights, many of these recruits come from regions where law enforcement is viewed with contempt. In countries like El Salvador, where violence is endemic, these recruits bring their disregard for the rule of law with them. "It's like no big deal," McBride says, referring to the violent tendencies that many of these recruits carry over from their homelands. The result is a police force that is not feared, not respected, and certainly not trusted—either by the public or by the criminals they are meant to police.

Symbol of a Broken System

The integration of DACA recipients into the LAPD is not merely a policy change—it is a symbol of the broader collapse of law enforcement. In a state where political virtue has supplanted public safety, the hiring of noncitizens to uphold laws they themselves exist in defiance of is the ultimate insult to the institution of policing. This new face of the LAPD is one that reflects the disintegration of authority, the erosion of standards, and the complete breakdown of the relationship between law enforcement and the communities it serves.

What's left is a hollowed-out institution where ideology triumphs over practicality, and the badge—once a symbol of authority—has become a mere accessory in a political costume. The public, meanwhile, is left to pay the price for this madness, as the streets grow more dangerous, the criminals more emboldened, and the police more impotent. The DACA cops are just the latest manifestation of a force in decline—a force no longer capable of protecting the very society it was created to defend.

Breaking Point: How Reform Betrayed Justice in Two Acts

In the unraveling crisis of morale among law enforcement, two cases stand as stark illustrations of how the very fabric of policing is being torn apart by the ideological zeal of political actors. These case studies reveal the dangerous consequences of criminalizing police actions and prioritizing criminal leniency over public safety. From the prosecution of Torrance officers Matthew Concannon and Anthony Chavez, to the tragic deaths of El Monte officers Joseph Santana and Michael Paredes, we see a justice system no longer rooted in fairness, but in the shifting winds of political expediency. These cases are not isolated tragedies; they are the predictable results of policies that elevate ideology above the rule of law and leave those tasked with protecting society vulnerable to both legal and mortal peril.

The Torrance Travesty: Criminalizing Policing in the Age of Ideological Prosecution

The prosecution of Torrance police officers Matthew Concannon and Anthony Chavez in 2023, orchestrated by Los Angeles District Attorney George Gascón, represents the disturbing new frontier of ideological prosecution. What we see unfolding here is not the pursuit of justice, but a calculated political maneuver designed to vilify law enforcement under the pretense of accountability. This case is a microcosm of a broader crisis in American policing—one fueled not by the misdeeds of officers, but by a zeal to criminalize the very act of enforcing the law in an age where political optics now eclipse facts.

In December 2018, Concannon and Chavez confronted Christopher Deandre Mitchell, a gang member seated in a stolen vehicle, a modified .22-caliber rifle between his legs. When Mitchell's movements suggested he was reaching for the weapon, the officers responded with lethal force. Their actions were immediately investigated, and District Attorney Jackie Lacey deemed the shooting justified based on a clear, fact-driven assessment of the situation.[29]

But this was not enough for George Gascón. Upon assuming office, he saw an opportunity to exploit the case for political gain, reopening it not because of any new evidence but because of a desire to pander to the radical, anti-police narrative that has swept across California. Despite no new revelations, Gascón charged the officers with voluntary manslaughter—a brazen act of political posturing.[30] John Lewin succinctly captures the essence of this travesty: "Gascón reopened the case despite the lack of new exculpatory evidence. . . . This prosecution is emblematic of a broader strategy to undermine the police." Gascón's actions reflect not a pursuit of justice, but an allegiance to an anti-law enforcement ideology that thrives on demonizing those sworn to protect.

Body-cam footage, which shows the officers issuing clear commands to Mitchell—commands he ignored—only reinforces their defense. The officers, perceiving a legitimate threat, acted accordingly. The special prosecutor's review, crucially, did not reveal any evidence that contradicted the original decision to clear the officers. Yet, Gascón's office persisted, determined to drag these officers through the mud of public disgrace in an effort to appease those who demand police blood in the name of "justice reform."[31]

Moreover, Gascón's office attempted to smear Concannon and Chavez by associating them with a racist text-messaging scandal within the Torrance Police Department—a cynical attempt to paint the officers as guilty by mere proximity to wrongdoing. There is no evidence tying either officer to the offensive messages, yet the suggestion alone serves as a smear in the court of public opinion. It is clear that the aim was never to achieve justice, but to weaponize the justice system for political ends.

What makes this case truly insidious is not merely the unjust prosecution of officers who had already been cleared, but the broader message it sends to all law enforcement in Los Angeles: no officer is safe from being retroactively criminalized if the political winds shift. Gascón has made it clear that even when officers are exonerated after a thorough investigation, their actions can be revisited and criminalized based on the prevailing political mood. This is not justice; this is persecution dressed in the garb of prosecutorial ambition.

The implications of this are chilling. As veteran officer Mike Maher points out, "The pendulum is coming back slowly . . . but this kind of prosecution could lead to hesitation in critical moments." And hesitation in the face of danger is a death sentence—not just for the officers involved, but for the public they are tasked with protecting. An officer unsure of whether their split-second decisions will later be criminalized by an overzealous prosecutor may hesitate at a crucial moment, with catastrophic consequences.

This case, therefore, is not merely about two officers. It signals a turning point—a watershed moment where lawful policing is retroactively criminalized to serve an ideological agenda. The prosecution of Concannon and Chavez is emblematic of the broader trend in California, where justice has been subverted by politics, and where the lives of officers are sacrificed on the altar of political expediency. George Gascón, in his war on law enforcement, has chosen ideology over justice, and the consequences for society are dire.

Blood Sacrifice in El Monte: The Deadly Cost of Crime-Equity

While the Torrance case illustrates how ideological prosecutors weaponize the justice system against officers, the tragic deaths of El Monte Police Officers Joseph Anthony Santana and Michael Paredes offer a more visceral example of the real, lethal cost of crime-equity. These officers' lives were sacrificed at the altar of a justice system that now prizes criminal comfort over public safety. And at the center of this moral catastrophe stands George Gascón, whose policies unleashed Justin William Flores, a violent felon, back into society—where he would ultimately claim the lives of these two officers.[32]

In June 2022, Santana and Paredes responded to what should have been a routine domestic violence call at a motel in El Monte. Instead, they were ambushed and murdered by Flores, a career criminal who should never have been free. Flores's rap sheet was extensive: stints in state prison for vehicle theft and burglary, convictions for violent offenses, and in 2020, a firearm and narcotics charge that should have put him behind bars for years.[33] But under the reign of Gascón, whose self-styled progressive policies favor leniency over justice, the charges were inexplicably reduced to probation.[34]

The pain of this catastrophic failure was captured by the mother of Officer Santana, Olga Garcia, who stood before reporters at a press conference and uttered the truth that Gascón's apologists refuse to confront: "I blame the death of my son and his partner on Gascón. Gascón will never know how he destroyed our families."[35] Her words resound as a damning indictment of a system that has lost its moral compass. This is not a tale of criminals as victims; it is about the real victims—officers and civilians—who face repeat offenders emboldened by a system unwilling to protect society from their violence.

Flores's criminal record was a clear warning sign. The law, if followed, would have kept him locked away, yet Gascón's policies ignored this. As a "striker," Flores should have been subjected to California's Three Strikes Law and given a mandatory state prison sentence. Instead, Gascón's office granted him a plea deal, avoiding prison altogether. Two weeks after serving a paltry 20-day jail stint, he gunned down two officers in cold blood.[36]

Eric Siddall, Vice President of the Association of Los Angeles Deputy District Attorneys, delivered a blunt assessment of the situation: "George Gascón said when he came into office, he would break the system. He broke it, and now he owns it—he owns these two killings."[37] Siddall's words cut to the core of the matter. Gascón, in his reckless pursuit of reform, shattered the very system designed to protect the public, leaving officers like Santana and Paredes to pay the ultimate price.

The deaths of these officers serve as a grim reminder that criminal justice reform, when enacted without any regard for the realities of crime and violence, is not merely misguided—it is deadly. Flores should have been in prison, serving the sentence that the law demanded for a violent, repeat offender. But under the twisted logic of Gascón's policies, where even the most dangerous criminals are given another chance, it was Santana and Paredes who paid the price.

The blood of these officers stains not only Gascón's hands but the hands of every legislator, judge, and bureaucrat who has enabled this experiment in criminal leniency. As Detective Jamie McBride chillingly observed, "You can take that and put it directly at the feet of George Gascón and his policies." This is no exaggeration. It is the stark reality of a state that has tipped the scales so far in favor of criminality that it has all but abandoned the very notion of public protection.

This travesty also reflects a broader systemic failure. Gascón's office, in a desperate attempt to rationalize its actions, has tried to deflect responsibility by insisting that Flores's sentencing was consistent with his criminal history. But this is a lie thinly veiled in bureaucratic jargon. Flores was a violent felon with multiple offenses, yet was granted probation when the law clearly mandated prison time. The grotesque reality is that Gascón's policies reduced a man who should have been imprisoned for years to a mere slap on the wrist—a probationary sentence for a violent repeat offender.

At the heart of this failure is a dangerous ideological blindness that views enforcement of California's Three Strikes Law as an archaic relic rather than a safeguard for public safety. Flores's case is not an outlier but a symptom of a broader disease infecting the justice system—a misguided belief that coddling criminals somehow rectifies societal wrongs. But when that belief translates into policy, it is officers like Santana and Paredes who are forced to confront the consequences.

Janine Paredes, the widow of Sergeant Michael Paredes, has filed a $25 million claim against Gascón and other officials responsible for her husband's death. It is a lawsuit steeped in the harsh reality that these officers are dead because of a system that has abdicated its responsibility to protect them.[38] The reckless leniency that allowed a man like Flores to roam free— and kill—cannot be ignored or excused away as a byproduct of reform.

The price of this experiment in so-called reform is paid in blood. And in the case of El Monte, it was the blood of two officers who deserved better from the system they served. The balance between justice and public safety has been shattered, and the deaths of Santana and Paredes stand as a warning that until the scales are tipped back, more lives will be needlessly lost.

Conclusion: The Abyss of California's Moral Abdication

California is not stumbling towards chaos; it is being deliberately steered into an abyss of lawlessness by those who have hijacked its institutions. The systematic undermining of law enforcement, the perversion of the judicial process, and the prioritization of criminal rights over victim protection are not policy missteps but components of a radical ideology that seeks to dismantle the very concept of ordered society.

California is not simply wandering into chaos; it is being actively steered there, by a leadership that has abandoned its duty to uphold the law in favor of a new ideological orthodoxy—one that elevates criminals to the status of victims and sacrifices public safety on the altar of progressive idealism. This is not the result of mere incompetence or policy missteps. It is the calculated culmination of a worldview that seeks to dismantle the very foundations of ordered society. The state's institutions, once pillars of justice, are now compromised, their purpose perverted to serve the demands of identity politics and the increasingly corrosive narratives of victimhood.

A Bay Area prosecutor who has witnessed this erosion firsthand, puts it with chilling clarity, "I blame the uneducated voter . . . I blame everybody in California who has jumped on the liberal bandwagon." Her indictment is damning, but it is also tragically accurate. The voters, content to be spoon-fed slogans like "mass incarceration" and "rehabilitation," have become complicit in their own undoing. It is not that the public is unaware of the state's problems—crime rates, rampant drug use, and the pervasive sense that the streets are no longer safe—it is that they refuse to acknowledge the root cause. In a culture where feelings outweigh facts and ideological purity triumphs over reason, the truth has become an inconvenient casualty.

This, as the prosecutor argues, is not a failure of leadership alone but a profound failure of the electorate itself. "Everybody's so upset with the problems, but nobody is actually really interested in solutions," she observes with an almost surgical precision. The electorate, unmoored from reality, continues to swallow the pieties of progressive politicians who, as she rightly notes, play into the music of radicalism because that is what keeps them in power. "I actually know Gavin [Newsom]," she says. "He's not as liberal as what he says he is, but he plays right into it . . . because that's what keeps you elected." This is the ultimate betrayal—not of ideology, but of the truth itself.

The Californian leadership has become adept at weaponizing ignorance, crafting policies not to solve the state's endemic issues but to perpetuate the very crises from which they profit politically. Law enforcement, already demoralized, finds itself in the impossible position of being both demonized and expected to maintain order in a society that no longer believes in the rule of law. The case studies we have examined, from the Torrance travesty to the blood sacrifice in El Monte, underscore the broader cultural and institutional rot that now defines California's justice system. Prosecutors like Gascón are not enforcers of justice; they are ideologues masquerading as reformers, trading the safety of the public for the approval of activist mobs.

The implications of California's descent are not confined to its own borders. The state, long seen as a bellwether for national trends, now threatens to export its ideological lunacy across the country. This is no longer a question of left versus right; it is a question of whether we, as a society, will tolerate the deliberate destruction of our institutions in the name of progress. As a Prosecutor from Oakland so insightfully warns, "The world is being prescribed the way the far right and the far left is saying it . . . but none of the voters know what they're talking about." In a state where facts are dismissed as inconvenient obstacles to ideological purity, the truth itself has become the first casualty of this cultural war.

California stands at the precipice, and the nation watches with bated breath. Will it continue its suicidal march toward a future where lawlessness reigns and the police are forced into inaction by the constant threat of prosecution? Or will it wake up, reject the siren call of radicalism, and restore some semblance of order and sanity to its institutions? The answer to this question will determine not only the future of California but the fate of a nation increasingly influenced by its example.

There is no room for compromise in this battle. Either we restore the rule of law and demand accountability from those in power, or we accept our descent into a Hobbesian nightmare, where life becomes nasty, brutish, and short. It is not enough to hope that reason will prevail; it must be fought for, unapologetically. As framed by an Alameda County Deputy DA, "Nobody's actually telling anybody what the truth is." The future of California, and perhaps America itself, depends on whether we can still tell the truth—and act on it before it is too late. The choice is stark: confront this madness head-on or resign ourselves to the dystopia that is rapidly becoming our new reality.

CHAPTER 18

BANALITY OF EVIL

Kamala Harris is not the architect of California's collapse—she is its most perfect creation. In a state where political success is measured not by competence but by a talent for survival, Harris has ascended, not through leadership or vision, but by mastering the art of political inertia. She has done nothing remarkable, yet risen everywhere. Her career is the embodiment of a political culture where ambition is an end in itself and governing is merely a means to another rung on the ladder.

Her tenure as a prosecutor and later as California's Attorney General was neither one of radical reform nor steadfast commitment to justice, but of studied opportunism. She championed "tough-on-crime" policies when it suited her, jailing thousands for minor drug offenses while selectively looking the other way when enforcement was politically inconvenient. She later rebranded herself as a progressive reformer when the political winds shifted, discarding past positions with all the conviction of a bureaucratic memo. Her policies, from dismantling California's Bureau of Narcotic Enforcement to backing disastrous criminal justice "reforms," have left a legacy of crime, lawlessness, and institutional decay—a legacy she has never been forced to answer for.

This chapter is not just an indictment of Harris's record but of the system that produced her. She is a case study in the banality of political evil—not a grand ideologue but a functionary of a machine that rewards obedience and punishes principle. Her career is a warning: not just of the

351

consequences of her own ambition, but of what happens when a state, and eventually a nation, is governed by those who value power above all else.

Totem of Patronage: The Willie Brown Machine

To chart the course of Kamala Harris's political rise is to unravel the intricate and sordid web of political patronage under the stewardship of former San Francisco Mayor Willie Brown, a titan of California politics. Brown's influence on Harris was neither incidental nor peripheral—it was foundational. Her early ascent, from unremarkable Oakland prosecutor to positions of influence, was driven by his patronage. In classic Brown fashion, Harris was appointed to lucrative but low-responsibility positions on state boards like the California Medical Assistance Commission and the California Unemployment Insurance Appeals Board. These sinecure roles provided substantial pay with minimal oversight, granting Harris not only financial security but the political visibility she needed to catapult herself into public life.[1] Brown's largesse extended beyond appointments; he even gifted Harris a BMW, a symbol of the transactional nature of their relationship.[2]

Steve Cooley, former District Attorney of Los Angeles, captures this dynamic with biting clarity: "Willie assembled his machine, got her a lot of money." Harris's rise was not the result of some organic swell of support or a principled stand on justice (indeed, very few people liked her personally), but a calculated maneuver orchestrated by Brown's extensive network of political allies and donors. Her victory over incumbent District Attorney Terence Hallinan was emblematic of this strategy, a victory fueled by support from Brown's well-connected inner circle.[3]

Cooley's recollection of Harris's rise carries even darker implications. A corruption inquiry related to Brown's development projects "vanished" once Harris took office as District Attorney. "That's the last I heard of it," Cooley quips, pointing not just to a quashed investigation, but to a political culture where power and patronage routinely overrule accountability. Harris's victory as San Francisco District Attorney did more than just mark her personal ascent—it signaled the continued entrenchment of corruption that had long festered under California's political elite.

The ethical compromises in Harris's entanglement with Brown's machine are stark. Investigative reports from the *San Francisco Chronicle* outlined how Brown's political apparatus operated through backdoor deals and campaign contributions, which often coincided with lucrative city contracts awarded to his benefactors.[4] Companies such as URS Corporation and Bechtel Corporation, which had contributed significantly to Brown's campaigns, secured major contracts for infrastructure projects like airport expansions.[5] This pervasive "pay-to-play" system raised troubling questions about the integrity of political decision-making in San Francisco.[6]

Brown's ability to deliver large-scale development projects, such as the Mission Bay redevelopment and the Hunters Point Shipyard revitalization, was built on his preternatural instincts for political maneuvering.[7] Developers with close ties to his administration seemed to benefit disproportionately, raising serious concerns about fairness and transparency in the approval processes.[8] The selection of Catellus Development Corporation as the master developer for Mission Bay—following generous contributions to Brown's campaigns—serves as a prime example of how political influence and financial contributions were intertwined in the Brown era.[9]

In this environment, Harris's rise must be seen as a product of political patronage, where success was not determined by merit but by strategic alliances and loyalty. Harris may have later branded herself as a reform-minded prosecutor, but her trajectory was undeniably shaped by a system that rewarded ambition over ethics and loyalty over competence.

The stark contrast between Harris's later rhetoric as a progressive reformer and her early alliances cannot be overstated. Her rise was not a testament to individual merit, but a product of a political ecosystem fueled by favor-trading, loyalty, and a selective application of justice. The forces shaping Harris's career reflect a broader malaise within California's political culture—where power flows not from integrity but from patronage and opportunism.

Ultimately, Harris's early political life is a sobering reminder that unchecked ambition, devoid of ethical restraint, corrupts the very institutions it seeks to serve. Brown's political machine did not just propel Harris—it defined the parameters of her career, casting a long shadow over her attempts to rebrand herself as a reformer. Her career, far from being a beacon of progressive change, reveals the hollowness of a political ascent built on patronage and expediency.

Origins of a Hollow Career

If the foundation of Kamala Harris's career was laid by Willie Brown's patronage, then its superstructure was built on the opportunism and political expediency that have long defined California's governance. Beyond the initial boost from Brown, Harris navigated a political landscape where the line between public service and personal ambition was not merely blurred but frequently erased.

The *San Francisco Chronicle* has meticulously documented the mechanisms by which power operates in the city. Journalists like Phil Matier and Andrew Ross exposed a municipal ecosystem in which alliances functioned as currency and loyalty often trumped merit.[10] Under Brown's administration, governance became an extension of personal networks, and positions of authority were routinely allocated based on fealty rather than competence.[11]

In this environment, Harris's rise symbolized a broader trend: the ascent of individuals whose careers were not driven by ideological conviction but by adeptness at navigating political currents. The accusations of nepotism and cronyism that surrounded Brown's administration cast a long shadow over those who benefited from his largesse. The appointment of allies to key city positions diluted accountability, as oversight mechanisms were undermined by those responsible for upholding them.[12]

The *Chronicle* also reported on how contracts and city resources were often channeled to favored businesses and individuals, raising deep questions about the equitable application of the law and the ethical obligations of public officials.[13] These practices did not occur in a vacuum; they were symptomatic of a political culture that prioritized the consolidation of power over the principles of transparency and fairness.

Harris's campaign for District Attorney was significantly bolstered by this environment. As reported by the *San Francisco Chronicle*, she received substantial financial backing from Brown's extensive network, as well as strategic guidance that was instrumental in navigating the labyrinthine politics of San Francisco.[14] This support was not merely a matter of endorsements; it was emblematic of her deeper integration into a political machine that wielded considerable influence over the city's affairs.

Terence Hallinan, the incumbent District Attorney whom Harris unseated, had earned a reputation for challenging corruption and confronting established power structures.[15] His defeat marked a decisive shift in the prosecutorial landscape of the city.

The abrupt cessation of corruption investigations into Brown's administration after Harris's election did not escape notice.[16] While direct evidence of interference is lacking, the correlation between Harris's ascent and the dwindling pursuit of municipal corruption inquiries raises pressing questions about the interplay between political loyalty and the administration of justice.

Lance Williams's investigative reporting cast an unforgiving light on the malleability of prosecutorial discretion under political patronage. Williams exposed how connections to influential figures often ensured favorable treatment, suggesting that justice—ostensibly blind—could see quite well when directed by vested interests.[17] Although not all these patterns can be traced directly to Harris, they contributed to the broader disillusionment with a legal system vulnerable to manipulation by entrenched power.

But the problem goes beyond isolated cases of selective prosecution; it speaks to a deeper betrayal of the principles of impartial governance, compromised not by accident, but by the calculated demands of political survival. In a political climate where allegiance acts as both currency and armor, Harris's career was shaped by the pressure to conform, as much as by her own ambitions. Her rise reflects not just the art of political survival, but the dangers inherent in a single-party system where power and principle are perpetually at odds.

Understanding Harris's rise requires confronting the systemic dynamics that not only influenced her leadership but actively shaped it. The alliances she forged and the environment of political patronage were not peripheral but central to her ascent. These were not mere contexts to be managed—they were forces that shaped decision-making at every stage of her career.

The inherent tension between personal ambition and public responsibility defines this landscape. Dissecting Harris's trajectory reveals that her advancement was not merely enabled but engineered by a network of influence that both empowered and constrained her. While this path is common in public life, the degree to which it skewed the administration of justice during her tenure requires critical examination.

The perception of a "hollow career" stems not only from the absence of accomplishments or intelligence—both of which, in Harris's case, often appear more rumor than fact—but from the yawning chasm between publicly avowed ideals and the realities of power. Harris's rise is a stark case study in how the mechanisms of political power can elevate individuals while hollowing out the institutions they are meant to serve.

San Francisco District Attorney (2004–2011): The Art of the Climb

Kamala Harris's tenure as San Francisco District Attorney (2004–2011) exposed the fundamental contradictions in her political persona. Self-styled as a "progressive prosecutor," Harris vowed to balance the need for justice reform with public safety. However, her actions often revealed a stark gap between her rhetoric and the reality of her decision-making. Her prosecutorial choices were frequently guided not by a coherent ideology, but by a calculated political ambition that adapted to the winds of San Francisco's progressive landscape while maintaining a foothold in the broader, more traditional law-and-order framework.

One of the clearest examples of this political balancing act came with her refusal to seek the death penalty for David Hill, a gang member who murdered police officer Isaac Espinoza. On the surface, Harris's opposition to the death penalty seemed consistent with her stated beliefs, yet the political backlash that followed—most notably from Senator Dianne Feinstein—revealed the broader political calculus behind her stance. Feinstein, representing a wing of the Democratic Party more aligned with law-and-order politics, viewed Harris's decision not as a principled stand but a calculated gesture designed to appeal to San Francisco's progressive base.[18] This episode revealed Harris's adeptness at navigating political waters while remaining careful not to alienate key constituencies.

The death penalty decision, in particular, highlighted the tension between Harris's professed ideals and her political calculations. While she garnered praise from progressive circles for opposing capital punishment, Feinstein's public rebuke exposed the risks of being seen as soft on crime, especially within a Democratic Party that, at the time, still had strong law-and-order factions. The conflict underscored a recurring theme in Harris's career: her talent for presenting herself as a reformer while shifting positions to align with establishment interests whenever politically convenient and lucrative.

Contradictions in Criminal Justice Reform

Despite her reformist branding, Harris's prosecutorial record reveals contradictions that undermine her claims of championing justice reform. Throughout her tenure, she aggressively pursued low-level drug offenses, disproportionately targeting minority communities. Data from the California Department of Justice shows that non-violent drug prosecutions surged under her leadership.[19] This prosecutorial approach stood in stark contrast to her later positioning as a reformer, challenging systemic inequities. Instead of addressing these disparities, Harris's actions reinforced the very structures of injustice she would later claim to oppose. The gap between her public persona and her prosecutorial record reveals a politician who was willing to maintain the status quo when it served her political trajectory.

Steve Cooley's assessment of Harris during this period is particularly revealing. "She was always looking for something to gain from any situation, never to lead. It wasn't about reform; it was about what could advance her career," Cooley remarked, underscoring the perception that Harris's decisions were driven more by political calculation than by any genuine commitment to justice reform or, for that matter, a coherent legal philosophy.[20]

The 2010 Crime Lab Scandal: A Test of Accountability

Another glaring example of Harris's political expediency was her handling of the 2010 San Francisco crime lab scandal. The debacle, which involved widespread evidence tampering and led to the dismissal of hundreds of criminal cases, severely damaged public trust in the DA's office.[21] Rather than taking responsibility for the scandal, Harris distanced herself from it, avoiding public accountability and opting for deflection rather than leadership. This crisis should have been a turning point for Harris—an opportunity to demonstrate her commitment to transparency and justice.

Instead, she navigated the fallout without addressing its root causes, allowing her political ambitions to emerge unscathed while the integrity of the
DA's office took the hit.

Sanctuary Policies and Undermining ICE

Harris's tenure as District Attorney was also marked by her strong advocacy for sanctuary city policies, which included actively shielding illegal
immigrant criminals from Immigration and Customs Enforcement (ICE).
Steve Cooley's criticism of Harris in this regard is damning: "She affirma-
tively, actively concealed illegal immigrant criminals, primarily dope dealers from Central American countries, from ICE when they should have
been referred for deportation." According to Cooley, Harris went so far as
to relocate illegal immigrant criminals to Southern California counties to
keep them from ICE's reach, further exacerbating public safety concerns.

The *Los Angeles Times* revealed that San Francisco authorities had been
relocating convicted juvenile felons to unsecured group homes outside
the city—sometimes in counties like San Bernardino—without notifying
federal authorities. This practice allowed many of these offenders to escape
supervision, with some going on to commit serious crimes. One particularly tragic case involved an undocumented juvenile convicted of assault
who was placed in a group home, only to abscond and later be involved
in a gang-related triple homicide. The *San Francisco Chronicle* reported in
July 2008 on the city's eventual revision of its sanctuary policy, acknowledging its fatal flaws in the wake of the killings.

Harris defended these policies under the guise of rehabilitative justice,
yet their consequences spoke volumes. While she argued that protecting
undocumented individuals was a moral imperative, the reality was far grimmer. The recidivism of offenders shielded from federal authorities put the
public at risk. Harris's own words, however, reveal the broader disconnect
between her policies and public safety. In 2015, as California's Attorney
General, she denounced the notion that illegal immigration should be
considered a crime: "I'm a career prosecutor," Harris told CBSLA. "I've
personally prosecuted everything from low-level offenses to homicides.
Unfortunately, I know what crime looks like. I know what a criminal
looks like who's committing a crime. An undocumented immigrant is not

a criminal."[22] While this rhetoric played well with progressive audiences, it obscured the very real consequences of her policies, particularly in cases involving violent offenders.

Ambition at Any Cost

Harris's tenure as District Attorney is a case study in the dangers of political ambition divorced from principled governance. Her refusal to pursue the death penalty in high-profile cases, aggressive prosecution of non-violent offenders, mishandling of the crime lab scandal, and sanctuary policies reveal a politician more interested in optics than outcomes. Harris's decisions were not made in isolation; they reflected a calculated ambition that often prioritized her career over the principles of justice she claimed to champion.

Her rise in politics, while impressive, left in its wake a series of contradictions that call into question the authenticity of her reformist claims. As she moved on to higher offices, the mechanisms of power that accelerated her ascent also hollowed out the integrity of the institutions she was meant to serve. Her career is a testament to how political ambition can erode the very values upon which it is supposedly built.

California Attorney General (2011–2017): A Legacy of Abdication and Failure

Kamala Harris's rise to California Attorney General in 2011 was hailed by her supporters as the dawn of progressive reform in the state's justice system. Yet, as with many lofty promises in her career, the reality of her tenure was marked by a pattern of political expediency and mismanagement that left California's law enforcement weaker and its citizens less safe. Far from ushering in a new era of justice reform, Harris's time as Attorney General was defined by decisions that prioritized optics over governance, and ambition over accountability.

Dismantling the Bureau of Narcotic Enforcement

One of the most catastrophic decisions of Kamala Harris's tenure as Attorney General was her choice to dismantle the Bureau of Narcotic Enforcement (BNE) in 2012. This 100-year-old institution had been at the forefront of California's efforts to combat organized crime and drug cartels.[23] Harris, who was responsible for overseeing the California Department of Justice's budget, framed the decision as a fiscal necessity, citing Governor Jerry Brown's $71 million cuts.[24] Yet the dismantling of the BNE was not just a response to budgetary pressure—it was strategic abandonment of the very infrastructure needed to protect California from the scourge of narcotics and violent crime; negligence at its worst.

The Sacramento Bee captured the alarm felt by law enforcement officials at the time: "We understand the state is facing tough economic times, but the elimination of these units severely hampers our ability to combat drug trafficking organizations that operate across jurisdictional boundaries."[25] The decision neutered California's capacity to coordinate anti-drug efforts, leaving local agencies to grapple with the consequences. Steve Cooley was unsparing in his critique: "She wiped out the BNE, and California paid the price. It was a monumental failure of leadership."[26]

What followed was predictable: narcotics trafficking surged, and regions once protected by the BNE's coordination were left vulnerable to the violent influence of drug cartels.[27] A 2018 survey by the California Peace Officers' Association (CPOA) found that 72% of respondents believed the elimination of the BNE had "severely weakened" the state's ability to combat organized drug crime.[28] Law enforcement officers, have said that California has no statewide coordination of major narcotics enforcement and it's been absolutely disastrous.

Local law enforcement officials echoed these concerns, noting that without the BNE's specialized agents and intelligence-sharing capabilities, they were left to address large-scale drug operations with limited resources and fragmented coordination. Many police chiefs, including those cited in The Sacramento Bee, voiced frustrations about the vacuum left by the BNE's disbandment. Without a central agency to coordinate operations across jurisdictions, California's law enforcement efforts became increasingly disjointed.[29]

Community leaders in areas hardest hit by narcotics-related violence were equally dismayed. In a 2017 Fresno Bee report, residents from California's Central Valley, a region known for its battles with drug cartels, expressed frustration over the state's failure to protect them. "We lost a critical line of defense," remarked one Fresno community leader. "The state left us to fend for ourselves."[30] The growing influence of drug cartels in these communities underscored the long-term damage caused by Harris's decision to dismantle the BNE, a move that left California exposed to the very dangers the bureau was established to combat.

The repercussions of the BNE's elimination were not confined to rural regions. In urban centers like Los Angeles and San Francisco, drug-related arrests surged as criminal syndicates exploited the absence of state-level coordination. According to data from the California Department of Corrections and Rehabilitation, drug-related homicides increased by 18% between 2012 and 2015, with narcotics trafficking spiking in areas that had previously relied on the BNE's oversight.[31,32]

By dismantling the BNE, Harris did more than cut a line item from the budget—she crippled California's most critical tool in the fight against narcotics and organized crime. In doing so, she left local law enforcement agencies overwhelmed, under-resourced, and unprepared to confront the rising tide of violence and drug trafficking that followed in the wake of her decision. Rather than adapting to the changing realities of drug enforcement, Harris's leadership created a vacuum that criminal organizations were eager to exploit.

AB 109: Shifting the Burden, Ignoring the Consequences

Shortly after disbanding the BNE, Harris threw her support behind AB 109, a controversial law aimed at reducing prison overcrowding by shifting the responsibility for housing lower-level felons from state prisons to county jails. The predictable result, as noted in chapter 6, was that overcrowded jails began releasing inmates early, with violent crime rising by 12% as a consequence. Property crimes also saw a notable increase, with a 7.6% rise in the first year alone, according to the Public Policy Institute of California.[33] This data should have served as a critical warning signal, but Harris remained steadfast in her defense of the bill, downplaying its role in the rising crime rates and its failure to protect public safety.

Harris's endorsement of AB 109 starkly contrasted with the warnings from law enforcement officials, including police chiefs, sheriffs, and district attorneys, who foresaw the risks of transferring long-term offenders to local jurisdictions. The California Deputy District Attorneys Association (LADAA) openly criticized the bill, implying that it would be a shell game that would place dangerous criminals back on the streets under the guise of rehabilitation.[34]

One of the most glaring criticisms of Harris's role in AB 109 was her failure to secure the funding or resources necessary for counties to properly implement realignment. This shortfall led to increased strain on local systems, resulting in early releases of offenders who should have remained incarcerated. The Los Angeles Police Protective League (LAPPL) condemned the bill, stating that the "legislature in fact gutted punishment as a consequence of crime."[35] Harris's position placed her in the difficult role of defending a policy that many law enforcement officials believed was a direct threat to public safety.

AB 109 not only released offenders back into communities but did so while depriving law enforcement of the necessary tools to ensure those communities remained safe. The LAPPL issued a scathing rebuke of the law, stating that "Harris's support for this bill ignored the very real threats these released offenders posed to public safety. Realignment prioritized criminals over the citizens and officers sworn to protect them."[36] Harris's decision to support AB 109, despite these clear failings, exemplified her commitment to a progressive agenda that focused on reducing incarceration rates at all costs, even at the expense of public safety, exposing a troubling pattern: Harris consistently embraced the rhetoric of reform without addressing the practical implications of the policies she championed.

The most damning aspect of Harris's involvement with AB 109 was her dismissal of the real-world consequences it had on public safety. Under the guise of reform, offenders with violent histories were reclassified as "low-risk" and released into communities ill-equipped to supervise them. Recidivism rates soared, and counties struggled with limited oversight and resources to manage the influx of offenders. Yet Harris, with the authority and responsibility to address these failures, continued to promote the law as a success.

Ultimately, Harris's endorsement of AB 109 reflects a dangerous philosophy that seeks to reduce incarceration while ignoring the consequences of releasing offenders early; it also serves as yet another example of political opportunism. Although the law was framed as a progressive solution to California's prison overcrowding crisis, the reality was that Harris, as Attorney General, had a duty to ensure public safety was not compromised. Instead, her silence was deafening as communities bore the brunt of rising crime rates, overcrowded jails, and early releases. Harris signaled her willingness to compromise the welfare of California's communities for her career advancement. Steve Cooley put it succinctly: "The policies she supported had real, tangible consequences for public safety, and she never took responsibility for them." While Harris may have argued that realignment was necessary to comply with federal mandates, her failure to address the public safety concerns raised by law enforcement—and her continued defense of the legislation despite overwhelming evidence of its flaws—cement her role in what many see as one of the most reckless criminal justice policies in recent California history.

Proposition 47: Legalizing Theft

If AB 109 undermined public safety, Harris's support for Proposition 47 in 2014 all but dismantled it. And her role in the passage of Proposition 47 is a telling illustration of the calculated confluence of personal ambition and political strategy. Though her involvement is often conveniently downplayed, it reveals her alignment with the broader progressive movement that seized California during her tenure as Attorney General. After a narrow victory in 2010, Harris was entrusted with the duty of drafting the official titles and summaries for all state propositions—a role that should have been neutral but was, in her hands, an instrument of profound influence. In one of her most pivotal acts, Harris gave life to a proposition that promised to improve public safety and education. In reality, it did the opposite.

While Harris may not have led the campaign for Proposition 47 openly, her fingerprints are unmistakably all over its passage. The measure was crafted, funded, and driven by the same Bay Area criminal justice reformers who had been instrumental in her political rise. More damningly, Bearstar Strategies, the very consulting firm that managed her re-election, was charged with spearheading the campaign for Proposition 47.[37] This was no mere coincidence; it was a cynical alignment of progressive reform and political maneuvering. It was a marriage of convenience between her ambition and the reckless policies that have since devastated the very communities she claimed to serve.

Proposition 47 was a proposition designed to appeal to voters through its hollow promises of safety and social benefit. Brazenly branded as the "Safe Neighborhoods and Schools Act," it was not reform; it was a marketing campaign.

The consequences of Harris's involvement in Proposition 47 were not theoretical or long-term—they were immediate and disastrous. By raising the felony threshold for theft to $950 and reclassifying drug possession as a misdemeanor, the law triggered a wave of property crime and rampant drug use that swept across California. A 2018 study in the Journal of Criminology found that property crimes surged by 9% following the passage of Prop 47, with vehicle thefts and burglaries showing the most significant increases. Public spaces once shared by citizens became havens for open drug abuse, with law enforcement stripped of their ability to intervene effectively.

Far worse, Proposition 47 dealt a crippling blow to the state's ability to solve violent crimes. The number of DNA samples collected plummeted from 15,000 to 5,000 per month, a staggering decline that has severely undermined efforts to solve rapes, murders, and other violent offenses. As the *Sacramento Bee* editorial board scathingly remarked, "If she was aware of the DNA issue, Harris could have exchanged some of the verbiage for the following nine words: 'Will curb law enforcement's authority to collect DNA samples.' If she wasn't aware, she was not doing her job."[38]

But beyond its immediate failings, Proposition 47 is a symbol of a far deeper rot—a disconnect between the political elite and the brutal realities on the ground. Harris, by engineering a proposition that sold voters a myth, helped unleash the very crime wave she purported to address. The supposed "savings" from reduced incarceration costs were quickly eclipsed by the immense social and economic toll of increased petty crime, rampant drug use, and the overall erosion of public safety. Californians, deceived by a title and summary designed to mislead, were left to bear the brunt of Harris's cynical manipulation of the democratic process. As Cooley so aptly summarized, "The damage has been untold and, in a sense, irreparable."[39]

Steve Cooley spoke the truth without hesitation, calling Harris's actions "fraud by misrepresentation"—a deliberate deception crafted to obscure the real and immediate dangers the law would unleash. Cooley rightly condemned the proposition for "baiting" voters into believing it would improve public safety when, in fact, it handed criminals a golden key to operate with impunity and shackled the police from doing their jobs.

In the aftermath, as communities grapple with the wreckage left by Proposition 47, the reality becomes clearer: this was not reform, it was the systematic dismantling of public safety. By stripping the justice system of its ability to meaningfully deter these offenses, Harris's policies emboldened criminals who now faced little more than token consequences.[40] Steve Cooley was once again scathing: "The policies Harris championed were about optics, not outcomes. California paid the price, and continues to pay."[41]

Kamala Harris's role in this legislation, though shrouded in political posturing, stands as a stark reminder that ambition, when unchecked, will sacrifice even the most basic principles of governance. She may have risen in the ranks of the Democratic Party, but her fingerprints remain indelibly imprinted on one of the most dangerous policies to emerge from California's recent history—a policy that has led to a rise in theft, drug-related crimes, and an eroded trust in the state's ability to maintain law and order.

Prop 47, sold as a measure to alleviate prison overcrowding, reclassified a range of felonies—including theft, drug possession, and other "non-violent" crimes—as misdemeanors. While it was praised by criminal justice reformers, the real-world consequences were far more damaging.

Kamala Harris and Prop 57: "Top Cop-Out"

As if Prop 47 had not already done enough damage, Harris's support for Proposition 57 in 2016 further weakened California's justice system and serves as another glaring testament to her dangerous flirtation with far-left criminal justice reform. As California's Attorney General, Harris wielded considerable power in shaping the language that framed Proposition 57 for voters. Her office crafted the ballot title and summary, deliberately describing serious violent crimes as "non-violent." This act was not mere negligence; it was a deliberate misrepresentation—a deception that exposed California's most vulnerable citizens to avoidable harm.

Loretta Sanchez, a fellow Democrat who ran against Harris for the Senate, was one of the few in her party who dared to call out this deception: "The ballot title and summary, written by Attorney General Kamala Harris, calls serious violent crimes 'non-violent,' including crimes such as rape by intoxication and human trafficking involving minors," Sanchez declared.[42] Her words were not hyperbole; they were a brutal indictment of a law that allowed rapists and traffickers to exploit legal loopholes for early release. Sanchez went further, branding Harris as the "top cop-out," an incisive rebuke that perfectly captured the hypocrisy of Harris touting herself as California's "top cop" while actively undermining the very public safety she was sworn to protect.[43]

And Sanchez was right. The California Department of Corrections and Rehabilitation reported a significant increase in inmates eligible for parole under Prop 57, including individuals convicted of serious offenses who posed clear risks to public safety.

Law enforcement agencies across California, from police unions to district attorneys, warned Harris and her supporters of the dangers of Proposition 57. They knew that the law would tie their hands, preventing them from keeping violent offenders off the streets. Yet Harris, ever loyal to the radical criminal justice reform movement (and the billionaire class funding it), ignored these warnings. Her priority was not public safety—it was the optics of reducing incarceration numbers to appease a progressive base, regardless of the cost to California's citizens.

Harris's ties to Proposition 57 were deeply intertwined with her political allies. While Harris did not openly campaign for Proposition 57, the measure was funded and supported by a network of progressive donors and organizations, many of whom were integral to the broader criminal justice reform movement that Harris championed. Major financial backing for Proposition 57 came from billionaire philanthropists such as George Soros, Tom Steyer, and Mark Zuckerberg's advocacy organization, FWD.us—all of whom have been vocal proponents of reducing incarceration rates through reform initiatives. These donors, who played a pivotal role in shaping California's justice policies, were key allies of Harris throughout her political rise, backing many of the progressive reforms she supported during her tenure as Attorney General.

This alliance between Harris and the well-heeled backers of Proposition 57 was no coincidence. Their shared vision for criminal justice reform, often to the detriment of public safety, created a dangerous synergy. Proposition 57 fit neatly into Harris's broader agenda, where the focus on reducing incarceration overshadowed the very real concerns of law enforcement professionals and the communities they served. The passage of Proposition 57, funded by these powerful interests, was not an isolated example of poor judgment. It exemplified Harris's willingness to align with political forces that sought to reduce incarceration at any cost.

The surge in violent crime, the early release of hardened criminals, and the devastation wrought by offenders like Smiley Martin are not anomalies—they are the inevitable outcomes of a policy that treated incarceration as the problem and criminals as the victims.

California's citizens were deceived by a law that promised safety but delivered chaos. Proposition 57 will forever be associated with Harris's failure to lead, her failure to protect, and her betrayal of the people she was meant to serve. The state now bears the scars of this failed policy, and the lives lost as a result are its gravest indictment.

A Career of Calculation, Not Conviction

Kamala Harris's tenure as California Attorney General stands as a testament to the perils of political ambition unchecked by principle. From the dismantling of the BNE to her support for AB 109, Prop 47, and Prop 57, Harris's decisions weakened California's criminal justice system, leaving communities vulnerable and emboldening criminals. The rise in violent and property crime, the overwhelming of local jails, and the release of dangerous offenders were all direct results of her policies.

Yet, instead of taking responsibility for the damage done, Harris used her position as a stepping stone, carefully crafting her narrative as a "reformer" on the national stage. But the evidence tells a different story. Far from reforming California's justice system, her tenure as Attorney General revealed a politician who consistently prioritized ambition over public safety, and optics over outcomes. The legacy of Kamala Harris in California is not one of progress—it is one of abdication.

Transition to National Politics (2016–Present): Unburdened by What Has Been

In 2017, Kamala Harris ascended to the U.S. Senate, carrying with her the complex legacy of her prosecutorial and Attorney General career.[44] As she transitioned into national politics, the country's discourse on law enforcement had shifted dramatically. The rise of the Black Lives Matter movement, increased public awareness of mass incarceration, and a growing outcry over police brutality created an environment where Harris's record became both a source of authority and a point of contention.[45]

On the surface, Harris's experience in law enforcement gave her a veneer of credibility on issues of criminal justice reform. As a senator, she co-sponsored the FIRST STEP Act, a bipartisan bill aimed at reducing mandatory minimum sentences and expanding rehabilitation programs for inmates.[46,47] But while Harris positioned herself as a leader in the criminal justice reform movement, her support for this legislation did little to erase the deeper contradictions of her record.[48] Her past was riddled with aggressive prosecutions of non-violent offenders and a clear reluctance to embrace key criminal justice reforms when she had real power as California's Attorney General.

Yet, Harris's prosecutorial past became a double-edged sword. As she pursued national office, her record as both a prosecutor and Attorney General came under intense scrutiny, particularly from activists and political opponents. Her role in overseeing aggressive prosecutions of non-violent offenders, as well as her reluctance to endorse certain criminal justice reforms during her time as Attorney General, clashed with her more recent progressive rhetoric. Critics pointed to her past defense of the death penalty despite personal opposition and her resistance to independent investigations into police shootings.[49] This inherent tension—between her past as an enforcer of the law and her current posture as a reformer—revealed the contradictions that would follow her through her national political career.[50]

The Brett Kavanaugh Show Trial and National Spotlight

Harris's defining moment on the national stage came during the Brett Kavanaugh Supreme Court confirmation hearings in 2018. Her sharp, prosecutorial interrogation style earned widespread praise, casting her as a tough, no-nonsense figure willing to hold powerful individuals accountable.[51] It was during these hearings that Harris's reputation as a forceful advocate was cemented, propelling her onto the shortlist of presidential contenders for 2020. This performance was pivotal in elevating her national profile and setting the stage for her presidential ambitions.[52]

However, as her 2020 presidential campaign unfolded, Harris struggled to reconcile her prosecutorial past with the progressive base she needed to win over. Loretta Sanchez, her opponent during her 2016 U.S. Senate race, had already sharpened these criticisms during a debate at California State University, Los Angeles, when she lambasted Harris for her reluctance to seek the death penalty for a convicted cop killer while serving as San Francisco District Attorney. "If you're not going to stand with law enforcement, if you're not going to stand with the families of victims, where do you stand?" Sanchez charged. This criticism resonated with some voters, who viewed Harris's decision as part of a broader pattern of leniency in her approach to crime, while others saw it as a principled stand against capital punishment.

Throughout the 2020 Democratic primary, these criticisms reemerged. Activists and opponents alike seized upon Harris's past as evidence of her failure to fully embrace transformative criminal justice reform.[53] An analysis by the American Civil Liberties Union (ACLU) highlighted Harris's resistance to certain reforms during her time as Attorney General, including her opposition to independent investigations of police shootings.[54] This discord between her record and rhetoric became a focal point for progressives who questioned her commitment to systemic change.[55]

Kamala Harris's prosecutorial background, far from being an asset, became an emblem of the very contradictions that define her career. Despite her attempts to position herself as a champion of reform, Harris's record is one of political opportunism—balancing tough-on-crime posturing with the progressive rhetoric necessary to navigate the Democratic Party's evolving base.[56] It was this malleability—and her biology—rather than any real commitment to change, that made her an appealing choice for Joe Biden's running mate in 2020.

But Harris's tenure as Attorney General, when examined through the lens of her actions rather than her rhetoric, reveals a politician willing to sacrifice public safety for political expediency. Far from reforming California's criminal justice system, Harris weakened it, leaving local communities vulnerable to the consequences of her failed policies. While she now claims to be a leader in criminal justice reform, her record tells a different story—one of rising crime, deteriorating public safety, and a state overwhelmed by the unintended consequences of her opportunism.

For Harris, reform is merely a talking point. Her record as Attorney General demonstrates that when given the opportunity to enact meaningful change, she instead embraced policies that decimated California's law enforcement capabilities and led to a surge in crime. The "reforms" she championed served only to bolster her political ambitions, leaving a trail of broken communities and rising violence in their wake. Harris is not the reformer she claims to be—she is a product of a system that rewards expediency over principle, image over substance.

As Vice President, Harris continues to claim the mantle of a reformer, but her past remains an anchor she cannot escape. The gap between her rhetoric and reality widens with every public statement. Her ability to straddle both sides of the political aisle—appeasing progressives while claiming to stand for law enforcement—speaks not to leadership, but to a chameleon-like political survival instinct.

While Harris's allies hailed her co-sponsorship of the FIRST STEP Act as evidence of her commitment to criminal justice reform, her critics point to the stark reality of her tenure as Attorney General. Harris's selective embrace of reform measures was not about fixing a broken system but about positioning herself for higher office, at any cost.

Conclusion: Avatar of a Failed State

Kamala Harris's career is not a mere chronicle of political ambition; it is the emblem of California's descent into chaos. Her rise, from a mediocre prosecutor propelled by Willie Brown's patronage, to her tenure as Attorney General, was marked by a pattern of opportunism and mismanagement that mirrors the dysfunction of the state she left behind. At every stage, Harris's leadership has been characterized by hollow rhetoric, failed policies, and a relentless pursuit of personal power at the expense of California's citizens.

Steve Cooley observed how Harris's policies undermined public safety: "The consequences of her decisions weren't just theoretical—they were felt on the ground. People were less safe because of the laws she backed." Harris is not merely complicit in California's decline; she embodies it. Her career is a study in political survival at any cost, a testament to how cronyism and corruption can elevate the undeserving while dismantling the structures meant to protect the public.

The chaos unleashed by the dismantling of the BNE, the flood of criminals released under her so-called "reforms," and the erosion of public safety are the tangible outcomes of a political career devoid of responsibility. Harris has proven, time and again, that she is not a reformer but a skilled opportunist, a figure who cloaks her ambition in the guise of justice while leaving ordinary citizens to pay the price. Harris has never been a leader. She has been a political chameleon, shifting her positions and allegiances with the winds of expediency, leaving behind a trail of destruction.

The damage Harris has wrought is not confined to California. As she positions herself for even greater national power, her tenure serves as a chilling warning: unchecked ambition, devoid of principle, leads only to ruin. The wreckage of California's justice system, now barely functioning under the weight of rising crime and weakened law enforcement, is her true legacy—a legacy that threatens to extend far beyond the borders of the Golden State.

As the specter of a Harris presidency looms, the nation should take heed. Her political ascent is a blueprint for failure—a blueprint built on cynical compromises, deflection, and the abandonment of the very principles she claims to uphold. California has borne the brunt of her leadership, and it continues to unravel as a result. Should Harris's influence expand to the global stage, we can expect more of the same: leadership without conviction, policies without foresight, and a country left to clean up the mess.

Kamala Harris is not the future of leadership—she is a warning of its decline. Her career, a triumph of expedience over substance, stands as a grim reminder that when ambition goes unchecked, it leaves behind only devastation.

CHAPTER 19

THE OLIGARCHY

California no longer functions as a democracy in any meaningful sense. It is an aristocracy, governed not by the electorate but by a ruling class whose influence spans generations. The Browns, Newsoms, Pelosis, and Gettys have not merely held power; they have institutionalized it, ensuring that the state's political and economic machinery serves their interests first. Through inherited wealth, patronage networks, and institutional capture, they have transformed California into a modern patrician order—where elections occur, but real political change does not.

This is not a system of crude political dominance but of refinement— one that maintains the outward rituals of democracy while neutralizing genuine opposition. The state's political structure is a closed circuit: elections managed to contain dissent, media narratives curated to protect the established order, and the Democratic Party functioning less as an ideological movement than as an apparatus of control. Its strength lies not in suppressing alternatives but in ensuring they never emerge.

California has long marketed itself as a progressive utopia, yet it is defined by its rigid hierarchy. The rhetoric of diversity obscures a stark divide: an expanding underclass dependent on state programs, a vanishing middle-class strangled by taxation and regulation, and an elite permanently insulated from the consequences of its own policies. Social justice serves not as a corrective force but as an ideological veil, allowing the ruling class to present its consolidation of power as moral duty rather than self-interest.

This chapter exposes the incestuous machinery of California's political economy—a system of patronage and exclusivity that operates beyond the awareness of its citizens, who, in this construct, are not participants but subjects. The Brown family laid its foundations, the Newsoms inherited its spoils, and the Pelosis ensure its perpetuation. These are not mere political dynasties in the traditional sense but custodians of a self-sustaining order in which policy is not a means of governance but an instrument for entrenching power and wealth. Housing remains artificially scarce to the benefit of generational landowners, energy policy is dictated by investment imperatives rather than public necessity, and crime laws are sculpted by an elite insulated from the consequences of their own decrees.

This is not the natural course of politics but the deliberate consolidation of an aristocratic order. California is not merely an outlier but a prototype. It has demonstrated that once an oligarchy cements itself within institutions, it does not fade—it expands.

The House of Brown—The Sacramento Monarchy

The origins of California's modern political aristocracy can be traced directly to the Brown family. Pat Brown, the state's governor from 1959 to 1967, was more than just a successful politician—he was the architect of the state's ruling dynasty. His tenure laid the groundwork for the consolidation of power that would later define California's political landscape. In Pat Brown's era, the Democratic Party was still, at least in theory, a coalition of competing interests. But his political machine was something more enduring: an apparatus that would not merely win elections but structure the state's governance around a tight circle of allies and patrons.[1]

The relationship between the Browns and the Newsoms is not a recent alliance but a generational pact. William Newsom II, the grandfather of Gavin Newsom, played a pivotal role in Pat Brown's campaigns, forging a bond that would span decades. This was not simply a matter of political support; it was a fusion of family and power, an entanglement of financial and political interests that would shape California for generations.[2]

Pat Brown's tenure was characterized by the kind of grand infrastructure projects that defined mid-century governance—highways, water systems, and universities—but it was also an era in which the foundations of the modern oligarchy were laid. His administration's awarding of lucrative contracts, its cultivation of a donor class that would wield influence for decades, and its close ties to business magnates ensured that California's political leadership would remain in familiar hands.[3]

Jerry Brown, his son, carried this legacy forward with a different style but the same fundamental objective: the perpetuation of a ruling class. If Pat Brown's era was marked by the expansion of the state, Jerry Brown's was defined by its consolidation. First elected governor in 1974, Jerry quickly positioned himself as the intellectual architect of modern California liberalism. While publicly cultivating an image of austerity and skepticism toward power, his tenure was anything but detached. His appointments, alliances, and policy decisions were deeply intertwined with the interests of those who had propelled his family into power.[4]

His governorship in the 1970s was the moment when the familial alliances that define California politics truly took shape. It was Jerry Brown who elevated Bill Newsom, Gavin's father, first to the Placer County bench and then to the California Court of Appeal.[5] These appointments were more than political favors; they were the cementing of a dynasty, ensuring that the Brown-Newsom alliance would not be a passing political arrangement but a multigenerational fixture.

But perhaps Jerry Brown's most enduring legacy was his role in shepherding Gavin Newsom's rise. By the time Brown returned to the governor's office in 2011, the transition was already underway. His final years in office were not just about governance; they were about succession. Newsom, then lieutenant governor, was the heir apparent. The path had been cleared, the machinery aligned. When Brown's term ended in 2019, the transfer of power was as seamless as any dynastic succession.[6]

What distinguishes the Brown dynasty is not just its longevity but its adaptability. Unlike political families that rise and fall with electoral cycles, the Browns have remained embedded within the machinery of the state. Their influence is not confined to office-holding; it extends through judicial appointments, regulatory agencies, and the vast donor network that has long sustained their power. Theirs is not a name that simply appears on the ballot; it is one that is woven into the very structure of California's governance.

The Brown dynasty, however, does not exist in isolation. It is part of a broader network, one in which political and financial power are inextricably linked. The Newsoms, the Gettys, and the Pelosis are not separate entities; they are extensions of the same oligarchic structure. What began as political alliances have hardened into a system of governance in which a handful of families dictate the trajectory of the state.

This is not a matter of conspiracy or coincidence. It is the natural consequence of a system in which power, once attained, is not relinquished but passed down. In a state that prides itself on progressivism, the most fundamental form of privilege—hereditary political control—remains unchallenged. And at the center of this inheritance stands the Brown family, the original architects of California's modern oligarchy, whose influence continues to shape the state long after their names have disappeared from the ballot.

The Newsom Dynasty—Heir to the Throne

If the Brown family built California's modern political order, it was the Newsoms who inherited it. Unlike Jerry Brown, who cultivated an image of ascetic detachment, Gavin Newsom embodies the seamless fusion of wealth and power that defines the state's ruling class. His ascent was not a product of ideological fervor or political struggle but of lineage, patronage, and the quiet maneuverings of an aristocracy that selects its successors with meticulous care.

Gavin Newsom was groomed for public life not through the traditional rites of political apprenticeship but through the careful stewardship of family connections and the beneficence of one of America's wealthiest dynasties. His rise is a case study in the mechanics of California's political aristocracy—how economic privilege translates effortlessly into political dominance. His career has been defined by an easy familiarity with the corridors of power, a sense of entitlement that comes from knowing that the pathways have already been cleared.[7]

The Getty family was instrumental in this project. Gordon Getty, son of the oil magnate J. Paul Getty, did more than merely support Newsom— he and his family functioned as his patrons, underwriting both his business ventures and his early political career. Newsom's father, Bill Newsom, was not only a close confidant of Gordon Getty but also the administrator of the Getty family trust, ensuring that the relationship between the two families was one of financial interdependence as much as political alliance.[8]

It was through Getty backing that Newsom built PlumpJack, the boutique winery and hospitality brand that would serve as the foundation for his wealth. But this was not a typical entrepreneurial endeavor. The venture was financed with seed money from the Getty trust, an arrangement that ensured Newsom's wealth accumulation was not the product of market competition but of aristocratic patronage. From the outset, he was insulated from the vicissitudes of economic risk, granted a platform from which to launch his political career.[9]

His entry into politics was similarly choreographed. Newsom did not claw his way into public office; he was placed there. His initial appointment to San Francisco's Parking and Traffic Commission was engineered by then-Mayor Willie Brown, a veteran power broker whose influence extended deep into the state's political infrastructure. From there, the trajectory was set: a seat on the Board of Supervisors, a stint as mayor of San Francisco, and eventually the role of lieutenant governor—a position that served less as an office of governance and more as a holding pattern until the governorship became available.[10]

By the time he ascended to the state's highest office in 2019, Newsom's authority was never in question. The machinery of the Democratic Party, the financial backing of the Gettys, and the political infrastructure of the Brown family had ensured that no serious opposition would emerge. His election was less a contest than a coronation, the final step in a succession plan that had been in place for decades.

Yet Newsom's power is not merely a function of inherited privilege—it is the embodiment of a political model in which wealth and governance are inseparable. His administration has been marked not by radical departures from the status quo but by its reinforcement. Housing policy, environmental regulations, and economic directives all operate within a framework that ensures the continued prosperity of the elite while managing—rather than resolving—the crises that afflict the working and middle classes.

Nowhere is this dynamic more evident than in the state's approach to economic policy. Newsom, like his predecessors, presides over a California that is increasingly uninhabitable for those outside the governing class. The state's policies—ostensibly designed to promote sustainability and social equity—function in practice as barriers to economic mobility. Housing restrictions, punitive taxation, and regulatory overreach serve not to democratize prosperity but to consolidate it, ensuring that wealth remains concentrated in the same hands that have controlled it for generations.

Newsom's tenure is not an aberration but a confirmation of California's transformation into a state governed by a closed elite. He is not an innovator or a reformer but a custodian of an order that predates him and will endure long after he leaves office. His career is a testament to the reality that in California, political power is not won—it is inherited.

The Gettys—California's Medici

Behind the Browns and Newsoms, California's governing dynasty, stands the Getty family—its sponsors and financiers, the invisible hand guiding policy and patronage from behind the curtain. Unlike the state's political families, who cycle through public office, the Gettys do not seek power through elected positions. They wield it through wealth, ensuring that the political order remains firmly aligned with their interests. Their role is not to govern directly but to underwrite governance itself—a model less akin to traditional American political dynasties than to the Medici banking empire.

J. Paul Getty, the oil baron who became the world's richest man, built the family's financial empire, but it was his son, Gordon Getty, who transformed that fortune into a mechanism for political control. His relationship with Bill Newsom, Gavin Newsom's father, was not mere social camaraderie; it was the foundation of a patronage network that would endure for generations. Bill Newsom was more than a friend—he was a financial steward of the Getty trust, managing its assets and strategically deploying its wealth to shape California's political landscape.[11]

This patronage was instrumental in Gavin Newsom's ascent. The Getty trust seeded his PlumpJack businesses, forging a direct pipeline between oligarchic wealth and political power. Between 1996 and 2001, Newsom's personal income—largely derived from Getty-backed ventures—exceeded

$400,000 annually. By 2000, his income spiked to $1.3 million, bolstered by a lucrative Getty-supported real estate deal. The family's financial support extended beyond business: at least 18 Gettys poured over half a million dollars into Newsom's various political campaigns, ensuring their influence over California's future leadership.[12]

Yet the Getty reach extends far beyond Newsom. Their financial empire has shaped the state's political trajectory in ways that transcend any single candidate. Through philanthropic foundations, university endowments, and cultural institutions, they have embedded themselves within California's elite decision-making apparatus. They hold seats on the boards of Stanford, UC Berkeley, and the San Francisco Museum of Modern Art—institutions that do not merely reflect political discourse but shape it. Their wealth sustains the California Democratic Party, allowing them to dictate policy direction while remaining shielded from scrutiny.[13]

Nowhere is their influence more apparent than in economic policy. The very politicians they bankroll have imposed some of the most restrictive land-use and environmental regulations in the country, ensuring that real estate remains artificially scarce and prohibitively expensive—except for those who already own it. Beneath progressive rhetoric, these policies serve a singular purpose: entrenching the economic primacy of families like the Gettys, whose vast holdings appreciate under conditions of controlled scarcity. Their fingerprints are equally evident in California's energy policy, where subsidies and mandates are structured to benefit well-capitalized investors while burdening the middle class with soaring costs.

Unlike the Browns and Newsoms, who operate in the public arena, the Gettys exert power in a manner both more elusive and more permanent. Their wealth is untouched by electoral cycles, their influence immune to shifts in public sentiment. They are the architects of California's financial aristocracy, ensuring that those who hold office—regardless of their ideological posturing—remain tethered to the interests of those who fund them.

The Gettys do not govern California in name. But in practice, they do.

The Pelosi Machine—Old Money Meets Political Power

While the Browns and Newsoms have dominated California's executive branch, and the Gettys have bankrolled its ruling class, the Pelosis have extended their influence beyond the state, operating as the bridge between California's oligarchy and the entrenched power centers in Washington. Their wealth and political acumen have allowed them to function as the enforcement arm of the ruling elite, securing federal resources, shielding their allies, and ensuring that California's dynastic order remains unchallenged at the national level.

The Pelosi connection to California's aristocracy is not incidental. Paul Pelosi, the financier and businessman, is the son of John Pelosi, a longtime business partner of William Newsom, Gavin Newsom's grandfather. Their joint venture—the concession to develop Squaw Valley for the 1960 Winter Olympics—was one of the earliest instances of how political connections in California translated into lucrative economic arrangements.[14] Though the business partnership formally ended, the political ties endured.

Nancy Pelosi, while not a product of California's old-money dynasties, became one of its chief protectors and enablers. She married into the Pelosi fortune and built her political career in San Francisco, rising to national prominence not through ideological vision but through her mastery of the political patronage system. She did not simply represent a congressional district; she became the gatekeeper for California's political machine in Washington, leveraging her control of fundraising and committee appointments to maintain party discipline.

The extent of her influence was most evident in her role as a kingmaker. She did not merely support Newsom's rise; she actively cultivated it. Her fundraising networks ensured that he had access to the financial resources necessary to dominate elections. The relationship between the two was more than political convenience—it was dynastic continuity.[15]

The Pelosi family's reach extends beyond electoral politics. Like the Gettys, they have used philanthropy and institutional control to cement their influence. They have deep ties to Stanford, UC Berkeley, and the San Francisco Museum of Modern Art—cultural and academic centers that function as ideological strongholds for California's ruling class. These institutions serve not only as incubators for the next generation of political operatives but as gatekeepers of acceptable discourse, ensuring that challenges to the status quo remain marginal.

Perhaps the clearest example of the Pelosi family's aristocratic role was the 2021 wedding of Ivy Getty, Gordon Getty's granddaughter. The event, held in San Francisco's City Hall, was officiated by Nancy Pelosi, with Kamala Harris in attendance.[16] It was less a wedding than a coronation, a demonstration of the seamless merger between California's old-money dynasties and its political establishment. It symbolized the permanence of the ruling class, the extent to which wealth and governance had become indistinguishable.

Through a combination of financial leverage, institutional control, and political enforcement, the Pelosi family has ensured that California's oligarchy is not merely sustained but expanded. While others operate behind the scenes, they wield power openly, their dominance undisguised. They are not merely beneficiaries of the system—they are its architects.

The Architecture of Power—A Fortress of Privilege and Control

The endurance of California's ruling elite is not simply a matter of family legacy or wealth—it is the result of a system carefully designed to maintain control. The state's political machine does not rely on crude authoritarianism; instead, it ensures that real power remains inaccessible to outsiders by controlling the avenues through which influence is attained. Elections, regulations, and economic policies are all structured in ways that make challenges to the oligarchy functionally impossible.

One of the most effective tools of elite preservation is the manipulation of the electoral process. California has not elected a Republican to statewide office since 2006, a statistic often attributed to demographic and ideological shifts. But the reality is more complex. The combination of top-two primaries, ballot harvesting, and an overwhelming financial advantage for Democratic candidates has turned the state's elections into a series of formalities. Nominal competition exists, but it is largely cosmetic. The same donor networks fund both wings of intra-party disputes, ensuring that regardless of who wins, the governing class remains unchanged.

Beyond the ballot box, the state's regulatory framework serves as another instrument of control. California's labyrinthine business and housing regulations, often justified as environmental or consumer protections, have the effect of insulating the elite from competition. The same families and firms that champion these restrictions are rarely subject to them—whether through exemptions, legal maneuvering, or sheer financial resilience. These policies do not hinder the wealthy; they cripple the aspirational class, ensuring that wealth remains concentrated rather than dispersed.

This extends into the housing market, where restrictive zoning laws and environmental review processes have made development prohibitively expensive. The consequences are twofold: home ownership remains out of reach for the majority of Californians, ensuring a permanent class of renters dependent on state intervention, while existing landowners—often members of the elite—watch their property values soar. The ruling class has no interest in solving the housing crisis because it is not a crisis for them—it is an asset.

California's media ecosystem plays a crucial role in maintaining this order. The state's major newspapers, including the *Los Angeles Times* and the *San Francisco Chronicle*, are controlled by a small cadre of oligarchs who have financial stakes in the policies they cover. Media narratives are shaped not by journalistic inquiry but by the interests of those who fund them. Opposition voices exist, but they are confined to the periphery, dismissed as reactionary or extremist. The press does not function as a check on power—it functions as its amplifier.

The same is true of California's academic institutions. Stanford, UC Berkeley, and UCLA produce not just the intellectual justifications for the state's political model but the personnel who administer it. The pipeline from elite universities to political office is seamless, ensuring that those who govern are drawn from a pre-selected class of individuals who have been vetted for ideological conformity. This is not merely a Democratic stronghold—it is a closed system, one in which dissent is filtered out long before it reaches positions of influence.

All of these mechanisms work in concert to create a self-replicating order. The families who have ruled California for generations do not hold power simply because of their wealth or name recognition; they hold power because they have built a structure that ensures their continued dominance. The barriers to entry are not explicit, but they are insurmountable for those outside the system. This is not the product of electoral preferences or shifting demographics—it is the logical outcome of a political and economic system designed to exclude.

California's ruling class has perfected the art of governance without accountability. They do not need to suppress opposition; they have simply ensured that none can emerge.

The Intersection of Old Money and Big Tech

California's oligarchy has evolved. The old-money families—the Browns, Newsoms, Pelosis, and Gettys—once ruled alone, their power rooted in land, finance, and political machinery. But in the past two decades, a new force has emerged, one that has not replaced them but merged with them: Big Tech.

The rise of Silicon Valley's billionaire class has not disrupted the state's ruling order; it has reinforced and modernized it. The titans of the tech industry—figures like Mark Zuckerberg, Larry Page, and Reid Hastings—have not supplanted California's old aristocracy but have been absorbed into it. The old money's political influence and institutional control have proven invaluable to the new digital elite, who, despite their fortunes, lacked the governing infrastructure to fully assert power. The result is a merger of interests: old money provides the political machinery, new money provides the capital.

This alliance is visible in the overlapping networks of venture capital firms, think tanks, and philanthropic organizations that dominate California's policymaking. The same institutions that have historically served as vehicles for Getty and Pelosi influence—the San Francisco Museum of Modern Art, Stanford University, the UC system—are now bolstered by the financial and technological resources of Silicon Valley's billionaires. These partnerships are not philanthropic in the traditional sense; they are investments in ideological and political control.

One of the clearest examples of this is the relationship between tech firms and the state's regulatory apparatus. Despite the ostensible hostility of California's political class toward corporate excess, the reality is that the state's labyrinthine regulations disproportionately benefit those who can afford to navigate them. Large tech companies, with their vast legal and lobbying resources, thrive in an environment that suffocates smaller competitors. The result is a system where only the largest firms—those with the closest ties to the political elite—can survive.

Elections, too, have been reshaped by this partnership. The vast wealth of Silicon Valley's elite has been funneled into political campaigns, non-profit initiatives, and media organizations that function as de facto arms of the Democratic Party. Tech billionaires, despite their self-styled libertarian origins, have found common cause with California's old guard, recognizing that an entrenched political monopoly serves their long-term interests. The regulatory state, far from being an obstacle, is a tool—one that ensures that challengers to the existing order remain structurally disadvantaged.

California's oligarchy has always adapted to preserve its dominance. The incorporation of Big Tech into its ranks is the latest and most sophisticated iteration of this process. The state is no longer ruled solely by the heirs of industrialists and political dynasties—it is now governed by a fusion of legacy power and digital authority, a regime in which the traditional instruments of control have been augmented by algorithmic enforcement and economic monopolization.

This is not a transition; it is an evolution. The same families remain in power, but their methods have been modernized. The result is a political order more absolute than ever before—one in which wealth, technology, and governance are seamlessly merged, ensuring that opposition remains not just ineffective, but imperceptible.

Neo-Feudal Order—A Bifurcated State

California has ceased to function as a middle-class society. It has become a bifurcated state, where the ruling class lives in fortified prosperity while an ever-expanding underclass struggles beneath them. The policies of the state's elite—whether on housing, crime, taxation, or immigration—have not merely eroded the middle-class; they have actively engineered its elimination.

Nowhere is this stratification more evident than in California's urban centers. The state's cities have devolved into stark contrasts: luxury enclaves of wealth surrounded by landscapes of destitution. In San Francisco, the political class dines at exclusive, Michelin-starred restaurants while fen-tanyl-addled vagrants collapse on the sidewalks just blocks away. In Los

Angeles, gated communities remain untouched by the policies that have turned entire neighborhoods into lawless encampments. This is not dysfunction—it is the natural consequence of governance that serves only the interests of those insulated from its failures.

The elimination of the middle-class has been accomplished through deliberate policy choices. Housing restrictions, driven by a combination of environmental bureaucracy and municipal obstructionism, have ensured that homeownership remains the privilege of those who inherited property or possess generational wealth. The taxation regime—one of the most punitive in the country—makes upward mobility all but impossible for the average citizen, while offering carve-outs and loopholes for those with the right legal and financial connections.

This economic stratification is mirrored in education. California's public schools, once the pride of the state, have been systematically degraded, with literacy and math proficiency rates now ranking among the lowest in the nation. Yet the children of the elite are unaffected; they attend exclusive private institutions, where they are groomed to take their place in the next iteration of the ruling class. The very politicians who decry inequality have ensured that their own offspring remain untouched by the collapse of public education.

Crime policy has followed the same pattern. The state's ruling class, shielded by private security and insulated neighborhoods, has embraced a criminal justice agenda that punishes the law-abiding while excusing the violent. The consequences are borne not by those who craft these policies but by the working-class families who cannot afford to live behind gates. Crime is not simply tolerated; it is functionally endorsed as a form of redistributive justice, a means of enforcing a new social order in which property rights and personal safety are privileges, not guarantees.

What has emerged is a system that bears little resemblance to the postwar prosperity once associated with California. Instead, it resembles the economic and social structures of Latin American oligarchies—of failed states—where a wealthy, insulated elite presides over a vast population that is either financially dependent on the state or trapped in a cycle of economic and social decline. This is neo-feudalism: a political economy where power is not merely concentrated but hereditary, where the barriers to mobility are not merely economic but structural.

The ruling class does not fear this arrangement; they prefer it. The middle-class, historically, has been the greatest threat to aristocracy. It is the middle-class that demands accountability, that challenges political monopolies, that insists upon the rule of law. By reducing the state's economic landscape to a binary of dependent poor and untouchable rich, the oligarchy has secured its position. There is no significant political opposition because those who might have constituted it have either left or been economically neutralized.

California's transformation into a neo-feudal state is not an accident, nor is it reversible under its current leadership. It is the logical conclusion of a system in which the ruling class is no longer accountable to the people but only to itself.

Prosopography of the Elite—A Closed Network

To understand how California is governed, one must look beyond elections, legislation, or policy debates. The true structure of power lies in the relationships between its ruling families, financial patrons, and institutional stewards. Political office is merely a revolving door for a class that does not change; it merely regenerates.

The term *prosopography*—the study of elite networks—offers the most accurate lens through which to examine California's ruling structure. The same names appear across generations, reemerging in different roles but always within the same system. The Browns, Newsoms, Pelosis, and Gettys are not distinct entities; they are interwoven, bound by blood, marriage, and financial entanglement. Their dominance is not a coincidence, nor is it the result of electoral competition—it is the product of a deliberate and self-sustaining hierarchy.

This oligarchy does not merely exist within government. It extends into academia, media, law, and finance. These connections are reinforced through philanthropic foundations, think tanks, and cultural institutions. The Gettys fund not just politicians but entire ecosystems of influence— museums, university departments, and media organizations that shape public discourse in ways that serve their interests. The Pelosis, through their extensive donor networks, control the flow of political capital at the federal level, ensuring that California's power structure remains intact regardless of national political shifts. The Newsoms, deeply embedded in both business and politics, serve as the liaison between corporate interests and governance.

Even internal conflicts within the Democratic Party do not threaten this order. What appear to be ideological disputes—between "moderates" and the more radical progressive wing—are, in reality, controlled opposition. The party functions less as a coalition of competing ideas and more as a managed enterprise, where disputes are resolved within the framework of an oligarchy that does not permit genuine upheaval. The system allows for the appearance of political struggle while ensuring that the results do not disrupt the balance of power.

This is why, despite its failures—on crime, housing, taxation, and education—California's ruling class remains unchallenged. The mechanisms of opposition have been neutralized before they can take shape. Electoral competition is stifled by structural advantages. Economic independence, which would allow new challengers to emerge, is eroded by regulatory burdens and taxation. The media, rather than scrutinizing the system, functions as its defender.

The result is a political order in which change is illusory. Names shift, titles change, but power remains where it has always been. This is not the rule of law or the consent of the governed. It is aristocracy, thinly disguised as democracy.

The One-Party System—Voting as Ritual, Rule as Certainty

California is often described as a deep-blue state, as if its political landscape is simply a reflection of the electorate's will. This is a convenient fiction. In reality, the state operates under a single-party system that has been engineered to function without serious opposition. Elections are held, ballots are counted, but the outcomes are foregone conclusions—not because of outright fraud, but because the mechanisms of power have been so thoroughly fortified that genuine competition is structurally impossible.

The dominance of the Democratic Party in California is not the result of ideological consensus; it is the product of institutional control. The ruling elite has mastered the art of political inertia, ensuring that power, once consolidated, does not meaningfully shift. This is accomplished not through overt authoritarianism but through a combination of legal maneuvering, financial monopolization, and media gatekeeping.

The first layer of this control is electoral engineering. California's top-two primary system, implemented under the guise of promoting bipartisanship, has instead eliminated it. In most statewide races, Republicans do not even make it to the general election. Instead, voters are presented with two Democratic candidates, carefully selected from within the acceptable spectrum of the ruling class. The illusion of choice remains, but the result is predetermined: no matter which candidate wins, the system remains unchanged.

Ballot harvesting, a practice legalized and expanded under Democratic rule, further consolidates power by ensuring that voter mobilization efforts are controlled by the dominant party. While framed as an effort to increase participation, its practical effect is to give well-funded political machines an overwhelming advantage, allowing them to collect and submit votes in a manner that all but guarantees their preferred candidates prevail.

But electoral engineering is only one piece of the puzzle. Financial control is another. The cost of running a competitive campaign in California is prohibitive, requiring tens—if not hundreds—of millions of dollars to be viable. The state's donor class, led by figures in Hollywood, Silicon Valley, and old-money families like the Gettys, ensures that only candidates who align with the existing order receive the funding necessary to compete. Corporate interests, too, fall in line, recognizing that contributing to the ruling party is not merely a matter of ideology but of survival.

The final layer of control is cultural. The state's media institutions function less as independent watchdogs than as ideological enforcers, reinforcing the prevailing narrative and silencing dissenting voices. The *Los Angeles Times*, the *San Francisco Chronicle*, and the dominant broadcast networks all operate within a narrow range of acceptable discourse, ensuring that alternative viewpoints—especially those challenging the state's ruling elite—are either marginalized or outright dismissed.

Policies that fail—on crime, housing, education, and infrastructure—persist not because the electorate demands them but because the mechanisms to overturn them have been rendered inoperable. The political monopoly of California's elite is not a temporary condition; it is the logical endpoint of a system designed to eliminate any trace of incipient opposition.

This is not democracy in any meaningful sense. It is a controlled democracy—a system in which power is retained through legal structures, financial barriers, and cultural dominance rather than through the will of the people. It is a political order where participation is permitted, but influence is reserved for those who have already been chosen.

California is no longer just a failed state; it is a prototype. A template for a new model of governance in which elections are a ritual, democracy a vestige, and power a self-replicating phenomenon, passed through bloodlines, financial monopolies, and ideological enforcement. It is what happens when liberalism, unmoored from opposition, metastasizes into its inevitable form: an aristocratic caste system cloaked in the language of progress.

Conclusion: The Fate of All Empires

California's oligarchy presents itself as invincible. It has engineered a system in which power is passed through families, where elections serve as pageantry rather than contests, and where opposition is neutralized before it can emerge. It does not fear economic decline, mass exodus, or public discontent—because it does not rely on a healthy state to maintain its rule.

But no empire, however insulated, can survive indefinitely when its foundations rot. The state the oligarchy governs is breaking down. The institutions that sustain its wealth and authority—real estate, technology, financial markets—are beginning to show signs of strain. The middle class has fled, but in their absence, the underclass is growing restless. Crime, once dismissed as a manageable side effect of progressive governance, has begun creeping into the enclaves of the elite. Even among the ruling class, fractures are forming, as competing factions struggle for control over an increasingly unstable system.

The illusion of permanence cannot hold forever. The architects of California's decline may believe they have secured their dominion, but history has little patience for those who mistake stagnation for stability. The same elites who built this order may soon find themselves trapped by it.

The question is not whether the oligarchy will fall. It is whether there will be anything left of California when it does.

AUTOPSY OF A FAILED STATE

A Master Called Law

Throughout history, there are certain moments that transcend time, reverberating across the ages with undiminished relevance. These moments do not merely pass into the pages of memory; they define the essence of civilization and the perpetual human struggle between order and chaos. Herodotus, the venerable chronicler of the ancient world, captures such a moment during the Greco-Persian Wars of the 5th century BC. The exiled Spartan king, Demaratus, is summoned before Xerxes, the supreme Persian emperor, who commands a realm of unrivaled wealth and power. Surveying his vast army of slaves, Xerxes is baffled: Why do the Greeks resist his overwhelming force? Why would free men, uncoerced by tyranny, choose defiance and likely death over submission and survival? Demaratus, with piercing clarity, replies: "They are free, yet not wholly free; for they have a master called Law, which they fear more than your subjects fear you."[1]

This exchange is more than a relic of ancient dialogue; it is a timeless indictment of societies that forsake the rule of law for the caprices of power. The Greeks' allegiance was not to a man but to the immutable principles of justice enshrined in their laws. It was this reverence for the

law—an embodiment of shared values and mutual obligations—that fortified them against both external conquest and internal decay.

As we reflect on the present condition of California, once the epitome
of American promise, we are compelled to ask: Have we abandoned our
"Master called Law"? Are we witnessing, in real time, the unraveling of
society that has forsaken the very principles that underpin its existence? Is
California a failed state?

The Greeks understood that freedom is anchored in a collective commitment to laws that transcend individual whims—a lesson lost on Xerxes
and, alarmingly, increasingly ignored in modern California.

The Breach of the Social Contract

The social contract, as envisioned by the great minds of the Enlightenment—
Hobbes, Locke, and Rousseau—forms the indispensable cornerstone of
civilized society. It is not merely an intellectual construct but the very
foundation upon which order rests, a binding pact between the citizen
and the state. In this pact, certain freedoms are sacrificed in exchange for
protection, the state's primary function. The state therefore liberates its
citizens from the anarchic "state of nature" where life, as Hobbes famously
wrote, is "solitary, poor, nasty, brutish, and short."[2] Security is not merely
a bureaucratic obligation—it is the state's sole justification for existence.

Hobbes argued that a government incapable of guaranteeing safety
has no moral claim to rule; its failure voids the social contract, plunging
society back into the anarchic "state of nature." Locke, with his resolute
focus on the protection of life, liberty, and property, contended that when
a state fails to safeguard these, it forfeits its legitimacy, rendering resistance—even overthrow—not merely justified but necessary.[3] Rousseau
introduced a collective dimension, asserting that the social contract is an
embodiment of the common good, the *Volonté Générale*. A government
that cannot shield its citizens from the predations of violence is not just
incompetent—it is illegitimate, having severed the very bond that con-
ferred its moral authority.[4]

Today, the current condition of California—and by extension, much
of the West—constitutes a breach of this social contract. Rising crime, the
normalization of lawlessness, and the state's unwillingness or inability to

protect its citizens are not mere failures of governance—they are acts of betrayal. they are a profound abdication of the state's most basic responsibility. This is a state that no longer serves its foundational purpose, a government whose legitimacy has crumbled under the weight of its own abdication.

When the state cannot guarantee the safety of its citizens, it ceases to be a state in any meaningful sense of the word. This is not some regrettable lapse in policy—it is a fundamental dereliction of duty, signaling the collapse of the social contract itself. Without the assurance of security, the social fabric unravels, and citizens are left to fend for themselves, abandoned to the Hobbesian nightmare from which the social contract was meant to deliver them. The state's monopoly on violence—the bedrock of its authority—has been ceded to criminal elements, operating with impunity.

Nowhere is this more apparent than in California's criminal justice system, which has devolved into a grotesque parody of justice. The scales have tipped disastrously in favor of offenders, with victims relegated to mere afterthoughts. District Attorney George Gascón's reign in Los Angeles is emblematic of this descent into chaos. His policies—eschewing prosecution for misdemeanors, refusing to enforce sentencing enhancements for violent crimes, and deliberately blocking cooperation with federal authorities—are not only reckless but a deliberate assault on the very notion of justice. The law, once revered as an impartial arbiter, now serves as little more than a cudgel for ideological whims.

As was expressed by the officers and prosecutors interviewed for this book, gangsters no longer fear the police or the criminal justice system. The erosion of deterrence has not only emboldened criminals—it has invited lawlessness into the very heart of civil society. A state that cannot or will not defend its citizens is a state that has abdicated its most sacred duty. It is no longer a protector; it is an accomplice to its own collapse.

Former Deputy District Attorney Kathy Cady warns of the inevitable consequences:

"People are angry and feel abandoned. When victims start to believe the system won't protect them, they will take the law into their own hands. The government, which is supposed to provide protection, is being prevented from doing so by radical policies. At some point, people will get tired of it."

Vigilantism is not the cause of societal breakdown; it is the symptom of a state that has already broken down. When the government fails to protect its people, it relinquishes the very claim to power that once legitimized its rule.

Echoes of Late-Stage Empire: California's Reckoning

The parallels between modern California and the late Western Roman Empire are as disconcerting as they are striking. As Victor Davis Hanson notes, by the early 5th century AD, Rome was already unraveling under the pressures of hyperinflation, rampant corruption, and the fragmentation of its empire. Commerce, trade, and travel were increasingly interrupted, and the empire's inability to secure its borders or assimilate diverse populations exacerbated the strain.[5] California, too, contends with unchecked immigration, economic stratification, and a cultural fragmentation that mirrors Rome's decline.

With nearly 27% of its population foreign-born, California's rejection of assimilation in favor of identity politics further erodes the shared values necessary for societal cohesion. Hanson points out that California "frowns on past melting-pot solutions," where schools once emphasized a common language and culture, fostering a collective sense of civic duty and responsibility. Without these unifying principles, California risks devolving into a mosaic of isolated communities, disconnected from any shared allegiance.

Just as Rome struggled to integrate disparate peoples under a common Latin tongue and shared values, California's multicultural experiment—lacking unifying principles—risks devolving into a mosaic of isolated communities, with scant allegiance to a common cause.[6] The result is a perilous trajectory toward balkanization, division, and eventual fragmentation.

Economic Regression and the Rise of *Luxus*

The Roman concept of *luxus*—a moral and material decadence that heralded societal decline—finds a strikingly parallel in California's growing economic disparities. Hanson observes that "the rapid expansion of Roman rule and its attendant enrichment from serial conquests led to what the Romans called *luxus*." This decadence manifested in "declining birth rates, promiscuity, materialism, fringe cults and religions, growing inequality, and the decline of the once independent agrarian middle-classes."

California exhibits similar symptoms. Parallel to the breakdown of law and order is an economic stratification that eerily mirrors Rome's late stage faltering empire. The financialization of the economy, a shift from tangible production to speculative ventures, has enriched a select few while hollowing out the middle class. California's economy increasingly resembles a neo-feudal landscape, with tech oligarchs and coastal elites ensconced in affluence, while vast swathes of the population grapple with poverty and precarity.

Hanson elucidates this divide: "California is increasingly a society of two classes—the richest zip codes of the coastal strip juxtaposed with a third of the nation's welfare recipients." The exodus of millions from the middle class, fleeing the state in search of affordable living and better opportunities, mirrors the depopulation that afflicted Rome, as citizens sought refuge from economic despair and the neglect of governance.

The state's reliance on illegal alien labor—akin to Rome's dependence on slaves and mercenaries—perpetuates a cycle of exploitation, suppressing wages for the most vulnerable workers. This model undermines the dignity of labor and deepens social tensions, eroding the cohesion necessary for a stable and just society.

Cultural Fragmentation and the Loss of Civic Virtue

Rome's decline was not merely economic or political; it was a cultural and moral collapse. The empire's failure to assimilate diverse populations under a common set of values, language, and laws led to its fragmentation, as civic virtue and social cohesion disintegrated. California faces a similar predicament. The rejection of the "melting pot" ideal in favor of identity politics and cultural relativism has balkanized society, weakening the shared civic identity necessary for societal resilience.

Educational institutions, once bastions of shared knowledge and critical inquiry, have become arenas for ideological indoctrination. The emphasis on grievance over gratitude, on division over unity, undermines the development of a common civic identity. Hanson observes that "a state that imports the foreign impoverished and exports its own successful middle-classes is incapable of reform." The result is a populace increasingly estranged from one another, lacking the mutual trust essential for collective action and societal resilience.

Collapse of Infrastructure and Public Trust

By the 5th century AD, Roman infrastructure was in a state of decay. Travel had become perilous, funding for public works had dried up, and the state could no longer maintain the vast infrastructure that had once symbolized its might. California now finds itself in a similar state of decay. Despite levying some of the highest income, gas, and sales taxes in the nation, the state suffers from chronic budget deficits. A quarter of its population struggles to pay their utility bills, home insurance companies are fleeing *en masse*, and California's freeways rank among the worst in the country.

Just as Roman citizens could no longer rely on stable infrastructure or competent governance, Californians are grappling with a government increasingly incapable of fiscal prudence. The erosion of infrastructure is paralleled by an equally corrosive decline in public trust. Californians, but indeed citizens across the nation, feel increasingly abandoned by the very institutions meant to safeguard their welfare, a betrayal reminiscent of the late Roman Empire's inability to protect its people.

Hanson notes that by 400 AD, "on a very fundamental level, things were falling apart. Residents were no longer able to travel as easily or safely. Sufficient funding for infrastructure expansion and upkeep was lacking." Citizens were increasingly unable to purchase once-common goods like pottery, foodstuffs, and glass, and were left vulnerable to unscrupulous local magistrates, operating with impunity far from the reach of Roman oversight. Likewise, Californians are coming to grips with a government that is both incompetent and indifferent, where even the most basic expectations of governance—safe roads, reliable utilities, and fiscal prudence—are no longer met.

Lawlessness and the Erosion of Justice

In the waning years of the Western Roman Empire, laws became ad hoc, subject to local customs rather than uniform Roman statutes. This legal fragmentation undermined the empire's cohesion, as central authority collapsed and regional warlords rose to fill the void. In California, selective enforcement of laws and the disregard for statutory mandates by progressive prosecutors mirrors this breakdown.

When prosecutors unilaterally decide which laws to enforce, they usurp the legislative function, undermining democracy and the rule of law. Hanson warns that "law became increasingly ad hoc" in the late Roman Empire, and California is following a similar trajectory. A society where laws are negotiable is a society teetering on the brink of chaos.

An even more alarming parallel is the rise of organized crime. Just as warlords carved up the remnants of Roman territories, Mexican drug cartels now operate with near impunity in California, controlling vast networks of narcotics distribution and exploiting porous borders. California's inability to maintain law and order has given rise to organized crime, cartels, and gang leaders who wield power in ways that parallel the warlords of late antiquity. This modern warlordism thrives in the vacuum created by ineffective governance and lax enforcement, posing an existential threat to California's sovereignty and the safety of its citizens.

A Society Incapable of Reform

Hanson delivers a damning verdict on California's political and institutional sclerosis: the state, he asserts, is "incapable of reform, or at least reform rapid and sweeping enough to preclude the general impoverishment and collapse of quality schools and infrastructure that is now emblematic of California." This incapacity for meaningful change is not a simple failure of governance; it is the inevitable outcome of a one-party monopoly that breeds complacency and smothers dissent. Without a credible opposition to challenge or scrutinize the ruling orthodoxy, the state has descended into stagnation, where inertia masquerades as governance.

This political paralysis is reminiscent of the late Western Roman Empire, where entrenched elites—isolated by their own privilege and divorced from the realities of a collapsing society—were either unwilling or unable to enact the reforms needed to stave off ruin. The result was not a gradual decay but an accelerated unraveling of the very structures that once upheld the empire. As Hanson points out, California's decay is not

gradual either; it is rapid, palpable, and, in some respects, already irreversible. The unwillingness to confront systemic failures has created a vacuum
where decline accelerates unchecked.

The political class, much like Rome's late-stage rulers, has insulated
itself from the consequences of its own ineptitude. The decimation of
the middle class, the collapse of infrastructure, and the deterioration of
public education are not abstract issues—they are the tangible markers
of a state spiraling toward collapse. Yet, the elites, ensconced in coastal
enclaves, remain untouched by the disintegration they have both enabled
and ignored. The absence of reform is not merely a failure of will; it is an
indictment of a political system that has become utterly detached from the
people it purports to serve.

Hanson's analysis underscores the grim reality: California's political
apparatus is trapped in a cycle of self-perpetuation, where power is maintained not through competence or accountability, but through ideological
conformity and the suppression of dissent. This is not governance; it is
bureaucratic inertia, propped up by a compliant media and a disengaged
electorate. The result is a state incapable of reforming itself, much like
Rome in its final years—a once-great civilization now paralyzed by its own
contradictions, sliding headlong into oblivion.

Lacking both the will and the capacity to confront its entrenched failures, California teeters on the edge of terminal decline. Its unraveling mirrors the swift decay of Rome, where a decadent elite, cocooned in complacency, presided over the empire's slow-motion collapse. The question is
no longer whether California can reform, but whether it will dictate the
terms of its own disintegration or be overtaken by the very forces it has
long refused to confront.

The Pathology of Decline and the Lessons Unheeded

The cumulative effect of these factors paints a grim portrait. California's
descent is not an isolated anomaly but the logical conclusion of a state that
has forsaken its foundational principles. The symptoms—economic dysfunction, legal incoherence, cultural fragmentation, and infrastructural
collapse—are not disparate phenomena but interconnected manifestations
of deeper societal decay. The state now mirrors late-stage Rome, where the

unraveling of political, social, and economic systems compounded one another, hastening the empire's collapse.

Hanson's analysis cuts through the notion of a "gentle decline," rejecting a that Rome—or, by extension, California—experienced a smooth transition into disarray. As he argues, "I don't find some of the arguments of the 'late antiquity' school of gradual and non-disruptive Western Roman transitions . . . all that convincing." History shows us that the tipping point comes abruptly, with little warning, and once the collapse begins, it accelerates with shocking speed.

California's inability to maintain basic governance—despite immense wealth—is a glaring indictment of its political class. In Rome's final years, elites were similarly insulated from the consequences of their failures, governing as though their world would continue indefinitely. But the parallels are unavoidable: both societies became paralyzed by their own contradictions, convinced of their permanence even as the cracks widened.

The state's infrastructure is the clearest metaphor for this broader decay. Despite high taxes, California's roads crumble, its power grids fail, and essential services falter. Rome, too, could no longer maintain its aqueducts, roads, or public works as the empire decayed, leaving its citizens to grapple with a state incapable of providing the very basics of civilization. The collapse of infrastructure, however, is not just physical; it is a reflection of deeper institutional decay, where once-stable systems become hollow and fragile, undermined by neglect and incompetence.

California's decline is not happening in isolation. It is the cumulative result of decades of misguided policies, unchecked political power, and an abandonment of the principles that once made it prosperous. The erosion is neither slow nor subtle. As Hanson warns, societies that ignore the lessons of history are doomed to repeat its harshest outcomes. The fall, when it comes, will not be gradual—it will be as catastrophic and final as that of Rome.

Looming Darkness: Post-Empire

The convergence of crises in California, and the broader West, signals an unsettling return to an age marked by the dissolution of cultural memory, institutional breakdown, and civilizational retreat. The symptoms are undeniable: a populace devoid of critical thought, the degradation of public discourse, entrenched economic stratification, and the erosion of the rule of law.

Hanson observes that "the general sense of chaos and breakdown is very late imperial Roman." The historical parallels are not academic abstractions—they are a clear indication of the precipice upon which we now stand. Collapse, when it arrives, is neither gradual nor orderly; it is sudden, chaotic, and devastating in its finality.

The forces that drove Rome into ruin—fragmented authority, political decay, and the rise of feudalism—are now unmistakably at play. The West, and California in particular, stands on the edge of this same abyss, beset by similar forces of fragmentation and decline.

Mass Illiteracy and the Degradation of Public Discourse
The early medieval period—the so-called "Dark Ages"—were characterized by a diffusion of illiteracy across western Europe as learning receded into the confines of monasticism. Today, however, we face a more insidious form of illiteracy—one not of letters but of thought. The proliferation of technology, the dominance of social media, and the incessant din of the 24-hour news cycle have created a populace inundated with information but starved of wisdom. The public is overwhelmed by noise, yet critically disengaged, ill-equipped to navigate the complexities of modern life. This intellectual atrophy is no less dangerous than the illiteracy of medieval Europe, leaving the populace vulnerable to manipulation and the dictates of an elite class, much like the masses under feudal lords.

Economic Stratification and Neo-Feudalism
California's current economic landscape bears an alarming resemblance to the stratified society of the medieval period. Just as the feudal system concentrated wealth and power in the hands of a few, the rise of tech oligarchs and the entrenchment of economic power among an elite few has created a new form of neo-feudalism. The erosion of the middle class—a stabilizing force in any society—has led to increasing social instability and the potential for unrest, as the wealth gap widens and the majority are left to labor in a system that no longer offers upward mobility.

Warlordism and the Breakdown of Central Authority

As the Roman Empire disintegrated, regional warlords emerged, filling the power vacuum left by the collapse of central authority. Today, the state's inability to maintain law and order has given rise to a modern form of warlordism—drug cartels, gangs, and organized crime syndicates that wield power with near impunity. These entities, often operating in tandem with corrupt elements of the state, reflect a deeper breakdown of governance, mirroring the feudal lords of old who ruled their territories with little interference from a distant and weakened central authority.

Peasantry and the Dispossessed

The homelessness crisis in California, exacerbated by the influx of migrants living in precarious conditions, resembles the peasantry and serfdom of the medieval era. These modern-day serfs are increasingly detached from the economic and social structures that sustain a stable life, condemned to the margins of society. This new underclass is both a symptom of societal decay and a contributor to its acceleration, as social policies fail to address the underlying causes of their dispossession. The growing chasm between the wealthy elite and the destitute creates a stratified society where survival is the only ambition afforded to the most vulnerable.

Loss of History and Heritage

The Dark Ages were defined by a loss of connection to the classical heritage of Rome and Greece. Today, we see a similar disconnection—not through illiteracy, but through the deliberate erasure of history. The ideological deconstruction of the past, where history is rewritten or discarded rather than understood and learned from, is severing the cultural continuity that has long been the foundation of Western civilization. This cultural amnesia makes society more susceptible to decay, as the lessons of the past are forgotten or ignored, leaving the present vulnerable to the very forces that led to earlier collapses.

Reversing Course: A Manifesto for Renewal

Understanding the anatomy of a failed state is a prerequisite for its remedy. The path to recovery demands:

- **Reasserting the Rule of Law:** Laws must be enforced uniformly and impartially. Prosecutorial discretion should not morph into prosecutorial nullification. Justice must be blind to ideology and vigilant against favoritism.
- **Revitalizing the Middle Class:** Economic policies should encourage entrepreneurship, reduce burdensome regulations, and make the cost of living manageable. A robust middle class is the bedrock of a stable society.
- **Fostering Cultural Cohesion:** Embracing a common language and shared civic values does not negate diversity but enriches it through unity. Assimilation is not an erasure of heritage but an inclusion in a collective narrative.
- **Investing in Infrastructure:** Physical decay reflects institutional decay. Prioritizing infrastructure is both practical and symbolic—a commitment to the future and a respect for the present.
- **Restoring Public Virtue:** Leadership must transcend performative gestures and address substantive issues. Accountability, transparency, and a focus on effective governance over ideological purity are essential.

A Final Reflection

Anatomizing the decline of a state is not a lamentation of doom but an indictment of complacency. California's trajectory, like that of countless civilizations before it, illustrates the fatal consequences of abandoning foundational principles. The parallels to Rome's collapse are not mere historical curiosities but grim reminders of what happens when governance dissolves into ideological fantasy and social decay is met with bureaucratic indifference.

The choice before California is stark: continue its spiral of disintegration or undertake the brutal, often thankless task of reform. The former leads to the hollowing-out of society, the reduction of a once-prosperous state into irrelevance, much like the ruins of Rome—visually grand, functionally useless. As Michael Maher of the LA County Sheriff's Department bluntly observes, "People want help. People just want help." That such a plea should be necessary is itself an indictment of a state that, for all its wealth, cannot meet even the most basic expectations of governance.

At the heart of any functioning society lies not wealth or power, but law. Demaratus, in reminding Xerxes that the Greeks feared law more than the Persian whip, captures the essence of what sustains civilization. California must rediscover this truth. The "master called law" must be more than a nostalgic recollection—it must become the foundation of renewal, or else the descent into chaos is inevitable. As John Lewin, Deputy District Attorney in Los Angeles, observes, "As a society, we've got to make sure that people are safe. That's one of the number one jobs of government." Failure to fulfill this most basic duty renders the state illegitimate, a protector no longer, but a collaborator in its own undoing.

The systemic failures of California are laid bare, though the political class remains immune to their consequences, cushioned in enclaves of wealth and power. The public, meanwhile, is forced to navigate a state that oscillates between negligence and ideological insanity. Lewin points to the absurdity of those who seek to reduce the prison population based on demographic proportions rather than criminal behavior. "You've got to look at why that's happening," he insists. "But the solution is not simply, 'we need prisons to reflect society.'" Such ideological contortions reflect a government not interested in justice but in appearances—a ruling class more concerned with optics than with substance.

The decline of California is not the result of external forces; it is an entirely self-inflicted wound. The crumbling infrastructure, the lawless streets, the exodus of the middle class—these are the inevitable consequences of a state that no longer adheres to the principles of governance but panders to the worst instincts of its political and cultural elites. It is not just failure; it is betrayal, a willful destruction of the very mechanisms that make a society functional.

But decline, as history teaches, is not always inevitable—only when a society refuses to confront the rot. Whether California will make that choice remains unclear. The question is not whether the state can be saved, but whether it is willing to save itself. Time-tested principles—upholding the rule of law, protecting citizens from crime, and maintaining a functioning infrastructure—are not mere relics of a more stable age. They are the essential prerequisites of any functioning society. To abandon them is to embrace chaos.

The twilight of California is not a distant possibility; it is already here. Whether that twilight deepens into a night from which there is no recovery depends entirely on the will to confront the failures that have brought the state to this precipice. The choices made now will echo for generations, but the future need not be written by those who mistake inertia for governance. The rhetoric of progress is cheap, but the consequences of inaction are costly. History will not absolve those who watched as the state collapsed under the weight of its own contradictions.

THE EMPIRE FALLS, THE NATION AWAKENS

On January 24, 2025, President Donald Trump—freshly inaugurated and exuding the confidence of vindication—descended from Air Force One at Los Angeles International Airport. He stood as a towering personification of authority against the backdrop of California's chaos and ruin, a stark contrast to the rudderless state left exposed by the January fires. On the tarmac below, Governor Gavin Newsom hovered awkwardly, his presence uninvited—but he appeared painfully eager to attach himself to the moment. Newsom had visibly diminished in stature, his polished veneer cracking under the weight of cascading failures. He reeked of desperation, a man whose carefully cultivated aura had been burned along with the neighborhoods still smoldering in the Pacific Palisades. In the days following the fires, he obsessively bemoaned "misinformation," "disinformation," "politicization," but really, it was just *information* that he objected to, because for once the narrative had escaped him.

In California, power and prestige are commodities brokered and bestowed by the plutocratic gatekeepers of its one-party aristocracy. For nearly two decades, Newsom was groomed as the Golden State's Dauphin—a synthetic figure, manufactured by the Gettys and their oligarch peers, as if assembled in a Pacific Heights laboratory. He embodied privilege (*white privilege*, if ever the term applied) masquerading as merit—a paragon of inherited status elevated by a system in which the Democrat elite fail upward with almost comical obliviousness; here, competence is at best an afterthought, far below the priority of image.

Trump had already dispensed with the state's most farcical example of this charade—the now oddly sympathetic and lowly Kamala Harris—but Newsom represented the same contrived and ridiculous archetype, albeit in a much more advanced form. For Newsom, there had only ever been one ultimate promotion remaining: the Presidency. Yet now, as he lingered and paced beneath the shadow of Air Force One, that ambition seemed not only delusional but cruelly laughable, the punchline to a joke he could no longer control.

As Trump approached, Newsom extended his hand with an obsequiousness that bordered on humiliation, rendering him even smaller. His attempt to engage—the pointing, the fist pumps, the thumbs up—the signature gesticulations that seemed cheaply lifted from *Top Gun*, only served to amplify his cloying weirdness. He had once cast himself as Trump's antithesis, declaring California a "Trump-proof" state, wielding progressive tropes as both shield and sword. But the man standing there now was stripped of the pretense, reduced to a supplicant begging for federal aid from the very man he had so vociferously and vainly scorned. Newsom's officious theatrics, so often mistaken for leadership, had curdled into farce. He was not the "Trump-slayer" his handlers once envisioned; he wasn't even the heir to Kamala's dubious legacy. His desperation was the death knell of a political career that had always been more performance than substance and which had overlapped with the precipitous degradation of America's greatest state.

Trump's demeanor, by contrast, was resolutely calm—unyielding but magnanimous in his willingness to shake the hand of a strident rival. If there was satisfaction in this reversal of fortunes, he revealed none of it. Instead, he moved past Newsom with the deliberate authority of a man who had come to deliver solutions, not indulge flattery. Yet, the extraordinary circumstances of the disaster, which were so plainly drawn from the folly of political negligence, could not be ignored. And the President's tour of the smoldering city began to feel less like a routine inspection and more like a reversal of the Maoist "struggle sessions" favored by California's leftists. Only now, the roles reversed: those who had slandered Trump as a rapist, insurrectionist, and fool stood diminished, their own incompetence laid bare against the backdrop of ashen ruin.

Nowhere was the humiliation more striking than when Karen Bass, Mayor of Los Angeles, sat across from Donald Trump. The meeting unfolded with the surreal gravitas of a courtroom scene, though one where the defendant remained painfully unaware of the inevitable verdict. Seated at the far edge of a long conference table, Bass punctuated her rushed platitudes with rehearsed gestures, a frantic attempt to project authority she clearly lacked. Her tone betrayed desperation cloaked in a brittle façade of performative confidence, as though she were trying to convince herself as much as anyone else that she was still in control. Wearing a purple power suit—tired habiliments of "girlboss" theatrics—Bass seemed both cliché and notably out-of-step with the solemnity of the moment. This discordance haunted her throughout the crisis, amplified by her perplexing return to Los Angeles from Ghana, a spectacle marked by a jarring mix of blank silence and inconsonant cheerfulness that only underscored her empty detachment.

Trump sat behind the Presidential Seal, a black MAGA hat with its gold embroidery perched atop his head like a crowning inevitability. In any other context, the hat might have seemed swaggering and theatrical, but here, against the ruin of California's misrule, it carried an unspoken resonance. It was not a symbol of bravado but of finality—an implicit statement that the chaos of the Golden State, no less American than the rest of the nation, would now be folded back into order, whether its leaders liked it or not.

To the President's right, Melania Trump sat in perfect, implacable stillness, her own black hat casting a shadow that framed her stoic, statuesque features. The shadow seemed to stretch across the table like an unspoken commentary, lending her an air of quiet arbitration that carried weight without effort. Her presence was neither ornamental nor commanding; it was something subtler, a composed stillness that seemed to observe and measure, amplifying the gravity of the scene by her dignity and restraint.

Between the President and First Lady rested the object that silently dominated the room: a gleaming white firefighter helmet, emblazoned with the number "47." It was more than a gift from the firefighters; it was a symbol of competence and resolve, a quiet rebuke of the failures that had left California in ruin. The helmet amplified Bass's futility, making her hollow motions and bromides seem even smaller. Once again, frontline defenders—the gritty and hardened union cadres, Democrat in heritage and MAGA in effect—made it clear where they stood; and it was not with Bass, not with Newsom, and certainly not with the limp-wristed mandarins of a party that long abandoned working men. For those watching at home, many who had once voted for Harris, Newsom, and/or Bass, the image likely brought an unspoken sense of relief: an actual boss was finally at the table. In that moment, the emptiness of the past few years was unmistakable, and what had been missing was painfully clear. Mel Gibson, whose home was incinerated in the Palisades fire, remarked, "I'm glad Trump's here at the moment. It's like daddy arrived and he's taking the belt off, you know? So, I think he'll get some results here quickly."[1]

As Bass stumbled through talking points about "slashing regulations" and "expediting permits," her words tumbled over each other, revealing her frantic need to grasp for relevance. "You can hold me to it!" she insisted, wagging her finger in a desperate bid for credibility. Trump remained motionless, his eyes fixed on Bass, betraying neither amusement nor approval.

He let her finish, and when he finally spoke, his clarion voice cut through the room like a blade: "They should be able to start [clearing debris] tonight."

Bass faltered. "No, no. That will not be the case," she stammered, her tone defensive and unconvincing.

"You have emergency powers just like I do," Trump replied, his tone calm, unflinching. "I'm exercising mine—you need to exercise yours." Each word landed with the weight of a sledgehammer, and Bass's façade crumbled further.

"I *did* exercise them. Yes," Bass insisted, her claims tenuous and defensive, betraying the weakness of her position and false presumption of her power. And still her hurried words collapsed under the silent gravity of the gleaming firefighter helmet, which now seemed to sit in quiet judgment of her obvious incompetence.

Outside, the aftermath of the Palisades and Eaton Fires served as an undeniable indictment of California's failures. Over 23,000 acres had burned in the Pacific Palisades and more than 40,000 acres across Los Angeles County. Once-affluent neighborhoods were reduced to skeletal ruins. Hydrants ran dry, leaving firefighters to battle flames with dwindling resources. Evacuation routes became death traps, hopelessly clogged and poorly maintained. Trump's blunt assessment cut through the excuses: "The hydrants didn't work. People want to start rebuilding, but they're being told to wait 18 months. This doesn't need to take 18 months. It should start tonight."[2] His words weren't just a critique; they were a condemnation of decades of mismanagement that had left the state vulnerable to catastrophe.

Bass's attempts to defend herself only magnified her inadequacy. "We absolutely need your help, we need federal help," she pleaded, her voice edging toward the latent reality of her obvious ineptitude.

"You've got it. I told you, you will have no permit problem, there will be zero delay," Trump reassured, generous and confident. He continued, "I am much more worried because I met at least eight groups of homeowners that said its 18 months [before they can rebuild] and that we're going to go through a whole series of questions on determining what's hazardous." Trump pointed to the frustrated homeowners in the room who affirmed the veracity of his claim with exhausted acknowledgment.

Bass, now bearing witness to the irrelevance of her position, defensively interrupted, "Nooo. No, no."

Trump, unmoved, pressed on with unwavering clarity: "You have to allow people to go on their site and start the process tonight."

Bass answered, "As we will . . . You can come back and check!" None believed her, least of all Trump.

"You already have the permits," he said. "Let them clear their own debris. Contractors will take two years. People can have it done in 24 hours." The room itself seemed to recoil from Bass's excuses, her authority crumbling under the weight of Trump's unrelenting scrutiny of bureaucratic bullshit.

This wasn't a meeting—it was an autopsy. The fire had consumed more than homes—it had incinerated the last vestige of California's stability.

Hydrants didn't fail because of climate change—they failed because of mismanagement and waste. Neighborhoods didn't burn because of bad luck—they burned because of neglected infrastructure. Trump and Melania departed the room with an air of finality, their black hats casting shadows that seemed to echo the reckoning left behind. Bass, shrinking in her chair, had been reduced to the scale of her negligible accomplishments, her purple suit now a risible emblem of futility, stripped of the gravitas her curated identity was supposed to convey.

In a *FOX News* interview on January 22, President Trump excoriated California's leadership over the Los Angeles wildfires, painting a damning picture of negligence and incompetence. "Los Angeles looked like a nuclear weapon went off," he said. "The fires raged for four or five days, and nobody was even fighting them because they didn't have any water. Firefighters, brave as hell, turned on hydrants, and nothing came out, while flames rushed at them at 30, 40 miles an hour. Their fire departments aren't funded properly. Some of the wealthiest, most powerful people in the country lost their homes, and it looked like America was helpless. We looked so weak."[3]

Indeed, for all its natural splendor and cultural magnetism—the profound love we natives feel for its beauty and the searing heartbreak we endure at its decline—California has become an albatross, dragging the nation down with the weight of its dysfunction. In this moment, the truth of Trump's admonition was undeniable: we didn't just look weak; we *were* weak. Nowhere was this fragility more starkly revealed than in the inferno that consumed Los Angeles. The fires of January 2025 did not merely reduce homes and hillside to ash; they immolated the last pretense of California's competence. Illusions of safety, governance, and order disintegrated in the blaze, exposing a hollowed-out state incapable of defending its people or its promises. The Pacific Palisades, once a glittering vision of Southern California's aspirational grandeur, now stood as a haunting monument to the neglect and failure which the absence of leadership kindles into inferno, raging like the desiccated hills of the Santa Monica Mountains.

Against the backdrop of destruction, billionaire real-estate developer Rick Caruso emerged as a rare symbol of pragmatism and resilience.

Caruso, deeply embedded in Los Angeles politics and commerce, had long distinguished himself through decisive and results-oriented leadership. At just twenty-six he became the youngest commissioner in the history of the Los Angeles Department of Water and Power, later serving as President of the Los Angeles Board of Police Commissioners. In 2022 he ran as a Democrat for mayor (though he had been a Republican and Independent), only to be narrowly defeated by Karen Bass. Yet while Bass's leadership faltered amid the crisis, Caruso's foresight and action stood in sharp contrast.

Caruso's properties in the Pacific Palisades, including his prized Palisades Village, survived the inferno—not through luck, but by design. Anticipating the inevitability of state failure in a disaster, he invested in private fire suppression systems, a decision that underscored his proactive management. While politicians deflected and bureaucrats evaded accountability, Caruso was on the ground, coordinating relief efforts, mobilizing private resources, and most notably, telling the truth in a landscaped parched by obfuscation.

"It wasn't breaking news that there may be a fire here," Caruso told *FOX11*. "And because of the negligence of our government leaders and our government officials, we have the Santa Monica Mountains, the density of that brush was fuel just waiting to explode. And that's when it did. And then, on top of the high winds, you just had everything come together. Could it have been prevented? Probably not. Could it have been mitigated? There's no doubt in my mind."[4]

As the smoke cleared, Caruso's critique of California's governing class grew sharper. "Career politicians have 'making excuses' down to a fine art," he said. "You see it rolling out and trying to explain why there wasn't water—nobody wants excuses why they lost their homes, why they lost their business."[5] Caruso's bluntness exposed what many Californians already knew: their leaders had failed them. His focus on tangible solutions, rather than excuses, offered a stark contrast to the hollow promises they had grown tired of hearing.

In the aftermath of the blaze, Dr. Patrick Soon-Shiong, owner of the *Los Angeles Times*, called the paper's endorsement of Karen Bass a "mistake," citing her failed leadership during the wildfires.[6] His criticism, however, was more than a moral reckoning—it was a calculated business decision. Soon-Shiong, like Jeff Bezos at the *Washington Post*, who declined to endorse a candidate in the last election, recognized the shifting political winds and the risks of alienating a disillusioned public.[7] His move reflected an understanding that his customers—readers and advertisers—were growing impatient with California's failing governance and progressive orthodoxy. By distancing himself from Bass, Soon-Shiong signaled an awareness of the market's pivot and the need to align with a growing demand for accountability. It was an acknowledgment that the state's political strategies were increasingly untenable—not just as governance, but as a product sold to an audience unwilling to further excuse preventable and catastrophic failures from its elected leaders.

Even before the fires swept through Los Angeles, there was smoke on the horizon of California's political landscape, signaling a potential shift in the winds emanating from the people. Yet in Sacramento and the state's other major cities, Kamala Harris's decisive electoral defeat was not met with reflection, but with yet more posturing. For California Democrats, the loss was not a wake-up call but an opportunity to double down on the empty spectacle of progressive governance. For California's top democrat, Gavin Newsom, the opportunity seemed particularly ripe.

In the "Brat Summer" of 2024, as Harris's doomed campaign hit peak "vibes" following the Democratic Convention in Chicago, a source close to Newsom described him as "inconsolable" and "not talking to anyone." Newsom's disdain for Harris was hardly a secret—nor an isolated viewpoint across California's political circles—and his frustration at her selection over him as the party's nominee was palpable. In an interview during the convention, when asked for his thoughts on the controversial nomination process post-Biden, Newsom offered a cutting, thinly veiled response, saying dryly that he'd been "told to say" it was "a very inclusive process." The remark betrayed not only his antipathy toward Harris but also his simmering resentment at being sidelined in favor of someone he clearly deemed unworthy of the presidency.[8]

Gavin Newsom stood to gain the most from Kamala Harris's political implosion, and he wasted no time capitalizing on her defeat. Without missing a beat, he maneuvered to cast himself as the Anti-Trump, the self-anointed leader of the "resistance." What Newsom failed—or refused—to acknowledge was that the election was not just a rejection of Harris, but a damning indictment of the California political machine she represented. Harris's defeat laid bare the hollow promises and moral preening that defined the state's governance. But Newsom, blind to the broader repudiation, saw only an opening to position himself for his next act in 2028.

On November 7, 2024, just days after Trump's re-election, Newsom convened a special legislative session, declaring, "The freedoms we hold dear in California are under attack—and we won't sit idle." Promising to "Trump-proof" the state, he unveiled measures to insulate California's progressive fortress from federal interference. "We are prepared," he proclaimed, "and we will do everything necessary to ensure Californians have the support and resources they need to thrive."[9] But to those living amid rampant homelessness, rising crime, and collapsing infrastructure, his words were as empty as the Santa Ynez reservoir, which had failed to supply the Palisades with life-saving hydration. Support? Resources? Preparedness? If only . . . The irony, of course lost on Newsom, hit with all the subtlety of Nancy Pelosi's facelifts.

To "Trump-proof" California, Newsom diverted millions in taxpayer dollars into a legal war chest designed to underwrite ideological litigation. The legislature approved a $50 million package to challenge Trump administration policies deemed hostile to the state's sanctuary laws, near-limitless abortion access, and its anti-growth labyrinth of environmental regulations. The package also earmarked funds to defend illegal aliens facing deportation.[10]

Remarkably, this initiative was passed just days after the LA fires—while the embers still smoldered—and as state and local officials begged Trump for federal disaster relief. "Today's actions are about real people, keeping families together, making sure diversity thrives," proclaimed State Senate Pro Tem Mike McGuire, who represents California's 2nd Senate district, stretching from San Francisco to the Oregon border, including Marin and Sonoma Counties. He added, "As a parent, I cannot imagine the fear and anxiety millions feel across the state today."[11]

Yet, as a Californian, one wonders if McGuire *can imagine* the fear and anxiety millions of "real people" and "families" endure when: their cities are engulfed in flames? When their homes are invaded by illegal alien death cults? When their insurance policies are cancelled overnight? When they can't afford basic necessities? When homeless drug addicts turn their streets into latrines? When Mexican drug cartels flood their neighborhoods with fentanyl? When fire hydrants sputter dry as their homes burn? When they blow a tire hitting a pothole at 60 mph? When they surrender over 12% of their income to fund welfare for illegal aliens? When they're taxed into oblivion to bankroll gender-affirming care for prisoners? When their businesses are ransacked, their cars repeatedly broken into, and the police never respond? Or, ultimately, when justice and competence feel like relics of a bygone era, forever out of reach? These are not hypotheticals; they are the daily realities of millions in a state that abandoned functional governance in favor of ideological vanity.

Expounding on Newsom's agenda, McGuire declared, "California has come too far and accomplished too much to simply surrender and accept [Trump's] dystopian vision for America. This is why we're moving with speed and investing in our legal defense. This is an important first step in protecting our progress and the values that make this state great."[12] Yet for most Californians, the dystopia McGuire spoke of was already their lived reality—one not imposed by Trump but forged by decades of Democratic single-party rule, riddled with corruption and shielded from accountability. For "real people," the state's promises had become meaningless platitudes. Increasingly, they were taking matters into their own hands, abandoning the hollow assurance of leadership and safeguarding themselves from the chaos those leaders had unleashed.

In Huntington Beach—Surf City USA—the city council issued a bold and unprecedented declaration on January 23, 2025, officially proclaiming the Orange County city, just forty-five minutes southwest of Downtown Los Angeles, a "non-sanctuary city." Councilmember Casey Burns articulated the weight of the decision: "We have the right, we have the responsibility to do better. Upholding the U.S. Constitution isn't just some abstract idea." He went further during the council meeting, asserting: "We are going to provide the best safety for our citizens, plain and simple. It's going to be what's best for Huntington Beach. Huntington Beach first."

The phrase "Huntington Beach first" reverberated far beyond the city's borders. It wasn't just local rhetoric but a sharp rebuke of the state's warped priorities, an unapologetic embrace of the "America First" ethos that had redefined national politics and brought renewal to an exhausted country. While Sacramento busied itself with performative legislative battles—mandating gender-neutral toy aisles, funding slave reparations studies in a state that never had slavery, and sanctifying the delta smelt—Huntington Beach focused on essentials: safety, sovereignty, and the rights of its citizens.[13,14] This was the real resistance—not the sanctimonious grandstanding of figures like Newsom and McGuire, but a small city drawing a hard line against the ideological overreach of California's political elite. It was a declaration that its residents mattered more than the approval of the Bay Area-Sacramento power bloc that had long scorned Southern California.

City Attorney Michael Gates reinforced this defiant stance, stating, "In California in particular, fighting crime is difficult enough with the relaxed criminal laws and lack of enforcement. The State should get out of the way of local law enforcement, stop handcuffing our police officers and California's cities, and get back to the business of protecting innocent citizens. Emphatically, the State should not take a position of violating federal immigration laws or encouraging cities to violate federal immigration laws."[15]

The contrast with other jurisdictions was striking. While Huntington Beach prioritized the safety and sovereignty of its citizens, San Diego County doubled down on its sanctuary status in December 2024, and Los Angeles finalized its own sanctuary city policy.[16] In Los Angeles, the rhetoric of officials remained utterly detached from the stark realities voters had expressed in the November election, and from the surging crime that cast a shadow over daily life in the county. Councilmember Hugo Soto-Martinez, who introduced the sanctuary motion in 2023, declared, "We're going to send a very clear message that the city of Los Angeles will not cooperate with ICE in any way. We want people to feel protected and be able to have faith in their government."[17] Protecting Americans, however, appeared nowhere in Soto-Martinez's calculus; his pronouncement reflected the priorities of a state more invested in shielding illegal aliens from Trump than safeguarding its own citizens from cartels. Soto-Martinez himself made it clear: both his parents were illegal aliens, as were many of his constituents.[18] These, then, are the guiding principles of governance in Los Angeles.

Huntington Beach's defiance transcended local politics, signaling a broader shift in California's political landscape. It wasn't just rebellion for rebellion's sake—it was a pragmatic assertion of priorities that Sacramento had long neglected. While the state pursued its ideological agenda, Huntington Beach acted with clarity and focus, asserting its right to self-determination in the face of a failing system. This was a city not only rejecting the hollow policies of the state but also charting a new path forward, one rooted in accountability and tangible results. And as cracks in California's political façade continued to widen, this act of defiance paved the way for another seismic shift: Proposition 36.

Ten years after California voters effectively legalized theft and drug possession with Proposition 47, the public's patience finally snapped, and its sanity was restored. In a decisive rebuke of the state's permissive approach to crime, Proposition 36, officially titled *"Allows Felony Charges and Increases Sentences for Certain Drug and Theft Crimes,"* (a notable contrast from the *"Safe Neighborhoods and Schools Act"* that marketed Proposition 47), passed with overwhelming support, garnering approximately 70.6% of the vote.[19] This landslide marked a dramatic pivot in the state's criminal justice priorities and sent an unmistakable message: Californians were no longer willing to tolerate the unchecked lawlessness Proposition 47 had unleashed.

Proposition 36 reintroduced accountability to crimes that had gone virtually unpunished for a decade, addressing offenses that Californians had come to see as emblematic of the state's decay. Key provisions included:

Repeat Shoplifting: Individuals with two or more prior theft convictions can now face felony charges for thefts under $950, punishable by up to three years in prison.

Organized Theft: Crimes involving three or more individuals committing theft or property damage may result in enhanced felony sentences, targeting the coordinated retail theft rings that have plagued California businesses.

Drug Possession: Possession of certain illegal drugs, including metham-phetamine and fentanyl, can now be charged as a "treatment-mandated felony." Offenders who complete court-ordered rehabilitation may have their charges dismissed; failure to comply could lead to up to three years in prison.

Drug Distribution Resulting in Death: Courts must now warn offend-ers that providing drugs resulting in someone's death could lead to mur-der charges, a sobering acknowledgment of the fentanyl crisis ravaging California communities.

Opposition to Proposition 36 came from predictable quarters. Gavin Newsom and progressive activists argued that the measure would undo years of criminal justice reform and exacerbate systemic inequities. Critics claimed that stricter sentencing could disproportionately impact margin-alized communities and strain California's already overcrowded prisons.[20] But these arguments, once politically effective, fell flat against the back-drop of emboldened theft rings, rampant drug-related deaths, and the visible erosion of public safety that Proposition 47 had enabled.

For voters, Proposition 36 wasn't about political ideology; it was about survival. It repudiated policies that had prioritized ideology over enforce-ment, compassion over consequences, and rhetoric over results. California's streets, once synonymous with opportunity, had become symbols of dys-function, and voters had reached their breaking point. Proposition 36 was their unequivocal response: enough is enough.

The immolation of Proposition 47 was mirrored in the political collapse of California's worst offenders—the Soros-backed rogue prosecutors George Gascón and Pamela Price. Once celebrated as transformative reformers, their tenures instead became synonymous with reckless permissiveness and systemic corruption which plunged millions of Californians into a grim reality imbued with fear and exhaustion. Cloaked in the language of social justice and criminal justice reform, these once-touted "visionaries" instead unleashed chaos, leaving in their wake emboldened criminals, broken com-munities, and the shattered remnants of public trust.

George Gascón's tenure as Los Angeles District Attorney was defined by policies that reframed crime as a societal inequity, dismantling the pillars of public safety in the largest jurisdiction in the United States. Under his watch, violent offenders walked free, organized theft rings flourished, and the law itself seemed to stand trial for daring to exist. His approach rendered victims invisible and emboldened criminals, transforming Los Angeles into a dystopian landscape where streets became battlegrounds and homes targets for an increasingly unchecked criminal underclass. By November 2024, LA residents had reached their breaking point. In a decisive repudiation of his warped policies and ideology, 61% of voters pushed Gascón out of the DA's office.[21] Gascón was ousted, not in a fit of outrage but in weary resignation. The people of Los Angeles were done living in fear, watching a legal system designed to protect them be repurposed into an experiment in ideological indulgence.

Nathan Hochman, a former U.S. Attorney and political independent, emerged as Gascón's successor, marking a sharp departure from the chaos of the preceding years. Hochman, widely regarded as a pragmatic and seasoned prosecutor, eschewed ideological posturing in favor of a straightforward message: "Crime is crime, and criminals should pay." His election signaled a seismic shift in California's directional trend on criminal justice. Voters didn't just reject Gascón's permissive policies; they delivered a resounding mandate to restore accountability in a state where public safety had been sacrificed on the altar of equity. Hochman's landslide victory—winning by a staggering twenty-point margin—was a twenty-seven-point swing from Gascón's 2020 win, underscoring the depth of the electorate's discontent.[22]

The backlash against Gascón was most pronounced in affluent cities like Manhattan Beach and Santa Monica, reliable Democratic strongholds but increasingly terrorized by the waves of criminals emboldened by his policies. In Santa Monica, where Gascón had once enjoyed nearly two-to-one support, voters decisively turned to Hochman. Manhattan Beach delivered an even more scathing rebuke, with Hochman trouncing Gascón by fifty points—a nearly forty-point collapse for Gascón compared to his 2020 performance. These shifts highlighted a glaring disconnect: voters in rich, white, liberal enclaves who had backed Democrats like Kamala Harris at the top of the ticket categorically rejected Gascón's criminal justice policies when faced with their real-world consequences. The result was an eighty-point disparity between support for Harris and Gascón in some areas.[23]

Hochman's victory wasn't just a rebuke of Gascón—it was a referendum on the lunatic policies that, in just four years, had left Los Angeles unsafe and ungovernable. Voters demanded leadership that prioritized their safety over ideological experiments, rejecting a tenure that had turned the law into an accomplice to chaos.

Meanwhile, in Northern California, Alameda County District Attorney Pamela Price faced her own reckoning. Elected in January 2023 as the county's first Black woman district attorney, Price ran on a platform of sweeping progressive reforms, pledging to end the death penalty and prioritize police accountability. But her tenure quickly unraveled. By August 2023, a recall campaign was underway, fueled by growing outrage over her extreme leniency toward crime. Price's policies prioritized violent offenders over victims—including children. She seemed to almost bask in the grateful reception of emboldened criminals pinning for a prosecutorial reprieve granted by "Auntie Pam." During her reign of terror, Price profoundly destabilized the City of Oakland, plunging Alameda County into a hellscape of open-air gun fights and heinous gang violence. By November 2024, 62.9% of voters had had enough, decisively removing her from office.[24]

Price's downfall underscored a shift in the political currents of California. Even in traditionally progressive Alameda County, voters had grown disillusioned with leaders who prioritized abstractions over realities. Her defeat signaled the breaking point for a state worn thin by policies that left victims unprotected and neighborhoods in disarray. The revolt against Price mirrored broader frustrations with the criminal justice reform wave, which had promised equity but instead delivered terror.[25]

The twin collapses of Gascón in Los Angeles and Price in Alameda weren't just about failed leadership; they were the rejection of an entire framework that had dominated California's criminal justice system. Voters, faced with the grim consequences of unchecked crime and declining safety, demanded a reorientation toward governance rooted in practicality and results. These defeats didn't just close the door on two controversial figures—they signaled the collapse of an era in which ideology came first and Californians came last.[26]

Even in San Francisco, the ninth circle of California's progressive damnation, reform shattered leftist entrenchment that November. Daniel Lurie, heir to the Levi Strauss fortune, unseated incumbent mayor London Breed in a race that laid bare the public's exhaustion with a city unraveling under the weight of its own policies.[27] Breed's tenure had become synonymous with dysfunction: sprawling homeless encampments engulfed iconic neighborhoods, open-air drug markets operated unchecked, and residents navigated streets littered with used syringes and human feces. The city's crime rate soared as organized theft and violent assaults became everyday realities. Even for many liberals, Breed's tenure came to embody a government paralyzed by ideology and incapable of addressing the crises it had created.

Lurie's campaign broke through with promises of accountability and pragmatism, presenting him as a reformer untainted by the bureaucratic rot and ideological paralysis that defined Breed's administration.[28] His victory wasn't just a rebuke of her leadership but a dramatic rejection of the political orthodoxy that had governed San Francisco for decades. Even the city that symbolized California's progressive ethos could no longer ignore the demand for competence over ideology.

Lurie's victory reflected a broader reckoning sweeping California, from Pamela Price's recall to the passage of Proposition 36. Californians, worn down by relentless chaos and urban decay, were no longer placated by lofty progressive rhetoric—they demanded tangible action. In an unexpected twist, this mounting discontent extended beyond local and state elections. For the first time, California voters began to reconsider a figure once deemed irreconcilable with the state's politics: Donald Trump.

In 2024, Donald Trump made surprising inroads in California, securing over 6 million votes—74,000 more votes than in 2020—and capturing 38.3% of the statewide vote.[29] Trump improved his performance in forty-five of the state's fifty-eight counties, flipping several that had previously supported Democrats.[30] Meanwhile, Kamala Harris, the sitting vice president and a California native, performed significantly worse than Joe Biden in 2020, losing vote share in all but one of the state's fifty-eight counties. Harris garnered almost 2 million *fewer* votes in California than the 11 million previously claimed by Biden.[31]

Trump's gains were particularly striking in Southern California. In Riverside and San Bernardino counties, he narrowly defeated Harris, winning 49.2% and 49.5% of the vote, respectively, and significantly increasing his margins from 2020. In Imperial County, which shares a border with Mexico and faces acute immigration challenges, Trump achieved an eleven-point swing, flipping the county from blue to red. Even in Los Angeles County, a Democratic stronghold, Trump's vote share rose from 21.4% in 2020 to 31.9% in 2024—marking the first time since 2004 that a Republican surpassed 25% in the county.[32]

Among Hispanic and Asian voters, Trump's appeal gained significant traction. Southeast Los Angeles County, home to a 90% Latino population, saw a dramatic 40% decline in Democratic support since 2016. Trump went from receiving less than 10% of the vote there in 2016 to nearly 30% in 2024, tripling his share and highlighting a seismic shift among working-class voters.[33] In historically reliable Democratic Asian enclaves like Monterey Park and Rosemead, the party's margins eroded by twenty to thirty-five points, reflecting growing frustration over rising costs, public safety concerns, and a sense that Democratic policies no longer addressed their priorities.[34]

This shift was most pronounced in working-class communities grappling with economic hardship and surging crime, where frustration with Democratic leadership ran deep. Huntington Park Mayor Karina Macias described the growing reliance on food stamps among her ethnic constituents and their mounting discontent over the state's failure to provide meaningful relief.[35] A December 2024 *Mother Jones* report, titled "Los Angeles County Shows Why Democrats Lost," captured this sentiment with a strikingly poignant anecdote. In a small shop in Southeast Los Angeles, a Guatemalan shopkeeper lamented the soaring costs of daily life and the disorder overtaking her neighborhood. She spoke wistfully of the relative economic stability during Trump's first term. When asked if she had voted, her quiet reply: "Soy illegal."[36]

Yet this realignment was not universal. In wealthier coastal enclaves like Manhattan Beach, Redondo Beach, and Hermosa Beach, Democrats maintained or even modestly expanded their margins of victory, high-lighting the growing political divide between working-class minorities and affluent white voters. Los Angeles County, once a monolith of progressive dominance, now mirrored a broader national trend: working-class frustration is shifting to the right, while progressive politics finds its safest harbor in the gated affluence of America's elite communities.

Trump's gains exposed widening cracks in California's Democratic stronghold, signaling that Democratic dominance in the state may no longer be guaranteed.[37] Up and down the ballot and across California, the November 2024 election results marked a growing disillusionment with the state's entrenched leadership and progressive policies; in surprising actuality, California stood at the forefront of a national political realignment that, against all odds, had resurrected MAGA.

Donald Trump's second term began with a forceful challenge to California's chronic mismanagement. Among his first priorities was addressing the state's disastrous water policies, which he publicly lambasted for prioritizing rigid, environmental dogma over urgent, practical solutions. He criticized California's longstanding practice of releasing billions of gallons of storm water into the ocean, while Central Valley farms suffered, and cities like Los Angeles faced crippling shortages. The image of dry fire hydrants in the Pacific Palisades during the January fires became a searing indictment of a state that had squandered its resources while deflecting blame onto climate change.[38]

Within hours of his inauguration, Trump ordered federal officials to draft plans to redirect water to California's Central Valley and urban centers. Two days later, he escalated his demands, warning that federal disaster aid could be withheld unless Sacramento committed to overhauling its water policies.[39, 40] This ultimatum sent shockwaves through California's political establishment, challenging decades of entrenched environmental orthodoxy that prioritized fish populations over the safety and livelihoods of millions. By directly confronting these policies, Trump forced state leaders to reckon with the systemic negligence and misplaced priorities that had left California so vulnerable.

Trump's focus extended beyond water management to another crisis that California's leadership had long ignored: the unchecked influence of Mexican drug cartels. By designating these cartels as Foreign Terrorist Organizations, the Trump administration reframed the issue as a national security threat rather than mere criminal activity. This designation unlocked powerful federal tools to dismantle cartel operations, from targeting their financial networks to aggressively combating the fentanyl epidemic that has ravaged California's communities. For a state where sanctuary policies ultimately shield organized crime, the administration's bold declaration marked a seismic shift in restoring the peace, while further exposing the bloody cost of California's permissive and negligent governance.

With former ICE Director Tom Homan as his border czar and Santa Monica native Stephen Miller shaping immigration policy, Trump will intensify federal enforcement against sanctuary cities like Los Angeles, bringing an end to the madness, an end to the unbridled migration treasonously sanctioned by Joe Biden, and which in short order had driven California and the nation into a tailspin of dereliction, misery, and death. California's defiant and criminally-complicit cities would finally face heightened scrutiny measured against the full weight of the federal government and the unshakable resolve of Donald Trump. Indeed, within days of retaking the presidency, federal agents initiated crackdowns on criminal illegal aliens—as promised. The administration even signaled that abuses of birthright citizenship, exploited to bolster California's population, would no longer be treated as an untouchable sacred cow. Finally, the government would treat this lunatic judicial loophole not as an inevitability but as a constitutional corruption demanding reform.

The January fires underscored the urgency of implementing large-scale infrastructure investment in California, and more broadly across the nation; Trump has seized the opportunity to propose transformative solutions that have direct bearing on the disaster in Los Angeles. Early discussions within the Trump team centered on the establishment of a federal sovereign wealth fund, modeled on successful programs in Norway and Singapore. Such a fund could harness public and private capital to invest in long-overdue critical infrastructure projects.[41] For California, this could mean billions of dollars for coastal desalination plants, modern aqueducts, nuclear power plants, and new reservoirs and dams to address the state's perennial gaps in energy resource fulfillment. Trump has also long championed the cause of large-scale urban renewal, a cause that indeed launched his early career amidst the blight of 1970's Manhattan. For MAGA, restoring America's broken cityscapes represents a paramount initiative to herald growth, prestige, and ultimately happiness. One could reasonably presume that the new administration would support a responsible, pro-growth federal incentive regime earmarked for revitalizing urban centers like downtown Los Angeles and San Francisco, which have been so shamefully decimated by rampant and humiliating crime, homelessness, and managerial neglect. America First starts at home.

By January 23, 2025, Trump announced his intent to use an energy emergency declaration to fast-track federal approvals for critical infrastructure, including power stations needed to support artificial intelligence (AI) centers.[42] Applied to California, this framework could bypass the state's infamous regulatory bottlenecks, transforming once-impractical projects into achievable realities under federal oversight.

Early estimates suggest that the fires may have caused an estimated $150 billion in damages, overwhelming insurance companies and escalating rebuilding costs.[43] Yet Trump's streamlined approach may offer a path forward, cutting through the state's regulatory quagmire to accelerate construction. Trump's policies may very well spur a dramatic realignment in California's relationship with the federal government. For decades, and certainly through the Trump years, California cast itself as a self-styled resistance state, defiantly opposing Washington while descending into chaos. This time, however, as Trump benefits from the apogee of his political capital and executive authority, Californians may witness his administration indomitably reversing the state's most toxic elements using federal authority to impose accountability on a state long mired in ideological vanity and corruption. The balance of power shifted decisively in November 2024, finally offering Californians a chance to escape their leaders' failures with a long-overdue lifeline from President Trump.

These and other measures emanating from the administration could represent more than just a temporary response to a sudden disaster by offering a blueprint for reversing a percolating catastrophe imbued in California's decline. By confronting water mismanagement, dismantling sanctuary state policies, and investing in transformative infrastructure via emergency powers—wholly warranted under the circumstances of California's failed state—Trump stands poised to directly challenge and counterbalance structural failures at the root of the state's dysfunction. Whether California's leaders would ultimately accept this lifeline or continue clinging to failed ideologies remains uncertain. But for a state on the brink, the choice is stark: adapt or collapse.

The significance of Kamala Harris's defeat cannot be overstated. It was not just the political demise of an emblematic figure of California's failed experiment; it was the nation's unequivocal rejection of the policies that had left California mired in crime, homelessness, and economic decline. Harris's campaign was less a presidential bid than a referendum on the California model—an attempt to nationalize the identity politics, permissiveness, and hollow moral posturing that had rendered her home state a shadow of its former promise.

California's failures were Harris's failures, inseparable from her political identity. The state she claimed as her legacy had become a grim emblem of ideological excess—a place where public safety, functional infrastructure, and economic mobility were sacrificed at the altar of equity. Her defeat was not just personal; it was systemic, a repudiation of the ethos that governance should be a stage for moral posturing while the foundations of society crumble beneath it. The American people had seen the consequences of this experiment, and they decisively rejected its export.

Harris presented herself as a unifier, a champion of equity and justice. Yet her campaign could not escape the glaring contrast between the rhetoric she espoused and the dystopia she had helped create. Under leaders like Harris, California had devolved into a place where basic governance was treated as an afterthought, and the essentials of civic life—public safety, housing, and economic opportunity—were subordinated to ideological zeal. Her defeat underscored the fundamental disconnect between her promises and the lived realities of those left to navigate the chaos she helped perpetuate.

Trump's victory, by contrast, was not just a rejection of Harris but of the California political model itself. Where Harris symbolized the failures of performance politics, Trump represented a return to first principles: action over rhetoric, accountability over excuses, and pragmatism over ideological dogma. His win was a mandate not only to halt the spread of California's dysfunction but to chart a path of renewal—a blueprint for addressing the deeper structural failures that California's leaders had refused to confront.

As Trump toured the devastation of the January fires, his presence highlighted the stark contrast between his vision and that of his defeated rival. Where Harris and her allies had offered "vibes" and bromide, Trump offered clarity, solutions, and a promise to cut through the bureaucratic paralysis that had left California vulnerable. Standing alongside Gavin Newsom, Trump's message was resolute: federal support would be swift, permitting requirements would be waived, and rebuilding would not be mired in the endless delays that had become synonymous with the state's governance.

Trump's words on the smoldering ruins of California cut through the haze of devastation: "There can be no Golden Age without the Golden State."[44] They were neither an empty platitude nor a fleeting soundbite. They were a challenge—and a reckoning.

For decades, California had sold itself as the vanguard of American progress, a utopia of innovation, equity, and enlightenment. But beneath its glittering façade lay a state rotting from within, undone by the very ideologies it claimed as virtues. The fires that swept through its hills and cities were not an anomaly—they were the final, searing indictment of a leadership that had traded governance for theater, abandoning its people to the chaos of their own neglected systems.

But if California has taught us anything, it is this: collapse is never sudden. It is a slow unraveling, masked by the inertia of past success until the cracks become chasms. The state's failures are not unique; they are the logical endpoint of a governing philosophy that values lies over truth, government over god, image over substance, grievance over governance, equity over morality, and anarchy over accountability. And while California may have led the nation into this abyss, it now stands as a cautionary tale—a living warning of what happens when a society confuses virtue-signaling with virtue itself.

Yet even here in California, second chances are possible. California's unraveling does not preclude its redemption. Fire may reduce a forest to ash, but it also clears the way for new growth. The ruins of this failed state offer the chance for reinvention, not just for California but for the nation as a whole. Redemption, like collapse, is a choice—one that requires the courage to rebuild, not just what has burned, but what has been broken.

Trump's second term is more than a response to California's collapse; it is a litmus test for the nation's future. Will we learn from the failures laid bare in the Golden State, or will we allow their contagion to spread, unchecked and unchallenged? Will we confront the difficult, unglamorous work of governance, or will we continue down the path of ideological indulgence that brought California to its knees?

As the embers of January cooled, one undeniable truth emerged: California is not merely a state—it is a mirror. Its collapse reflects the choices we make as a nation, the values we prioritize, and the lies we are willing to accept. California's fate is America's warning, its ruins a monument to the cost of mistaking ideology for governance. Whether its story ends in redemption or further ruin will depend not on California's leaders but on the collective will of a nation that must decide whether to rebuild or succumb.

The time for illusions has passed. The path forward is ours to chart, but it requires facing the fire, the failures, and the truths we can no longer ignore. California's warning has been delivered. The only question left is whether we will listen.

ENDNOTES

Foreword

1 https://nypost.com/2025/01/14/us-news/drained-la-reservoir-in-worst-fire-ravaged-area-has-repeatedly-needed-repairs/.

2 https://www.firerescue1.com/fire-service-staffing/records-show-lafd-did-not-increase-staffing-engines-before-wildfire?

3 https://ktla.com/news/local-news/why-did-fire-hydrants-go-dry-for-crews-fighting-the-palisades-fire/.

4 https://www.dailymail.co.uk/news/article-14286121/los-angeles-fire-union-chief-department-freddy-escobar.html.

5 https://www.yahoo.com/news/acts-kindness-seen-during-devastating-180014195.html?

6 https://people.com/steve-guttenberg-home-survived-los-angeles-wildfires-8773885?

7 https://www.ft.com/content/af92842a-24f9–4e9f-8332-ee0c17be5a01?

8 https://www.ft.com/content/af92842a-24f9–4e9f-8332-ee0c17be5a01?

9 https://www.enca.com/opinion/inmates-battling-la-wildfires-see-chance-redemption?

10 https://www.pbssocal.org/shows/lost-la/the-devil-wind-a-brief-history-of-the-santa-anas.

11 Ibid.

12 https://www.pbssocal.org/shows/lost-la/the-devil-wind-a-brief-history-of-the-santa-anas.

13 Didion, Joan. "The Santa Ana Winds." Slouching Towards Bethlehem, New York: Farrar, Straus and Giroux, LLC.

14 Ibid.

15 https://www.newsweek.com/controlled-burns-california-forest-management-los-angeles-fires-2012492.

16 https://www.city-journal.org/article/la-wildfires-forest-management-regulatory-reform.

17 https://www.newsweek.com/endangered-plant-pacific-palisades-fire -2016053.

18 https://www.theepochtimes.com/us/three-quarters-of-a-trillion-gallons-of -stormwater-washes-away-annually-in-california-5600490.

19 https://pacinst.org/announcement/new-pacific-institute-report-finds-substantial -opportunity-for-urban-stormwater-capture-to-enhance-water-resilience -in-communities-across-the-united-states/.

20 https://www.turnto23.com/news/state/californias-rain-bounty-slips-into -the-ocean-and-drought-shocked-central-valley-farmers-want-an-explanation.

21 https://www.whitehouse.gov/presidential-actions/2025/01/putting-people -over-fish-stopping-radical-environmentalism-to-provide-water-to-southern -california/.

22 https://nypost.com/2025/01/08/us-news/how-la-ran-out-of-water-in-the -middle-of-the-palisades-fire/.

23 https://www.theguardian.com/us-news/2024/nov/19/klamath-river-dam -removal-salmon.

24 https://www.courthousenews.com/california-completes-largest-dam -removal-in-us-history/.

25 https://lao.ca.gov/Publications/Report/4922.

26 https://apnews.com/article/california-medicaid-expansion-undocumented -immigrants-34d8deb2186e9195b253f499e81a3d77.

27 https://lao.ca.gov/Publications/Report/4885#:~:text=Over%20the%20 past%20three%20budget,due%20to%20their%20immigration%20status.

28 https://www.foxnews.com/politics/california-spent-500m-dei-initiatives -race-equity-fish-nonprofit.

29 https://www.newsweek.com/fact-check-did-california-donate-firefighting -equipment-ukraine-2012160.

30 https://www.kqed.org/science/1994972/forest-service-halts-prescribed -burns-california-worth-risk.

31 https://www.americaunwon.com/p/why-los-angeles-burned?utm_campaign =post&utm_medium=web.

32 https://nypost.com/2025/01/15/us-news/victims-sue-los-angeles -department-of-water-and-power-over-palisades-fire/.

33 https://capitalisminstitute.org/l-a-water-chief-faces-scrutiny-over-offline -reservoir-during-critical-fire-season/.

34 https://nypost.com/2025/01/19/opinion/la-fires-reveal-democrat-run -californias-ridiculous-number-of-catastrophes/.

35 https://nypost.com/2025/01/08/us-news/la-mayor-karen-bass-cut-fire -department-funding-by-17–6m/.

36 https://lafd.org/sites/default/files/pdf_files/LAFD-2023–2026 -STRATEGIC-PLAN-04042023%20.pdf.

37 https://www.nbcnews.com/news/us-news/california-wildfires-what-we
-know-palisades-eaton-los-angeles-rcna188239.

38 Ibid.

39 https://www.cbsnews.com/losangeles/news/palisades-and-eaton-fires-now
-among-most-destructive-wildfires-recorded-in-california-history/.

40 https://www.nbcnews.com/news/us-news/california-wildfires-what-we
-know-victims-killed-rcna188240.

41 https://www.laalmanac.com/fire/fi07.php?

42 https://www.forbes.com/sites/alanohnsman/2025/01/13/la-fires-150
-billion-price-tag/.

43 https://www.nbcnews.com/news/us-news/los-angeles-wildfires-rage-as
-homeowners-battle-insurance-crisis-rcna186783.

44 https://laist.com/news/housing-homelessness/los-angeles-palisades-fire
-housing-rent-price-gouging-law-california-zillow-listing.

45 https://www.instagram.com/la_chron/reel/DEn7pJlylh4/.

46 https://www.latimes.com/california/story/2025–01-13/prosecutors
-looting-arson-charges-los-angeles-fires#:~:text=One%20trio%20of%20
men%20is,Nathan%20Hochman.

47 https://nypost.com/2025/01/19/us-news/2-people-detained-for-using
-firetruck-bought-at-auction-to-impersonate-firefighters-in-pacific-palisades/.

48 https://nypost.com/2025/01/18/us-news/california-firefighters-stop
-alleged-looters-stealing-emmy-award-from-altadena-home-destroyed-by
-eaton-fire/.

49 https://www.cbsnews.com/losangeles/news/santa-monica-declares-local
-state-of-emergency-looks-to-enact-curfew-for-residents/.

50 https://www.latimes.com/california/story/2025–01-09/curfew-national
-guard-crackdown-on-looting-la-fires.

51 https://www.police1.com/arrests-sentencing/up-to-60-suspected-looters
-arrested-in-fire-ravaged-l-a-9-charged-so-far.

52 https://enewspaper.latimes.com/infinity/article_share.aspx?guid=b11c
21f2–1c86–46c3–9969-6b884c55e7aa.

53 https://nypost.com/2025/01/18/us-news/pam-shrivers-tennis-trophies
-stolen-after-evacuating-la-palisades-fire/.

54 https://abc7.com/live-updates/15771235/entry/15797014/.

55 https://www.latimes.com/california/story/2025–01-13/prosecutors-looting
-arson-charges-los-angeles-fires.

56 Ibid.

57 https://www.foxla.com/news/azusa-arson-suspect-arrested-la-wildfires.

58 https://www.latimes.com/california/story/2025–01-10/ventura-county-officials
-kenneth-fire-person-of-interest.

59 https://nypost.com/2025/01/13/us-news/suspect-arrested-with-flame
thrower-near-kenneth-fire-is-an-illegal-immigrant-report/.

60   https://nypost.com/2024/11/19/us-news/la-unanimously-passes-sanctuary
      -city-ordinance-to-protect-migrants-ahead-of-trumps-planned-deportations/.
61   https://nypost.com/2025/01/13/us-news/suspect-arrested-with-flame
      thrower-near-kenneth-fire-is-an-illegal-immigrant-report/.
62   https://www.yahoo.com/news/2-more-firebugs-charged-las-200852542.html.
63   Ibid.
64   https://www.cnn.com/2025/01/21/us/arson-los-angeles-wildfires/index
      .html.
65   https://www.cnn.com/2025/01/21/us/arson-los-angeles-wildfires/index
      .html.
66   https://34c031f8-c9fd-4018–8c5a-4159cdff6b0d-cdn-endpoint.azureedge
      .net/-/media/calfire-website/images—misc/arson-stats_aug-2024.jpg?rev=9
      17125103f2148d9b4c6125ca8cc5fe3&hash=F9E649DF3B383C58B43F
      A5164697221A.
67   https://34c031f8-c9fd-4018–8c5a-4159cdff6b0d-cdn-endpoint.azureedge.
      net/-/media/calfire-website/images/arson-acres-burned-2023.png?rev=6aa3
      554831784fdc8f298d31d4ea3656&hash=949F7CD7173B72BB3840B30
      7F207A68C.

Chapter 1

1   https://www.ppic.org/blog/whos-leaving-california-and-whos-moving-in/.
2   69 Perez, C. A. and Johnson, H. (2024) *How has California's immigrant
      population changed over time?*, *Public Policy Institute of California*. Available
      at: https://www.ppic.org/blog/how-has-californias-immigrant-population
      -changed-over-time/ (Accessed: September 28, 2024).
3   Pelchen, L. (2023) *Why are people leaving California? Stats that may sur-
      prise you*, *Forbes*. Available at: https://www.forbes.com/home-improvement
      /moving-services/california-moving-statistics/ (Accessed: September 28, 2024).
4   Pew Research Center. *Immigration and Political Realignment in the U.S.* 2020
      at: https://www.pewresearch.org/topics/immigration/(Accessed September
      2024).
5   Mayda, A. M., Peri, G. and Steingress, W. (2016) Immigration to the U.S.: A
      problem for the Republicans or the Democrats? Cambridge, MA: National
      Bureau of Economic Research. https://www.nber.org/papers/w21941.
6   Ibid.
7   https://www.forbes.com/sites/navathwal/2016/04/18/what-san-franciscos
      -tech-boom-means-for-bay-area-real-estate.
8   https://www.hoover.org/research/diversity-illegal-immigration.
9   Hanson, V. D. (2020) *California is a cruel medieval state, Tennessee Star*.
      The Tennessee Star. Available at: https://tennesseestar.com/commentary
      /commentary-california-is-a-cruel-medieval-state/admin/2020/03/10
      (Accessed: September 28, 2024).

10   Perez, C. A. and Johnson, H. (2024) *How has California's immigrant popu-lation changed over time?*, *Public Policy Institute of California*. Available at: https://www.ppic.org/blog/how-has-californias-immigrant-population -changed-over-time/ (Accessed: September 28, 2024).

11   *Facts about English learners in California* (no date) *Cde.ca.gov*. Available at: https://www.cde.ca.gov/ds/ad/cefelfacts.asp (Accessed: September 28, 2024).

12   Shelley, S. (2024) "Can California afford health care for undocumented immigrants?," *Los Angeles Daily*, 6 January. Available at: https://www.daily news.com/2024/01/06/can-california-afford-health-care-for-undocumented -immigrants/ (Accessed: September 28, 2024).

13   California Department of Healthcare Services (2024) *Ages 26 through 49 Adult Full Scope Medi-Cal Expansion| En Español*. Available at: https: //www.dhcs.ca.gov/services/medi-cal/eligibility/Pages/Adult-Expansion .aspx (Accessed: September 28, 2024).

14   George Orwell, *1984* (New York: Harcourt Brace Jovanovich, 1949), 220.

15   Johnson, H. and McGhee, E. (2024) *Who's leaving California—and who's moving in?*, *Public Policy Institute of California*. Available at: https://www .ppic.org/blog/whos-leaving-california-and-whos-moving-in/ (Accessed: September 28, 2024).

16   Schrupp, K. (2024) "Outmigration cost California $24B in departed incomes as poorer people move in," *Washington Examiner*, 6 July. Available at: https://www.washingtonexaminer.com/news/3071957/outmigration-cost -california-24b-in-departed-incomes-as-poorer-people-move-in/ (Accessed: September 29, 2024).

17   Schrupp, K. and The Center Square (2024) *California population rises after long slump; immigration offset birth decline, The Center Square*. Available at: https://www.thecentersquare.com/california/article_37faf972–0728-11ef -8f0c-83456341839a.html (Accessed: September 29, 2024).

18   Vranich, J. and Ohanian, L. E. (no date) *Why company headquarters are leaving California in unprecedented numbers, Hoover.org*. Available at: https: //www.hoover.org/sites/default/files/research/docs/21117-Ohanian-Vranich -4_0.pdf (Accessed: September 28, 2024).

19   Pelchen, L. (2023) *Why are people leaving California? Stats that may sur-prise you, Forbes*. Available at: https://www.forbes.com/home-improvement /moving-services/california-moving-statistics/ (Accessed: September 28, 2024).

Chapter 2

1   See "17 gangs targeting Los Angeles' mega-rich," Los Angeles Times (April 12, 2022), available at https://www.latimes.com/california/story/2022–04 -12/17-gangs-targeting-los-angeles-mega-rich; see also "South Los Angeles follow-home robberies: Crime in LA, gangs," ABC7 (date), available at

https://abc7.com/south-los-angeles-follow-home-robberies-crime-in-la
-gangs/11745547/.

2   E.g. 2 arrested in more than 90 car break-ins by Westchester and Playa
del Rey, NBC Los Angeles, Lloyd (April 2024), https://www.nbclosangeles
.com/news/local/2-arrested-in-dozens-of-car-break-ins-in-westchester-and
-playa-del-rey/3395309/.

3   https://xtown.la/2024/01/16/los-angeles-sees-murders-decline-in-2023
-but-property-crime-is-up/.

4   https://xtown.la/2024/01/29/a-closer-look-at-the-327-murders-los-angeles
-suffered-in-2023/.

5   The City of Los Angeles has removed this information from its online public records, and not without controversy. In its place, the City provides a
Maintenance Update and/or "The Page You Requested Cannot be Found."
https://catalog.data.gov/dataset/crime-data-from-2020-to-present.

6   Ibid.

7   Ibid.

8   Ibid.

9   Ibid.

10   Ibid.

11   https://www.fbi.gov/news/press-releases/fbi-releases-2022-crime-in
-the-nation-statistics.

12   https://data-openjustice.doj.ca.gov/sites/default/files/2024–07/Crime%20
In%20CA%202023f.pdf.

13   https://www.statista.com/statistics/191219/reported-violent-crime-rate
-in-the-usa-since-1990.

14   https://data-openjustice.doj.ca.gov/sites/default/files/2024–07/Crime%20
In%20CA%202023f.pdf.

15   https://www.statista.com/statistics/191243/reported-burglary-rate-in
-the-us-since-1990.

16   https://www.statista.com/statistics/191237/reported-property-crime-rate
-in-the-us-since-1990.

17   https://www.statista.com/statistics/191216/reported-motor-vehicle-theft
-rate-in-the-us-since-1990.

18   The City of Los Angeles has removed this information from its online public records, and not without controversy. In its place, the City provides a
Maintenance Update and/or "The Page You Requested Cannot be Found."
https://catalog.data.gov/dataset/crime-data-from-2020-to-present.

Chapter 3

1   https://www.britannica.com/event/Reign-of-Terror.

2   https://soviethistory.msu.edu/1917–2/state-security/state-security-texts
/resolution-on-red-terror.

3 https://academic.oup.com/hwj/article-abstract/doi/10.1093/hwj/dbac017.

4 https://doi.org/10.1093/acrefore/9780190264079.013.650.

5 https://as.nyu.edu/content/dam/nyu-as/ir/documents/Mngomezulu.Sizwebanzi.2016ThesisAward.pdf.

6 https://www.britannica.com/place/Zimbabwe/Rhodesia-and-the-UDI.

7 https://www.accord.org.za/ajcr-issues/farm-attacks-or-white-genocide-interrogating-the-unresolved-land-question-in-south-africa.

Chapter 4

1 https://nlgmass.org/nlg-national-history.

2 https://www.jstor.org/stable/20099137.

3 https://www.newyorker.com/magazine/2021/09/20/the-man-behind-critical-race-theory.

4 https://www.americanbar.org/groups/crsj/resources/human-rights/archive/lesson-critical-race-theory.

5 https://digitalcommons.law.mercer.edu/cgi/viewcontent.cgi?article=3116&context=jour_mlr.

6 https://www.researchgate.net/publication/343113059_Comment_on_An_Empirical_Analysis_of_Racial_Differences_in_Police_Use_of_Force_by_Roland_G_Fryer_Jr.

7 https://www.fbi.gov/news/press-releases/fbi-releases-2023-crime-in-the-nation-statistics.

8 Heather Mac Donald, "The Great Stop-and-Frisk Fraud," *Manhattan Institute*, April 1, 2023, https://manhattan.institute/article/the-great-stop-and-frisk-fraud.

9 Jonah Newman, "Stop-and-Frisk Down 80% in Chicago, but Black and Latinx People Still Hit the Hardest, Judge Finds," The Chicago Reporter, June 15, 2020, https://www.chicagoreporter.com/stop-and-frisk-down-80-in-chicago-but-black-and-latinx-people-still-hit-the-hardest-judge-finds/.

10 Michael Barba, "SF Crime: Police Call Pandemic, Mission District Behind Rise in Crime," *San Francisco Standard*, January 26, 2022, https://sfstandard.com/2022/01/26/sf-crime-police-pandemic-mission-district.

11 Charles Stimson, "Four Reasons for the Crime Increase," The Heritage Foundation, June 29, 2022, https://www.heritage.org/crime-and-justice/commentary/four-reasons-the-crime-increase.

12 Liz Sawyer, "Minneapolis Violent Crimes Soared in 2020 Amid Pandemic, Protests," *Star Tribune*, January 25, 2021, https://www.startribune.com/minneapolis-violent-crimes-soared-in-2020-amid-pandemic-protests/600019989.

13 Dean Moses, "Mayhem in May: NYPD Reports 22% Crime Spike and 73% Shooting Surge," amNewYork, June 2, 2021, https://www.amny.com

/new-york/mayhem-in-may-nypd-reports-22-crime-spike-and-73-shooting
-surge/.

14   Alan Greenblatt, "Cops and the Perils of De-escalation," *Governing*, May 18,
      2021, https://www.governing.com/management-and-administration/cops
      -and-the-perils-of-de-escalation.

15   See generally Penal Code § 1000 (West 2024); Penal Code § 100.36 (West
      2024); Penal Code § 1001.81 (West 2024).

16   Wright, Alex. "Long-Term Recidivism Studies Show High Arrest Rates."
      Prison Legal News, 3 May 2019, https://www.prisonlegalnews.org/news
      /2019/may/3/long-term-recidivism-studies-show-high-arrest-rates/.

17   United States Department of Justice, Bureau of Justice Statistics. 2018
      Update on Prisoner Recidivism: A 9-Year Follow-Up Period (2005–2014).
      May 2018, https://bjs.ojp.gov/library/publications/2018-update-prisoner
      -recidivism-9-year-follow-period-2005–2014.

18   Florida Sentencing and Offender Release Report, "New Study Published
      Regarding Florida's Prisoner Release Reoffender Law," Florida Department
      of Law Enforcement, July 15, 2023, https://www.flsa6.gov/New-study
      -published-regarding-Florida-s-Prisoner-Release-Reoffender-law-1–11806
      .html.

19   California Department of Corrections and Rehabilitation, "Recidivism
      Reports," accessed October 3, 2024, https://www.cdcr.ca.gov/research
      /recidivism-reports/.

20   Travis C. Pratt and Francis T. Cullen, "Assessing Macro-Level Predictors and
      Theories of Crime: A Meta-Analysis," *Journal of Quantitative Criminology* 29,
      no. 2 (2013): 195–236, https://link.springer.com/article/10.1007/s10940
      –012-9166-x.

21   David S. Abrams, "Estimating the Deterrent Effect of Incarceration Using
      Sentencing Enhancements," *National Bureau of Economic Research*, February
      2017, https://www.nber.org/papers/w22648.

22   National Institute of Justice, "Reentry Research at NIJ: Providing Robust
      Evidence for High-Stakes Decision-Making," *National Institute of Justice*,
      June 2022, https://nij.ojp.gov/topics/articles/reentry-research-nij-providing
      -robust-evidence-high-stakes-decision-making.

23   Compare California Judicial Branch, "California Judicial Branch: An
      Overview" (nonpartisan election of judges), available at https://www.courts.
      ca.gov/documents/California_Judicial_Branch.pdf.

24   Brandon Martin and Joseph Hayes, "California's Violent Crime Rate Is
      Diverging from the National Trend," Public Policy Institute of California,
      February 22, 2023, https://www.ppic.org/blog/californias-violent-crime
      -rate-is-diverging-from-the-national-trend/#:~:text=When%20we%20
      look%20at%20county,least%2030%25%20in%2028%20counties.

Chapter 5

1   https://en.wikipedia.org/wiki/Murder_of_Polly_Klaas.
2   https://www.lao.ca.gov/2005/3_strikes/3_strikes_102005.htm.
3   Ibid.
4   Ibid.
5   See generally "Reforming San Francisco's Criminal Justice System," Alameda
    County Probation Department, p. 3 (Believes that mass incarceration is
    due to a "war on crime" and decades of "mass incarceration" of a policy
    agenda in criminal justice reform. Believe that mass incarceration is not
    the reason for lower incarceration rates but aging population, decreased
    alcohol consumption, decreased unemployment, and increased hiring of
    police officers), available at https://probation.acgov.org/probation-assets
    /files/resources-info/Reforming%20San%20Franciscos%20Criminal%20
    Justice%20System-JA4.pdf; see also George Gascón's campaign website,
    "George Gascón's plan to expand diversion, reduce incarceration, and pre-
    vent recidivism in Los Angeles County," available at https://georgegascon
    .org/campaign-news/george-gascons-plan-to-expand-diversion-reduce
    -incarceration-and-prevent-recidivism-in-los-angeles-county/#_ftn
    ref3 (providing information on alternatives to arrest, prosecution, and
    incarceration).

    See "Los Angeles D.A. race could be reshaped by national calls for crim-
    inal justice reform," *Los Angeles Times* (July 1, 2020), available at https:
    //www.latimes.com/california/story/2020–07-01/los-angeles-da-race-could-
    be-reshaped-national-calls-criminal-justice-reform; see also "Amid weeks
    of protest expressing outrage at police brutality, demonstrators target D.A.
    Jackie Lacey," *Los Angeles Times* (June 10, 2020), available at https://www
    .latimes.com/california/story/2020–06-10/amid-weeks-of-protest-expressing
    -outrage-at-police-brutality-demonstrators-target-d-a-jackie-lacey.
6   https://www.cdcr.ca.gov/news/2024/02/13/cdcr-recidivism-report-finds
    -recidivism-rates-drop-2.
7   https://lasd.org/transparency/crimeandarrest/.

Chapter 6

1   Legislative Analyst's Office, "The 2013–14 Budget: Overview of Criminal
    Justice Proposals," February 15, 2013, https://lao.ca.gov/reports/2013/crim
    /criminal-justice-proposals/criminal-justice-proposals-021513.aspx.
2   Magnus Lofstrom and Brandon Martin, "Public Safety Realignment and
    Crime Rates in California," *Public Policy Institute of California*, September
    2015, https://www.ppic.org/publication/public-safety-realignment-and-crime
    -rates-in-california/.
3   California Department of Corrections and Rehabilitation, "2014
    Outcome Evaluation Report," August 2014, https://www.cdcr.ca.gov

/research/wp-content/uploads/sites/174/2019/08/Outcome-Evaluation
-Report-2014.pdf.

4   Paige St. John, "Early Releases Rising: Thousands Are Leaving Prison Under
New Federal Rules," *Los Angeles Times*, July 20, 2015, https://www.latimes
.com/local/crime/la-me-ff-early-release-20150720-story.html.

5   Michael Gomez, "California-Mexico: Ike Souzer and the Murder that Shook
Orange County," *True Crime News*, August 14, 2024, https://truecrime
news.com/2024/08/14/california-mexico-orange-county-ike-souzer-murder
-vandalism-parole-violation/.

6   Orange County District Attorney, "Man Who Stabbed His Mother to Death
at 13 Years Old Indicted on Felony Charges for Manufacturing a Weapon in
Jail," April 20, 2024, https://orangecountyda.org/press/man-who-stabbed
-his-mother-to-death-at-13-years-old-previously-escaped-from-custody
-indicted-on-felony-charges-he-manufactured-a-weapon-in-jail-ike-souzer
-has-violent-history-of-attacking-correct/.

7   Legislative Analyst's Office, "The 2013–14 Budget: Overview of Criminal
Justice Proposals," February 15, 2013, https://lao.ca.gov/reports/2013
/crim/criminal-justice-proposals/criminal-justice-proposals-021513.aspx.

8   Center on Juvenile and Criminal Justice, "Realignment and Recidivism:
Some Key Facts," February 12, 2014, http://www.cjcj.org/news/8113.

9   Douglas Schoen, "Kamala Harris Avoiding Responsibility," The Hill,
March 7, 2024, https://thehill.com/opinion/campaign/4860542-kamala
-harris-avoiding-responsibility/.

10   Mia Bird et al., "The Impact of Proposition 47 on Crime and
Recidivism," Public Policy Institute of California, October 2018, https:
//www.ppic.org/publication/the-impact-of-proposition-47-on-crime-and
-recidivism/#:~:text=While%20the%20reform%20had%20no,residents)
%20compared%20to%20other%20states.

11   Guy Marzorati, "Prop 47's Impact on California's Criminal Justice System,"
KQED News, May 25, 2024, https://www.kqed.org/news/11975692
/prop-47s-impact-on-californias-criminal-justice-system.

12   Staff Report, "U.S. Drug Overdose Deaths Skyrocket," San Francisco
Chronicle, July 15, 2024, https://www.sfchronicle.com/projects/us-drug
-overdose-deaths/.

13   Ibid.

14   Rowena Itchon, "Prop 47 Never Stood a Chance," Pacific Research
Institute, April 5, 2024, https://www.pacificresearch.org/prop-47-never-stood
-a-chance/.

15   Walters, D. (2022) *Tricky measure allows release of violent felons, CalMatters*.
Available at: https://calmatters.org/commentary/2022/12/tricky-measure
-allows-release-of-violent-felons/.

16   California Attorney General's Office, "Props 47 and 57 May Have Led to an Increase in Crime," California City News, March 18, 2022, https://california citynews.org/2022/03/california%E2%80%99s-attorney-general-says -props-47-and-57-may-have-led-increase-crime.html.

17   Rowena Itchon, "Prop 57 Contains a Loophole for Violent Criminals," Pacific Research Institute, July 20, 2024, https://www.pacificresearch.org /prop-57-contains-a-loophole-for-violent-criminals/.

18   Gabriel Dillard, "Sacramento Mass Shooting Suspect Served Less Time Due to Prop 57," GV Wire, April 8, 2024, https://gvwire.com/2022/04/08 /sacramento-mass-shooting-suspect-served-less-time-due-to-prop-57/.

19   Thalia Gonzalez, "How California's Criminal Justice Reform Highlights Racial Disparities," Race and Justice Network, April 20, 2024, https://racism .org/articles/law-and-justice/criminal-justice-and-racism/373-criminal-justice -reform/11138-how-california.

20   Stanford Law School, "The California Racial Justice Act of 2020 Explained," Stanford Law School, April 22, 2024, https://law.stanford.edu/2024/04/22 /the-california-racial-justice-act-of-2020-explained/.

21   Ibid.

22   Staff Report, "Judge Dismisses Special Circumstances in Antioch Murder Case in Wake of Racist Text Scandal," KQED News, May 2, 2024, https: //www.kqed.org/news/11977602/how-the-racial-justice-act-could-shake -up-californias-criminal-court-system.

23   Guy Marzorati, "How the Racial Justice Act Could Shake Up California's Criminal Court System," KQED News, May 25, 2024, https://www.kqed .org/news/11977602/how-the-racial-justice-act-could-shake-up-californias -criminal-court-system.

24   Open Society Foundations, "Racial Justice in the United States," March 1, 2024, https://www.opensocietyfoundations.org/newsroom/racial-justice -in-the-united-states.

25   Open Society Foundations, "Open Society Foundations Announce $220 Million for Building Power in Black Communities," July 13, 2020, https: //www.opensocietyfoundations.org/newsroom/open-society-foundations -announce-220-million-for-building-power-in-black-communities.

26   Jeremy B. White, "Four Wealthy Donors Fuel Overhaul of California's Criminal Justice System," Politico, July 17, 2021, https://www.politico .com/states/california/story/2021/07/17/four-wealthy-donors-fuel-over haul-of-californias-criminal-justice-system-1388261.

27   See AB 3070 (passed 09/2020), available at https://legiscan.com/CA/text/ AB3070/id/2211008 (detailing the purpose of the bill to increase diver- sity in jury selection by prohibiting attorneys from using peremptory chal- lenges based on protected characteristics such as race, ethnicity, gender, sexual orientation, national origin, or religious affiliation); see also "AB

3070 prohibiting attorneys from removing juror may have negative impact, crime victims say," Fox LA (January 2022), available at https://www.foxla .com/news/ab-3070-prohibiting-attorneys-from-removing-juror-may -have-negative-impact-crime-victims-say (reporting on concerns raised by crime victims regarding the potential negative impact of AB 3070, which went into effect in January 2022).

28 See Wilson, David. "Oakland's DA urges more lenient sentences even amid fears over crime." *The Washington Post*, March 20, 2023. https://www.washing tonpost.com/nation/2023/03/20/oakland-prosecutor-crime-prison/.

29 Bill Melugin, "AB 3070 Prohibiting Attorneys from Removing Juror May Have Negative Impact, Crime Victims Say," Fox News Los Angeles, March 18, 2023, https://www.foxla.com/news/ab-3070-prohibiting-attorneys-from -removing-juror-may-have-negative-impact-crime-victims-say.

30 California Code of Civil Procedure, Section 203 (Revised 2020), Senate Bill 310; CA Civ Pro Code § 203 (2023).

Chapter 7

1 https://www.theguardian.com/us-news/article/2024/jul/01/2100-deaths -in-10-years-how-fentanyl-is-devastating-los-angeles-unhoused-community.

2 Los Angeles County, "New Public Health Report Shows Sharp Rise in Mortality Among People Experiencing Homelessness," May 12, 2023, https://lacounty.gov/2023/05/12/new-public-health-report-shows-sharp -rise-in-mortality-among-people-experiencing-homelessness/.

3 Ibid.

4 https://www.latimes.com/california/story/2024–11–21/nearly-half-of-los -angeles-homelessness-budget-went-unspent-controller-finds.

5 https://www.lahsa.org/news?article=927-lahsa-releases-results-of-2023 -greater-los-angeles-homeless-count.

6 https://www.laalmanac.com/social/so14.php?utm.

7 https://www.huduser.gov/portal/sites/default/files/pdf/2023-ahar-part-1. Pdf?utm.

8 https://www.lahsa.org/news?article=944–2023-greater-los-angeles-homeless -count-data&utm.

9 https://www.cato.org/blog/evidence-also-calls-californias-housing-first -homelessness-strategy-question?utm.

10 https://ens.lacity.org/cao/cao_budget_memo/caocao_budget_memo 2925180190_05082024.pdf.

11 https://laist.com/news/housing-homelessness/los-angeles-homeless-services -authority-lahsa-audit-2024-november-county?utm.

12 https://homeless.lacounty.gov/service-providers/.

13 https://da.lacounty.gov/media/news/la-councilman-curren-price-charged -pay-play-scheme?utm.

14 https://www.justice.gov/usao-cdca/pr/former-los-angeles-politician-jose -huizar-sentenced-13-years-federal-prison?utm.

15 https://www.justice.gov/usao-cdca/pr/former-los-angeles-politician-jose -huizar-sentenced-13-years-federal-prison?utm.

16 https://www.nbclosangeles.com/investigations/la-mayor-inside-safe -homeless-housing-program/3281201/?utm.

17 https://www.reuters.com/world/us/cities-crack-down-homeless -la-offers-them-hotel-room-2024–12-13/?utm.

18 https://calmatters.org/housing/homelessness/2024/10/inside-safe/?utm.

19 Office of the Governor, "California Seizes Record 62,000 Pounds of Fentanyl," California Governor's Office, February 27, 2024, https://www.gov .ca.gov/2024/02/27/california-seizes-record-62000-pounds-of-fentanyl/.

20 https://www.fox26houston.com/news/california-seizes-record-62000 -pounds-of-fentanyl?utm_.

21 http://lapublichealth.org/sapc/MDU/SpecialReport/Fentanyl-Overdoses -in-Los-Angeles-County.pdf.

22 https://www.theguardian.com/us-news/article/2024/jul/01/2100-deaths -in-10-years-how-fentanyl-is-devastating-los-angeles-unhoused-community/.

23 Ibid.

24 http://lapublichealth.org/sapc/MDU/SpecialReport/Fentanyl-Overdoses -in-Los-Angeles-County.pdf.

25 https://americafirstpolicy.com/issues/protecting-americas-retailers -from-theft.

26 https://www.latimes.com/california/story/2019–11-14/homeless-housing-poll -opinion.

27 https://www.texastribune.org/2019/07/02/why-homelessness-going -down-houston-dallas/.

Chapter 8

1 See "Sophisticated 'burglary tourists' fly from South America to rob wealthy homes, LAPD says," *Los Angeles Times*, Winton (March 2023), available at https://www.latimes.com/california/story/2024–03-16/los-angeles -police-south-american-crime-tourism.

2 See Winton, "Sophisticated 'burglary tourists' fly from South America to rob wealthy homes, LAPD says" (March 16, 2024), *Los Angeles Times*.

3 See Eight arrested in multimillion-dollar retail theft operation, Los Angeles County sheriff officials say, LA Times, Petersen (May 2024) ("Authorities investigating retail theft refer to people who buy stolen goods and then resell them for a profit as "fences."").

4 Id.; "West LA home hit by smash and grab robbers in broad daylight," Fox 11 Los Angeles (Feb. 2024), available at https://www.foxla.com/news/west -la-home-hit-by-smash-and-grab-robbers-in-broad-daylight (allegedly stole more than $25,000 worth of valuables).

5   "Flocking: Is The New Trend in L.A. Burglaries," Miranda (April 2017),
       available at https://www.mirandarightslawfirm.com/blog/flocking-is-the
       -new-trend-in-l-a-burglaries/#:~:text=It's%20called%20flocking%20because
       %20of,affluent%2Dlooking%20homes%20to%20burglarize ("gang mem-
       bers "flock" to the neighborhoods where residential burglaries provide the
       biggest payoffs").
6   "4 Arrested After Allegedly Being Caught in the Act of 'Knock Knock'
       Burglaries," NBC Los Angeles (October 2019), available at https://www
       .nbclosangeles.com/news/4-arrested-knock-knock-burglary-caught-in-the
       -act/1966634/ ("[the] driver was observed approaching the front door of
       the victim's home, in an apparent 'door knock' tactic. He then returned to
       his Mercedes-Benz and remained seated. Detectives then saw the Chevrolet
       arrive and park nearby, and saw two additional suspects exit that Chevy
       SUV and walk to the rear yard of the victim's property.

       "Shortly thereafter, those two suspects are seen quickly walking out of
       the front door and re-entering their SUV. Both vehicles simultaneously
       pulled away from the victim's residence and left the vicinity.")
7   See "Houston, We Have A Problem: LAPD Nabs 2 Jugging Suspects Who
       Hail From Texas," CBS News (March 2019).

Chapter 9

1   See generally Gang Recruitment Increasing with Younger Kids, Yahoo!
       Finance (Jan. 2024), https://finance.yahoo.com/news/gang-recruitment
       -increasing-younger-kids-153700015.html (stating that children join gangs
       as young as 9 years old; but the average age is 15 years old).
2   See Man, 12-year-old girl arrested for string of armed robberies across
       LA County, CBS News, Fioresi (April 2024), https://www.cbsnews.com
       /losangeles/news/man-12-year-old-girl-arrested-for-string-of-armed
       -robberies-across-la-county/. 18 year old and a 12 year old.
3   Compare PnB Rock: Father and son pair charged with rapper's murder,
       BBC (Sept. 2022), https://www.bbc.com/news/newsbeat-63088361. (He
       was from Philadelphia and the two suspects got away in a getaway car. Child
       was 17 years old.)
4   https://www.sfchronicle.com/bayarea/article/oakland-robberies-crime
       -18116829.php.
5   https://www.nbclosangeles.com/news/local/2-arrested-in-dozens-of-car-break
       -ins-in-westchester-and-playa-del-rey/3395309/.
6   https://data-openjustice.doj.ca.gov/sites/default/files/2023-06
       /Juvenile%20Justice%20In%20CA%202022f.pdf.
7   See generally Gang Recruitment Increasing with Younger Kids, Yahoo!
       Finance (Jan. 2024), https://finance.yahoo.com/news/gang-recruitment
       -increasing-younger-kids-153700015.html (stating that children join gangs
       as young as 9 years old; but the average age is 15 years old).

8 See Special Directive 20–09, Youth Justice, from Los Angeles District Attorney George Gascón to all Deputy District Attorneys (Dec. 7, 2020), https://da.lacounty.gov/sites/default/files/pdf/SPECIAL-DIRECTIVE-20–09.pdf.

9 Proposition 57 Public Safety and Rehabilitation Act of 2016.

10 https://data-openjustice.doj.ca.gov/sites/default/files/2023–06/Juvenile%20Justice%20In%20CA%202022f.pdf.

11 https://data-openjustice.doj.ca.gov/sites/default/files/2024–07/Juvenile%20Justice%20In%20CA%202023f.pdf.

12 https://data-openjustice.doj.ca.gov/sites/default/files/2024–07/Crime%20In%20CA%202023f.pdf.

13 https://data-openjustice.doj.ca.gov/sites/default/files/2023–06/Crime%20In%20CA%202022f.pdf.

14 https://www.cbsnews.com/sanfrancisco/news/oakland-crime-data-2023-complex-picture-property-crimes-homicides/

15 https://data-openjustice.doj.ca.gov/sites/default/files/2023–06/Juvenile%20Justice%20In%20CA%202022f.pdf.

16 Ibid.

17 Ibid.

18 Ibid.

Chapter 10

1 http://www.lacp.org/2010-Articles-Main/041510-GangCrimes-LACounty-SomeFacts.htm.

2 https://www.nationalguard.mil/About-the-Guard/Army-National-Guard/#:~:text=Today%2C%20with%20more%20than%20325%2C000,America%20at%20home%20and%20overseas.

3 https://www.justice.gov/archive/ndic/pubs23/23937/dtos.htm.

4 https://www.theguardian.com/world/2007/mar/18/usa.paulharris.

5 https://tarrant.tx.networkofcare.org/kids/library/article.aspx?id=1813.

6 https://nationalgangcenter.ojp.gov/survey-analysis/measuring-the-extent-of-gang-problems?utm.

7 https://oag.ca.gov/system/files/media/ag-annual-report-calgang-2023.pdf.

8 See U.S. Department of Justice, Crips and Bloods: An Informational Guide for the Investigator (1988), available at https://www.ojp.gov/ncjrs/virtual-library/abstracts/crips-and-bloods-informational-guide-investigator#:~:text=The%20Crips%20and%20Bloods%20are,than%20they%20had%20ever%20known (stating that the large sums of money produced from criminal activity by gangs gives them their power and influence).

9 https://www.ppic.org/wp-content/uploads/jtf-prison-population-jtf.pdf.

10 https://www.cdcr.ca.gov/research/wp-content/uploads/sites/174/2024/01/Fall-2023-Population-Projections-Publication.pdf.

11 See generally Center for Urban Research, "Population Change: Urban Regions Beyond NYC," available at https://www.urbanresearchmaps.org /plurality/othercitymaps.htm#tabs-1a.

12 See *Washington Post*, Foster-Frau, "In Black-Led Compton, a Latino majority fights for political power" (May 2023), available at https://www .washingtonpost.com/nation/2023/05/15/compton-latinos-black-political -power/ (stating that in the 1990s the population in Compton was 74% Black, now its nearly 70% Latino).

13 See generally *Los Angeles Times*, Ormseth, "Crackdown on Harbor-area gangs reveals ties to Mexican Mafia" (May 2023), available at https://www .latimes.com/california/story/2023–05-17/crackdown-on-harbor-area -gangs-reveals-ties-to-mexican-mafia; The Daily Beast, Ferranti, "The Mexican Mafia Is the Daddy of All Street Gangs" (Apr. 2017), available at https://www .thedailybeast.com/the-mexican-mafia-is-the-daddy-of-all-street-gangs.

14 See Department of Justice Archives, National Drug Intelligence Center, "Attorney General's Report to Congress on the Growth of Violent Street Gangs in Suburban Areas" (April 2008), available at https://www.justice .gov/archive/ndic/pubs27/27612/gang.htm.

15 Southern Poverty Law Center, Mock, "Latino Gang Members in Southern California Terrorizing and Killing Blacks" (Jan. 2007), available at https: //www.splcenter.org/fighting-hate/intelligence-report/2007/latino-gang- members-southern-california-are-terrorizing-and-killing-blacks (the racial hatred among Mexican Mafia Leaders is due to a long-standing race war between the Mexican Mafia and the Black Guerilla family, a rival African-American prison gang that has lead to the Mexican Mafia issuing a "green light"on all blacks).

Chapter 11

1 See Scott Marcano, The World's Most Dangerous Drug Cartel is a Fortune 500 Company (July 2016), LinkedIn Article, https://www.linkedin.com/pulse /worlds-most-dangerous-drug-cartel-fortune-500-company-scott-marcano/.

2 https://www.cato.org/testimony/cost-border-crisis.

3 See generally Dezenski, Sessions: many unaccompanied minors are 'wolves in sheep's clothing', Politico (Sept. 2017), https://www.politico.com /story/2017/09/21/jeff-sessions-border-unaccompanied-minors-wolves -242991.

4 Verza, "Over 2,000 migrants kidnapped in Mexico last year," AP News (May 2023), available at https://apnews.com/article/mexico-migrants-gangs -kidnappings-900d889c38aebd5e6daa35a4456f4a5a.

5 https://schoolsforchiapas.org/global-diaspora-of-mexican-drug-trafficking/.

6 https://www.cbp.gov/newsroom/local-media-release/man-made -smuggling-tunnel-discovered-border.

7 https://www.npr.org/2022/02/19/1081948884/mexican-drug-cartels-are-getting-into-the-avocado-and-lime-business.

8 https://www.geopoliticalmonitor.com/why-mexican-cyber-cartels-threaten-u-s-national-security/?utm.

9 Ibid.

10 https://www.theguardian.com/world/2020/dec/07/mexico-cartels-drugs-spying-corruption?utm.

11 https://www.brookings.edu/articles/mexican-cartels-are-providing-covid-19-assistance-why-thats-not-surprising/?utm.

12 https://www.e-ir.info/2011/12/16/the-rise-of-the-la-familia-michoacana-the-impact-of-structural-adjustment-policies-on-state-institutions-and-the-agriculture-sector/?utm.

13 https://www.cbsnews.com/news/narco-sub-cocaine-intercepted-pacific-ocean-mexican-navy/.

14 https://edition.cnn.com/2012/01/15/world/mexico-drug-war-essay/index.html.

15 https://homeland.house.gov/2023/07/19/chairman-green-every-dollar-the-cartels-rake-in-comes-at-the-cost-of-an-american-life-or-livelihood/#:~:text=Cartels%20have%20made%20a%20record,sold%20for%20%2410%2D%2430.

16 https://www.cfr.org/backgrounder/mexicos-long-war-drugs-crime-and-cartels.

17 https://www.washingtonpost.com/graphics/2020/world/mexico-losing-control/mexico-disappeared-drug-war/.

18 https://apnews.com/article/mexico-migrants-cartels-smuggling-chiapas-us-border-67d4851eefa60981bceb772bf26d7204.

19 LA County, "Los Angeles County's Efforts to End the Commercial Sexual Exploitation of Children and Youth: Human Trafficking," available at https://lacounty.gov/residents/public-safety/human-trafficking/ (describing over the last decade a significant amount of time, energy, and resources have gone to address human trafficking in LA).

20 https://bjs.ojp.gov/library/publications/human-trafficking-data-collection-activities-2024?utm.

21 https://nypost.com/2024/08/21/us-news/biden-harris-admin-loses-track-of-320000-migrant-children/?utm.

22 https://deliverfund.org/blog/facts-about-human-trafficking-in-united-states/?utm.

23 https://www.reuters.com/world/we-bought-everything-needed-make-fentanyl-3600-2024-07-25/?utm.

24 https://www.unodc.org/pdf/WDR_2006/wdr2006_chap5_cocaine.pdf.

25 https://www.justice.gov/archive/ndic/pubs/654/meth.htm.

26   Congressional Research Service, "Mexico's Drug Cartels and Their Impact on U.S. National Security," February 10, 2023, https://crsreports.congress .gov/product/pdf/R/R41576.

27   Global Guardian, "Risk Map: Mexico 2024," *Global Guardian*, April 2024, https://www.globalguardian.com/newsroom/risk-map-mexico.

28   Knowledge@Wharton, "Drug Trafficking, Violence, and Mexico's Economic Future," *Wharton School of the University of Pennsylvania*, March 2024, https://knowledge.wharton.upenn.edu/article/drug-trafficking-violence -and-mexicos-economic-future/.

29   Ibid.

30   Congressional Research Service, "Mexico's Drug Cartels and Their Impact on U.S. National Security," February 10, 2023, https://crsreports.congress .gov/product/pdf/R/R41576.

31   https://www.reuters.com/investigates/special-report/mexico-drugs -remittances/.

Chapter 12

1   https://www.nytimes.com/1977/02/19/archives/aztec-sacrifices-laid-to -hunger-not-just-religion.html.

2   https://www.bbc.com/culture/article/20150227-a-place-for-human-sacrifices.

3   https://www.eluniversal.com.mx/english/sacred-religious-and-cannibalistic -origins-pozole/#:~:text=Its%20name%20derives%20from%20the,What %20is%20your%20favorite%20pozole?

4   https://www.gutenberg.org/files/42661/42661-h/42661-h.html.

5   https://study.com/learn/lesson/aztec-god-xipe-totec-rituals-symbolism .html#:~:text=The%20Aztecs%20performed%20several%20rituals,in%20 a%20massive%20gladiatorial%20contest.

6   https://www.historyonthenet.com/aztec-warriors-the-flower-wars.

7   Díaz del Castillo, B., Burke, J., & Humphrey, T. (2012). The true history of the conquest of New Spain.

8   Ibid.

9   Freidel, David: and Schele, Linda (1992). *A Forest of Kings: the Untold Story of the Ancient Maya.*

10   Ibid.

11   Ibid.

12   Herschel Smith, "Sicario: Human Sacrifice to Santa Muerte," The Captain's Journal, October 21, 2018, https://www.captainsjournal.com/2018/10/21 /sicario-human-sacrifice-to-santa-muerte/.

13   E. B. Tylor, *Primitive Culture* (Murray, London, 1871), explores the devel- opment of human societies through the concept of cultural evolution, emphasizing the transition from "primitive" to more complex social struc- tures. Tylor introduced the idea of animism as the earliest form of religion,

framing it as a key element in understanding the progression of human thought and societal development within anthropology.

14 Tylor, E. B. (1889). *Primitive culture: Researches into the development of mythology, philosophy, religion, language, art and custom* (3rd American from 2nd English ed.). Henry Holt and Company. https://doi.org/10.1037/12987-000.

15 Bronislaw Malinowski, *A Scientific Theory of Culture* (1944), argues for a functionalist approach in anthropology, where cultural practices and institutions are seen as adaptive responses to the basic needs of individuals within a society. Malinowski's emphasis on fieldwork and his theory of functionalism significantly influenced the development of social anthropology, situating culture as a dynamic system fulfilling biological and psychological needs.

16 Bourdieu, P. (2003). "Symbolic Violence" in Beyond French Feminisms, edited by R. Célestin, E. DalMolin, and I. de Courtivron. Published by Palgrave Macmillan, New York.

17 Ralph Grillo, *Anthropologies of the Present: Postmodernity and Ethnographic Practice* (2011), discusses the symbolic nature of violence, particularly in the context of terror tactics such as beheadings and public dismemberments. Grillo highlights how these acts serve dual functions, instilling fear and asserting power through symbolic gestures, reflecting both the psychological and political dimensions of violence in various societies.

18 Payne, Stanley G. "A History of Fascism, 1914–1945." University of Wisconsin Press, 1996.; Payne's analysis of fascism provides a framework for understanding how cultural atavism surfaces during periods of sociopolitical crisis.

19 Juergensmeyer, Mark. "Terror in the Mind of God: The Global Rise of Religious Violence." University of California Press, 2003; This book explores the role of religious and cultural atavism in contemporary violence, providing a broader context for understanding cartel violence.

20 Valdez, J. (2010). The deadly consequences: How violence shapes drug trafficking in Mexico. University of Texas Press.

21 This practice mirrors historical acts of political control and terror, as seen in ancient Roman and medieval displays of executed bodies, which served to project authority and instill fear (Foucault, 1977). Similarly, cartels employ these tactics as a reaction to modern instability, reviving ancient methods of reinforcing social order through fear (Grillo, 2011; Campbell, 2009). These acts reflect sociological theories of power and discipline, as explored by Michel Foucault in *Discipline and Punish,* where public executions and displays were intended to reinforce the authority of the state through symbolic violence.

22 The rise of Mexican drug cartels is intertwined with a period of intense political corruption, economic inequality, and social unrest during the

late 20th century. According to Campbell (2009), these conditions, combined with weak state institutions and the collapse of the PRI's political dominance, created a fertile environment for the cartels to gain power. Widespread poverty and lack of government accountability further exacerbated the violence, contributing to a pervasive sense of lawlessness. Campbell notes that this environment allowed criminal organizations to flourish, exploiting the instability to control lucrative drug trade routes. Campbell, H. (2009). *Drug War Zone: Frontline Dispatches from the Streets of El Paso and Juárez.* University of Texas Press.

23 https://www.taylorfrancis.com/chapters/edit/10.4324/9780429431517–5 /preconquest-consciousness-richard-sorenson.

24 Rod Dreher, "Santa Muerte: The Spiritual Realities of the Drug War," The American Conservative, July 15, 2019, https://www.theamerican conservative.com/santa-muerte-the-spiritual-realities-of-the-drug-war/; see also Parker Asmann, "Narco Culture and Mexico's Drug Gangs," InSight Crime, November 8, 2019, https://insightcrime.org/news/analysis /narco-culture-and-mexico-s-drug-gangs/.

25 Joshua J. McElwee, "Narco Cultura Explores Meaning of the War on Drugs," National Catholic Reporter, February 21, 2020, https://www .ncronline.org/blogs/ncr-today/narco-cultura-explores-meaning-war-drugs.

26 Grillo, Ioan. "El Narco: Inside Mexico's Criminal Insurgency." Bloomsbury Press, 2011; This book provides a detailed account of the operations and cultural underpinnings of Mexican drug cartels.

27 Almonte, R. (n.d.). Santa Muerte and the rise of narco saints. Stars Insider. Retrieved from starsinsider.com.

28 John P. Sullivan, "El Centro Field Note No. 1: Ciudad Juárez Prison Interview on Sicario Human Sacrifice and Santa Muerte," Small Wars Journal, March 2020, https://smallwarsjournal.com/jrnl/art/el-centro-field -note-no-1-ciudad-juarez-prison-interview-sicario-human-sacrifice-santa.

29 Federal Bureau of Investigation, "Santa Muerte-Inspired and Ritualistic Killings," FBI Law Enforcement Bulletin, September 2020, https://leb.fbi .gov/articles/featured-articles/santa-muerte-inspired-and-ritualistic-killings.

30 Robert McCoppin, "Santa Muerte Defendants in Court in Chicago," *Chicago Tribune*, May 9, 2017, https://www.chicagotribune.com/news /breaking/ct-santa-muerte-defendants-20170509-story.html.

31 Joshua Rhett Miller, "Religious Saints of Murderers, Outlaws Worshiped by Cartels," *New York Post*, December 21, 2021, https://nypost.com/2021/12 /21/religious-saints-of-murders-outlaws-worshiped-by-cartels/.

32 Varese, Federico. "Mafias on the Move: How Organized Crime Conquers New Territories." Princeton University Press, 2011; Varese's analysis of how different organized crime groups expand and maintain their influence provides valuable comparative insights.

33 Bowden, Mark. "Killing Pablo: The Hunt for the World's Greatest Outlaw." Atlantic Monthly Press, 2001. Bowden's work on the Colombian cartels highlights the differences in operational strategies compared to Mexican cartels.

Chapter 13

1 https://constitution.congress.gov/browse/essay/artIII-S3-C1–4 /ALDE_00013527/#:~:text=Article%20III%2C%20Section%20 3%2C%20Clause,on%20Confession%20in%20open%20Court.

2 https://www.law.cornell.edu/constitution-conan/article-3/section-3/clause -1/treason-clause-doctrine-and-practice.

3 Sanford Levinson, *Framed: America's 51 Constitutions and the Crisis of Governance* (Oxford University Press, 2012). Levinson explores the evolving interpretation of constitutional provisions, advocating for a flexible approach that can be applied to modern security issues, including non-military threats; Robert Natelson, *The Original Constitution: What It Actually Said and Meant* (Tenth Amendment Center, 2011). Natelson discusses the historical context and broad application of constitutional guarantees, which could extend to contemporary issues like illegal immigration; Justice Clarence Thomas, *Arizona v. United States*, 567 U.S. 387 (2012), concurring opinion. Justice Thomas reflects on the importance of state sovereignty and the federal government's duty to protect states from both external and internal threats under the Guarantee Clause.

4 *New York v. United States*, 505 U.S. 144 (1992).

5 https://www.myfloridalegal.com/newsrelease/ag-moody-wins-major -immigration-case?utm.

6 https://crsreports.congress.gov/product/pdf/R/R43708?utm.

7 Anderson, J. H. (2023) *Impeachable?*, *City Journal*. Available at: https: //www.city-journal.org/article/bidens-border-policy-is-an-impeachable -offense (Accessed: October 1, 2024).

8 *Arizona v. United States*, 567 U.S. 387 (2012).

9 Ibid.

10 *Texas v. Biden*, No. 21–10806 (5th Cir. 2021).

11 https://www.senate.gov/about/origins-foundations/senate-and-constitution /constitution.htm#a4_sec4.

12 https://uscode.house.gov/view.xhtml?req=(title:8%20section:1231%20 edition:prelim)

13 https://www.law.cornell.edu/uscode/text/8/1231.

14 https://judiciary.house.gov/sites/evo-subsites/republicans-judiciary.house .gov/files/evo-media-document/scott-testimony.pdf.

15 https://homeland.house.gov/wp-content/uploads/2024/09/September -2024-Border-Report.pdf.

16   https://www.perseus.tufts.edu/hopper/text?doc=Perseus%3Atext%3A1999.
     02.0019%3Atext%3DCatil.%3Aspeech%3D1%3Achapter%3D1.

17   https://www.yorku.ca/comninel/courses/3025pdf/Locke.pdf.

18   https://winstonchurchill.hillsdale.edu/english-speaking-peoples5
     -charles-civil-war/.

19   https://winstonchurchill.hillsdale.edu/english-speaking-peoples5-charles
     -civil-war/.

20   https://origin-rh.web.fordham.edu/halsall/mod/1791burke.asp.

21   https://archive.org/details/in.ernet.dli.2015.184486.

22   https://www.senate.gov/about/powers-procedures/impeachment/impeachment
     -johnson.htm.

Chapter 14

1   https://franpritchett.com/00islamlinks/txt_jinnah_lahore_1940.html.

2   See https://www.redcross.org.uk/stories/our-movement/our-history/india
     -partition-the-red-cross-response-to-the-refugee-crisis; see also, https://www
     .1947partitionarchive.org/collections/.

3   https://www.sciencespo.fr/mass-violence-war-massacre-resistance/en/document
     /mass-crimes-under-stalin-1930–1953.html?

4   https://www.rfa.org/english/news/uyghur/settlers-04132020172143.html?

5   https://www.statista.com/statistics/886209/foreigner-numbers-germany/.

6   https://www.legislation.gov.uk/ukpga/2003/21/section/127?

7   Orwell, George. *Politics and the English Language.* Horizon, vol. 13, no.
     76, April 1946, pp. 252–265. The Orwell Foundation, https://www.orwell
     foundation.com/the-orwell-foundation/orwell/essays-and-other-works
     /politics-and-the-english-language/.

8   See https://www.ijesd.org/papers/29-D438.pdf; see also, https://www.pewre
     search.org/religion/2017/11/29/europes-growing-muslim-population/?

9   https://www.cfr.org/report/venezuelan-refugee-crisis.

10   https://www.icc-cpi.int/sites/default/files/2024–05/Rome-Statute-eng.pdf?

11   https://www.un.org/en/genocideprevention/documents/atrocity-crimes
     /Doc.1_Convention%20on%20the%20Prevention%20and%20Punishment
     %20of%20the%20Crime%20of%20Genocide.pdf.

12   https://constitution.congress.gov/constitution/article-4/.

13   https://www.ppic.org/publication/immigrants-in-california/?

14   https://en.wikisource.org/wiki/California_Proposition_187_(1994).

15   https://leginfo.legislature.ca.gov/faces/billNavClient.xhtml?bill_id=2011
     20120AB131.

16   https://leginfo.legislature.ca.gov/faces/billNavClient.xhtml?bill_id=2013
     20140AB4.

17   https://www.aclusocal.org/en/know-your-rights/california-values-act-sb-54.

18   https://oag.ca.gov/news/press-releases/attorney-general-kamala-d-harris
-urges-us-senate-oppose-immigration-legislation.

Chapter 15

1   https://www.foxnews.com/politics/illegal-immigrants-biden-admin
-amount-greater-population-36-states.
2   https://www.history.com/topics/immigration/immigration-united-states
-timeline.
3   https://www.oxfordacademic.com/book/9780195325416.
4   https://www.gutenberg.org/files/25717/25717-h/25717-h.htm.
5   https://www.worldhistory.org/Chang%27an/.
6   https://www.britannica.com/summary/An-Lushan.
7   https://turkishstudies.net/economy?makale_id=46455&mod=makale
_ing_ozet.
8   https://www.bbc.com/news/world-europe-45269764.
9   https://www.brookings.edu/articles/understanding-urban-riots-in-france/.
10   https://www.npr.org/2023/06/30/1185394143/france-teen-police
-shooting-protests-nahel.
11   https://ctc.westpoint.edu/al-qaidas-involvement-in-britains-homegrown
-terrorist-plots/.
12   https://data.worldbank.org/indicator/NY.GDP.MKTP.CD?utm.
13   https://www.fairus.org/issue/publications-resources/fiscal-burden-illegal
-immigration-united-states-taxpayers-2023.
14   Ibid.
15   https://www.fairus.org/issue/publications-resources/fiscal-burden
-illegal-immigration-united-states-taxpayers-2023.
16   https://www.texaspolicy.com/trump-can-fix-the-illegal-immigration-crisis-
and-make-them-pay-for-it-too/.
17   Federation for American Immigration Reform, "Fiscal Burden of Illegal
Immigration on United States Taxpayers 2023," FAIR, June 2023,
https://www.fairus.org/issue/publications-resources/fiscal-burden-illegal
-immigration-united-states-taxpayers-2023.
18   https://www.fairus.org/issue/publications-resources/fiscal-burden
-illegal-immigration-united-states-taxpayers-2023.
19   Ibid.
20   Federation for American Immigration Reform, "Los Angeles Mayor Says
Sanctuary Designation Not an Invitation for Illegal Immigration," FAIR,
September 2023, https://www.fairus.org/legislation/state-and-local/los-angeles
-mayor-says-sanctuary-designation-not-invitation-illegal.
21   https://www.hks.harvard.edu/publications/wage-impact-marielitos
-reappraisal-0.

22 California Department of Water Resources, "Water Use and Efficiency Program," April 2023, https://water.ca.gov/Programs/Water-Use-And-Efficiency.

23 South Coast Air Quality Management District, "2022 Air Quality Management Plan," November 2022, http://www.aqmd.gov/docs/default-source/clean-air-plans/air-quality-management-plans/2022-air-quality-management-plan/final-2022-aqmp.pdf.

24 Texas A&M University, "Congestion Data," Texas A&M Transportation Institute, January 2023, https://mobility.tamu.edu/umr/congestion-data/.

25 Steven A. Camarota, "The Cost of Illegal Immigration to United States Taxpayers," Center for Immigration Studies, June 2023, https://cis.org/Report/Cost-Illegal-Immigration-United-States-Taxpayers.

26 Arizona Department of Water Resources, "Biennial Report 2018–2020," Arizona Department of Water Resources, February 2021, https://new.azwater.gov/sites/default/files/media/Biennial_Report_2018_2020.pdf.

27 https://cis.org/Oped/Immigrants-already-tip-scales-US-elections-without-even-voting.

28 https://www.americanimmigrationcouncil.org/research/immigrants-in-california.

29 https://www.lausd.org/cms/lib/CA01000043/Centricity/Domain/468/2022–2023%20TDemo.pdf.

30 https://www.uscis.gov/military/naturalization-through-military-service.

31 https://www.pewresearch.org/social-trends/2015/05/12/english-proficiency-on-the-rise-among-latinos/.

32 https://encyclopedia.1914–1918-online.net/article/nationalities-austria-hungary/.

33 https://www.icty.org/en/about/what-former-yugoslavia/conflicts.

34 22 CFR § 40.21—Crimes Involving Moral Turpitude and Controlled Substance Violators.

35 See *Los Angeles Times*, Drugs, Deportation and You: A Los Angeles Case Study (Apr. 10, 2015), https://www.latimes.com/local/politics/la-me-pol-drugs-deportation-20150410-story.html.

36 Faira, "Los Angeles doesn't want to prosecute criminals if they are illegal immigrants," *Washington Examiner* (Dec. 2022), https://www.washingtonexaminer.com/opinion/2324598/los-angeles-doesnt-want-to-prosecute-criminals-if-they-are-illegal-immigrants/ (according to the policy, "All charging determinations shall be undertaken with the goal of avoiding or mitigating the adverse immigration consequences of a decision.").

37 See U.S. Immigration and Customs Enforcement, NYC Sanctuary Policies Continue to Shield Criminal Aliens (Jan. 2020), https://www.ice.gov/news/releases/nyc-sanctuary-policies-continue-shield-criminal-aliens.

38 See generally Hersher, Rebecca. "Los Angeles Officials To ICE: Stop Identifying Yourselves As Police." NPR, February 24, 2017, available at

https://www.npr.org/sections/thetwo-way/2017/02/24/517041101/los
-angeles-officials-to-ice-stop-identifying-yourselves-as-police.

39   https://www.breitbart.com/immigration/2024/01/15/l-a-police-department
-wants-to-give-badges-and-guns-to-illegal-aliens/

Chapter 16

1   *Justice for Sale: How George Soros Put Radical Prosecutors in Power*, Law
Enforcement Legal Defense Fund, June 2022, https://www.policedefense
.org/leldf-justice-for-sale/.

2   Ibid.

3   Moore, M., Menezes, R. and Queally, J. (2020) "L.A. County district attorney
race: Who are the top donors?," *The Los Angeles Times*, 1 October. Available
at: https://www.latimes.com/projects/la-district-attorney-race-top-donors.

4   Schwager, Jack D. (1992). *The New Market Wizards: Conversations with
America's Top Traders*. HarperCollins Publishers.

5   Soros, George. *The Alchemy of Finance*. Wiley, 1987.

6   Weiss, S. (2020) "Feel unsafe in NYC? You can hire a personal bodyguard
on demand," *New York Post*, 26 October. Available at: https://nypost
.com/2020/10/26/feel-unsafe-in-nyc-you-can-hire-a-personal-bodyguard
-on-demand.

7   Zilber, A. (2023) "eBay founder gives nearly $2M to defund police— while
funding private security startup," *New York Post*, 26 May. Available at:
https://nypost.com/2023/05/26/ebay-founder-pierre-omidyar-gives-nearly
-2m-to-defund-police/ (Accessed: September 25, 2024).

8   *Justice for Sale: How George Soros Put Radical Prosecutors in Power*, (June
2022) Law Enforcement Legal Defense Fund, June 2022, https://www.police
defense.org/leldf-justice-for-sale/.

9   Stimson, C. (January 2023) *The Soros Rogue Prosecutor Movement
and the Insurance Industry*, The Heritage Foundation. Available at:
https://www.heritage.org/crime-and-justice/lecture/the-soros-rogue
-prosecutor-movement-and-the-insurance-industry/.

10   *Los Angeles County Sherriff's Department Crime Statistics by Department 2022
vs 2023* (2023). Available at: https://lasd.org/wp-content/uploads/2024/03
/Transparency_Crime_and_Arrest_2023_Department.pdf.

11   *Los Angeles County Sherriff's Department Crime Statistics by Department 2021
vs. 2022* (2022). Available at: https://lasd.org/wp-content/uploads/2023/01
/Transparency_DEPARTMENT-CurrentMonth-YTD_012623–1.pdf.

12   *LAPD statistics show increase in violent crimes and robberies compared to last
year* (2024) *ABC7 Los Angeles*. Available at: https://abc7.com/lapd-reports
-increase-in-violent-crimes-robberies-compared-to-2023/14577521
(Accessed: September 26, 2024).

13 Buckley, T. (2024) *DA Gascon's 'lower crime' claims false—state stats show increases, Californiaglobe.com*. Available at: https://californiaglobe.com/fr /da-gascons-lower-crime-claims-false-state-stats-show-increases/.

14 *LAPD statistics show increase in violent crimes and robberies compared to last year* (2024) *ABC7 Los Angeles*. Available at: https://abc7.com/lapd-reports -increase-in-violent-crimes-robberies-compared-to-2023/14577521 /(Accessed: September 26, 2024).

15 Swan, R. (2024) "'Pure fear': Violent crime in Oakland rose 21% last year. Residents worry it will define the city," *The San Francisco Chronicle*, 25 January. Available at: https://www.sfchronicle.com/crime/article/oakland -violent-crime-robbery-18615820.php.

16 See "Los Angeles D.A. race could be reshaped by national calls for criminal justice reform," *Los Angeles Times* (July 1, 2020), available at https: //www.latimes.com/california/story/2020–07-01/los-angeles-da-race-could -be-reshaped-national-calls-criminal-justice-reform; see also "Amid weeks of protest expressing outrage at police brutality, demonstrators target D.A. Jackie Lacey," *Los Angeles Times* (June 10, 2020), available at https://www .latimes.com/california/story/2020–06-10/amid-weeks-of-protest-expressing -outrage-at-police-brutality-demonstrators-target-d-a-jackie-lacey.

17 See generally Wilson, "LA's Soros-Backed DA Sitting on 10,000 Cases," The Washington Free Beacon (May 2023), https://freebeacon.com/democrats /las-soros-backed-da-sitting-on-10000-cases/ (stating that one of several progressive prosecutors funded by billionaire George Soros).

18 See LinkedIn, George Gascón, available at https://www.linkedin.com/in /george-gasc%C3%B3n-b3440745/details/experience/ (listing Gascón's experience, including 28 years as Assistant Chief of Police LAPD, Chief of Police in Mesa and San Francisco for a total of 5 years, 8 years as a District Attorney in San Francisco, and 1 year as a Justice reform advocate at Summit before taking the position at LA in 2020).

19 *Los Angeles County Sherriff's Department Crime Statistics by Department 2021 vs. 2022* (2022). Available at: https://lasd.org/wp-content/uploads/2023/01 /Transparency_DEPARTMENT-CurrentMonth-YTD_012623–1.pdf.

20 *District attorney George Gascón issues statement on money bail* (no date) *Lacounty.gov*. Available at: https://da.lacounty.gov/media/news/district-attorney -george-gascon-issues-statement-money-bail (Accessed: October 3, 2024).

21 Santi Ruiz, "L.A.'s Soros-Backed DA Sitting on 10,000 Cases," The Washington Free Beacon, January 15, 2024, https://freebeacon.com /democrats/las-soros-backed-da-sitting-on-10000-cases/.

22 Stoltze, F. (2021) *Gang, gun charges plummet under DA gascón, sparking debate over justice and safety, LAist*. Available at: https://laist.com/news /criminal-justice/gang-gun-charges-plummet-under-da-gascon-sparking -debate-over-justice-and-safety (Accessed: September 26, 2024).

23   See generally "Gascon pressed at Los Angeles County DA debate over lax policies on gang-related crime enhancements," Fox LA (date), available at https://www.foxla.com/news/gascon-pressed-at-los-angeles-county-da-debate-over-lax-policies-on-gang-related-crime-enhancements (discussing lax policies on gang-related crime enhancements).

24   422 See Right Choice Law, "Enhancement—Gang," available at https://www.fredthia.com/criminaldefense/enhancements/gang-enhancement/#:~:text=Penal%20Code%20section%20186.22%2C%20also,conduct%E2%80%9D%20by%20other%20gang%20members; see also Cal. Pen. Code § 186.2(d) (defining "Criminal Profiteering activity"), available at https://casetext.com/statute/california-codes/california-penal-code/part-1-of-crimes-and-punishments/title-7-of-crimes-against-public-justice/chapter-9-criminal-profiteering/section-1862-definitions.

       See Gorin, "What is a PC 1275 Hold?" (Nov. 2023), available at https://www.egattorneys.com/pc-1275-hold.

       See Los Angeles County District Attorney's Office, January 5, 2021, "District Attorney George Gascon Issues Statement on Money Bail," available at https://da.lacounty.gov/media/news/district-attorney-george-gascon-issues-statement-money-bail. (quoting "money bail is as unjust as it is unsafe.")

25   "Why DA Gascon reversed decades of parole policy to support release in most cases," LAist, available at https://laist.com/news/criminal-justice/why-da-gascon-reversed-decades-of-parole-policy-to-support-release-in-most-cases.

       "Recall and Resentencing," California Department of Corrections and Rehabilitation, available at https://www.cdcr.ca.gov/family-resources/recall-resentencing/.

       See "George Gascon packing Los Angeles DA office with former public defenders: sources," *New York Post* (October 20, 2023), available at https://nypost.com/2023/10/20/george-gascon-packing-los-angeles-da-office-with-former-public-defenders-sources/.

26   LAist, DA Gascon's Push For Shorter Prison Terms Runs Into Resistance From Judges, Prosecutors (Stolze) (Dec. 2020), https://laist.com/news/da-gascons-push-for-shorter-prison-terms-runs-into-resistance-from-judges-prosecutors.

27   See Special Directive 20–09, Youth Justice, from Los Angeles District Attorney George Gascón to all Deputy District Attorneys (Dec. 7, 2020), https://da.lacounty.gov/sites/default/files/pdf/SPECIAL-DIRECTIVE-20–09.pdf.

28   District Attorney Gascón Addresses Police Accountability on the 2nd Anniversary of George Floyd's Death (Santiago), Los Angeles County District Attorney's Office Press Release, May 25, 2022, https://da.lacounty.gov/media/news/district-attorney-gasc-n-addresses-police-accountability-2nd-anniversary-george-floyd-s.

29   See *The New York Times*, He's Remaking Criminal Justice in L.A. But How Far Is Too Far? (Bazelon & Medina) (Nov. 2021), https://www.nytimes .com/2021/11/17/magazine/george-gascon-los-angeles.html (noting that he had never tired a case in court).

30   Marks, M. (no date) *Los Angeles DA George Gascon's ignites more controversy with chief of staff appointment, Californiaglobe.com*. Available at: https://californiaglobe.com/fr/los-angeles-da-george-gascons-ignites-more -controversy-with-chief-of-staff-appointment/ (Accessed: September 30, 2024).

31   Williams, M. (2023) "Woke LA DA George Gascon's new chief of staff is proud former LOOTER who wants to abolish prisons and defund 'barbarian' police: Backed ransacking of shops during 2020 BLM riots," *Daily Mail*, 16 December. Available at: https://www.dailymail.co.uk/news/article -12871841/LA-DA-George-Gascons-chief-staff-Tiffiny-Blacknell-riots .html (Accessed: September 30, 2024).

32   Melugin, B. (2020b) *Gascón adviser accused of offering "sweetheart" deal to gang murder suspect behind back of prosecutor, FOX 11 Los Angeles*. Available at: https://www.foxla.com/news/gascon-adviser-accused-of-offering-swee theart-deal-to-gang-murder-suspect-behind-back-of-prosecutor (Accessed: September 30, 2024).

33   See LA Association of Assistant Police Officers, (Dec. 2023) Controversial Chief of Staff Selection Amplifies Criticism of DA Gascon's Leadership, https://laapoa.com/2023/12/controversial-chief-of-staff-selection-amplifies -criticism-of-da-gascons-leadership/ (she was a rioter).

34   Compare/See YouTube video: Shirt is Police are trained to Kill Us, https://www.youtube.com/watch?v=ywFl9602fK0; Fox 11 DA candidate calls on Gascon to fire Chief of Staff.

35   Spiegelman, I. (2022) "Trans Child Molester Tried as Minor by D.A. Gascón Charged with Murder," *Los Angeles Magazine*, 11 May. Available at: https://lamag.com/news/trans-child-molester-tried-as-minor-by-d-a-gascon -charged-with-murder.

36   Ibid.

37   Hernandez, M. (2022) "California child molester sentenced to two years in juvenile facility," *New York Post*, 27 January. Available at: https://nypost.com/2022/01/27/hannah-tubbs-sentenced-to-california-juvenile -detention-facility.

38   *Gascon acknowledges sentence not adequate for convicted child sex abuser Hannah Tubbs* (2022) *CBS Los Angeles*. Available at: https://www.cbsnews .com/losangeles/news/la-da-george-gascon-acknowledges-sentence-not -adequate-for-convicted-child-sex-abuser-hannah-tubbs.

39   Ibid.

40   *Woman sentenced to juvenile custody in LA county charged in Kern county murder* (2022) *NBC Southern California*. Available at: https://www

.nbclosangeles.com/news/local/hannah-tubbs-murder-charge-kern-county
-robbery-juvenile-case-george-gascon/2890931/ (Accessed: September 25,
2024).

41 See generally Office of Governor Gavin Newsom, "Governor Newsom
Deploys California Highway Patrol to Oakland and East Bay, Launches
Law Enforcement Surge Operations" (February 6, 2024), https://www.gov
.ca.gov/2024/02/06/chp-surge-east-bay/ (violent crime rose 21%, robbery
increased 38%, and vehicle theft increased 45%; while crime has decreased
around California, Crime in Oakland are doing the opposite).

42 See generally Hill, Fox News, "Alameda County DA Pamela Price facing
recall as special election looms: The 'people have spoken'" (May 2024),
https://www.foxnews.com/media/alameda-county-da-pamela-price-recall
-special-election-looms-people-spoken (stating far-left Alameda County
District Attorney Pamela Price, a Soros-funded DA).

43 Accord Noyes, ABC 7 News, "EXCLUSIVE: Inside Alameda Co. DA Pamela
Price's closed-door meeting; I-Team obtains recordings" (March 2023),
https://abc7news.com/alameda-county-district-attorney-pamela-price
-oakland-arena-closed-door-meeting/13060331/ (stating she has gotten rid
of more than 20 experienced prosecutors, 6 still on administrative leave); see
also Hill, Fox News, May 2024.

44 Barnard, C. (2023) *Jasper Wu: Suspects charged in I-880 freeway shooting death
of toddler now eligible for parole*, ABC7 San Francisco. Available at: https:
//abc7news.com/jasper-wu-suspects-parole-oakland-freeway-shooting
-ivory-bevins-trevor-green-johnny-jackson/13360364.

45 *2 suspects in fatal shooting of Jasper Wu face murder charges with gang enhancements* (2023) *CBS San Francisco*. Available at: https://www.cbsnews.com
/sanfrancisco/news/2-suspects-in-fatal-shooting-of-jasper-wu-face-murder
-charges-with-gang-enhancements.

46 Raguso, E. (2023) *Jasper Wu murder suspects now face less time, DA decides*,
The Berkeley Scanner. Available at: https://www.berkeleyscanner.com/2023
/06/08/courts/jasper-wu-murder-suspects-face-less-time-pamela-price
/ (Accessed: September 25, 2024).

47 Ibid.

48 *Pamela's 10-point platform* (no date) *Pamela Price for Alameda County District
Attorney*. Available at: https://www.pamelaprice4da.com/platform?ref=berkeley
scanner.com.

49 "Two Torrance police officers charged in connection with death of
Christopher Deandre Mitchell," Los Angeles County District Attorney's
Office (date), available at https://da.lacounty.gov/media/news/two-torrance
-police-officers-charged-connection-death-christopher-deandre-mitchell.

50 See "Jury awards L.A. prosecutor $1.5 million in retaliation suit against
D.A. George Gascon," *Los Angeles Times* (March 6, 2023), available at https:

//www.latimes.com/california/story/2023–03-06/jury-awards-l-a-prosecutor
-1–5-million-in-retaliation-suit-against-d-a-george-gascon; see also "George
Gascon's illegal retaliation costs continue to add up," Association of Deputy
District Attorney (March 8, 2023), available at https://www.laadda
.com/2023/03/08/george-gascons-illegal-retaliation-costs-continue-to-add
-up/; c.f. "LA County settles with veteran prosecutor after FOX 11 report
details allegations of Gascon retaliation," Fox LA, available at https://www
.foxla.com/news/la-county-settles-with-veteran-prosecutor-after-fox-11-report
-details-allegations-of-gascon-retaliation; c.f. "Gascon loses retaliation case,"
Yahoo News, available at https://news.yahoo.com/gasc-n-loses-retaliation
-case-011938480.html.

51 California Globe, "Too bad there isn't a three-strikes law for DAs: Gascon
goes 0 for 2," available at https://californiaglobe.com/fr/too-bad-there-isnt
-a-three-strikes-law-for-das-gascon-goes-0-for-2/ (providing details of the
retaliation case against District Attorney George Gascon, including the shift
of one of his deputies from a lead juvenile prosecutor position to the parole
department).

52 See "Prosecutors' union files unfair labor practices complaint against
Gascon," Daily News (February 27, 2024), available at https://www.daily
news.com/2024/02/27/prosecutors-union-files-unfair-labor-practices
-complaint-against-gascon. *More than a dozen, prosecutors have sued
Gascón, alleging they faced retaliation and demotion and, in some cases,
were denied promotions for defying his controversial sentencing directives).
This does not bode well for either Gascon or the Los Angeles taxpayer as
the district attorney face 16 more similar lawsuits plus another 11 separate
civil service actions, (after 2 already). The number is 2.3 not 2.4; see also
"George Gascon's illegal retaliation costs continue to add up," Association of
Deputy District Attorney (March 8, 2023), available at https://www.laadda
.com/2023/03/08/george-gascons-illegal-retaliation-costs-continue-to-add
-up/ (reporting that the costs of illegal retaliation by George Gascon amount
to $2.5 million).

Chapter 17

1 See "Los Angeles D.A. race could be reshaped by national calls for criminal justice reform," *Los Angeles Times* (July 1, 2020), available at https:
//www.latimes.com/california/story/2020–07-01/los-angeles-da-race
-could-be-reshaped-national-calls-criminal-justice-reform; see also "Amid
weeks of protest expressing outrage at police brutality, demonstrators target
D.A. Jackie Lacey," *Los Angeles Times* (June 10, 2020), available at https:
//www.latimes.com/california/story/2020–06-10/amid-weeks-of-protest
-expressing-outrage-at-police-brutality-demonstrators-target-d-a-jackie-lacey.

2   See "Los Angeles D.A. race could be reshaped by national calls for crim-
     inal justice reform," *Los Angeles Times* (July 1, 2020), available at https:
     //www.latimes.com/california/story/2020–07-01/los-angeles-da-race-could
     -be-reshaped-national-calls-criminal-justice-reform; see also "Amid weeks
     of protest expressing outrage at police brutality, demonstrators target D.A.
     Jackie Lacey," *Los Angeles Times* (June 10, 2020), available at https://www
     .latimes.com/california/story/2020–06-10/amid-weeks-of-protest-expressing
     -outrage-at-police-brutality-demonstrators-target-d-a-jackie-lacey.

3   Sean Kinney, "What Really Impacts Morale in Policing?" Police1,
     September 18, 2023, https://www.police1.com/chiefs-sheriffs/articles/what
     -really-impacts-morale-in-policing-N2BXxCUe0iedEF23/.

4   See Fichera, "Posts distort California bill allowing non-citizen police officers"
     (Apr. 2022), AP News, available at https://apnews.com/article/fact-checking
     -046640064186 (stating that the bill would allow non-citizens who are
     authorized to work in U.S. to become police officers).

5   Anna Giaritelli, "Kamala Harris Finally Comments on Jussie Smollett after
     'Modern-Day Lynching' Reaction to Alleged MAGA Attack," Washington
     Examiner, March 5, 2020, https://www.washingtonexaminer.com/news
     /1590536/kamala-harris-finally-comments-on-jussie-smollett-after-modern
     -day-lynching-reaction-to-alleged-maga-attack/.

6   Louise Hall, "Kamala Harris's Role as California's Top Cop under Scrutiny,"
     The Independent, August 15, 2020, https://www.independent.co.uk/news
     /world/americas/us-election/kamala-harris-police-biden-vp-pick-california
     -senate-a9662801.html.

7   Christopher Cadelago, "Kamala Harris's California Record in the
     Spotlight as She Eyes a Political Future," Politico, July 19, 2024,
     https://www.politico.com/news/2024/07/19/kamala-harris-california
     -record-political-future-00169103.

8   Louise Hall, "Kamala Harris's Role as California's Top Cop under Scrutiny,"
     The Independent, August 15, 2020, https://www.independent.co.uk/news
     /world/americas/us-election/kamala-harris-police-biden-vp-pick-california
     -senate-a9662801.html.

9   Andrew Buncombe, "Biden Delivers Speech in the Wake of George Floyd
     Verdict," The Independent, April 21, 2021, https://www.independent.co
     .uk/news/world/americas/us-politics/biden-speech-today-george-floyd-verdict
     -b1834840.html.

10   Joshua Rhett Miller, "Kamala Harris Blasted for Praising BLM as 'Essential
     and Brilliant' Amid Violence," *New York Post*, September 26, 2020, https:
     //nypost.com/2020/09/26/kamala-harris-blasted-for-praising-blm-as
     -essential-and-brilliant-amid-violence/.

11   Bill Melugin, "Kamala Harris Supported BLM Protests in Louisville," Fox
     News, September 18, 2020, https://www.foxnews.com/politics/kamala
     -harris-blm-protests-louisville.

12   Michael Scherer, "Kamala Harris Tweeted Support for Bail Fund, Which Didn't Just Assist Protestors," *Washington Post*, September 3, 2020, https://www.washingtonpost.com/politics/2020/09/03/kamala-harris-tweeted-support-bail-fund-money-didnt-just-assist-protestors/.

13   Lyden, T. (2020) *Minnesota nonprofit with $35M bails out those accused of violent crimes*, FOX 9 Minneapolis-St. Paul. Available at: https://www.fox9.com/news/minnesota-nonprofit-with-35m-bails-out-those-accused-of-violent-crimes=.

14   Kamala Harris, Interview on Defund the Police Movement, June 2020, YouTube video, 15:47, https://www.youtube.com/watch?v=3OWiRuJgtVE.

15   Steakin, W. and Charalambous, P. (2024) *Harris, in 2020, said "we have to redirect resources" from police, ABC News*. Available at: https://abcnews.go.com/US/harris-2020-redirect-resources-police/story?id=112378103.

16   Staff Report, "Kamala Harris Praised Defund the Police Movement in June 2020 Radio Interview," KION 546, July 26, 2024, https://kion546.com/politics/cnn-us-politics/2024/07/26/kamala-harris-praised-defund-the-police-movement-in-june-2020-radio-interview-2/.

17   https://www.cnn.com/2024/07/26/politics/kfile-kamala-harris-praised-defund-the-police-movement-in-june-2020/index.html.

18   https://www.congress.gov/bill/117th-congress/house-bill/1280/cosponsors.

19   https://www.congress.gov/bill/117th-congress/house-bill/1280.

20   See generally "LA County DA George Gascón in the hot seat at candidates' debate," LAist (date), available at https://laist.com/news/politics/la-county-da-george-gascon-in-the-hot-seat-at-candidates-debate (stating morale at an all-time low and internal strife within the DA's office).

21   "Roughly 120 prosecutors have left since Gascon took office, has led caseloads to balloon," *Los Angeles Times* (May 3, 2022), available at https://www.latimes.com/california/story/2022–05-03/la-da-internal-strife#:~:text=Roughly%20120%20prosecutors%20have%20left,has%20led%20caseloads%20to%20balloon (detailing the departure of prosecutors from the DA's office and some caseloads have tripled or doubled since resignations and COVID backlogs).

22   Greg Friese, "What Officers Said Were the Biggest Challenges of 2023," Police1, January 15, 2024, https://www.police1.com/year-in-review/what-officers-said-were-the-biggest-challenges-of-2023.

23   Bill Melugin, "California Police Unions Blast WalletHub's Ranking of the State as Top for Police Officers," Police1, September 5, 2024, https://www.police1.com/police-recruiting/california-police-unions-blast-wallethubs-ranking-of-the-state-as-top-for-police-officers/.

24   Ibid.

25   See generally "Rodney King: 'How many more years do I have to live through this history repeating itself?'" The Guardian (March 2, 2021), available at https://www.theguardian.com/us-news/2021/mar/02/rodney-king-lapd-police-30-years-later.

26　See "LASD employees are now mirroring LA County demographics," Los Angeles County Sheriff's Department (date), available at https://lasd.org /lasd-employees-are-now-mirroring-la-county-demographics/ (providing statistics on the demographics of LASD personnel in 2020: 68% LASD were minorities, 18.3% were females; 52.5% were Hispanics).

27　See generally ABC7, Bass says city trying to grow LAPD after years of shrinking Force, Haskell (Dec. 2023), https://abc7.com/lapd-mayor-karen -bass-police-chief-michel-moore/14151750/ (reporting a lack of resources for Health and Human Services has now forced law enforcement to deal with the ills of society such as substance abuse which they are not equipped to take on).

28　See Police 1, "California police unions blast WalletHub's ranking of the state as top for police officers" (May 2024), available at https://www.police1 .com/police-recruiting/california-police-unions-blast-wallethubs-ranking -of-the-state-as-top-for-police-officers (stating that historic low police staffing has led to dangerous safety situations, mandatory overtime that equate to low officer morale)

　　Leonard, "LAPD moves to accommodate new DACA who can't personally own guns" (Dec 2023), available at https://www.nbclosangeles.com /investigations/lapd-daca-officers-guns/3288740/.

29　https://da.lacounty.gov/sites/default/files/pdf/JSID_OIS_10_2019 _Mitchell.pdf.

30　Staff Report, "Torrance Officers Plead Not Guilty to Manslaughter in 2018 Fatal Shooting," MyNewsLA, April 17, 2023, https://mynewsla.com /crime/2023/04/17/torrance-officers-plead-not-guilty-to-manslaughter-in -2018-fatal-shooting-2/.

31　Staff Report, "Torrance Police Officers Charged with Manslaughter in 2018 Shooting," California City News, April 17, 2023, https://www.california citynews.org/2023/04/torrance-police-officers-charged-manslaughter -2018-shooting.html.

32　https://www.nbclosangeles.com/news/local/el-monte-police-officers-killed -justin-flores-criminal-history-da-george-gascon/2917215/

33　https://abc7.com/george-gascn-district-attoreny-el-monte-officers-killed -investigation-motel/11985492/

34　https://www.nbclosangeles.com/news/local/el-monte-officers-murdered -alleged-killer-on-probation-for-illegal-gun/2917849/

35　Staff Report, "Mother of Slain El Monte Officer Blames DA Gascon for Son's Death," NBC Los Angeles, October 5, 2023, https://www.nbclosangeles .com/news/local/mother-of-slain-el-monte-officer-blames-da-gascon-for -sons-death/2918755/.

36　See AP News, Wife says she tried to warn before deadly shooting, (Dazio) (June 2022), https://apnews.com/article/politics-california-los-angeles-gun -violence-shootings-e31f94e01b224ea436ef3a676d304ee0.

37 Staff Report, "Mother of Slain El Monte Officer Blames DA Gascon for Son's Death," NBC Los Angeles, October 5, 2023, https://www.nbclosangeles .com/news/local/mother-of-slain-el-monte-officer-blames-da-gascon-for -sons-death/2918755/.

38 https://abc7.com/el-monte-police-sergeant-george-gascon/12506627/.

Chapter 18

1 Alana Goodman, "Kamala Harris launched political career with $120K 'patronage' job from boyfriend Willie Brown," Washington Examiner, January 28, 2019.

2 William Cummings, "Former S.F. Mayor Willie Brown Writes about Dating Kamala Harris, Appointing her to Posts," USA Today, January 27, 2019.

3 Scott Bland, "'Ruthless': How Kamala Harris Won Her First Race," Politico Magazine, January 25, 2019.

4 Phillip Matier AR. "Board appointee's credentials," *San Francisco Chronicle*, Jan 25 1999.

5 Rachel Gordon and Lance Williams, "S.F. Airport Contractors Gave Big to Brown," *San Francisco Chronicle*, August 6, 2000.

6 Chuck Finnie and LW, "Brown friends thrive as lobbyists 3 associates of mayor earned $2.6 million in fees for contacting S.F. officials during his term," *San Francisco Examiner*. Oct 20 1999.

7 Dan Levy, "Mission Bay Deal Makes History," *San Francisco Chronicle*, November 17, 1998.

8 Ibid.

9 Dan Levy, "Catellus to Develop Mission Bay," *San Francisco Chronicle*, November 17, 1998.

10 Phillip Matier AR. "Mayor's friends keep on getting jobs at S.F. parking dept." *San Francisco Chronicle*. March 7, 1997.

11 Elizabeth Lesly Stevens, "The Power Broker," Washington Monthly, July 7, 2012, https://washingtonmonthly.com/2012/07/07/the-power-broker/.

12 Phil Matier and Andrew Ross, "San Francisco's Political Landscape," *San Francisco Chronicle*, as referenced in Randy Shaw, "Phil Matier's Powerful Impact," Beyond Chron, accessed September 2024, https://beyondchron .org/phil-matiers-powerful-impact.

13 Ibid.

14 Rachel Gordon, "Kamala Harris Campaign," Politico Magazine, January 25, 2019, https://www.politico.com/magazine/story/2019/01/25/kamala-harris -2020-senate-profile-224174.

15 Lance Williams, "Political Dynamics in San Francisco," *San Francisco Chronicle*, 2004, as cited in Beyond Chron, https://beyondchron.org.

16 Peter Schweizer, Profiles in Corruption: Abuse of Power by America's Progressive Elite (New York: HarperCollins, 2020).

17   Lance Williams, "Guest Speaker: Investigative Reporting on Political Influence
      in San Francisco," San Francisco State University, March 29, 2022, https:
      //journalism.sfsu.edu/guest-speaker-lance-williams-investigative-reporter.

18   Murphy, Dean E. "Killing of Officer Stirs Death Penalty Debate." *The New
      York Times*, 12 June 2004, https://www.nytimes.com/2004/06/12/us/killing
      -of-officer-stirs-death-penalty-debate.html.

19   *California Department of Justice*, "Statistical Overview of Drug Prosecutions:
      2004–2011," State Reports.

20   Steve Cooley quoted in *Los Angeles Times*, "Criticism of Harris's Performance
      as District Attorney," March 2011.

21   Kranish, Michael. "Crime Lab Scandal Rocked Kamala Harris's Term as San
      Francisco District Attorney." *The Washington Post*, March 6, 2019.

22   *"Undocumented immigrant not A criminal," California attorney general says*
      (2015) *CBS Los Angeles*. Available at: https://www.cbsnews.com/losangeles
      /news/undocumented-immigrant-not-a-criminal-california-attorney-general
      -says/.

23   McGreevy, Patrick. "Budget cuts threaten state's anti-drug units." *Los Angeles
      Times*, May 20, 2011.

24   York, Anthony. "Brown unveils plan to slash state budget deficit." *Los Angeles
      Times*, January 10, 2011.

25   "Police chiefs: State budget cuts could endanger public safety." *The
      Sacramento Bee*, June 1, 2011.

26   Cooley, Steve. Interview with *Los Angeles Daily News*, February 17, 2016.

27   "2011 National Drug Threat Assessment." *U.S. Department of Justice*,
      National Drug Intelligence Center, August 2011.

28   "State budget cuts to eliminate Bureau of Narcotic Enforcement." *KCRA
      News*, June 2, 2011.

29   "California DOJ to eliminate anti-drug task force." *The Sacramento Bee*,
      June 3, 2011.

30   Rodriguez, Joe. "Central Valley battles meth resurgence as funding drops."
      Fresno Bee, March 15, 2015.

31   "Crime in California 2015." California Department of Justice, 2016.

32   "Public Safety Realignment Fact Sheet." California State Sheriffs'
      Association, 2013.

33   Brandon Martin and Magnus Lofstrom, "Realignment and Crime in
      California," Public Policy Institute of California, September 2015, https:
      //www.ppic.org/publication/realignment-and-crime-in-california/.

34   California District Attorneys Association, "Realignment," April 14, 2015,
      https://www.cdaa.org/realignment.

35   https://www.lapd.com/blog/ab-109-delivers-insult-justice.

36   Los Angeles Police Department, "Public Safety Realignment Impact," February
      17, 2018, https://www.lapd.com/article/public-safety-realignment-impact.

37 Bearstar Strategies, "Case Study: California Ballot Measures," June 14, 2024, https://bearstarstrategies.com/case_study/ballot-measures/.

38 Editorial Board, "California's Criminal Justice Disaster," *Sacramento Bee*, February 20, 2015, https://www.sacbee.com/opinion/editorials/article1049 2628.html.

39 Adiel Kaplan, "Kamala Harris's Criminal Justice Policies in California," NBC News, September 26, 2024, https://www.nbcnews.com/investigations /kamala-harris-criminal-justice-policies-california-rcna163518.

40 Bird, Mia, et al. "The Impact of Proposition 47 on Crime and Recidivism." Public Policy Institute of California, May 2018.

41 Cooley, Steve. "Opinion: Prop. 47 and Realignment have made us less safe." *Los Angeles Daily News*, February 17, 2016.

42 Libby Denkmann, "Moving Further to the Right: Sanchez Accuses Harris," LAist, October 20, 2020, https://laist.com/news/kpcc-archive /moving-further-to-the-right-sanchez-accuses-harris.

43 Editorial Board, "The Kamala Harris Problem," *Sacramento Bee*, October 10, 2024, https://www.sacbee.com/news/politics-government/capitol-alert /article105877347.html.

44 "California U.S. Senate Election Results." *The New York Times*, November 8, 2016.

45 Buchanan, Larry, et al. "Black Lives Matter May Be the Largest Movement in U.S. History." *The New York Times*, July 3, 2020.

46 Wagner, John. "Kamala Harris releases criminal justice reform plan emphasizing executive actions." *The Washington Post*, September 9, 2019.

47 S.756 - First Step Act of 2018." *Congress.gov*, 115th Congress (2017–2018).

48 Nelson, Steven. "Kamala Harris Touts Criminal Justice Reform Record Despite Criticism." *U.S. News & World Report*, January 21, 2019.

49 Fuller, Thomas. "As Attorney General, Kamala Harris's Office Tried to Keep Inmates Locked Up for Cheap Labor." *The New York Times*, February 11, 2019.

50 Lopez, German. "Kamala Harris's criminal justice record scrutinized as she joins Biden ticket." *Vox*, August 11, 2020.

51 Scott, Eugene. "Kamala Harris's questioning of Brett Kavanaugh made her a 2020 contender." *The Washington Post*, September 7, 2018.

52 Merica, Dan. "Kamala Harris launches 2020 presidential bid." *CNN*, January 21, 2019.

53 Krieg, Gregory. "Kamala Harris' record as prosecutor faces new scrutiny from liberals." *CNN*, January 21, 2019.

54 "ACLU Comment on Sen. Kamala Harris Being Named as Vice Presidential Running Mate." *American Civil Liberties Union*, August 11, 2020.

55 Steinhauer, Jennifer, and Stephanie Saul. "Kamala Harris's Criminal Justice Record Killed Her Presidential Run. Maybe That Was the Plan." *The New York Times*, December 3, 2019.

56 Reston, Maeve. "Why Joe Biden picked Kamala Harris as his running mate." *CNN*, August 12, 2020

Chapter 19

1 "Jerry Brown, Gavin Newsom and Democratic history"—SFGATE (Published: November 9, 2010) https://www.sfgate.com/bayarea/matier-ross /article/Jerry-Brown-Gavin-Newsom-and-Democratic-history-3247234 .php.

2 Dan Walters, Gavin Newsom's Keeping It All in the Family, CalMatters (Jan. 9, 2019), https://calmatters.org/commentary/2019/01/gavin-newsoms -keeping-it-all-in-the-family.

3 "Jerry Brown, Gavin Newsom and Democratic history"—SFGATE (Published: November 9, 2010) https://www.sfgate.com/bayarea/matier-ross /article/Jerry-Brown-Gavin-Newsom-and-Democratic-history-3247234 .php.

4 Ibid.

5 "William Newsom, 84, California Judge and Governor-Elect's Father, Dies." *The New York Times*. December 13, 2018.

6 "Jerry Brown, Gavin Newsom and Democratic history"—SFGATE (Published: November 9, 2010) https://www.sfgate.com/bayarea/matier -ross/article/Jerry-Brown-Gavin-Newsom-and-Democratic-history -3247234.php.

7 Byrne, Peter (April 2, 2003). "Bringing Up Baby Gavin." SF Weekly. p. 1–2.

8 Jack Royston, The Surprising Newsom, Pelosi and Harris Ties With the Getty Oil Dynasty, Newsweek (June 30, 2022), https://www.newsweek .com/surprising-newsom-pelosi-harris-ties-getty-oil-dynasty-1717810.

9 Ibid.

10 Chuck Finnie; Rachel Gordon; Lance Williams (March 23, 2003). "Newsom's Portfolio: Mayoral hopeful has parlayed Getty money, family ties and political connections into local prominence." *The San Francisco Chronicle*.

11 Jack Royston, The Surprising Newsom, Pelosi and Harris Ties With the Getty Oil Dynasty, Newsweek (June 30, 2022), https://www.newsweek .com/surprising-newsom-pelosi-harris-ties-getty-oil-dynasty-1717810.

12 Ibid.

13 Ibid.

14 "William Newsom, father of Gavin Newsom, dies at age 84." *The San Francisco Examiner*. December 13, 2018.

15   Dan Walters, Gavin Newsom's Keeping It All in the Family, CalMatters (Jan. 9, 2019), https://calmatters.org/commentary/2019/01/gavin-newsoms -keeping-it-all-in-the-family.

16   Jack Royston, The Surprising Newsom, Pelosi and Harris Ties With the Getty Oil Dynasty, Newsweek (June 30, 2022), https://www.newsweek .com/surprising-newsom-pelosi-harris-ties-getty-oil-dynasty-1717810.

Conclusion

1   https://origin-rh.web.fordham.edu/Halsall/ancient/herodotus-xerxes.asp.

2   https://www.bartleby.com/lit-hub/hc/of-man-being-the-first-part-of -leviathan/chapter-xiii-10/.

3   https://housedivided.dickinson.edu/sites/teagle/texts/john-locke-second -treatise-on-government-1689/.

4   https://www.britannica.com/topic/social-contract/The-social-contract -in-Rousseau.

5   All references to Hanson's analysis are derived from personal correspondence on September 20, 2024.

6   Hanson, email message.

Afterword

1   https://www.usatoday.com/story/entertainment/celebrities/2025/01/25 /mel-gibson-trump-california-visit-daddy-arrived/77945877007/.

2   https://www.youtube.com/watch?v=l_IREnqjttw.

3   https://www.youtube.com/watch?v=I6ns70m_6r4.

4   https://www.foxla.com/news/palisades-fire-rick-caruso-excuses.

5   Ibid.

6   https://www.newsweek.com/karen-bass-endorsement-mistake-says-los -angeles-times-owner-2014435.

7   https://www.cnn.com/2024/10/25/media/washington-post-wont-endorse -presidential-candidate/index.html.

8   https://www.dailymail.co.uk/news/article-13775065/Gavin-Newsom-dig -Kamala-Harris-DNC-nominating-process.html.

9   https://www.gov.ca.gov/2024/11/07/special-session-ca-values/.

10   https://calmatters.org/newsletter/california-trump-legal-fees-fund/.

11   https://www.kcra.com/article/california-senate-money-legal-battles-trump -administration/63530616.

12   https://www.gov.ca.gov/2024/11/07/special-session-ca-values/.

13   https://www.cnn.com/2024/01/01/us/gender-neutral-toy-aisles-are-now -law-in-california/index.html.

14   https://oag.ca.gov/ab3121/report.

15   https://www.huntingtonbeachca.gov/news_detail_T4_R269.php.

16 https://www.theepochtimes.com/us/san-diego-county-votes-to-prohibit
    -support-for-immigration-enforcement-5774431.
17 https://apnews.com/article/sanctuary-city-trump-deportations-immigrants
    -los-angeles-836cf68a756c64800bbeb0270e8a965c.
18 Ibid.
19 https://nypost.com/2024/11/06/us-news/californians-overwhelmingly
    -pass-anti-crime-proposition-36/.
20 Ibid.
21 https://www.latimes.com/california/story/2024–11-05/2024-california
    -election-la-da-race-hochman-Gascón-race-election-night.
22 https://www.latimes.com/california/story/2024–11-05/2024-california
    -election-la-da-race-hochman-gascon-race-election-night.
23 https://www.motherjones.com/politics/2024/12/los-angeles-county-voter
    -data-latino-asian-wealthy-swing-southeast-working-class-2024-trump
    -harris-biden/.
24 https://ballotpedia.org/Pamela_Price_recall%2C_Alameda_County%2C
    California%282023–2024%29.
25 https://www.nbcbayarea.com/news/local/east-bay/alameda
    -county-district-attorney-pamela-price-recall-results/3713155/.
26 https://nypost.com/2024/11/17/us-news/oakland-mayor-da-booted
    -in-revolt-against-soft-on-crime-policies/.
27 https://www.sfchronicle.com/election/article/daniel-lurie-sf-mayor
    -19901110.php.
28 https://www.sfgate.com/politics/article/levis-heir-daniel-lurie-wins-sf-may
    ors-race-19898585.php.
29 https://calmatters.org/politics/elections/2024/12/california-election
    -results-trump-vote-2024/.
30 https://abc7news.com/post/data-shows-political-shift-higher-percentage
    -bay-area-ca-residents-voting-trump-2024/15538720/.
31 https://calmatters.org/politics/elections/2024/12/california-election
    -results-trump-vote-2024/.
32 https://abc7.com/post/higher-percentage-la-county-voters-favored-donald
    -trump-2024-election-2020-data-shows/15541547/.
33 https://www.motherjones.com/politics/2024/12/los-angeles-county-voter
    -data-latino-asian-wealthy-swing-southeast-working-class-2024-trump
    -harris-biden/.
34 Ibid.
35 Ibid.
36 Ibid.
37 Ibid.
38 https://www.reuters.com/world/us/trump-directs-us-government-override
    -california-water-policies-if-necessary-2025–01-27.

39   https://www.dailymail.co.uk/news/article-14320329/Gavin-Newsom-plot
      -ruin-Trump-presidential-visit-tour-LA-fire-wreckage-new-blazes-erupt
      -Southern-California.html/.
40   https://apnews.com/article/donald-trump-republicans-taxes-eea4754a0f
      580d451aa0588f0639d52c/.
41   https://www.forbes.com/sites/antoniopequenoiv/2024/09/05/trump
      -proposes-sovereign-wealth-fund-for-us-what-to-know-about-the-state
      -owned-budget/.
42   https://thehill.com/policy/energy-environment/5103917-trump-ai-power
      -centers-energy-emergency-declaration/./
43   https://www.forbes.com/sites/alanohnsman/2025/01/13/la-fires-150-billion
      -price-tag/.
44   https://www.politico.com/news/2025/01/24/trump-longtime-california
      -antagonist-praised-the-state-during-la-fires-visit-00200609/.